Thinking Feminist: Key Concepts in Women's Studies

Thinking Feminist

Key Concepts in Women's Studies

Edited by

Diane Richardson

and

Victoria Robinson

THE GUILFORD PRESS
New York

Individual chapters © Kum-Kum Bhavnani, Gill Frith,
Jalna Hanmer, June Hannam, Jenny Hockey,
Stevi Jackson, Margaret Marshment, Mary Maynard,
Paula Nicolson, Diane Richardson, Victoria Robinson,
Christine Skelton, Jackie Stacey, Anna Witz 1993

Published by The Guilford Press
A Division of Guilford Publications, Inc.
72 Spring Street, New York, NY 10012

Printed in Hong Kong

This book is printed on acid-free paper

Last digit is print number: 9   8   7   6   5   4   3   2   1

Library of Congress Cataloging-in-Publication Data

Thinking feminist: key concepts in women's studies /
    edited by Diane Richardson and Victoria Robinson.
        p.   cm.
    Includes bibliographical references and index.
    ISBN 0–89862–989–6.   ISBN 0–89862–160–7 (pbk.)
    1. Women—Social conditions.   2. Women's studies.   3. Feminist
theory.   I. Richardson, Diane, 1953–   .   II. Robinson, Victoria.
HQ1154.T475   1993
305.42'0973—dc20   92–28106
                                                              CIP

Contents

List of Figures

List of Tables

Acknowledgements

We would like to thank all those involved in the preparation of this book. Special thanks go to Sylvia Parkin, who helped with the typing of the manuscript, and to our publishing editors Frances Arnold and Jo Campling. I also want to thank Wendy Bolton for her help. For part of the time spent working on the book I was Visiting Scholar in Women's Studies at Murdoch University, Perth, Western Australia. Various people there made my time a stimulating and enjoyable one, and I would especially like to thank Lynne Alice, Bev Thiele, Lynn Star and Rehana Ghadially. I must also thank, for sharing their ideas and enthusiasm, the students at the University of Sheffield who have taken the Sex and Gender course over the last nine years. My colleague Chris Middleton has also been an important source of support and deserves to be thanked. I'm also grateful to Vicki Robinson, who originally had the idea of writing this book, for asking me to co-edit it with her. It's been a lot of hard work, but enormous fun at times as well. Finally, my thanks, as always, to my friends for their emotional support, in particular Ann Watkinson, Libby Hawkins, Jackie Davis, Jean Carabine and Carol Standish.

Sheffield   DIANE RICHARDSON

I would firstly like to acknowledge the perseverance and imagination of my students on the Women's Studies Certificate and Diploma courses in the Division of Adult Continuing Education at the University of Sheffield from 1987 to 1992. Many of the ideas in this book have been discussed with them. My thanks to Maggie Murdoch for her support and comments on my own chapter, as well as to Jenny Hockey and Heather Symonds for being with me on this project from the beginning, Louise Parsons for her love of feminist theory, and Bill Hampton for his initial encouragement. I also acknowledge the commitment of Hilary Eadson,

Diane Bailey, Alison McKenzie, Jenny Greatrex and Sue Whitney in their efforts to establish Women's Studies at degree level in the community at Rotherham College of Arts and Technology. Diane Richardson has provided both intellectual and literal sustenance as well as the benefit of her experience in terms of our conversations on feminist thought, life's other pleasures and an endless supply of sandwiches. My thanks also to Colin.

Sheffield   VICTORIA ROBINSON

Notes on the Contributors

Kum-Kum Bhavnani has been teaching Social Psychology and Women's Studies since 1975. She has taught at Leeds Polytechnic, Preston Polytechnic and Bradford University in Britain, as well as working at the Open University and as an Educational Psychologist in Sheffield. She was recently a Visiting Associate Professor of Women's Studies at Oberlin College, Ohio, in the USA, and is presently at the University of California at Santa Barbara. Her PhD is from King's College, Cambridge University.

Gill Frith is a Lecturer in English Literature at the University of Warwick. She has worked extensively in adult education, specialising in women's writing and feminist theory, and has published several essays on the relationship between reading and gender. She is currently completing *The Intimacy Which Is Knowledge*, a book about female friendship in novels by women writers.

Jalna Hanmer is a Reader in Women's Studies and Co-ordinator of the MA/Dip. Women's Studies (Applied) at the University of Bradford. She studied Sociology at the University of California, then worked as a community worker and in Women's Aid. She researches and writes on violence against women, and biological reproduction.

June Hannam teaches British Social History and Women's Studies at Bristol Polytechnic where she is Head of History. She has published articles on feminist and socialist politics in the nineteenth and early twentieth centuries and has written a biography, *Isabella Ford, 1855–1924*. She is now working on a study of women's political activity in Bristol, c. 1830–1920.

Jenny Hockey graduated from Durham University as a mature student in social anthropology in 1978. Her postgraduate research was published in 1990; as *Experiences of Death: an anthropological account*. She has taught at both Sheffield University and Polytechnic, Teesside Polytechnic and is currently employed as a Senior Lecturer in Sociology at Humberside Polytechnic. Her teaching and research interests include Women's Studies, popular culture, health, ageing and death.

Stevi Jackson is Principal Lecturer in Sociology and course leader of the BA in Women's Studies at the Polytechnic of Wales. She is the author of *Childhood and Sexuality*; *Family Lives: a Feminist Sociology*; and several articles on sexuality and family relations.

Margaret Marshment lectures in Media and Cultural Studies at Liverpool Polytechnic. She has also taught on the Women's Studies MA at the University of Kent, and the Popular Culture and Changing Experience of Women courses for the Open University. She is co-translator, with Grazyna Baran, of *Fat Like the Sun*, a volume of Anna Swir's poetry; and co-editor, with Lorraine Gamman, of *The Female Gaze*. Her research interests are in the fields of feminism, representation and popular culture.

Mary Maynard is a Senior Lecturer in Sociology and Co-ordinator of the postgraduate Centre for Women's Studies at the University of York. She is co-author of *Sexism, Racism and Oppression* (with Arthur Brittan); co-editor of *Women, Violence and Social Control* (with Jalna Hanmer); and author of *Sociological Theory*. She has also written a number of articles on Women's Studies issues, particularly in relation to housework, violence, and theory and methodology. She is currently completing a book on feminist thought.

Paula Nicolson is Lecturer in Medical Psychology at the University of Sheffield Medical School. She is both a feminist and a psychologist: two characteristics that are not always compatible. She has done research and written on the psychology of women, particularly in relation to postnatal depression and the menstrual cycle, and is currently working on a study of female sexuality. She was one of the founder members of the Psychology of Women section of the British Psychological Society.

Diane Richardson is Senior Lecturer in the Department of Sociological Studies at the University of Sheffield, and has been a Visiting Scholar in Women's Studies at Murdoch University, Australia. Her other books include *Women and the Aids Crisis* (1989), *Safer Sex: The Guide for Women Today* (1990) and *Women, Motherhood and Childrearing* (1992).

Victoria Robinson lectures in Women's Studies and has established it as a field of study in the Division of Adult Continuing Education at the University of Sheffield. She has also worked with women in further education to develop Women's Studies at degree level in local communities. Her research interests include the development of Women's Studies, feminist theory, sexuality, masculinity, film and cultural studies.

Christine Skelton is a lecturer in Education at the University of Newcastle upon Tyne, where she teaches on Primary and Secondary PGCE (Post Graduate Certificate in Education) courses. Her previous research includes an ethnography of an initial teacher education programme and a life history study of the careers of male teachers of young children. She is conducting PhD research on masculinities in the primary school.

Jackie Stacey teaches in the Sociology Department at Lancaster University. She is co-editor (with Sarah Franklin and Celia Lury) of *Off-Centre: Feminism and Cultural Studies* (1991), (with Hilary Hinds and Ann Phoenix) of *Working Out: New Directions for Women's Studies* (1992) and author of *Star Gazing: Female Spectatorship and Hollywood Cinema in 1940s and 1950s Britain* (1993). As a result of her recent experience of having cancer, she is presently working on a chapter about gender, cultural taboo and discourses of the body for a book on women and cancer, edited by Patricia Duncker.

Anne Witz is Lecturer in Sociology in the Department of Social Policy and Social Work at the University of Birmingham. She is the author of *Professions and Patriarchy*, and the co-editor of *Gender and Bureaucracy*. She has published several articles on the history of women's work in the professions and in coal-mining in Britain. Her current research is on gender and colonialism, and she is conducting research into white women doctors in colonial India. She is also involved in a collaborative research project on gender, careers and organisations, which examines the career strategies of women and men in nursing, banking and local authority employment.

Introduction

Over the past two decades Women's Studies has become established as an important field of study in many countries across the world. It is now a rapidly expanding area both in terms of the number of courses available and in the proliferation of feminist theories from a variety of perspectives. Other academic disciplines such as Sociology and Literature are also in the process of being transformed as a result of the debates and ideas coming from within Women's Studies.

Despite these developments, there have been few attempts to provide a Women's Studies textbook that offers a comprehensive overview of past, present and future developments in feminist knowledge and theory. Many tutors have been unable to recommend an introductory text which covers the major debates, and consequently students have often found themselves without an accessible source book. This is one of the reasons why, having taught Women's Studies at different levels for a number of years, we felt it was important for this book to be written.

A number of textbooks for Women's Studies have been published (for example Gunew, 1990 and 1991; the Open University series, *Issues in Women's Studies*; and Humm, 1992) as well as books dealing specifically with current debates about the teaching and learning process in Women's Studies (for example, Aaron and Walby, 1991; and Hinds, Phoenix and Stacey, 1992). However, these are different in style and intention from this book, which is not a reader and sets out to provide students with a basic introduction to Women's Studies. Inevitably in a book such as this there are gaps and omissions, for instance feminist critiques of science and technology, and the absence of specific chapters on social policy and cross-cultural perspectives. However, no one book can do justice to the variety and richness of the diversity of feminist ideas available within the broad scope of Women's Studies. What this book does offer is a comprehensive overview of the key themes and issues in major subject areas within Women's Studies, from an interdisciplinary perspective. It introduces the main feminist ideas and perspectives on such issues as sexuality, the family, work, 'race', history, violence, reproduction, feminist theory, motherhood, health, education, literature, representation, and debates within Women's Studies itself to students of Women's Studies, and those studying feminism and gender relations on other courses. Each chapter benefits from the writer's specialist knowledge of their subject, and contains a summary of the research and a critique of the main arguments, highlighting differences between feminists. At the end of each chapter there are suggestions for further reading. These recommended texts are useful overviews or collections, allowing the reader to explore the issues raised in each chapter in more depth.

For those new to Women's Studies there are a number of dictionaries available which are useful in helping to explain and expand upon concepts and terminology used in this book (Kramarae and Treichler, 1985; Tuttle, 1987; and Humm, 1989a). The use of the term 'race' in quotes is to indicate that 'race' is a socially constructed category rather than a biologically determined one. Also, the word Black with a capital is used to indicate that it is a political category rather than purely a descriptive term, referring to the common experiences of racism directed at non-white people. The term Women of Colour rather than Black is preferred by some authors, particularly in the United States.

Finally, we would hope that this book clearly demonstrates that the idea that we have entered a post-feminist age is far from a reality for women throughout the world. Our aim is that this book will stimulate further discussion and analysis and show that feminist thought and action are constantly developing and informing each other in the process of working towards an end to women's oppression.

VICTORIA ROBINSON
DIANE RICHARDSON

1

Introducing Women's Studies

Victoria Robinson

> But if I wish to define myself, I must first of all say: 'I am a woman';
> on this truth must be based all further discussion – de Beauvoir, 1949,
> p. 15.

Simone de Beauvoir's assertion that her being a woman was not irrelevant, but fundamental to the endeavour to theorise women's position, is
a simple but revolutionary idea. Looking back, as an undergraduate
student, my frustration and lack of a vital and passionate connection to
my studies – which saw men's experience and definitions of themselves
and the world as defining my experiences as a woman – could be
understood. It was not until I became a postgraduate student of Women's
Studies that the previously uninspiring intellectual landscape was irrevoc-
ably transformed. Later, as a teacher of Women's Studies in further,
adult and higher education, traditional classroom practices such as a
notion of the tutor as an unchallengable expert and an unquestioning
acceptance of the 'founding forefathers' of knowledge such as Karl
Marx and Sigmund Freud, which characterised traditional learning, were
inappropriate to the collective learning experience which was Women's
Studies.

If Women's Studies is not about learning to cook an economical dish
for a family of four nor about embroidery courses for women with a little
time on their hands (the value of women's traditional skills accepted),
then what is it? Why has it emerged as a dynamic, fast-growing and
popular area of study?

Women's Studies has been difficult to define, partly because of the
diversity of feminist thought and positions and also because it has no

1

straightforward parallel to other subjects. Feminist voices from the early
1980s attempted to explain why Women's Studies had been necessary:

> Fundamental to feminism is the premise that women have been 'left
> out' of codified knowledge; where men have formulated explanations
> in relation to themselves, they have generally either rendered women
> invisible or classified them as deviant . . . The description and ana-
> lysis of the omission of women as autonomous human beings has
> been one of the most significant contributions made by feminism.
> (Spender, 1981, p. 2)

This recognition has entailed the setting up of Women's Studies programmes and also attempts to characterise them:

> To introduce feminist insights means to challenge radically the gen-
> eration and distribution of knowledge; it means changing the whole
> shape of the course, or the problem – or the discipline . . . Auto-
> nomous Women's Studies, as we define it, has the potential to alter
> fundamentally the nature of all knowledge by shifting the focus from
> androcentricity to a frame of reference in which women's different
> and differing ideas, experiences, needs and interests are valid in their
> own right and form the basis for our teaching and learning. (Bowles
> and Klein, 1983, p. 3)

If a fundamental feature of Women's Studies is the simple yet radical
belief in an approach to knowledge which places women at the centre of
analysis (challenging an androcentric/phallocentric notion of knowledge
which can be defined as men's experiences and priorities being seen as
central and representative of *all*), then this realisation of a theoretical
dishonesty has profound implications for how we organise, structure,
teach and research within the disciplines and the academy in general.
This 'simple' shift in theorising and teaching recognises the politics of
theory in terms of the so-called objectivity of knowledge, which has
failed to recognise and validate the diversity of experience of over half
of humankind. The emphasis on a feminist perspective meant a realisation of the power relations inherent in current knowledge frameworks
and practices, in terms of who had access to that knowledge, how it was
distilled and evaluated and how meanings were 'encoded', so creating
'men's studies' (Spender, 1981). Though we have made use of past male
theorists despite their gender blindness, it was recognised that we needed

to develop feminist theories and concepts which see women as primary to theorising.

In this chapter I will briefly situate the development of Women's Studies, particularly in Britain and the United States, in an historical context before raising some epistemological issues (that is, theoretical issues and problems in the production of knowledge) and discussing some of the central characteristics of Women's Studies as a subject area. As suggested, the radical implications of feminist theory and practice inform the curriculum and teaching and learning, so it is necessary to examine the relationship of students and teachers to Women's Studies and the dynamics of the classroom. Central debates both between Women's Studies and the academy and within the subject itself, are discussed, followed by a consideration of emerging subjects such as gender studies and men's studies.

What is Women's Studies?

The women's movement of the 1960s and 1970s in the Western world had a fundamental impact on the establishment of Women's Studies courses in adult and higher education. This connection of the academic world to a social movement meant that the setting up and teaching of such courses was a profoundly political act; theoretical analysis was seen as being intimately connected to social change, which was broadly defined as the recognition and analysis of women's oppression, and therefore how to end their subordination in patriarchal and capitalist societies.

There has been debate over whether Women's Studies is an extension of the women's movement or if 'it is now structurally (and, some would maintain, ideologically) distinct from that movement' (Sheridan, 1990, p. 36). So it could be argued that the links with the women's movement have changed or lessened (see Chapter 3). But it must be acknowledged that the feminist insistence on the importance of sisterhood, the personal being political, the false separation of public and private spheres, a recognition of the common oppression of women and their diversity in terms of 'race', ethnicity, sexuality, class, age and levels of disability, as well as the acknowledgement of the importance of women's historical and immediate experience and the idea of the development of a feminist consciousness, were central concepts to the women's movement and began to inform the development of Women's Studies in the establishments. (Though some of these assumptions, such as a universal sister-hood, the use of the category 'woman', and a simplistic notion of difference and diversity have been challenged and inform contemporary debates within Women's Studies (see Chapters 2 and 3).)

Women's Studies as a formal area of study emerged in the United States in the late 1960s (see Boxer, 1982 for a comprehensive account of its development there). In Britain, women involved with left politics and the women's movement in the 1960s and 1970s began to set up Women's Studies courses within higher education and in an adult educa-tion context, and it was in the latter where, for instance, women's health, history and self-assertiveness courses developed. The constraints of for-mal assessment and required qualifications which characterised higher education did not apply to community-based education, allowing women more control over the educational process (Hughes and Kennedy, 1983).

Though some courses in Britain had been established within poly-technics and universities, it was not until 1980 that the first MA was offered in Women's Studies, at the University of Kent. Gradually other postgraduate courses followed and then undergraduate programmes, so that it is now possible to study for a full degree in Women's Studies in Britain. (For more detail on course development from the 1970s on-wards, see Klein (1983); see Zmroczek and Duchen (1989, 1991) for a discussion of Women's Studies progress in the UK in a European con-text; see Sheridan (1991) for Australian developments.) Access courses and further/adult education programmes have also been important in terms of entry to higher education for groups such as Black and working class women (Kennedy and Piette, 1991) and so have feminist higher education courses in local communities (Haywoode and Scanlon, 1987).

Despite hostile political and economic conditions, Women's Studies exists as both autonomous programmes and as courses and modules within different disciplines in further, adult and higher education. It is established in varying degrees in North and South America, Europe, Australia and New Zealand, Asia and the Arab world, where feminist scholars are seeking to transform both academic disciplines and women's lives (Klein, 1991). Many of these courses, however, are often established despite underfunding, opposition and prejudice against Women's Studies and through intense and prolonged struggle with the system (Brunt, Green, Jones and Woodward, 1983; Hanmer, 1991).

Women's Studies encompasses the deconstruction of traditional dis-ciplines in terms of their subject matter and their structure. Teaching, learning and research are all transformed by a questioning of conventional knowledge claims to objectivity and 'truth' and the separation of experience from theory. Women's Studies practitioners have also attempted to produce theories and concepts which reflect feminist concerns and principles. Most, though not all, research has been within the social sciences and arts/humanities areas, though there has been a recognition that the sciences and technology need to be reconceptualised from a feminist perspective (Zmroczek and Duchen, 1989).

Feminist perspectives seek to address the fact that individual disciplines themselves are gender blind – presenting male values and experience as human ones. Pamela Abbott and Clare Wallace argue that within the discipline of sociology there have been three steps in this reconceptualising of knowledge. The first is integration where 'malestream' sociology is purged of bias by including women to fill in the gaps of existing knowledge. The second stage is separatism, which requires the construction of new sociological theories for women, by women. Both these stages are seen as inadequate in that such approaches continue to marginalise women through tokenism and lip service, and by malestream sociology being left to carry out the 'real' theorising and research. The discipline itself remains untouched by feminist criticisms and concerns. What is seen as necessary is the third approach, one of reconceptualisation, which recognises that we need research 'by women and for women' but also that we need what amounts to a revolution:

> Instead it is seen as necessary to reconceptualise sociological theories – revolution, not reform, is necessary. This is both because existing theories are sexist beyond reform by mere tinkering and because feminist research actually challenges assumptions and generalisations made from malestream research. What is needed is a total and radical reformation of sociology so that it is able to incorporate women adequately. (Abbott and Wallace, 1990, p. 10)

Other women writing of different disciplines have argued that the acceptance of the feminist critique in their specific knowledge frameworks has varied (Spender, 1981). Henrietta L. Moore (1988) asserts that the feminist critique has been marginalised within the social sciences. Her argument for this, however, is because of 'the identification of feminist concerns with women's concerns' (p. vii) rather than one which stresses gender, not women as the structuring principle. But Sue Wilkinson (1991) argues in terms of a woman-centred feminist psychology, and poses the question that though psychology needs feminism, does feminism need psychology, with its resistance to feminist interventions and its insistence on itself as a science?

There is, then, variation in how existing paradigms of knowledge have reacted to and been informed by feminist scholarship and disagreement over the reasons for this. But even in areas such as cultural studies and sociology, for instance, where feminist research is not only finding new answers but posing new questions about the invisibility and marginalisation of women and their relationship to culture and the social world, a total intellectual revolution in the concepts, perspectives and methodologies of the subject areas is far from being achieved.

Whilst some disciplines such as the natural sciences and psychology remain (to different degrees) untouched, generally, a token acceptance of a feminist perspective in the form of 'added in' lectures on women or a cursory mention of gender relations in seminars, remains the rule rather than the exception. Gender, 'race' and sexuality are still not established as ways of seeing the world in the way that class is within politics or history. More positively, though, if Women's Studies and feminist theory has only been in existence (in an institutionalised context) for twenty years, then even small shifts in malestream thought can be seen as beginning to displace centuries of male academic bias and power.

The organisation of knowledge into separate and distinct disciplines meant that the new questions and methods of feminist enquiry that emerged from putting women at the centre of theoretical discourse were not adequately answered or dealt with. The crossing of theoretical boundaries – multidisciplinary, interdisciplinary or transdisciplinary (going beyond the disciplines) – allows an issue or area to be examined from a variety of intellectual standpoints and has been seen as the most appropriate to Women's Studies. Some women have questioned the possibility of a truly interdisciplinary approach, or have pointed out the potential difficulties of such an approach with scholars trained in single disciplines (Bowles, 1983). (For a comparison of disciplinary, interdisciplinary and transdisciplinary approaches and the debates involved, see Sheridan, 1991).

It has also been argued that Women's Studies itself constitutes an academic discipline, both for intellectual reasons and for survival within the institutions (Coyner, 1983). Other feminists would not wish to see feminist scholarship constrained by the limits of a discipline and prefer to see it as a field of study. Some non-feminists within the academic world would still argue that Women's Studies is not a distinct, legitimate subject area, given that it 'thieves' like a magpie from a diversity of sources, but the new generation of students who now hold undergraduate and postgraduate degrees (including PhDs) would suggest otherwise.

Women's Studies started by filling in the gaps and exposing the silences, adding women into disciplines which were not reformulated from a feminist perspective. This 'add on' approach was not sufficient, though, and it was necessary to develop autonomous Women's Studies with its emphasis on the *feminist* basis of its evolving theories and methodologies; the recognition of men's power to define knowledge and practice. This is not merely adding another piece to the patriarchal jigsaw, but it is in effect starting a personal, educational and political revolution at both an individual and a structural level. This being the case, there is an argument for using the term 'Feminist Studies' instead of Women's Studies, but it is often avoided for practical reasons (for example, the academy's resistance to the term) and because it is not self-evident which 'feminisms' are being referred to. Whatever name is used, the male educational hierarchy should both fear and welcome these transformations in theoretical certainty – for to truly take on the full implications of this means the giving up of power as well as gaining in intellectual integrity.

Who engages with Women's Studies?

Studying Women's Studies can be simultaneously exhilarating and painful, as well as illuminating and disconcerting, making women's experience of oppression, which was once seen as opaque and individual, into something approaching a collective sense of oppression and struggle. So who decides to engage with it and why do they choose to?

Women's historical exclusion from education for ideological reasons and practical ones, such as lack of child-care facilities, as well as their under-achievement at different levels, has been well documented (Spender and Sarah, 1988; Chapter 14). Another central reason for the relative lack of working class and/or Black women in education, for instance, has been that intellectually the subject matter has not spoken directly to their experiences. The idea that traditional subjects and research have been *about* and not *for* women is counteracted by Women's Studies' insistence of the notion that women's experience as workers, mothers and carers is not left outside the classroom, separate from the 'serious' job of theorising. Learning therefore connects with the 'mundane' world of women's daily lives as well as with their sexuality and emotional life.

Women who left education at an early age or who have been on traditional courses speak of the vital nature of learning in the feminist classroom which contrasts with earlier experiences.

Students of Women's Studies vary in terms of 'race', ethnicity, age,
class, sexuality, able-bodiedness and nationality. They may be connected with the women's movement and associate strongly with a diversity of feminist ideas or they may not view or define themselves as
feminist, even subscribing to media stereotypes of feminists as 'strident,
man-hating harridans'. Sue Lees points out that the accounts of women
students who came on to a foundation course in Women's Studies in the
mid-1980s reveal reasons that are similar to those of women joining
consciousness groups in the late 1960s. The accounts quoted reveal
women's different reasons and relationship to feminism. She concludes:

> Do these accounts suggest we have reached the period of post femin-
> ism? Over and over again women maintain that they come on courses
> for themselves, for their own development, rather than to gain any
> particular qualifications. Some are already graduates, some even have
> postgraduate qualifications, but do not feel their previous education
> has had relevance to their lives. (Lees, 1991, p. 94)

Some students, however, have an image of feminism which stereotypes not only Women's Studies courses but also their students and
tutors (Auchmuty, Borzello and Langdell, 1983). What is important is
that the feminist classroom affords the possibility of dialogue between
women with different conceptions of and relationships to feminism, and
that the idea of contradiction between women's lived experience and
perceived feminist ideas is creatively explored.

As Women's Studies becomes more mainstream and students start to
take Women's Studies as just another course, as they would literature or
economics, rather than as a conscious political or exploratory act, then
the need for students and teachers to problematise this becomes imperative. This can lead to situations where women who define themselves as
feminist are in the minority (Davis, 1985). Theoretically, for example,
students can produce technically proficient essays covering all the right
issues but which in reality are only masquerading a supposed feminist
empathy, as they have not reflected on the debates in a personal context.
So the feminist insistence on the personal being political can be obscured
when students take Women's Studies purely for the qualification. Also,
first-year undergraduates' conceptions of Women's Studies may be vastly
different from mature students' engagement with feminist issues. If

currently the majority of students and teachers of Women's Studies are women, then we need to be aware and discuss the implications of more men being involved at various levels, as well as to recognise the diversity of Women's Studies students in general. Students then, choose to do Women's Studies for a variety of reasons (not necessarily mutually exclusive) and expect different things from the experience. They may take it for profoundly political reasons; out of a curiosity to engage with feminism, or to help them combat sexism at work; for a qualification, or because it looks like an interesting course and it becomes mainly an intellectual exercise. Some students use courses primarily for consciousness-raising, others as an opportunity for critical analysis of the situation of women, others still for both these reasons.

Students also have a range of home backgrounds and personal relationships so some may have support from family and partners for their studies, others may face hostility and misunderstanding of what Women's Studies is. The consciousness-raising aspect of Women's Studies in whatever context – a women's health course in the local community or an MA in Women's Studies – can and does change students, and this needs to be reflected on as part of the course itself (Bonder, 1985). Students initially hostile to feminist ideas may, at the end of a course, identify with feminist views. Students generally may find through Women's Studies a new confidence and become more articulate as a result. Students can also question and analyse the roles and relationships they are in as a consequence of taking on feminist ideas and it can have a profound impact on students' self-perceptions and values as well as on their conceptions of educational practices such as student–teacher relationships. Like tutors, they may bring into the classroom anti-lesbian and racist attitudes and assumptions, so course content and teaching methods need to acknowledge the problems and potential of exploring them. Women's Studies classrooms will be charged with a whole range of emotions and feelings: hurt, anger, passion and revelation, and both students and teachers need to incorporate these into feminist theoretical and pedagogical practices (Culley, 1985; Fisher, 1987). As Jalna Hanmer says: 'On Women's Studies courses, women students can behave in new ways. They often feel able to demand, discharge and disclose in ways unthinkable on traditional discipline, or interdisciplinary, or professional courses. This can be critical for student academic development' (Hanmer, 1991, p. 113). It is important, as Hanmer says, that the course gives students space and time for 'student-initiated informal groups with opportunities to sit and discuss anything and everything'. If the constraints of the course do not allow this, then students may form their own groups out of class time, which serve both a social and intellectual function.

Many Women's Studies courses are part-time, increasingly modularised, and allow students to combine work, family and study as effectively as possible. It is important that the needs of women, often mature students and part-time, are considered when planning courses. The timing of courses and the reasons why students are not always able to adhere rigidly to assessment deadlines are important to consider, along with the incorporation of study skills into courses, as women may have had negative educational experiences which reinforce feelings of inadequacy and lack of confidence in academic matters. Child-care provision, which has not been a priority in higher education (though adult and community courses have recognised the necessity), is crucial if women are not going to be denied access to education as in the past.

If students endeavour to theorise women's position in circumstances which are far from ideal, then the staff involved in setting up and teaching courses make decisions from similar contradictory positions, often in the context of resistance to and lack of understanding of what Women's Studies actually is.

Teachers of Women's Studies arrive at their intellectual destination from a variety of sources. Many have been working from within individual disciplines to transform the theory and methodology of their subject matter, as well as dealing with colleagues' resistance to feminist ideas. They often face the double burden of teaching within their own subject and developing Women's Studies in an intellectual and practical sense. Commitment by female staff, mirrored by students' perseverance, needs to be placed in the context of attitudes which have refused to see Women's Studies as academically respectable or rigorous, where an honest admitting of feminist bias is seen as evidence of political indoctrination and abandonment of objectivity and reason. Women teachers who have done postgraduate work in an interdisciplinary programme of Women's Studies and the new generation of women on current undergraduate programmes may well see themselves as scholars of Women's Studies as opposed to an economist or historian, for example, who has a specific interest in feminist theory. Such a woman would be able to teach courses on health, psychology, feminist theory, and women and the media, and would be a truly interdisciplinary person (Bowles, 1983). Tutors (like myself) may well be on part-time or temporary contracts without tenure, and access to the decision-making process as well as institutional and research resources is limited. So staff who are marginalised within the institution in terms of power because they are women, can be doubly so if involved with a subject which has neither status or support.

Teachers themselves come from different classes and 'races' and may be lesbian or heterosexual, struggling with their own and others racism and homophobia, and so the ways in which their personal identities interact with institutional constraints and student expectations are all part of the dynamics of the feminist and non-feminist classroom (McDaniel, 1985; Stetson, 1985; Squirrell, 1989).

If Women's Studies within the academic sphere has been seen as too radical, then some in the women's movement argue that teachers of Women's Studies (and Women's Studies itself) will be deradicalised as it enters the mainstream, in terms of its political vision and connection to the wider movement. Women's Studies' practitioners can be seen to be corrupted by a male hierarchy that demands obedience to a patriarchal orthodoxy and have been seen as careerists, or not connected to the women's movement, by those women who see them as merely token feminists (Taking Liberties Collective, 1989).

It is necessary to recognise, however, that to associate with feminism and Women's Studies can also be detrimental to women involved in courses in terms of careers and academic 'respectability'. Also, such distinctions between Women's Studies and the women's movement deny the political principles of women involved in setting up and teaching such courses: the fact that this can be a feminist political act; and it also ignores the political energy needed to survive in the institutions (see Stanko, 1991).

Teaching and learning in the Women's Studies classroom

If a feminist perspective on education means radically changing the curriculum, it also necessitates a reflection and transformation on how we teach and learn. From the beginning of the setting up of Women's Studies courses in the early 1970s, feminist pedagogy has been on the agenda, but it is only relatively recently that we have started to discuss the diversity and complexity of feminist approaches: 'It is vital, therefore, that we understand process and content to be inextricably linked and that we develop and share feminist pedagogical approaches that are democratic, cooperative, experiential, integrative of cognitive and affective learning, and empowering of students to create personal and social change' (Schniedewind and Maher, 1987, p. 4).

Ideally, the Women's Studies classroom is about creating a situation where students can engage with such feminist principles, where they can learn to evolve as autonomous scholars and listen to and respect others. What is the reality of such a classroom when the contradictions of struggling with our own prejudices, the difficulty of dismantling and reconstructing previously comforting educational practices and the diversity of student and teacher expectations, are ever present within far-from-radical establishments? The central relationship to receive consideration is the one of student and teacher.

The idea of the tutor as all-knowing expert with students as empty vessels to be filled with pearls of wisdom was criticised by 1970s theorists such as Paulo Freire in *Pedagogy of the Oppressed* (1970), but the gender dimension did not inform these reconceptions. There has been acknowledgement that students and teachers both enrich the classroom and theoretical discourse with the immediacy and vitality of their experience, and a dialogue should ensue, not a hierarchy of opinion. The concepts of authority and power associated with the relationship have been analysed, and the negative aspects of these dynamics: their misuse and antithesis to feminist philosophy in terms of hierarchical learning and non-collectivity, meant an initial rejection of, for example, the right of teachers to assess student's work. Claire Ungerson (1988) feels that we can now expect that some women have the experience to grade and judge written work. This has paralleled a feminist redefinition of power and authority to entail an acceptance of the teacher's role as both possessor of knowledge and nurturer, so that patriarchal pedagogic patterns are not reproduced (Culley *et al.*, 1985; Friedman, 1985). We need therefore to redefine our notions of power, and talk instead of empowerment. Carolyn M. Shrewsbury states: 'By focusing on empowerment, feminist pedagogy embodies a concept of power as energy, capacity, and potential rather than as domination' (Shrewsbury, 1987, p. 8). Power is seen as necessary for personal realisation and thus to achieve collective ends.

This recognition of power and attempts to challenge hierarchical notions of assessment and learning can be seen in the paradox of education's insistence on graded work to ensure standards of achievement. Students and teachers may attempt to challenge this by incorporating collective working methods with joint student essays and presentations, dissertations or research as opposed to exams, by team-teaching and by including non-traditional methods of discussion and assessment, such as collective marking, experiential accounts and women's autobiography, within courses. (See Maher, 1985; Sellers, 1989; Humm, 1991; and Lubelska, 1991 for a discussion of some of these issues.)

Students may choose not to know what grades they have been getting for their written work, but the paradox remains that teachers may well have to exercise institutional power and formally assess work and not to do so would devalue Women's Studies courses in terms of the status they have within institutions and in terms of students' need and desire for a qualification (de Wolfe, 1980; and Evans, 1983a). It is important that the process of evaluation and marking is discussed openly and the politics of the criteria used by teachers recognised. These issues of power are reflected in all aspects of Women's Studies, from entry to courses, curriculum development, the format of classes in terms of small group work (Hobby, 1989), in the planning of conferences (Bell, 1987), and in equal representation of all groups (in the production of journals, for example). It is necessary to problematise the contradictory position students and teachers occupy in relation to each other, the academic world, and the principles of the women's movement in course feedback and class discussion, so that 'Our classrooms need not always reflect an equality of power, but must reflect movements in that direction' (Shrewsbury, 1987).

Vital work in exploring the political implications of feminist pedagogic issues has been the recognition of the need for students and tutors to work creatively with difference between women and struggle to analyse and overcome racism, heterosexism, classism and ageism. Students and tutors may be heterosexual or lesbian (out or not). They may be struggling to address their own prejudices (or questioning their backgrounds and allegiances), and feminist theory is not sufficiently developed to fully account for the interactions of capitalism, 'race', age, heterosexism and gender, for example (Thompson, 1987). Working therefore with difference and women in a dynamic sense can lead to frustration and anger in the classroom. Racism in Women's Studies courses and the issue of a Black feminist pedagogy has been raised and discussed (Butler, 1985; Russell, 1985; Spelman, 1985; Washington, 1985; Omolade, 1987). Anti-lesbianism, heterosexism and lesbian students and tutors in the classroom have also been analysed (Gurko, 1982; McDaniel, 1985; Crumpacker and Vander Haegen, 1987). The needs of older and disabled students, long neglected, crucially need to be discussed in terms of feminist pedagogic issues.

As Women's Studies progresses into the mainstream and feminist students may become the minority, we need to make explicit the contradictions involved in feminist teaching and learning in the mixed (women and men) or mainstream classroom (Davis, 1985; Cayleff, 1988; and Cameron, 1989). Not only do we need to make explicit our teaching strategies, but we should develop feminist pedagogies at all educational levels, including teaching feminist issues in schools (Payne and Spender, 1980).

Debates within Women's Studies

The master's tools will never dismantle the master's house – Lorde (1984b)

Women's Studies is an evolving, fluid and dynamic area of study connected to the women's movement (even if that connection is conceptualised differently, as I have mentioned), with its own plurality of political positions and aims. It is also a political act against phallocentric knowledge-making, ironically being constituted within the walls of the academy it is attempting to transform through feminist perspectives. It is of little wonder then that there are intense debates within Women's Studies itself, and there are parallels with the dialogues taking place in different countries despite cultural differences.

The question of whether as women, we should engage with theory at all, was initially posed as Women's Studies developed (see Chapter 3). Theory was seen as a male weapon of oppression, wielded by those who would ridicule and silence women. Women's energy then was seen as best directed at practical moves to help the community of women. But such views, ignore the fact that women have always theorised, despite traditional parallels of men with logic and reason and women with intuition and emotion. Theory itself is not inherently male, even if it has been used to justify women's position of inequality (Spender, 1983b). What we need to do is to redefine theory and the act of theorising. What is necessary is accessibility to theory and the recognition that: 'Women's Studies has a most important part to play in ensuring that knowledge, itself a form of social power, is not produced solely in the interests of the powerful and influential' (Evans, 1983b, p. 228). For a further discussion of the 'suspicious pleasures' of teaching feminist theory, see Joan Cocks (1985).

Different countries have different traditions regarding feminism and its relationship to theory in terms of the relative importance attached to descriptive, empirical or analytical work (Marks and de Courtivron, 1981; and Moi, 1987). Some women feel that theory which is inaccessible to most women and elitist in terms of the language used is anathema to the women's movement principles of collective access and sharing of knowledge. For instance, theorists who have embraced a psychoanalytic theoretical language are sometimes seen to replicate male patterns of theorising, 'the equivalent of strapping on a phallus' (Greer, 1988). Other women insist on the importance of theory, which will sometimes of necessity be complex, but which needs to be made available to as many women as possible, combining subjectivity and objectivity, and at the same time ensuring that theory is connected to social action.

This reconceptualising of theory also extends to feminist research methods, which need, for example, to question the traditional barriers between researcher and researched and neutral, value-free methodology (Roberts, 1981a; Mies, 1983; Stanley and Wise, 1983). Liz Stanley (1990a) argues that within the general framework of an academic mode of production there are different feminist research methodologies as there are different kinds of feminists – but central to feminist research is an acceptance of 'knowledge *what*' and 'knowledge *for*'. By this she means that the point of feminist research for her 'is to change the world, not only to study it' (p. 15). She also stresses the need to acknowledge the important connectedness of methodology and theory. There has also been debate over whether qualitative or quantitative research methods are more suited to feminist methodologies. (Or both; see Jayaratne, 1983, for example.)

An epistemological issue which has been central to both feminist theory and research methodology has been the academic separation of theory and experience, and emotion and reason. A fundamental issue about the nature of feminist theorising has been the insistence by feminists of redefining an academic notion of objectivity. At one level, this has led to accusations that Women's Studies practitioners are 'biased' – indoctrinating students with political (and worse, feminist!) dogma, or that they are not sufficiently rigorous.

Dale Spender (1981) charts how women initially defended the subjective (and by implication women), and moved to a critique of objectivity, which was, in effect, a critique of men themselves:

> Women came to realise that the knowledge which men constructed about women (from their deviant physiology and psychology to the

definition of women as non-workers) was frequently rated as 'objective' while the knowledge women began to construct about women (which has its origins in the role of a participant rather than a spectator) was frequently rated as 'subjective'. (Spender, 1981, p. 5)

So feminists challenged 'the objectivity of objectivity' and recognised that subjectivity was a valid part of theorising. (For a discussion of whether that means feminism has to abandon objectivity, see Sydie, 1987.)

Personal experience, then, is a vital starting point to explore differences and similarities between women. Within the context of Women's Studies, women can locate that experience within a theoretical context, to combine reflection on the personal with analysis and critique. Such a combination is not without tension. Students sometimes feel that there is either too little or too much experience informing theoretical debate. Juliet Mitchell and Ann Oakley wrote:

> In the first place we feel that by its very nature the statement of personal experience and the glorification of sisterhood become repetitious. They are useful as starting points but after that they become distractions from another equally essential enterprise . . . Although political work is always on one level about personal lives, we feel the time for the drawing-board has come. (Oakley and Mitchell, 1976, p. 11)

If in the 1970s it was seen by some women as necessary to stress the theoretical side of feminist theorising in an attempt perhaps to achieve academic credibility, then in the 1980s the experience/theory debate was still an issue. Veronica Beechey asserts that 'the concept of "experience" which remains the bedrock of a feminist analysis for some writers is criticised by others for being subjectivist' (Beechey, 1986, p. 1). Certainly, individual experience which is not reflected on, or challenged, can be at best limiting, and could, for instance, be racist, if I as a white woman use only my experiences alone for constructing a theoretical framework or world view (see Chapter 2).

This tension between experience and theory has somewhat lessened as Women's Studies progresses (Ungerson, 1988), and we have begun to think about how experience and theory interact and indeed, why they have been thought of as separate entities. Women have reflected on ways to incorporate experience into the content of courses, for example by working imaginatively with students' autobiographies and analysing the concept of experience itself (Hoffman, 1985; and Humm, 1989b).

If we accept the need to theorise, where is the best place to offer a sustained and rigorous critique of patriarchal knowledge and women's position in society? Some women feel that the contradictions involved in situating Women's Studies within formal academic settings are too problematic in terms of accepting and working within imperfect conditions, and the concessions needed to remain there too great (Freeman, 1979). Women's Studies is seen as best constituted outside formal education, and within informal community-based situations where curriculum control and women-only spaces are easier to obtain. (Even Women's Studies itself is not seen as the most appropriate place for feminist scholars because women's energies, some argue, could be directed instead at, for example, helping women in the community.)

Virginia Woolf (1938) saw the dangers of entering male-dominated and male-defined educational institutions. Much later Hester Eisenstein (1984) interprets Mary Daly in Gyn/Ecology (1978) as asserting that Women's Studies programmes were merely 'gifts of the patriarchy, rather than concessions won in struggle' (p. 115).

In fact, some women initially left the academic sphere or have suggested that a separate women's academy or university would enable Women's Studies to realise its aims in a principled manner, ensuring control over curriculum, staff and resources – a return in a sense to women-only colleges. Others, like Sarah Hoagland (1978) and Gloria Bowles (1983) have acknowledged the contradictions of Women's Studies in higher education, but have stressed the necessity of engaging in mainstream institutions.

A central debate around Women's Studies within mainstream education evolved in the late 1970s and the 1980s over whether we should put our energies and resources into autonomous Women's Studies courses or into integrating feminist perspectives and methodologies within the other disciplines, and ultimately transforming them. Separatists have argued that separate Women's Studies does not necessarily mean a distancing from power in terms of status and resources, as supporters of integrated Women's Studies have argued. Separateness is seen as a political stance chosen from a position of strength, not marginality or weakness, and integration is viewed as assimilation, with the woman-centred aspects of Women's Studies being lost (Raymond, 1985). The 'mainstreaming' implications of integration are also discussed by Marian Lowe and Margaret Lowe Benston (1991) in terms of the contradictions involved regarding power and feminist principles. Autonomous Women's Studies means not having to rehearse old arguments and waste valuable time on anti-feminist views. Others, (Hoagland, 1978) have felt that the enclave of autonomous Women's Studies allowed the mainstream to assert that women have 'been done', leaving male-defined theories, methodologies and teaching practices untouched by feminist insights and allowing students and staff, both female and male, to refuse engagement with feminism.

These two stances simplify the debate as many women argue the need for the simultaneous development of autonomous Women's Studies and feminist approaches within the disciplines. Others see Women's Studies as a strategy, not as an end in itself – thus Women's Studies is, in effect, signing its own death warrant when the other subjects are truly transformed. Gloria Bowles and Renate Duelli Klein (1983) summarise the autonomy/integration debate, pointing out that supporters of both approaches have different views on how change takes place, that few women would want to argue for one strategy only, and how other factors such as the nature and size of the college, and the resources available, are important influences when deciding which course of action to pursue. If women from both sides of the debate, by necessity, need each other, then they also stress that autonomous Women's Studies is vital for the realisation of feminist visions. Susan Sheridan (1990), writing as an Australian, surveys the literature on the 'mainstreaming' or independent, interdisciplinary 'discipline' debate, particularly as it has emerged in the United States, and utilising D. Rosenfelt, concludes:

> There are few voices to be heard now defending the view that women's studies will 'wither away once the curriculum is transformed, should that happy event ever come to pass', while there is a variety of proposals about the kind of autonomous existence it might lead in the future as a discipline or body of knowledge (Rosenfelt, 1984, p. 168). (Sheridan, 1990, p. 49)

Moving in from the cold: problems and possibilities

Connected to this debate is the idea that Women's Studies is gradually moving in from the margins and becoming more mainstream. Though still very marginalised in some respects, for example in terms of the funding it attracts and understanding of what it is, Women's Studies is gradually gaining academic respectability and status within the institutions, and the growth of new courses at different levels is rapid. If it is accepted that Women's Studies wants to move out of the margins to the centre, towards acceptance, academic credibility, and arguably more power, then its development should be celebrated. But crucial questions such as where exactly we are shifting to, and whether such a move entails deradicalisation and co-option, need to be asked.

In 1981, Adrienne Rich wrote:

> The question now facing Women's Studies, it seems to me, is the extent to which she has, in the past decade, matured into the dutiful daughter of the white patriarchal university – a daughter who threw tantrums and played the tomboy when she was younger but who has now learned to wear a dress and speak almost as nicely as Daddy wants her to. (Rich, 1981, pp. 4–5)

The possibilities of respectability replacing rebellion, and of token Women's Studies courses, are real ones. Some Women's Studies courses distance themselves from the term feminist because of adverse reaction from the male establishment. Another irony inherent in the success of Women's Studies is that more male teachers and students, as well as anti-feminists, may have to or want to engage in it, so women-only, pro-feminist spaces will be lost. Lyndie Brimstone argues for the strategic importance of being in a marginal position, as going into the mainstream does not challenge the marginal/mainstream hierarchical conception, so that 'When we leave the margins it must be because they no longer exist' (Brimstone, 1991). It is important to recognise, though, that with the increasing acceptance of Women's Studies into the mainstream of scholarship, we need to develop strategies which enable us to use the power and position we gain from entering, and still authentically challenge the academy with a diversity of feminist approaches. This could be through independent Women's Studies programmes and transformation of individual disciplines.

A central question of the 1990s is whether we are developing and transforming as a distinct area of study without the diversity of women's experience which feminism in the 1980s claimed to represent. Reflecting debates and divisions within the women's movement, the most fundamental dilemma of Women's Studies has concerned the marginalisation of Black, working-class and lesbian perspectives, often in opposition to the prioritising of the needs and experiences of white, middle-class

Western women. The title of Adrienne Rich's book 'On Lies, Secrets and Silence' (1980a) could be used to illustrate how Women's Studies has largely been silent on the question of the diversity of women's experiences and interests. In a theoretical sense, for example, Black perspectives have often been ignored or added in a superficial manner without informing concepts or debate in a systematic way (Carby, 1982a; Hooks, 1991; Watt and Cook, 1991; and Chapter 2). Gloria T. Hull *et al.* (1982) reveal the existence of a diverse Black women's tradition and how Women's Studies has refused to be influenced or reconceptualised by this or to acknowledge Black women's contradictory position in the wider Black community. Even when subjects such as history recognised class and 'race' issues, the omission of Black women as opposed to Black men was still apparent (Higginbotham and Watts, 1988). If 'woman' is not seen as a unified category, then it becomes possible to see the differences between Black and white women in terms of their history, economic position and culture, for example. It also means that 'Black' is not a unified category either, revealing differences between Black women also.

Patricia Hill Collins in 'Black Feminist Thought', though specifically referring to African–American women, deliberately places Black women's experiences and ideas central to her analysis:

In this volume, by placing African–American women's ideas in the center of analysis, I not only privilege those ideas but encourage white feminists, African–American men, and all others to investigate the similarities and differences among their own standpoints and those of African–American women. (Collins, 1990, p. xiii)

Lesbians have also revealed the heterosexist nature of feminist theory in terms of course content and format which refuses to critique heterosexuality and which often conflates lesbianism automatically with radical separatist feminism. Lesbianism is often separated off from general feminist issues and discussed in the context of a narrow definition of sexuality. The insights gained from discussing heterosexuality, for example, in a sexuality module, often do not inform feminist theory generally (Franklin and Stacey, 1986). An absence of lesbian perspectives is to be found in the lack of lesbian teaching staff as well as in the content and style of what is taught on Women's Studies courses (Taking Liberties Collective, 1989). We also need to discuss how the categories of 'race', ethnicity, class, lesbianism and heterosexuality are connected and not necessarily mutually exclusive (Brah, 1991; Brimstone, 1991; and Chapter 2).

In the same way that Black feminists have argued that 'whiteness' needs to be deconstructed by white people as a social category, then it is also argued that heterosexuality should be discussed and theorised, so that even within feminist theory it is not taken for granted or assumed to be a 'natural' institution and experience. (See, for example, the special issue of *Feminism and Psychology*; on heterosexuality.)

Working-class women have illustrated how their needs and expectations of Women's Studies courses have been subsumed under the assumption that all women have the same access to courses in terms of finance, and that middle-class women have defined the feminist theoretical agenda (Taking Liberties Collective, 1989). Other groups of women such as revolutionary/radical feminists, older women, women with disabilities and women involved with feminism outside the academic arena have voiced dissatisfaction with Women's Studies courses' failure to include and validate their views and political situations.

Women's Studies has begun to recognise the need to work creatively with the concept of difference between women, which ensures that feminist theory is a synthesis of those differences in a dynamic sense – so we have meaningful dialogue around both differences and similarities, not guilty avoidance and angry accusations by women, or a hierarchy of oppressions, nor an undynamic pluralism of positions which does not recognise power differences. But if the 1980s was about an eventual recognition and reflection on this, the 1990s need to be about the need of Women's Studies to make those reflections become a reality in terms of feminist theorising: syllabus content, teaching methods and the involvement of all students and teachers in feminist projects. Some women (and men) have felt the necessity to establish separate Black, lesbian, and Jewish Women's Studies courses as well as gay studies, and we need to talk openly about the reasons for such programmes (for example, the failure of Women's Studies to adequately make visible these groups and their diverse perspectives, and the racism and heterosexism of the institutions) and the implications of them, both in theoretical and resource terms. (For discussion of some of these issues see Cruikshank, 1982; Hull *et al.*, 1982; and Escoffier, 1990). For example, should Lesbian Studies and Black Studies courses be integrated into Women's Studies programmes, or should they be autonomous?

The question of men, both male students and staff, and their relationship to Women's Studies, has gained in relevance as the subject has developed. Ironically, much feminist energy has been spent working out whether men can be feminists or not and devising strategies for coping with them, whether hostile or genuinely interested in Women's Studies. Men, like women, have a variety of reasons for taking up Women's Studies, which range from authentic interest to intellectual curiosity, and include negative reasons such as the wish to 'master' the theories involved, to put down the arguments of feminists more effectively, and the 'need to understand women better'!

An inherent danger is of men studying and teaching feminist perspectives, but not taking on their implications at a personal level, refusing to acknowledge their own power as men or how they use that power in their daily lives and relationships. Some male academics, for instance, appropriate feminist criticism but don't engage with it and their interest is for women, 'both gratifying and unsettling' (Showalter, 1987), given that most men do not even engage with feminist theory at all. Elaine Showalter proceeds to quote Gayatri Spivak who is 'sharply skeptical of the motives of "straight white male intellectuals" who have turned to feminism' (p. 118). Certainly, now that feminist theory has gained some respectability, and is even seen as fashionable, some men see feminist critiques as acceptable, and that engaging with them can perhaps be a good career move. Some have not acknowledged the theoretical debt they owe to Women's Studies in terms of the hard-won insights of feminist theory. Others reflect productively on their position as teachers of Women's Studies (Bezucha, 1985; Schilb, 1985; and Snoek, 1985), but the question arises of whether men should be teaching and studying Women's Studies at all.

However, supportive men have at times ensured that Women's Studies courses have flourished when non-feminist female staff's lack of interest has been apparent, or when no feminist women tutors have been available. Specific situations have meant the principle of only women teaching the courses has been impossible if Women's Studies courses were to be established at all, though many courses have tried to ensure that if men are teaching, then wherever possible, students choose through options whether to take a male-run course. Men, however sympathetic, do change the nature of the classroom in terms of what can be discussed, and what kind of atmosphere can be achieved. Some women, like Pat Mahony (1983), have argued the case that Women's Studies needs to be taught in single-sex groups because some men monopolise discussions. She further makes the point that women in mixed groups will themselves often come to this conclusion.

If it is accepted that men as socially constructed subjects need to examine the issues Women's Studies raises in both a personal and theoretical way, then the question arises of what is the best way for them to do this. Men can join Women's Studies classes, they can take options within their subject areas on feminist issues and some have asserted the need for the setting up of men's studies courses, where they can explore the deconstruction and reconstruction of masculinity, which traditional disciplines have not done (Brod, 1987, Introduction). Men have asserted that 'Men's studies doesn't seek to supplant women's studies. It seeks to buttress, to augment women's studies, to complete the radically re-drawn portrait of gender that women's studies has begun' (Kimmel, 1988, p. 20).

Though the United States has seen the initial growth of such courses, other countries such as Britain are starting to emphasise men's studies sections in bookshops and publishers' catalogues. Some women, whilst supporting the need for men to take responsibility for self-inspection and effecting personal change, as well as theorising male power, view such courses with suspicion. The very name is unfortunate, given that it assumes Women's Studies and men's studies are complementary, and its existence, before the security of Women's Studies courses is established, will, ironically, put the focus back on men, who may ignore feminist work and possibly divert resources away from Women's Studies. Feminists have asked where were the men who are involved in men's studies *before* it became academically advantageous to study masculinity, as well as pointing out that there are other ways men can show support for feminism and women's position, without creating their own area of study (Canaan and Griffin, 1990). The suggestion from Joyce E. Canaan and Christine Griffin is that men should 'Take on the Big Boys instead of the women', the 'Big Boys' being traditional disciplines, as there is still much more work to do there regarding gender and masculinity, despite traditional research being about men.

Another new development in the 1980s and 1990s is gender studies. Gender studies has been growing within the disciplines in Britain and more recently as an area of study in its own right. Increasingly, new journals are appearing which include the word 'gender' in the title. Any development which sees gender divisions as socially constructed, and therefore liable to change, is to be welcomed, the increase in awareness of gender as being as important a variable such as class in theory generally, is also to be seen as positive. But an emerging concern is for the growing tendency of gender studies to be seen as a more politically safe option than Women's Studies. Feminists have argued that the concentration on gender as opposed to placing women as the main category of analysis means that we see both women and men as equally oppressed, and the power imbalance is obscured, thus depoliticising the relationship between the sexes. Men's power and their personal and structural responsibility for women's oppression is no longer of primary importance, and individual men do not have to examine their own beliefs and behaviour, or confront male power at the level of society, if they feel they are equally subordinated. This can happen in both gender studies and men's studies. Some would argue that 'The object of analysis for many has shifted from "women" to "gender", with the implication that both women and men should be regarded as gendered subjects' (Beechey, 1986, p. 1). The acceptance of this shift can entail an arguing of the need for gender studies programmes.

Others, such as Mary Evans (1991), see the 'lure' of gender studies in terms of it being a part of the central concerns of institutions rather than at the margins, and by allowing men into the area so it becomes a complex rather than a narrow or restricted field, as Women's Studies may be perceived. But gender is 'a term which seems to suggest that the interests of the sexes have now converged and that the differences in life changes (not to mention economic rewards) that exist between women and men are matters of choice' (Evans, 1991, p. 73). She argues for the necessity of using the name Women's Studies as it allows the focus to remain on sexual difference 'because asserting the category of woman challenges the classless, genderless, raceless non-problematic person who is the perfect human actor of a consumer society' (p. 72) (see also Sheridan, 1990).

Conclusion

In the 1990s, it is still important that we continue to believe 'If knowledge is power and we hold on to this belief – then we must carefully scrutinize the roads we take in our quest for knowledge – the way we make our revolutions – and ask whether they are indeed suited to making our visions come to life' (Bowles and Klein, 1983, p. 13). This means that what and how we teach is reflected on by ourselves, and in our classrooms. The relationship between Women's Studies and the academic world, and with wider society, is also important. We are developing networks and connections between different institutions and courses, which include Women's Studies in higher education, in access and local community contexts and importantly we need to do this in schools, both secondary and primary. This is not only so that we can build up research links and resources, sharing information, but also to avoid isolation and have a full dialogue between all those involved. Also, so that the insights of Women's Studies are not just for those in higher education, in the development of it as a field of study, there must be awareness of the necessity of empowering girls and older women, whether in schools or community-based situations, in their intellectual and everyday lives.

We need to consider the image of Women's Studies, and without discarding any of the passion and radicalism, should think about ways to make as many women as possible aware of the diversity and richness of feminist thought. We need strategies to ensure that theory is effectively linked to action, including policy formation, thus affecting women's existence.

If the 1980s revealed to us that Women's Studies could be seen as white and Eurocentric in its theories and approaches, and the situation of women worldwide refutes the myth of post-feminism, then one of the most important tasks of Women's Studies is to be aware of its development internationally and the diversity of women's experience. Changes in Europe and the Eastern bloc, as well as elsewhere, afford women the chance to look imaginatively at the concept of difference as well as the commonalities between women, to foster connections, to learn from each other and to give support, so creating a truly global feminism.

Further reading

Jane Aaron and Sylvia Walby (eds), *Out of the Margins: Women's Studies in the Nineties* (London, Falmer Press, 1991). This book deals with a number of issues in Women's Studies, in terms of feminist theoretical concerns and classroom practices. It looks at Women's Studies and the feminist movement as well as diversity and Women's Studies, and its relation as a field of study to other disciplines. Another book which continues the discussions raised here is Hilary Hinds, Ann Phoenix and Jackie Stacey (eds), *Working Out: New Directions for Women's Studies* (London, Falmer Press, 1992).

For an earlier analysis of debates in Women's Studies which are still relevant in the 1990s see Gloria Bowles and Renate Duelli Klein (eds), *Theories of Women's Studies* (London, Routledge & Kegan Paul, 1983).

Sneja Gunew (ed.), *Feminist Knowledge: Critique And Construct* (London, Routledge, 1990); and Sneja Gunew (ed.), *A Reader in Feminist Knowledge*

(London, Routledge, 1991). These companion volumes have sections on feminist knowledge and Women's Studies, feminism and the disciplines, positions within the women's movement and feminism, and developments within feminist theory. The latter volume has a section on Black women and feminism.

Margo Culley and Catherine Portuges (eds), *Gendered Subjects: The Dynamics of Feminist Teaching*, (London, Routledge & Kegan Paul, 1985); and *Women's Studies Quarterly 'Special Feature: Feminist Pedagogy'*, XV (3) and (4) Fall/ Winter, 1987. Both these texts are concerned with the feminist classroom, and discuss a range of pedagogical questions and approaches within feminist theory. Integral to many of the individual essays in each is a consideration of gender, 'race', lesbianism and class in relation to students, teachers and feminist thought.

2

Talking Racism and the Editing of Women's Studies[1]

Kum-Kum Bhavnani

Women's Studies is starting to become established within further and higher education in many parts of the world. Often, however, it is rare to see Black women as students or teachers on such courses.[2] The question is, 'why?' In this chapter, I will argue that the racism embedded within contemporary and prevailing concepts of feminism and Women's Studies act as a powerful disincentive for Black women to participate in these courses. Racism is a system of domination and subordination based on spurious biological notions that human beings can be fixed into racially discrete groups. It is identified as a 'natural' process, and is seen to be a logical consequence of the differentiation of human beings into 'races'. Given that there is no sound evidence from the natural and biological sciences to justify the assumption that the human species can be divided up into separate 'races', both 'race' and racism come to be economic, political, ideological and social expressions. In other words, 'race' is not a social category which is empirically defined, rather it is created, reproduced and challenged through economic, political and ideological institutions.

Women's exploitation and oppression are created and reproduced through the domains of production, reproduction, care-giving and sexuality (Mitchell, 1971). Thus, the racialised structurings of capitalism and patriarchy, along with analyses of imperialism and colonialism, are central to discussions of women's exploitation and oppression. While, for example, the debates and arguments between socialist and radical feminists has always been on the curricula of Women's Studies courses, that some women are also implicated in the reproduction of racisms has rarely been a discussion which has been acknowledged, let alone engaged with; and sometimes, such discussions have been silenced. 'Woman-centred' approaches have been the order of the decade, with comparatively little explicit discussion of what such a phrase means, and what it is seen as signifying. 'We' are all assumed to both know what it means, and agree with the assumptions on which it is based. To follow through with this argument, the unity of women has often formed the theme through which sexuality, violence against women, and reproductive rights are discussed. While discussions of women's location within economic production, the role of the state and in the nuclear family has meant that 'class' inequalities have been engaged with, albeit in rather a limited way at times, rarely have these inequalities been noted for how they inform and are informed by both racialised *and* gendered inequalities. Further, I will suggest that as questions are raised as to why it is women are exploited and oppressed through racially constituted, patriarchal and capitalist formations, it may then be possible to consider how to continue the transformation of Women's Studies and the courses associated with it, as well as the projects of feminism more generally.

Women's Studies courses in colleges and universities have attempted to create a clear area of intellectual enquiry to be known as Women's Studies, or indeed Feminist Studies. Further, as Victoria Robinson discussed in the previous chapter, Women's Studies have also critiqued forms of academic enquiry within the 'mainstream'. The critiques, summarised in the chapters in this book, have examined how women's contributions have been erased from much academic work, as, for example, within history. While journals such as *History Workshop*, in defining themselves as socialist and feminist have attempted to put right this *Erasure*, it is still clear that this process must continue until gender divisions are located centrally within historical enquiry. An erasure of women's contributions means that another process comes into play – that of *Denial*. Here, writers have denied, and continue to deny, the particular ways in which women can both contribute to and challenge the existing social order. Marxist theory is often singled out for such a charge – that it denies the *differing* ways in which women and men can contribute in the creation of surplus value; and some of the writings on women and domestic labour attempt to confront that (Coulson, Magas and Wainwright, 1975). However, as gender divisions get erased in academic enquiry, denial remains respectable, and women become

Invisible. This invisibility is a familiar process; women are absent in much social theory. Yet it is often only noticed when feminists such as Nancy Fraser (1989) write about gender in contemporary social theory. Some work attempts to 'add women in' in order to avoid being categorised as 'malestream' (see Abbott and Wallace (1990) for examples and critiques of this approach). This way of acknowledging the existence of women can be criticised as *Tokenism* because, whilst it includes women as a topic, it does not recognise the power imbalance between women and men, nor does it place gender divisions as a central facet of analysing economic, political and social relationships.

The four processes of *Erasure, Denial, Invisibility* and *Tokenism* are clues in a work of detection of the mainstream and are basic to feminist critiques. Given that Women's Studies courses are centrally informed by feminist writings, these four processes also frequently form the organising principles for developing curricula in Women's Studies.

For many who are students and teachers of Women's Studies, these ideas are no longer new or controversial. In practice they represent part of the rationale for the existence and growing appeal of Women's Studies. Women's Studies is thus a challenge to much academic work; however, to write about *a* feminism, which analyses and challenges capitalism and patriarchy, implies that women have common interests. These assumed similarities of interest are then defined in such a way that they override the differences of interests amongst us.

Whatever our desires, hopes and visions for a global sisterhood, it is clear that such a sisterhood is to be struggled for; it has to be a goal rather than a starting point. Songs such as 'Are my hands Clean?' by 'Sweet Honey in the Rock', a group of African–American women living in the United States (words cited in Enloe, 1989, p. 158), which contain lines such as 'I wear garments touched by hands from all over the world' and 'Far from the Port au Prince palace/Third World Women toil doing piece work to Sears' specifications/For three dollars a day my sisters make my blouse' show in a pointed way how some women's exploitation works in the interests of other women who buy cheap clothes. What these words do, and most sociological texts do not, is highlight some of the tensions within feminist approaches. The song not only hints that women living in industrialised nations benefit from the sweated labour of women in other parts of the world, but it also suggests that within industrialised countries, both the Black and the white populations may benefit in similar ways from such exploitation. In this way, it shows that the interests of women the world over are not always the same on all issues. Women living in the Third World may have differing priorities from Black women living in industrialised nations, who, in turn, may have differing priorities and interests from white women. As Sweet Honey in the Rock is a group of Black singers, the words can thus act as a reminder to Black and Third-World women living in affluent countries that our interests can also clash with the interests of women living and working elsewhere. So, this example demonstrates that the category 'woman' is not a transhistorical or transgeographical one, for it shows that women's interests are not always and automatically coincident. Thus, if woman is not a transhistorical category, and all women's interests do not coincide, then it follows that feminism, the political movement which aims to liberate all women, is also historically and geographically specific. In other words, there need to be many feminisms, that is, many ways of understanding and analysing women's exploitation and resistances.

Just as 'woman' and 'feminism' are not concepts which have unchanging meanings, so the term 'race' has specific origins and a specific trajectory depending on its geographical and historical meanings. 'Race' does not have a biological validity, for all human beings are members of the same race, *Homo sapiens*. However, it is clear that 'race' does have a social power, for it is on the basis of assumed racial differences that human beings are categorised as Black or white in Britain. The development of 'race' as a spurious *scientific* category is a consequence of imperialism and colonisation; for it is this 'scientificism' which informed, and still informs, prevailing ideologies of biological superiority and inferiority among human beings on the basis of 'race'. But people are not merely categorised; racism, the consequence of 'race', means that there are power inequalities embedded within this historically specific system of domination. In other words, human beings are located within relationships of subordination and domination which are simultaneously framed by racialised, economic and gendered inequalities. That is, capitalist society is not only patriarchal and racially structured, but it is, by definition, also structured by class (Bhavnani and Coulson, 1986).

It is the ways in which 'race', gender and class are enmeshed and inscribed within each other which has led to forceful challenges to feminisms – whether Marxist, socialist, liberal or radical (see Chapter 3). And it is this racially unselfconscious feminism which often assumes that 'woman' is a unitary and singular category; that is, that there are no differences of interest amongst Black and white women. Even when the differences of interest are acknowledged by some feminists, it is rare for such differences to be actively engaged with – mere acknowledgement seems to be enough.

The challenges to feminism have come from a wide variety of perspectives and most have originated (but not exclusively so), from Black women. The initial direction of these challenges can be summed up as follows: 'By and large within the Women's Movement today, white women focus upon their oppression as women, and ignore differences of race, sexual preference, class and age. There is a pretence to a homogeneity of experience covered by the word *sisterhood* that does not in fact exist' (Lorde, 1984, p. 114). Audre Lorde, who has been described, for example, as 'a lesbian, feminist and activist poet' (Lewis, 1990, p. 101) and has described herself as a 'Black lesbian feminist socialist mother of two including one boy and a member of an inter-racial couple' (Lorde, 1984, p. 114), emphasises the creativity which differences among women can fuel. And in doing this, she addresses some of her writings to white women: 'Some problems we share as women, some we do not. You fear your children will grow up to join the patriarchy and testify against you, we fear our children will be dragged from a car and shot down in the street, and you will turn your backs upon the reasons they are dying' (Lorde, 1984, p. 119). This brief extract from Lorde's prose writing, in addressing white women, captures both an accusation of racial erasure ('some we do not') as well as her way of examining the differing and often contradictory experiences of Black and white women. Whilst she acknowledges that all women who are mothers have fears for their children, she is arguing that the fears of Black women simultaneously include a fear that white women will refuse to look at the *reasons* that may cause Black children to be shot.

Erasure is thus a key theme in critiques of feminism which are associated with Black women. bell hooks (1982) called her book *Ain't I A Woman?* to signal the ways in which Black women have been excluded from notions of feminism. The title of her book uses the now-famous words of Sojourner Truth, who was the only Black woman present at a Women's Rights Convention held in 1851 at Akron, Ohio, when, in her address to the Convention, she used that phrase as a refrain. The extract from her speech which is most frequently alluded to is as follows:

That man over there says that women need to be helped into carriages, and lifted over ditches, and to have the best places . . . and ain't I a woman? Look at me! Look at my arm! . . . I have ploughed and planted and gathered into barns, and no man could heed me – and ain't I a woman? I could work as much as any man (when I could get it) and bear the lash as well – and ain't I a woman? I have borne five children and seen them most sold off into slavery, and when I cried out with grief, none but Jesus heard – and ain't I a woman?

In this way, Sojourner Truth made the point that racism as well as class bias were embedded within the nineteenth-century women's movement (Davis, 1982). Recently, Patricia Hill Collins (1990) has elegantly shown that in questioning the norms by which white women were defined, that in demonstrating that femininity was actually specific to white middle-class women (for example, being helped into carriages, helped over ditches, not having strong arms), Sojourner Truth was, in fact, deconstructing 'woman' as a category. That is, this well-known speech can be understood as being a commentary on apparently universal notions of 'woman', of 'femininity', and not only as an assertion that Black women are different from white women. The implication of deconstructing 'woman', of challenging Erasure means that the 'solution' which follows is not a simplistic one of 'adding (Black in this case) women in'. Rather, by raising the charge of racial Erasure, Black feminists are presenting a means of redefining 'womanhood' and 'femininity'.

Such a lesson may also be drawn from Rosina Visram's (1986) historical account of Indians in Britain from 1700 to 1947, in which she demonstrates that the history of Britain is one which rests on the contributions of women and men from India, from at least two centuries ago. She notes that women frequently came as ayahs; they accompanied the British household on its return journey from India: 'Once on board, the ayah took complete charge of the children, the baggage and the memsahib. Good ayahs were not only meant to be clean, honest and trustworthy with children, but capable as nurses and excellent sailors too' (Visram, 1986, p. 29). The ayahs were then usually dismissed from their job when they arrived in England, and had to fend for themselves; as may be imagined, their lives were thus even more difficult than when employed as a carer. Visram's documenting of this pattern of migration for some Indian women shows clearly how the white women who were the memsahibs negotiated their roles as mother and homemaker by using the labour of poor, non-white women. It is this kind of example which has been hidden from history and which, when unearthed, can begin to show how imperialism, class, and 'race' inform the varieties of definitions of womanhood which are encountered. In other words, Black women servicing white households is a relationship which is embedded in the differing historical interests of women all over the world. It is still the case that many women are able to use/buy the labour power of poorer women (for example as child-minders, nursery nurses and domestic workers) precisely in order to lighten their own domestic and 'caring' responsibilities, these responsibilities having themselves been forged within patriarchal concepts of women's main role. I point to this set of arguments not because there are always easy political answers to changing the state of affairs, but because it can be seen that definitions of 'woman' are often contradictory; it is these contradictions which may become highlighted as the histories of Black women are examined and reflected upon.

As racial Erasure is examined, for example in historical analyses, so it becomes possible to see the ways in which white women themselves have been implicated in these racialised erasures. This is not only to say that white women can be, and are, racist, or implicated in institutionalised racism, but also to suggest that there is, at the same time, a *Denial* of white as a racialised category. White skin frequently signifies power and privilege – 'the rightness of whiteness' – and this can be accompanied by a resounding silence emanating from white women about this aspect of political, economic and ideological inequality (see Frankenberg (1988) for an outstanding exception to this denial). What such a silence does is to deny the need for many feminisms to view as central to their task that the manner in which a person develops into defining themselves as white is as important as focusing on the experience of Black women, and thus that one of the goals of feminism is to work towards the removal of the apparently natural power and privilege often accorded to white women in relation to Black women (and sometimes to Black men). If 'whiteness' is unpacked, it is then possible to see not only how gender relations are expressed in racialised contexts, but also how racialised structuring is informed by gender inequalities.

A silence and denial over the power and privilege which whiteness can often provide is most frequently encountered within certain strands of radical feminism. For example, Elly Bulkin (1980, cited in Jaggar, 1983, p. 122) has argued that Mary Daly wipes out the particular oppressions of poor women, colonised women and women of colour – that is, she argues that Daly operates with a false universalism in her work *Gyn/Ecology* (1978). As radical feminism argues that the key antagonism in human social relations is between women and men, which is often the experienced oppression of white Western middle-class women, then the political position that sisterhood is the primary, if not the only, potential to be strived for, is often the logical consequence of such a politics for Black and white radical feminists. This is not to say that liberal, socialist and Marxist feminisms do not strive for sisterhood, nor that they deal adequately with racism. My argument is, however, that a position such as that which is the basis of all forms of radical feminism, and which urges all women to unite as 'sisters' against the patriarchy, is the one that is the most likely to lead to a Denial of differing and contradictory interests between Black and white women.

The argument that the ways in which white women are often in a position of domination in relations to Black women, and so frequently have different and conflicting interests, has sometimes been conducted in a bitter and angry way between Black and white women. One strand within these debates is that the silences and denials to which I have just referred lead to an assumption that *all* women have material interests in common. But when a white woman falsely accuses a Black man of raping her, is she my sister? Do she and I have interests in common?[3] One of the clearest ways in which one can see what it is that is being argued by Black women is to read the Combahee River Collective's statement:

> A combined antiracist and antisexist position drew us together initially, and as we developed politically we addressed ourselves to heterosexism and economic oppression under capitalism . . . We believe that sexual politics under patriarchy is as pervasive in Black women's lives as are the politics of class and race. We also often find it difficult to separate race from class from sex oppression because in our lives they are most often experiences simultaneously . . . We struggle together with Black men against racism, while we also struggle with Black men about sexism. (Combahee River Collective, 1981, pp. 212–13)

To ensure that their point cannot be missed, perhaps another sentence could be included. This could read: 'We struggle together with white women against patriarchal oppression while we also struggle with white women about racism and imperial domination'.

The reasons for arguing that sisterhood is not global – for looking at the 'boundaries of sisterhood' (Carby, 1982a) – have been debated both in North America and in Britain. Angela Davis (1982) has shown how the campaigns for women's suffrage in the United States in the last century were based on attempts by many white women to privilege white women's suffrage above that of Black men. The history of these struggles is not a straightforward one. Davis shows how although Elizabeth Cady Stanton had strongly urged support for the anti-slavery campaigns when the Civil War began in the United States, Stanton also suggested, at the first annual meeting of the Equal Rights Association in 1867, that white Anglo-Saxon women ought to obtain the franchise before Black men received the vote: 'With the black man we have no new element in this government, but with the education and elevation of women we have a power that is to develop the Saxon race into a higher and nobler life' (Stanton, cited in Davis, 1982, p. 72).

It is this history of pitting white women's rights against those of Black men that underlies the charge of racism directed at many aspects of white women's campaigning. Gendered inequalities are set up so as to act in competition with racialised inequalities – *either* someone is Black *or* they are a woman. The consequence of this is that Black women are defined into or out of one of these categories, and those of us who refuse such a splitting, who argue uncompromisingly that 'race' and gender are inextricably enmeshed, often end up with our arguments not being heard. In this way, the denials elide into Invisibility – the *Invisibility* of Black women as racialised and gendered subjects simultaneously.

A racism within much of Women's Studies and feminist campaigns which is based on the Invisibility of Black women is the target of many critiques. For example, Hazel Carby (1982a) showed how 'feminist' analyses of the British Welfare State as reinforcing the dependency of women on men in Britain does not 'fit' for Black women. Many Afro-Caribbean women who were recruited to Britain after 1945 came as workers first and foremost. Thus, unlike white women, Black women were not suffocatingly 'protected' from the labour market: 'Rather than a concern to protect or preserve the black family in Britain, the state reproduced commonsense notions of its inherent pathology: black women were seen to fail as mothers precisely because of their position as workers' (Carby, 1982a, p. 219).

Black women of South Asian origin who were likely to enter Britain after 1945 as dependents of men were subject to the controls of the British immigration legislation, a set of legislation which legitimated internal examinations of women at entry to Britain, and which led to severe restrictions on family life for Black people (Bhavnani and Bhavnani, 1985). The point here is that while white women such as

Elizabeth Wilson (1977) demonstrated some of the ways in which the state reproduced patriarchal relationships, these ways were specific to white, and often English, women. Black women's relationships to the state, as workers as well as migrants, and the ways in which these interconnected with ideologies and political realities of women as dependents, were ignored. Thus, Black women were Invisible in such writings. More recently, Fiona Williams (1989) has reviewed the implications of the charge of racism and sexism in analyses of British welfare.

The Invisibility of Black women is, of course, not only present in many so-called feminist analyses. Just as it is often assumed that all women in the category 'woman' are white, so it is often assumed that all Black people are men (Hull *et al.*, 1982). Many analyses of the experience of slavery in the United States do just that. However, in 1971, Angela Davis wrote a piece, while she was in jail, called 'Reflections on the role of the black woman in the community of slaves', in which she analyses and so refutes the concept of the Black matriarch 'as its presumed historical inception' (Davis, 1971, p. 3). One section of her article deals with resistances within the lives of the enslaved, and she argues that it was only within the 'home' (out of sight of the slave owners and overseers) that it was possible for the enslaved to assert a small amount of freedom. Davis argues that it was the enslaved *women* who were doing domestic work within the communities of the enslaved, thus mirroring and reproducing the patriarchal routines of white society in North America. She then uses this insight to suggest that 'Domestic labor was the only meaningful labor for the slave community as a whole . . . the black woman in chains could help to lay the foundation for some degree of autonomy . . . She was therefore essential to the *survival* of the community. Not all people have survived enslavement; hence her survival-oriented activities were themselves a form of resistance' (Davis, 1971, p. 7).

In other words, Davis argues that through performing the domestic labour tasks for the enslaved, Black women were central in the creation of an arena through which some aspects of slavery could be resisted. Davis also shows not only how resistances within slavery were conducted by women, but also how the 'alleged benefits of the ideology of femininity did not accrue to her' (Davis 1971, p. 7). Rather, because she was treated as slave, she was also made equal by the slave owners, in terms of extraction of surplus value, to enslaved men – 'She shared in the deformed equality of equal oppression' (Davis, 1971, p. 8). Thus, 'It would appear that the intense levels of resistance maintained by black people . . . are due in part to the greater *objective* equality between the black man and the black woman (Davis, 1971, p. 15).

This argument could be further continued by suggesting that as ideologies of sexuality are racialised ideologies – although different for Black women than for Black men – this meant that Black men were more likely to be severely punished and/or lynched for apparently 'inappropriate' sexual behaviour (for example, sexual relations with white women), while Black women were more likely than Black men to be raped by slave owners who were men. From this it can be seen that interrogating the histories of Black women who were enslaved in the United States can provide insights into resistances to slavery. Such histories can also begin to suggest a means of reflecting upon the tense and contradictory interests between Black and white women, and their relationships to ideologies of femininity.

A key aspect of Women's Studies is that the academic enquiries and projects attempt to overcome the processes of Invisibility of many women, and thus stop us being hidden from history. Almost by definition, such work will not only 'add women in', but will also aim to understand women's myriad resistances and forms of exploitation. For example, Parita Trivedy (1984) documents some of the ways women were involved in peasant uprisings in India in the 1940s. In her article, she outlines the existence of the Mahila Samitis who organised around the specific forms of oppression experienced by peasant women, which included being couriers as well as being involved in armed struggle. She states that it is necessary to conduct such historical work because 'the characterisation of Indian history, Indian society and the Indian peoples continues to affect the way events in India are viewed today and continues to affect the way Asian communities in Britain are viewed' (Trivedy, 1984, p. 43). In other words, this type of approach may then allow the present to be understood as *dynamic* and *interpreted* rather than as being static and given.

But it is not only history which can prevent Invisibility. We must also learn to speak out when we can. For when we speak out against racism, we are then able to begin to create the conditions in which dignity and confidence for all people may occur. Take the example of lesbianism. Just as many white lesbians argue about the Invisibility of lesbianism within feminist analyses and campaigns, so Black lesbians also have commented on their invisibility: 'G: But I also feel a joy and strength at seeing any Black and Third World women coming out because they all help to shatter the myth that lesbianism is a "white thing"' (Carmen, Gail, Shaila and Pratibha, 1984, p. 56).

The process of becoming Invisible affects Black and Third-World Women in many ways. It is not only our histories in relation to the histories of white women which work in conflictual and contradictory ways, it is also that our sexualities and our ways of expressing them – whether in an interracial setting, whether with white children, whether we live as single women or whether we choose to live as lesbians – get informed and influenced by the invisibility. But that Invisibility can be challenged in two ways that can be used to complement each other – by working out *when* and *why* our voices are not heard, as well as by our learning how to project our voices more precisely. This is not just to obtain a more complete description, not a means for 'adding in' another issue, but to force the otherwise hollow and superficial distortions within much of feminist work to be heard and seen. As our voices are heard, so it is possible to lay out a more precise set of projections that can indicate the kinds of visions we have and want to create.

Erasure, leading to Denial, which becomes the precursor for Invisibility means that a solution which is often created is that of *Tokenism*. The inclusion of a 'token', the exception, for example a Black woman, can be one way to suggest that all is not as it seems. It can also be a means to indicate that human lives and human institutions, economic, political and ideological, can be organised in such a way that they do not have to conform to an apparent 'normality', a state of affairs which can exclude Black women, unless we are seen as either 'victims' or are 'pathologised'. But Tokenism can also mean a lack. The problem, though, is that the very same acknowledgement of a lack can often prevent any further analysis and exploration of why that lack occurs. A case in point is Dorothy Smith's exciting book *The Everyday World as Problematic: A Feminist Sociology*. In this book, Smith aims to analyse 'relations of ruling'. She suggests that such an analysis of the relations of ruling involves the taking on of 'the view of ruling and to view society and social relations in terms of the perspectives, interests and relevances of men active in relations of ruling. It is to know ourselves thus' (Smith, 1988, pp. 2–3).

Who is the 'ourselves' to which Smith refers? It does seem as if the 'ourselves' is synonymous with white women, but the question which then follows is, 'Why was it not specified that it was white women?' Smith has a footnote at this point. In it, she refers to the work by Edward Said, *Orientalism* (1978) which she says 'is valuable reading for feminists'. While Smith actively demonstrates men's interests as constituting relations of ruling, she does not explicitly state *which* men's interests are being analysed. Neither does she look systematically at the ways in which some (white?) women are implicated within these relations of ruling such that other (Black?) women are not. The footnote to Said[4] which I have quoted becomes an *acknowledgement* of the issue and so the footnote becomes the acknowledgement without the analysis. Towards the end of Smith's book she does, however, see that there is a problem: 'If the discourse of women is a discourse of white women, it is in large part because [this discourse] has become organised in institutional contexts that have excluded black and native women as a routine accomplishment of how they work' (Smith, 1988, pp. 221–2).

Smith has put her finger on something very important here, and she continues by quoting some poetry: 'the category human has no meaning/ when spoken in white' (Bannerji, quoted in Smith, 1988, p. 222). Smith then writes a thoughtful paragraph on the fact that 'the relevances crystallized in the discourse of white women may overlap with but are not the same as the relevances of black women' (Smith, 1988, 222). In the next seven sentences she hints at the complexity that the differing relevances create for 'feminist' theorising. The book ends three pages later. My point here is that Smith's potentially powerful and insightful analysis of the relations of ruling is weakened by Token acknowledgements to pertinent themes which are, however, only dealt with in passing or are 'added in' almost as an afterthought at the end.

I am anxious here to not appear to be setting a moral high ground about who can be more thoughtful on 'race' than whom. Catherine Stimpson (1988) wrote in the early 1970s: 'Race, to the dismay of many, to the relief of others has become a proper test for deciding who is best at certain intellectual as well as political activities' (p. 3). This sentiment captures a large amount of the tensions I feel when I write and argue about racism. It *is* proper that a racialised consciousness be central to all intellectual and political work. But I would not wish to caricature its importance to the point where my politics get understood as the politics of Black separatists. Further, it is clear that some (white) writers and political activists have taken racism seriously. For example, the journal *Feminist Review* gave over editorial control to a group of Black women in 1984, and *Signs* produced an important special issue (1989) called 'Common Grounds and Crossroads: Race, Ethnicity and Class in Women's Lives'. And yet I still see reviews of feminist theory which merely add Black women in (for example, Tong, 1989).

It is this 'adding in' which Elizabeth Spelman (1988) partly addresses in her book *Inessential Woman*. In one chapter in her book she closely examines the arguments, which, when comparing racism to sexism, often lead to questions such as 'which is more fundamental?' This, she points out, is an unhelpful question, for it implies that each is a clearly bounded, discrete category untouched by the other. The question is unanswerable, for it is like asking, of the product of a multiplication, which of the two numbers is more fundamental to the answer. In the same vein, it is not therefore possible to list a universal hierarchy of oppressions. Racism and sexism inform each other – all women are racialised and all human beings are gendered. In other words, each structures the other, with both being inscribed within unequal class relationships. And, of course, class is not just white or masculine. I am not simply a woman, nor Black, nor a university lecturer, nor Indian, nor someone who teaches research methods, nor an aunt, nor heterosexual, nor a socialist – for each of my apparently categorical identities are not what they appear. A Black woman university lecturer working in Britain, for example, is constantly negotiating some of the tensions and contradictions of symbolic and actual power, privilege, powerlessness and institutionalised discrimination when she is doing her job.[5] Some co-workers and students may want to categorise me as one or the other first, and I may elect, or have foisted upon me, a particular part of my identity in a particular situation. But as I opt for one category or identity, this very process of opting means that there is an acknowledgement that there are others which could have been selected. And if there are others which could have been selected, then the fact that there were possibilities must mean that those categories also inform my identity. So, categories of identity are not discrete and uninfluenced by each other – for human consciousness and language both create and are created by the relationship of the categories to each other. For example, when I walk down a street in Europe or North America wearing jeans and am harassed or abused, I cannot say that my sex is privileged above my Blackness or vice versa – because I don't know if it is.

Trivedy (1984) makes a similar point when she discusses campaigns by some Black women in Britain against deportation; the campaigns which she discusses began because the women's marriages ended while they were in Britain and the state deemed that the women therefore had no right to continue living in Britain. She points out that white women supported the campaigns because the campaigns were seen as a 'women's issue'. However, she says that this approach 'created tensions because they have failed to see that in reality racial and sexual oppressions operate at one and the same time . . . and it is only when the specificities of the different forms of oppressions are tackled as they manifest themselves in particular . . . situations can we begin to forge links and alliances in a rigorous and meaningful manner' (Trivedy, 1984, p. 46). Therefore, simply 'adding' race into gendered inequalities, rather than conceptualising them as enmeshed within each other can produce a tokenism of the most unhelpful sort: we come to be 'perceived as token women in Black texts and as token Blacks in feminist texts' (Giddings, 1984, p. 5).

Thus the very processes I have discussed above and which Women's Studies courses attempt to challenge – *Erasure, Denial, Invisibility* and *Tokenism* – act themselves as *EDIT*ors of Women's Studies. If the arguments I have outlined so far are taken seriously and reflected upon, these arguments may also point to routes away from the dead end of false promises provided by the unthinking ideas of sisterhood which I discussed earlier.

One way out may be to think about Black and white women as having different experiences. Spelman (1988), for example, argues that it is therefore crucial to take account (she scintillatingly calls it 'a lively regard') of the variety of women's experiences. While experiences are a key to giving Women's Studies its force and power, I think that having a 'lively regard' for different women's experiences is only one of many starting points. Whilst 'regard' implies both respect and affection – qualities which are antipathetic to racism – and 'lively' signifies the necessity for being actively involved in the processes, it is still the case that privileging experience could be a dead root rather than a blossom.

A key and major contribution of Women's Studies texts has been to record the importance of experience within academic analyses. By experience, I refer to the ways in which human beings describe and discuss individual and personal feelings. This is an important way by which feminists can tackle academic work in Women's Studies while retaining an overall direction for our politics, which to me includes the process of excavating suppressed and subjugated knowledges. But I find myself in a dilemma. Take the use of the word 'oppression'. A group of white women could tell me that they feel 'oppressed' by my determination to concentrate on 'difference' and its implication for challenging power inequalities, and I can say that I feel 'oppressed' by their refusal to consider 'difference'. In using the same word, does it mean that these are both the same types of experience? How does this experience of 'oppression' differ from the 'oppression' of the dispossessed poor – be they in London, New York, Johannesburg or Bombay? What use is a notion of global sisterhood when one thinks about 'home', for example:

> Where is home for starters? Can you call a country which has system-atically colonised your countries of origin, one which refuses through a thorough racism in its institutions, media and culture to even recog-nise your existence and your rights to that existence – can you call this country 'home' without having your tongue inside your cheek?
>
> For Black women who are political or economic exiles from coun-tries such as South Africa, Chile, Jamaica, India (the list could of course be endless) where is 'home'? . . . Home with such women becomes a place of mind, a place where she knows she cannot be. (Grewal *et al.*, 1988, p. 10)

One path through this problem of valuing and analysing different experiences is to reflect on how experience (and it is frequently, but not exclusively white) has become privileged, and has become *the* claim to an unchanging truth. Feminist critiques of academic knowledge have had to rely on challenging the notion of objectivity, and have therefore raised the question 'who can be a knower?' (Harding, 1987). There has therefore been a challenge to the notion of a value-free knowledge (see Chapter 1). Further, it has been argued that the different ways in which different knowledge is framed is an *ideological* issue rather than one of objective analysis (Alonso, 1988). As a result, it has often 'made sense' for some feminists to construct experience as being in opposition to objectivity. In order, then, to challenge patriarchal and spuriously objec-tive knowledge, so the argument goes, it is necessary to remove objectiv-ity as privileged knowledge. This, it is claimed, can be done by inverting the binary oppositions of experience and objectivity. In other words, within this framework, to privilege experience will mean that 'objectiv-ity' becomes downgraded. The result of this argument is that 'experi-ence' becomes *the* claim to truth, much as the 'objectivity' which is being railed against. Thus, 'experience' is used as a truth which silences and ends the right to argue with it.

Whilst an insight into differing meanings of experience is very import-ant for Women's Studies, the difficulty for me is that feminist projects can only have an impact, or be central in the creation of a new order, if inversion of these hierarchies of knowledge (the objectivity/experience hierarchy, which can imply unequal power relationships) are accompanied by a simultaneous subversion. For 'experience' can be a back door through which ideas of global sisterhood can remain unquestioned. Power inequalities therefore end up being sidestepped. In other words, I suggest that not only must a particular form of knowledge be 'dis-privileged', but, at the same time, it should not be replaced by some other form of knowledge which is to be defined as privileged. That is, it is not enough to value or privilege experience in relation to objective know-ledge/analysis; for one is still defined as more important than the other.

Rather, it is crucial to demonstrate that individual experience is created because it is in an *active relationship* with objectivity. Each both creates and informs and is created and informed by the other. For example, to continue with the idea of the dispossessed poor, my version of feminism leads me to *experience* anger about all human poverty, and this experience is informed by my *'objective' knowledge* that there is institutionalised injustice against poor people. In this way, my intellec-tual commitment to examine the causes and the perpetuation of poverty are informed by my experience of seeing people who have to beg for money being stripped of all human dignity and self-respect. I cannot say that my experience is more important than my 'objective' knowledge – each has informed the development and commitment of the other. It is this relationship that I suggest can undermine the privileging of one form of knowledge over another.

A similar point can be drawn from Barbara Christian's 1987 article called 'The Race for Theory'. In a discussion of the high status accorded to 'theoretical' work within many academic disciplines, including philo-sophy and literary studies, she suggests that 'some of our most daring and potentially radical critics (and by 'our' I mean black, female, Third World) [are] speaking a language and defining their discussion in terms alien to and opposed to our needs and orientation' (Christian, 1987, p. 52). While arguing that 'my folk . . . have always been a race for theory' she is not suggesting a privileging of 'pure experience' above criticism. Rather, she is arguing against an opposition between theory, which is treated as mediated *analysis*, and literature, which is treated as pure and authentic *expression*. The oppositions she discusses here are parallel to the ones of 'objectivity' and 'experience' which I discussed above. Her argument is partly about the academic status given to theo-retical analyses, which means that those who strive for the greatest of academic respectability have to be defined as doing theoretical work in order to achieve this respectability. The argument she presents is one which has seemingly always been present within Women's Studies in the academy, but does not seem to have been discussed very often in the past few years. (See Coulson and Bhavnani (1990) for one such recent attempt, however.)

But despite the cautionary note sounded above, I do not want to forget that analysing experience in the light of theory, and theory in the light of experience, must continue to remain central to the projects of Women's Studies. An outstanding example of such integrative writing is Avtar Brah's 'Journey to Nairobi' (1988). In this piece, the author begins with her return to East Africa (where she had not been since Idi Amin's expulsion of East African Asians from Uganda in the late 1960s) for the 1985 United Nations Decade for Women conference which marked the 'Women's Decade'. In writing about her return, Brah frames her experiences of return within an understanding of the imperialist, gendered and racialised history of countries in East Africa, and concludes the article with a comment on the differing and yet colliding racisms in contemporary Britain: 'Black women – Asian and Afro-Caribbean – have played a pivotal role in Black struggles in the past. We remain in a strong position to carry them forward' (Brah, 1988, p. 88).

The 'cause' of the EDITing I discussed earlier is not just because Black women's *experiences* are different from those of white women. For, if that were the case, then 'adding Black women in' would be the only solution. Rather, what also needs analysis is *why* the experiences are Erased, Denied or made Invisible. Merely 'adding in' does not facilitate the development of the questions which attempt to understand the processes behind the EDITing. Further, the provision of answers in the guise of individual responsibilities, that is that the individual should have thought harder about these issues, is not enough. It may be part of the explanation. But also part of the explanation is the way in which language, thought, common sense and ideologies are framed within imperialist, and therefore patriarchal, histories. As we have seen, 'adding in' is unsatisfactory, for it leaves the category of 'feminist' itself unquestioned and therefore intact. The issue is one of politics.

In order to discuss politics here, it seems to be necessary to define 'feminist'. However, to define feminism is in itself a political statement: 'The way in which feminism is defined is contingent upon the way the definer understands past, existing and future relationships between women and men' (Ramazanoglu, 1989, p. 7). And a political stance requires the naming of sources of power inequalities and resistances. If politics is 'the means by which human beings regulate, attempt to regulate and challenge, with a view to changing unequal power relationships'

(Bhavnani, 1991), then feminism must attempt to address political contexts and changes. Feminism, and its 'daughter' within the academy Women's Studies, is beautifully placed to understand and challenge the local and global directions and impetus of contemporary capitalism. In asking questions such as 'What is it that oppresses women? What shapes the lives and identities of women?' (Bhavnani and Coulson, 1986, p. 86), feminism can point to both the movement and organisation of capital across national boundaries (Mitter, 1986), as well as to aspects of contemporary life in Britain (for example, Bryan, Dadzie and Scafe, 1985). And while these two aspects, combined together, may appear to be literally very far apart, it is the local/global, theory/practice, and experience/analysis oppositions which feminism can disrupt, interrupt and hopefully subvert.

What is specific to feminism that makes me determined to keep hold of that word? Why do I still insist on calling myself a feminist (usually qualified by Black and Marxist/socialist, but I can imagine a time when I won't need to do that)? For me, the word retains a vision of *all* women challenging sexualised, gendered, racialised and economic control over our lives through ideology and politics. And because we have a variety of relationships with men, ranging from attempts at absolute separatism to working together with them, feminism must therefore be a starting point for women who aim to eradicate poverty and injustice for all human beings. That 'feminism' has taken on the mantle of being universal, while its shape has been specific is not reason enough to discard it. This is because feminism is associated with progressivism and a progressive politics; the task for Women's Studies must be to ensure feminism speaks both universally and specifically. 'Feminism is the political theory and practice that struggles to free *all* women: women of colour, working class women, poor women, disabled women, lesbians, old women – as well as white economically privileged heterosexual women' (Smith, 1982, p. 49). The next question which arises is, 'What is to be done?' The EDITing has to be negotiated, debated and discussed, and also inverted so that the process of subversion can become integral.

The goal is clearly for feminism to be *Transformed* in such a way that it is seen as a challenge to economic and racial, as well as sexual, exploitation and oppression (Bhavnani and Coulson, 1986). The means by which this can continue requires that *International* perspectives, rather than only national ones, be placed at the centre. Cynthia Enloe's (1989) examination of international politics by 'making feminist sense' of it, is an exciting venture. Just as Roberta Sykes' (1989) book on Black

Australians provides some telling insights for all of us, whether socialist, or feminist or both. In a different and stimulating manner, Lata Mani's (1990) article on the different ways in which her feminist historical work is received when discussed in the USA, in Britain and India, provides an instructive starting point through which we could all think about our own work, political and academic.

If transformation is possible by situating feminism in an International frame, then *Difference* comes to the front. Discussions of difference, often focusing exclusively on experience are certainly one part of Women's Studies. Whether it is discussions of 'Free Abortion on Demand' or 'A woman's right to control over her body', these discussions are known to be part of women's political experiences and differences. For feminism, Difference can help with the discussions which suggest that abortion can be viewed as a form of genocide and be used to legitimate eugenist practices in dealing with global issues (Davis, 1982). Difference may also help feminist work to reflect on the ways in which some feminisms reproduce colonial discourses, with the consequence of 'Third-World Woman' being defined as a unitary and unified subject (Mohanty, 1988). Building in Difference as a means to develop feminist projects also helps discussions of sexuality – by Black and Third-World women as well as white women (Alexander, 1991). Difference can also provide a guiding theme in analyses of women's relationships with the state which could include both issues of domestic violence (Mama, 1989) for Black and white women, as well as taking account of the ways in which the state and its agents deal with immigration (Phizacklea, 1983). Some Black women are also of the middle class throughout the world, which means that the discussion of class differences and, therefore, differences of interests become important in developing feminist projects. Different racisms are therefore an integral part of feminism too. Anti-Irish racism (for example, Hickman, 1990), anti-Semitism (for example, Bulkin *et al.*, 1984; Bourne, 1987) are just two examples, along with anti-Black racism. Definitions of culture, many of which are narrow in focus, are frequently restricted to ethnicity, and exclude racism, for example as Phoenix (1988) argues in her analysis of young motherhood.[6] Different ethnicities and their implications for how we organise our households need to be tackled, and negotiated. And differing identities must be analysed to see what discursive productions do in practice, as well as providing clues to our political differences (for example, Hall, 1990; Young, 1990).

All the above means that feminist projects are therefore *Epistemo-*

logical in nature. By this, I mean that feminist approaches to knowledge demand not only an inversion in the hierarchies of what is considered 'objective' knowledge and what is not, but they also create, in an integral way, a subversion of prevailing views of the world. For instance, Haraway's (1988) argument that objectivity is a 'particular and specific embodiment' rather than a 'false vision promising transcendence of all limits and responsibility' (p. 582), is one example of such subversion. She argues that 'partial perspectives' are 'privileged ones', because 'feminist objectivity is about *limited* location and *situated* knowledge' (p. 583; my emphasis). Limited location and situated knowledge are therefore the route into the creation of feminist objectivity. Such an elegant argument is relevant not only when reflecting upon written work produced within academic settings. This subversion is also part of the teaching/learning/discussing and acting which flows from, as well as initiates, feminist insights. It is in this way that I suggest feminist approaches may provide key starting points for ways in to new and reformulated beginnings.

In this way, feminism, in refusing the EDITing which I have discussed, will instead be inverted to become the TIDE from which knowledge flows. We will act, read and write with a confidence so that feminism becomes not only a movement about gendered inequalities, but that these gendered inequalities both inform and are informed by racialised, class-based and sexualised inequalities. 'The weapon of knowledge seems to be the most formidable weapon of all' (Mernissi, 1988, p. 20).

Notes

1. An earlier version of this chapter was presented at the University of Toronto in March 1989. Thanks to Jacqui Alexander, Meg Coulson, Ruth Frankenberg, Zavini Khan, Gail Lewis and Gillian Russell for their comments.
2. 'Black' is used in Britain as a political term to denote the common experiences of racism directed at non-white peoples. The phrase most frequently used in the United States is 'people of colour', for there, 'Black' refers specifically to African–Americans.
3. See Davis (1982) for her comments on just such a series of events, and for her critique of many white feminists' silence about racism in her analysis of rape.
4. 'Said's book is a clear documentation and analysis, using some themes

from Foucault, that the Orient is an institution within contemporary thought and that Orientalism refers to the systematic knowledge by which the Orient is constructed as the Other'.

5.   She may also get considerable pleasure from some of these contradictions when they create the conditions for some change, however small. Also, see Bhavnani (1990) for how these negotiations may proceed for a Black woman researcher.

6.   One of the most illuminating accounts of motherhood that I have ever read is *Beloved*, by Toni Morrison (1987). If difference is embedded into Women's Studies then a piece like that could be used to begin discussions of motherhood, not just 'Black motherhood'.

Further reading

Shabnum Grewal, *Charting the Journey: writing by black and third world women* (London, Sheba, 1988). This anthology of writings provides a wide range of arguments and discussions central to the issues raised by Black and Third-World women. Other similar texts would be Cherrie Moraga and Gloria Anzaldua (eds), *This Bridge Called My Back* (Watertown, Mass., Persephone Press).

Patricia Hill Collins, *Black Feminist Thought: Knowledge, Consciousness and the Politics of Government* (Boston, Mass., Unwin Hyman, 1990). This book reviews the epistemological implications of feminist thought. While it specifically focuses on African–American women, it raises issues which resonate with the points raised by many women of colour.

Rosina Visram, *Ayahs, Lascars and Princes* (London, Pluto Press, 1986). This book is a fascinating study of the historical underpinnings of Black people's (specifically Indians) presence in Britain. It therefore raises questions about the frameworks which are used to legitimate immigration legislation.

Cynthia Enloe, *Bananas, Beaches and Bases; Making Feminist Sense of International Politics* (London, Pandora, 1989). This is a stimulating and innovative book which explores how to make 'feminist sense of international politics'. She succeeds in showing the links between 'Third World' and 'First World' feminism, and so provides some interesting ideas for furthering international feminism.

Donna Haraway, *Primate Visions Gender, Race and Nature in the World of Modern Science* (London, Routledge, 1989). This book is a startlingly original and provocative analysis of the socially constructed frames of gender, 'race' and nature. It raises some very important questions about the ways in which scientific and social knowledges are created and reproduced.

3

Untangling Feminist Theory

Jackie Stacey

Women's Studies and the debate about theory

The question of feminist theory has produced heated debate on many Women's Studies courses. Indeed, there has frequently been a division between those who want to read theory and see it as vital for feminists to engage with in order to challenge existing forms of academic knowledge and practice, and those who have found it, at best, dry, boring and irrelevant, and at worst, so steeped in patriarchal traditions that any feminist engagement with it signifies complicity with the oppressors.

The former group criticises the latter for their rejection of 'theory', on the grounds that feminists need to develop rigorous analyses and explanations of women's oppression, and not simply to have consciousness-raising discussions which could take place outside educational institutions in other feminist contexts. They also argue that if we, as feminists, do not produce our own theories, we will continue to be defined by existing forms of patriarchal knowledge, which have confined us to the realms of nature, the home, or have defined us as the sexualised object of masculine desire. The latter group challenges the former for their attention to 'theory', which they see as elitist, inaccessible and inevitably producing a division between feminist academics and 'ordinary women'. Instead of producing hypotheses and general claims about how gender inequality operates (and the practical applications to the question of political change is often far from obvious), it is argued that feminists need to produce work about women's lives which is directly relevant to challenging women's oppression and improving women's position in society.[1]

49

This rather stereotyped dichotomy is, in part, rhetorical, but it refers to a phenomenon within Women's Studies which will be recognisable to many readers. These opposing responses to theory are a part of broader disagreements regarding the relationship of Women's Studies to the women's movement and feminist politics more generally. Unlike many other theories, feminist theory has a specific relationship to a political movement, and indeed to one in which women's experiences have often been the basis for radical activism and the force behind a desire for change. The centrality of personal experience within the women's movement has meant that the role of theory has been particularly critically debated within Women's Studies.

The term 'feminist theory' generally suggests a body of knowledge which offers critical explanations of women's subordination. By 'critical' I mean that the explanation does not seek to reinforce or legitimate, but rather attempts to undermine, expose or challenge, women's subordination. It also tends to operate at *some* level of abstraction, using analytical categories which move beyond the merely descriptive or anecdotal, and at some level of generalisation moving beyond the individual case. Typically, feminist theory offers some kind of analysis and explanation of how and why women have less power than men, and how this imbalance could be challenged and transformed. Feminists have produced diverse and competing theories about the general patterns of inequality and the broader structures, belief systems and institutions which produce and organise particular experiences, in order to analyse, understand and, hopefully, challenge women's subordination.

There are several ways in which I could have constructed a chapter on feminist theory. I could have chosen a handful of key texts,[2] or particular theorists whose contributions seemed especially influential, and analysed their importance to feminist theory. However, constructing such a list of 'feminist classics' would have been daunting because of the vast range of important feminist texts which exist (dating back to the seventeenth century and probably earlier!).[3] Such a selection of writers would also have constructed a rather individualistic story of feminist theorists, replacing 'Great Men' with 'Great Women'.

The 'key texts approach' would also have been problematic because of the hierarchies and exclusions which are so frequently established through such a selection. For example, a run-through of Simone de Beauvoir's *The Second Sex*, Betty Friedan's *The Feminine Mystique*, Kate Millet's *Sexual Politics*, Shulamith Firestone's *The Dialectic of Sex*, Germaine Greer's *The Female Eunuch* may offer some insight into one version of the 'classics' of post-1960s feminist thought, but misses out other feminist work which has been just as important. An alternative trajectory could have been Angela Davis's *Women, Race and Class*, Barbara Smith's (ed.) *Home Girls*, Cherrie Moraga and G. Anzaldua's (eds) *This Bridge Called My Back*, bell hooks' *Ain't I a Woman?*, Audre Lorde's *Sister Outsider*, and Alice Walker's *In Search of Our Mothers' Gardens*. Or yet another might have been Sidney Abbot and Barbara Love's *Sappho Was a Right-On Woman*, Jill Johnson's *Lesbian Nation*, Adrienne Rich's *Compulsory Heterosexuality*, Mary Daly's *Gyn/Ecology*, Lillian Faderman's *Surpassing the Love of Men*, Monique Wittig's *The Lesbian Body* and Luce Irigaray's *Speculum of the Other Woman*. Or indeed another, Sheila Rowbotham *et al.*'s *Beyond the Fragments*, Sheila Rowbotham's *Woman's Consciousness, Man's World*, Juliet Mitchell's *Psychoanalysis and Feminism*, Michèle Barrett's *Women's Oppression Today* and Terry Lovell's edited collection *British Feminist Thought*.

The selection of *key texts* is not simply a question of personal choice, but rather poses the problem of the establishment of a 'feminist canon'; in other words, the repeated selection of certain feminist texts can become part of the academic process which validates certain writers over others, and has led to the exclusion or marginalisation of, for example, lesbian and Black feminist writing. This is ironic when considered in the light of feminist critiques of the establishment of academic knowledge which excludes women generally.

An alternative to the 'key texts' approach would have been a chapter structured by a discussion of the similarities and differences between the standard feminist perspectives used on many Women's Studies courses – radical, Marxist and liberal feminist, with perhaps a passing reference to anarchist or eco-feminist. Black feminism is then usually attached, as if it were a unified category in need of no further differentiation. Typically, the three classic feminist positions are characterised as follows: radical feminism focuses on male violence against women and men's control of women's sexuality and reproduction, seeing men as a group as responsible for women's oppression; Marxist feminism, in contrast, sees women's oppression as tied to forms of capitalist exploitation of labour, and thus women's paid and unpaid work is analysed in relation to its function within the capitalist economy; and finally liberal feminism is distinctive in its focus on individual rights and choices which are denied women, and ways in which the law and education could rectify these injustices. In some accounts, socialist feminism and Marxist feminism

are distinct from one another, socialist feminism being less economically
deterministic, and allowing some kind of autonomy to women's oppression, yet retaining a belief that women's liberation and socialism are
joint goals.

However, like many other feminists, I have long felt dissatisfied with
this rigid categorisation which, firstly, excludes so much feminist thinking which eludes such distinctions; and secondly, fixes individual
writers and thinkers in a way that ignores the changes and developments
in their work, disregarding the complexities or contradictions in one
woman's feminism. Use of these categories frequently obscures more
than it reveals and can lead to the unhelpful stereotyping of feminist
ideas: for example, radical feminists are dismissed as essentialist, lesbians are all assumed to be radical feminists, socialist feminists are
assumed to be uninterested in sexuality, and liberal feminists are seen as
naïvely reformist.

Instead, I have decided to outline what I see as some of the key
theoretical debates within Women's Studies. What follows, then, is an
introduction to contemporary feminist theory through a selection of
some of the many debates which have posed particular theoretical
questions.

The patriarchy debate

One of the significant roles of feminist theory has been to try to account
for women's subordination in society. This has been important in terms
of producing some indications of how gender inequality could be challenged and transformed politically. Having read endless documentation
of the exclusions, marginalisations, pain and suffering of women which
exist in just about any discipline, women have asked 'Why?'; and 'How
can we begin to account for the existence of women's oppression?'
Feminists have produced a vast range of different explanations of how
and why women are oppressed and these competing accounts have been
widely debated within Women's Studies. One of the aims of this next
section, then, is to highlight the existence of many different feminist
theories, rather than one coherent body of work which can be named
feminist theory. The debate about patriarchy has been chosen as a case
study to illustrate this point, since it has been central to much feminist
analysis and continues to inform a great deal of feminist work, though
sometimes in an implicit rather than an explicit way.

The usefulness of the concept of 'patriarchy' has been widely debated.[4] Some feminists have found its definition so diffuse as to be ultimately unhelpful (Barrett, 1980), others have found it too general or too monolithic a term to be useful (Beechey, 1987; and Rowbotham, 1982). Others still have argued for its restriction to the specific social situation it originally described; Gayle Rubin (1975), for example, prefers the concept of a 'sex–gender system' which allows for variation and historical specificity to forms of women's oppression.

For many feminists, however, the term patriarchy has provided an important concept for the theorisation of how and why women are oppressed (Millett, 1970; Daly, 1978; Hartmann, 1979; Delphy, 1984b; and Walby, 1990). They have used the term 'patriarchy' to analyse the systematic organisation of women's oppression. It was seen to be a useful term because it gave some conceptual form to the nature of male dominance in society: 'the concept of 'patriarchy' was re-discovered by the new feminist movement as a struggle concept, because the movement needed a term by which the totality of oppressive and exploitative relations which affect women, could be expressed, as well as their systematic character' (Mies, 1986, p. 37).

It has also been an equally important term in feminist activism, as Michèle Barrett highlights in her retrospective analysis, in which she reflects upon her own previous dismissal of the usefulness of the concept:

> Many feminists said to me that it was completely wrong to suggest the abandonment of such an eloquent and resonant concept – and one so regularly used in feminist political activism – on rather academic grounds of inconsistent usage and so on. What is at stake, which I later came to see, was the symbolic status of using the concept of 'patriarchy' as a marker of a position that in general terms I was in fact taking – that we recognize the independent character of women's oppression and avoid explanations that reduce it to other factors. (Barrett, 1980, p. xiii)

Originally used to describe the power of the father as head of household, the term 'patriarchy' has been used within post-1960s feminism to refer to the systematic organisation of male supremacy and female subordination. However, the concept of patriarchy has not been used within feminist theory in any simple or unified way, but rather there are numerous definitions of the term, each with a slightly different emphasis:

our society, like all other historical civilisations, is a patriarchy. The fact is evident at once if one recalls that the military, industry, technology, universities, science, political office and finance – in short, every avenue of power within society, including the coercive power of the police, is entirely in male hands. As the essence of politics is power, such realization cannot fail to carry impact . . . If one takes patriarchal government to be the institution whereby that half of the populace which is female is controlled by that half which is male, the principles of patriarchy appear to be twofold: male shall dominate female, elder male shall dominate younger. (Millett, 1970, reprinted 1989, p. 25)

the control of women's fertility and sexuality in monogamous marriage and . . . the economic subordination of women through the sexual division of labour (and property). (McDonough and Harrison, quoted in Barrett, 1980, p. 17)

As well as various and competing definitions of patriarchy, there are also several different purposes for which feminists have used the term in analysing women's oppression. I shall discuss three of these as examples of the diversity even within the feminist work which agrees on the usefulness of the term: these are firstly historical, secondly material, and thirdly psychoanalytic. The first of these includes feminists who have used the term 'patriarchy' to identify the historical emergence of systems of male domination. These include the work of Gerda Lerner (1986); Maria Mies (1986); Kate Millet (1970); Kate Young and Olivia Harris (in Evans, 1982); and Mary Daly (1978). In very different ways they are all interested in tracing systems of male domination back through history to look either at the different and yet overlapping forms it has taken (Daly, 1978) or to analyse the context of its emergence (Young and Harris, 1982; and Mies, 1986).

The term patriarchy has been employed in feminist theory to trace the origins of women's subordination. According to Mies (1986, p. 38), the term 'patriarchy' signifies the historical emergence of particular forms of inequality between women and men, in contrast to the view that gender inequality is natural (which so frequently pervades dominant ideas about how society operates). Instead of accepting such justifications of male domination, many feminists have sought to explain the emergence of patriarchal societies in contrast to previous more egalitarian, or even matriarchal societies.

The search for the origins of patriarchy has led many feminists back to the work of Friedrich Engels, who, in his work *The Origin of the Family, Private Property and the State* attempts to account for the 'world historic defeat of the female sex'. Locating his analysis in changes in modes of appropriation, Engels argued that women lost power with the historical shift in the importance of production (the production of tools, food and commodities for exchange) over reproduction (the reproduction of the species, childbirth and rearing) (Engels, 1940). As productive activity generated surplus goods for exchange instead of direct use, it became necessary for those who owned such surpluses to ensure they were appropriately passed and thus legitimate heirs were ensured through the imposition of monogamous marriage.

As Moira Maconachie (1987), and others, have pointed out, there are numerous flaws in Engels' account, not least that he assumes what he sets out to explain: that is, the sexual division of labour. Why men and not women should begin to benefit from surplus goods in the sphere of production is not clear, neither is the reason for women's responsibility for reproduction; a biological determinism is simply assumed. Nevertheless, while there are many unanswered questions in Engels' account, it has proved significant in the development of the historical analysis of the emergence of patriarchy.

However, some feminists have questioned the purpose of tracing the origins of women's subordination and have challenged the notion that any conclusive evidence can be produced about the roots of patriarchy. Others have insisted that some kind of theoretical model of its origins is vital for a feminist analysis of how we might change society: if we do not know what caused women's subordinate position, then how can we begin to try to transform that position?

The second use of the term 'patriarchy' that I want to discuss here can be described as working within a materialist framework.[5] This clearly overlaps with the historical study of the emergence of patriarchy in some ways, but these theorists have a rather different purpose in their use of the concept. Rather than investigating the question of origins, these theorists seek to elaborate an explanation of how patriarchy works in terms of the different activities of women and men in society. These writers are frequently in dialogue with Marxist theory and debate the relationship or lack of one between patriarchy and capitalism. Sometimes referred to as dual systems theorists within sociology, writers such as Heidi Hartmann (1979) and Zillah Eisenstein (1979) have debated the roles of capitalism and patriarchy in the reproduction of women's oppression.

Christine Delphy's work (1984) has had a central place in feminist debates about patriarchy because of her insistence upon an autonomous system of patriarchal control defining women's position in contemporary society. Delphy challenges much Marxist feminist work that looks at the ways in which women's oppression results from, or is connected to, class inequality under capitalism, and puts forward instead a model of patriarchy as 'theoretically independent from capitalism'. With her emphasis on labour and modes of production, Delphy retains the materialism of a Marxist perspective in her analysis, but applies this to the expropriation of women's labour by husbands within the household.

According to Delphy, there are two modes of production: the industrial mode of production, which is the arena of capitalist exploitation; and the family mode of production, in which women's labour is exploited by men. Men benefit from women's provision of domestic services and unpaid child-rearing within the family, as well as their production of certain goods for use and exchange. Thus it is men's exploitation of women's reproductive and productive activities in the household which is the main form of women's oppression. Patriarchal exploitation is therefore seen as 'the common, specific and main oppression of women' (Delphy, 1984b, p. 74).

There have been extensive criticisms of Delphy's model of patriarchy, including her use (some would say misuse) of Marxist concepts, her generalisations based on French peasant households to elaborate a theory of patriarchy, and her reduction of marriage to a labour contract, ignoring ideologies of love and romance which play a role in women's decisions to marry (Barrett and McIntosh, 1979). However, despite these problems with Delphy's work, it remains an important contribution to feminist theories of patriarchy and offers an important challenge to Marxist models, which define women's class position through their husbands or solely in relation to capitalism.

Another contribution to the materialist debates about patriarchy is Sylvia Walby's work (1986, 1990) which attempts to produce an analysis of the structures of patriarchal society. Her argument is based on an analysis of what she calls the six structures of patriarchal society: employment; household production; the state; sexuality; violence; and culture. Walby outlines the ways in which these structures have changed from their private forms in the nineteenth century, 'based upon household production', to their more public forms in the twentieth century, 'based principally in public sites such as employment and the state' (Walby, 1990, p. 24).

However, it remains somewhat unclear in her analysis of what exactly constitutes a 'structure' of patriarchy: some structures are more clearly conceptualised than others (for example, paid employment and culture), and, given that such structures are not analogous, further consideration needs to be given to their interrelationship. In addition, the lack of space for any consideration of questions of identity and lived experience in this model leave it open to the criticisms of much structuralist analysis: it fails to explain how people negotiate such a system, how they resist or conform, and how and why it affects different women differently, according to class, 'race', ethnic and sexual identity.

Nevertheless, in offering an account of patriarchy which does not focus on one area of society, such as Delphy's on household production or Millett's on the family, but rather one which includes the breadth and diversity of patriarchal forms of control over women, Walby provides an all-encompassing account of the systematic oppression of women in society. Her account also successfully avoids the criticisms of universalism and essentialism so often levelled at generalised theories of patriarchy, by offering a model of patriarchy which identifies historically specific forms in particular periods.

A third use of the term 'patriarchy' has been within feminist reworkings of psychoanalytic theory. In particular, feminists such as Juliet Mitchell (1974, 1982); Jacqueline Rose (1982, 1986); Janet Sayers (1986, 1988); Nancy Chodorow (1978); and Dorothy Dinnerstein (1977) have advocated a re-evaluation of psychoanalysis, previously dismissed by feminists for its mysogynist ideas about female sexuality (for example, Greer (1971); Firestone (1971); and Millett (1970)). Instead, these later works have argued that psychoanalytic theory can help explain the deep-rootedness of patriarchy through an understanding of the unconscious. Rather than seeing patriarchy *solely* as a set of social structures or institutions which oppress women, psychoanalytic theory analyses the operations of patriarchy on a psychic, as well as a social, level.

Feminist work on the psychic dimensions of patriarchy has explored ways in which the broader structures of society operate within kinship relations in the formation of individual identities. Juliet Mitchell's influential work (1974) relates Jacques Lacan's concept of the 'law of the father' in the family to patriarchal power in society more generally (see Mitchell and Rose (eds) (1982)). She argues that the broader patterns of patriarchal exchange of women between men in society are reproduced within the individual psyche. Thus the valuing of the male over the female is something we all internalise, not simply as a conscious belief we have been socialised to accept, but in the formation of our earliest sexual identities which take place through unconscious as well as conscious processes.

This usage of the notion of patriarchy as operating at an unconscious, as well as a conscious level, appealed particularly to feminists who found that change was more difficult to achieve, both personally and politically, than much feminist theory suggested it would be. It helped to explain the investments women had in their existing identities, which notions such as false-consciousness, drawn originally from Marxism, had failed to explain.

However, as well as stressing the deep-rootedness of patriarchal culture (Sayers, 1986) the notion of the unconscious also, ironically, potentially affords a model which enables us to account for the 'failure' of patriarchy. This is seen to offer an important counter to the rather pessimistic accounts of the inevitability of the success of patriarchal domination. Jacqueline Rose's work, for example, emphasises the complexity of the processes through which we learn the meaning of sexual difference, and highlights the impossibility of fully or permanently achieving femininity within a patriarchal culture (Rose, 1986, pp. 29–31). Femininity, according to Rose, is a shifting signifier; its complete or successful embodiment is, happily, impossible. Since, according to this Lacanian position, identity is constantly disrupted by unconscious desires, women can never be totally successfully fixed within a patriarchal definition of femininity.

Feminist reworking of psychoanalytic theory to produce an understanding of patriarchal culture has been challenged from many different quarters. Many feminists find some of the basic assumptions (such as those found in theories of the Oedipus complex, the pathologisations of homosexuality or the construction of female frigidity) in Freudian thought so problematic that they believe all of it should be dismissed (Jeffreys, 1985, 1990). Others dislike the elitism of the institution of psychoanalysis in its practice today, or question the necessity of the obscurity of much contemporary psychoanalytic theory, especially from the Lacanian school. Others still see its usefulness to feminism limited by its focus on the psyche and fail to see any political significance in such a psychologically-based theory of the individual (Jackson, 1982; and Wilson, 1981).

In particular, the use of psychoanalysis to produce feminist theories of patriarchy has been criticised for its ahistoricism and universalism. Carolyn Steedman, for example, questions the general applicability of the psychoanalytic model, developed as it was on the basis of Freud's white, middle-class Viennese patients growing up in patriarchal families at the end of the nineteenth century. Whilst Steedman accepts the usefulness of Freud's analysis of the structures of patriarchy within the bourgeois, patriarchal family at the turn of the century, she is sceptical of its general application by feminists to all women from 'different class, cultural and geographical backgrounds in the nineteenth and twentieth centuries' (Steedman, 1986, p. 75).

All three of these theoretical uses of the concept of patriarchy, the historical, the material and the psychoanalytic, have produced generalised explanations of the subordination of women. In very different ways, and towards very different ends, all three have offered analyses of how patriarchy is organised and how power relations within it are reproduced at a general level.

Universal theories and the politics of difference

The debate about patriarchy raises important questions about the extent to which women's subordination is universal. Have women always had less power than men in all societies? If so, what are the common elements which might be identified in those societies? Does patriarchy take different forms in different societies, and if so, can *any* commonalities be found in those societies which extend across time and place? Within feminist anthropology for example, there are strong disagreements between universalists, who look for cross-cultural commonalities, and cultural relativists, who focus on the specificities of cultural meaning and organisation internal to one particular culture (MacCormack and Strathern (eds), 1980; Rosaldo and Lamphere (eds), 1974; and Moore, 1988).

This difference is replicated within feminist theory more generally. Much early feminist work emphasised the ways in which women in all cultures had less power than men, and were subjected to similar forms of patriarchal control. Indeed, feminist theorists from outside anthropology, seeking to make universalist arguments, also used evidence from cross-cultural analysis to make the case that women are universally oppressed.

Mary Daly (1978), for example, looked at fifteenth-century witch-burning in Europe, Chinese foot-binding, clitoredectomy in Africa, and American gynaecology and drew parallels in these forms of patriarchal control over women's bodies, sexuality and physical movement. Her analysis of these 'sado-rituals' across different cultures at different times emphasises the similarities in the forms of patriarchal control exercised over women universally. However, her work was also heavily criticised, not only by feminist anthropologists, who argued that cultural practices cannot be understood outside their particular cultural contexts, but also by some Black feminists who challenged the inclusion of Black women solely to document oppression. In 'An Open Letter to Mary Daly', Audre Lorde writes:

> it was obvious that you were dealing with non European women, but only as victims and preyers-upon each other. I began to feel my history and my mythic background distorted by the absence of any images of my foremothers in power. Your inclusion of African genital mutilation was an important and necessary piece in any consideration of female ecology, and too little has been written about it. To imply, however, that all women suffer the same oppression simply because we are women is to lose sight of the many and varied tools of patriarchy. (Lorde, 1984c, p. 67)

There are parallel debates within feminist history, some arguments emphasising the continuities in women's position throughout history, whilst others look at the historical specificity of the particular organisation of gender relations at any one time. For example, one debate within feminist history is the question of the extent to which the Industrial Revolution produced a fundamental restructuring of the sexual division of labour rather than simply intensifying pre-existing divisions (Hall and O'Day, 1983); another debate is about significance of the similarities between the changes in women's position in the home and in the labour market during and after the First and Second World Wars (Braybon and Summerfield, 1987).

The question of universals and particulars is not only relevant to looking at women's subordination, however; it has also been an important component in debates about women's resistance to patriarchal control. What are the parallels between feminism in the 1990s and feminism in the nineteenth century? Can arguments about pornography today be related to debates about sexual morality in the nineteenth and early twentieth century (Bland, 1990; and Hunt, 1990)? Or, looking even further back, have women always resisted patriarchal control and if so, has their resistance taken similar forms (Daly, 1978)? If not, what are the particular historical forces that have shaped women's resistances (Faderman, 1981; London Feminist History Group, 1983; and Graham *et al.*, 1989)?

Women's resistances have also been linked across national boundaries. Mitter (1986), for example, emphasises the importance of an international perspective on women's collective actions, since the sexual division of labour is linked to the international division of labour. Multinational corporations invest in women's cheap labour in 'First' and 'Third' World countries and the challenge to the exploitative conditions of those women's working conditions has been internationally organised. Some feminists have emphasised the similarities between women's position in different societies, challenging the narrow focus of some feminist analysis, which ignores the international dimensions of women's resistances.

The theoretical debate about the extent to which women's oppression and resistance is universal or not overlaps with an important debate about similarities and differences between women (Ramazanoglu, 1989). Some of the early generalisations about women's position in society produced by feminists have been criticised for the ways in which they were based on a very particular version of what it meant to be a woman. Typically, the accounts have been challenged for their lack of consideration of differences between women in relation to 'race', ethnicity, nationality, class and sexuality.

Much feminist theory has been concerned with explaining the position of white women in society. Black feminist work has frequently been marginalised within Women's Studies, and Black feminists have challenged existing agendas, arguing that many taken-for-granted issues within feminist debate have a different meaning for many Black women. From questioning the general applicability of particular categories such as 'reproduction', 'patriarchy' and 'the family' (Carby, 1982a) to rethinking feminist theories of work, violence, sexuality and parenting, (hooks, 1984), Black feminist work has provided a crucial challenge to the limits and exclusions of white feminist theory.

As well as challenging white feminist theory, Black feminists have also documented their own 'hidden histories' of racism, colonialism and imperialism, which have shaped all our lives in very different ways. Power differentials between women and men are cross-cut by differences in power between women depending on how they are positioned within these histories. Thus not only has the challenge come from Black women in industrial capitalist countries but it has also been raised by women in the so-called 'Third World', who have been written about by white feminists but have had little opportunity to develop or voice their own theories of their oppression. More recently Helen (charles) (1992) has turned the tables and challenged white feminists to theorise 'whiteness' and their relationship to white culture, instead of focusing on Black women when the issues of 'race' and ethnicity are raised.

Another example of the politics of difference which has had important implications for theorising women's oppression is the question of sexual identity. Some models of 'woman' employed within feminist theory have been challenged for their basis in heterosexuality. For example, theories of the sexual division of labour or of the regulation of female sexuality through contraception and abortion have frequently taken priority over analysis of custody for lesbian mothers, or the construction of public space as heterosexual.

The women's movement provided the forum for many lesbians not only to come out but also to feel positive about their sexual identities, about which many had previously been made to feel ashamed and negative. Many other women, previously heterosexual by practice, though not necessarily in their desires, began to have relationships with other women and saw this as a positive alternative to much-struggled-over relationships with men. Thus the difference between heterosexual and lesbian women has a particular historical and political significance, since the divide is not a fixed one, and has therefore produced anxiety on both sides for different reasons (Stanley (ed.), 1990a). Indeed, there has been a lack of heterosexual feminist work on heterosexuality, a topic which has tended to be critically addressed mainly by lesbian feminists.

Class differences between women have also been introduced into Women's Studies as a challenge to theories about the universality of women's oppression. The relationship between class and gender has been a difficult one to theorise, since women's class position, for married women, has frequently been defined by the type of paid employment done by their husbands. Despite these difficulties, important critiques of feminist theory have been made in terms of its middle-class assumptions: for example, the assumptions that to enter paid work will be liberating for women, or that women live in isolated nuclear family units, have been challenged for their basis within a middle-class model of women's position in society (Steedman, 1986).

Thus the questioning of some early generalisations about what women have in common and about the universality of women's oppression emerged in the political context of the women's movement, where debates about differences between women countered the earlier over-emphasis on sameness. However, the two debates, that of universalism and that of differences between women, cannot simply be mapped on to each other: for example, plenty of feminist theory which is not claiming the universality of women's oppression can be challenged for its racist assumptions, and likewise generalised theories of oppression are by no means the prerogative of white feminists (hooks, 1982, 1984). Similarly, much lesbian writing has produced generalised theory, and much feminist writing with a historically and culturally specific focus contains heterosexist assumptions. It would be an oversimplification to attach generalised theories of women's oppression solely to the most relatively privileged group: white, middle-class heterosexual women. Furthermore, it is important to distinguish between theorists who produce general explanations of women's oppression and those who make claims for the universal validity of models developed in particular contexts.

The focus on differences between women has been an important redress in a movement that built its momentum on a falsely universalistic understanding of women's oppression. However, there have also been some related complexities within this area of debate, with some troubling consequences for effective political and theoretical activity which relate back to the centrality of personal experience within feminism. There have been tensions and anxieties around the question of who has the right to speak for and about whom. The challenge to some of the early theoretical models within Women's Studies on the basis of the exclusions they reproduced (Spelman, 1988), and the challenge to who is included in the 'we' advocated in much feminist theory and activism, have led, in some cases, to a kind of 'identity politics' in which no one can speak for or even about anyone else, and no analysis can be made beyond one's own personal experience of oppression. There has also been a tendency towards specificity, in which the consideration of the class, 'race', ethnic, national, sexual and other identities of women can prevent any kind of generalisations being made about women at all.

These debates about differences between women have often been painful and fraught, and have frequently resulted in the collapse of projects, the destruction of groups and a disillusionment with feminist work. Audre Lorde has written powerfully about this issue:

we have *all* been programmed to respond to human differences between us with fear and loathing and to handle that difference in one of three ways: ignore it, and if that is not possible, copy it if we think it is dominant, or destroy it if we think it is subordinate. But we have no patterns for relating across our human difference as equals. As a result, those differences have been misnamed and misused in the service of separation and confusion. (Lorde, 1984, p. 115)

The challenge remains for difference to be an empowering exchange, rather than a threat. Audre Lorde continues by stressing the importance of the constructive negotiation of differences:

it is not those differences between us that are separating us. It is rather our refusal to recognize those differences, and to examine the distortions which result from our misnaming them and their effects upon human behaviour and expectation . . . It is a lifetime pursuit for each one of us to extract these distortions from our living at the same time as we recognise, reclaim, and define those differences upon which they are imposed . . . We need to develop tools for using human difference as a springboard for creative change within our lives. (Lorde, 1984, pp. 115–16)

The category woman

In addition to the political questions about differences between women, there have been corresponding developments within social and cultural theory which have opened up debates about the meaning of the category 'woman'. These stem primarily from the work of post-structuralists (for example, Henriques *et al.* (1984) and Weedon (1987)) who have had considerable influence in some areas of feminist analysis, such as cultural representation, sexuality and identity. In particular, the notion of any kind of fixed identity is problematised and thus 'woman', as a category, is regarded as a constantly shifting signifier of multiple meanings.

Some feminists have found this framework useful in their investigations of the social and cultural construction of what it means to be a woman in a patriarchal society. Rather than assuming 'woman' to be a given category of feminist analysis, which is considered to be a problematic form of essentialism, these feminists highlight the fluidity of the meaning of that category across time, place and context. Thus the assumption of a shared collective identity amongst women as a group who have a certain set of interests in common, which has been a part of so much feminist analysis and activism, is questioned.

This questioning is based upon a debate between post-structuralism and feminism in which the analysis of identity and subjectivity has been central concerns to both (Weedon, 1987). The term 'subjectivity' is being used here, not to refer to feelings, or emotional responses, as is often its meaning (in contrast to the notion of objectivity, which offers 'scientific facts'), but rather to refer to the ways in which we understand ourselves as subjects positioned by discourses or ideologies. Identity, I would argue, overlaps with subjectivity in that both concern one's sense of self and place in the world, but specifically refers to general groups of people and social categories such as gender, class, nationality, 'race', ethnicity, sexuality, region, religion, parental status and so on. Subjectivity would then be the particular configuration of those social and cultural identities in one person.

The term 'individual' is deliberately avoided by these frameworks, since it tends to be associated with the rather liberal belief that we are autonomous beings, unconstrained by power structures and institutions, who can choose our 'lot' in life. Indeed, individualism is seen as part of dominant ideology in a capitalist and patriarchal society, which encourages us to believe there are no external limitations on what we can do and who we can be, and if we 'fail' we only have ourselves to blame. In contrast to this view, feminists and Marxists have argued that the systems of inequality, such as patriarchy and capitalism, depend on the success of a few at the expense of the majority. In contrast to the term 'individual', then, subjectivity emphasises the ways in which our thoughts, feelings and activities are produced and limited by external constraints.

The engagement with post-structuralism needs to be understood in the context of existing feminist theory and some of its limitations. In particular, the model of subjectivity used in much feminist theory fails to answer crucial questions and restricts understanding of some of the contradictions and complexities involved in women's position in society. In answer to the question of why did women 'accept' their subordinate position in society, many feminists typically provide one of two replies: either women are forced into it by violence, or the threat of it, which is sometimes the case, but often is not; or women learn to accept their position through social conditioning and role models. The latter explanation is often implicit in much feminist thinking, even if it is not foregrounded as such.

Social conditioning has become a catch-all explanation for how and why women's oppression is reproduced. According to this model, women learn their subordination through familial relations, media representations of masculinity and femininity, or at school through books and praise or punishment for appropriately gendered behaviour by teachers. Social role theory has been the most obvious challenge to biological explanations of the differences between women and men. However, it also has severe limitations: how, for example, do we account for the many different forms of femininity which exist in society; how do we explain changes within the lives of individual women and in broader historical terms; and finally, how do we explain the emergence of resistance movements such as feminism if we have all been successfully socialised to accept our subordination (Henriques *et al.*, 1984)? Thus concern for diversity, change and resistance have led some feminists to be dissatisfied with this model of how power imbalances are reproduced in society and how we play our part in that reproduction.

Some feminists have turned instead to post-structuralist theories of power, ideology and subjectivity which offer a more complex model of how society operates, especially in terms of how our subjectivities are formed in relation to our subjugation. Within post-structuralism, subjectivity is seen as fluid and changing: thus the use of the category 'woman' has been criticised as essentialist in that it assumes that we all know what that category entails. Rather than reproducing a taken-for-granted and fixed meaning of the category 'woman', post-structuralist feminists have advocated the deconstruction of the category 'woman'. By this they mean that we need to pull apart the ways in which the different meanings of femininity have been cemented together, in order to expose the ways in which femininity has been constructed by patriarchal culture (Williamson, 1978, 1986; Coward, 1984; and Spivak, 1987). They argue that the unthinking use of the category 'woman' can, in fact, reinforce essentialist beliefs that the differences between women and men are given and fixed.

In an influential article and later book, *Am I that Name*, Denise Riley (1988) has looked at the category woman used within feminist history. She challenges the use of the category across different historical periods as if it had a common meaning throughout history. Instead, she argues for a deconstructionist position which acknowledges that the category 'woman' means different things in different historical periods, and thus rather than assuming we know, not to mention share, the experience of 'being a woman', Riley advocates the analysis of how that category is attributed meaning within different historical contexts.

Feminists using post-structuralist theory have been criticised for deconstructing the central categories for academic and political feminist activity. Instead of rejecting any use of such categories, Riley, like Gayatri Spivak (1985) argues for the strategic use of the category 'woman', sometimes using it and sometimes refusing it, but always foregrounding its constructedness and its diverse meanings.

Part of the post-structuralist challenge to liberal humanist models of the self within feminist theory, then, has been the assertion that subjectivity is, in fact, fractured and fluid. One way in which this fracturing has been theorised is through a feminist reworking of Freudian (for example, Sayers, 1982, 1986) or Lacanian psychoanalysis (for example, Mitchell, 1974; Mitchell and Rose, 1982; and Rose, 1986).

By emphasising the centrality of the unconscious in the formation of subjectivity, Lacanian psychoanalysis has introduced the notion of split subjectivity. In this model any sense of coherence or wholeness achieved by a person is merely fictional, since the unconscious contains fears and desires which continually threaten to disrupt such coherence or stability. What might appear rather a pessimistic approach, and indeed has been criticised for being so, has particular purchase for feminists, argues Jacqueline Rose, since it suggests that femininity is never fully achievable.

Thus, femininity is questioned still more fundamentally, not just in terms of the lack of fixity in its meaning, but also in terms of its coherence being constantly threatened by the unconscious. Psychoanalytic theory generally emphasises the ways in which all subjects are constituted in relation to both masculinity and femininity in the context of a whole series of complex desires and identifications within the familial context, the repression of which is necessary, but never fully successful. Resistance and refusal of femininity by women is thus explicable through a notion of the unconscious, and the idea that masculinity is not exclusively the privilege of men. Within this Lacanian model, then, feminists have challenged what they perceived as the essentialism of much feminist thinking, which saw femininity as a complete, unified and stable identity. This anti-essentialism of the Lacanian position belongs to a broader set of debates within feminist theory about social constructionism and essentialism.

Social constructionisms and essentialisms: a false dichotomy?

Within much feminist work the terms 'social constructionist' and 'essentialist' have become conceptual shorthand for important theoretical and political differences. In relation to analysing gender and sexuality, essentialism refers to arguments which appeal to biological or genetic determinism, universalism or explanations based on the idea of 'nature' or 'human nature'. Social constructionism, on the other hand, appeals to the idea that these are not natural, fixed or universal but specific to their social, cultural and historical context. Whereas essentialist explanations tend to suggest that change is difficult to achieve, social constructionism emphasizes change, discontinuity and contradiction (Franklin and Stacey, 1988).

Typically, feminists have seen themselves as advocating social constructionist perspectives in opposition to biological essentialism. Outside feminist circles, the most frequently voiced explanation for the differences between women's and men's position in society is biology, often returning to women's 'reproductive capacity'. In challenging biological explanations of women's position in society (such as that all women naturally feel maternal instinct, or that all women are naturally heterosexual), which ultimately justify existing inequality by fixing it in the realm of the supposedly given and unchangeable natural facts of biology, many feminists have sought to account for it in other ways. The disciplines of anthropology, sociology and history have offered feminists ways in which to challenge the fixity of the biological model of gender difference, and argue instead that the position of women in society was something which had been socially produced and organised: how else could the diversity of women's and men's roles in different societies in the world, and at different times in history, be explained? In opposition to such biological discourses, then, feminists have argued that women's position in society is established through particular sets of social and cultural forces which can be challenged and changed.

Within much feminist work the need to see gender and sexuality as socially constructed has been taken for granted. The emergence of the social constructionist position as dominant within feminist theory has been seen as a successful challenge to the inevitability and permanence of both heterosexuality and male dominance, previously naturalised within biologically deterministic beliefs systems (see Chapter 4).

However, the thorny question of essentialism extends beyond the relatively straightforward dismissal of biologically deterministic patriarchal discourses of gender and sexuality (Sayers, 1986). Indeed, it extends into all kinds of feminist theory and into internal debates between feminists. One of those most frequently accused of biological essentialism is Shulamith Firestone in her early work *The Dialectic of Sex* (1971), in which she sees the organisation of reproduction as the root of women's oppression. Firestone, in this bold and revolutionary text, argues that women are subordinated through their role in reproduction in this society. She argued that if biological reproduction could be reorganised through the use of technology, and thus externalised from women's bodies, women could be liberated from the restrictive role biology has assigned them. Firestone has been accused of essentialism because of the way in which she situates women's oppression firmly within biology itself (Barrett, 1988, p. 13). Rather than advocating the reorganisation of child-care or paid work, Firestone demands that women's relationship to reproduction be reorganised so that women's liberation can be achieved (see Chapter 10). Thus, even within feminist work, some theorists have been rejected for their biological essentialism.

Another feminist who has been accused of a very different form of essentialism, and who herself denies the validity of such a criticism, is the influential French feminist theorist, Luce Irigaray (1985a, 1985b). Her work attempts to highlight the patriarchal assumptions of existing theorists such as Jacques Lacan, whose theories of sexual difference are based on a model of masculine sexuality. Instead, Irigaray produces an ironic rewrite of the meanings of sexual difference based on feminine sexuality and the specificity of women's bodies. She, like many other French feminists such as Hélène Cixous, attempts to ground a radically different feminine culture in the specificity of the female body (Cixous, 1981). Irigaray's work has been widely appreciated for its inspirational challenge to the foundations of much patriarchal thought. But her critics consistently return to the problems of the essentialism in her work due to the ways in which the female body is seen to be the basis of this different feminine culture (see Chapter 7). However, her work, along with some other French feminist theorists, has been extremely important in investigating the specificity of a feminine writing, a feminine culture and a feminine sexuality.

In addition to these forms of biological essentialism within feminist theory, another form of essentialism which has been seen as problematic can be found in arguments about the historical and cross-cultural continuities in women's oppression. Feminist theorists who emphasise the universal existence of women's oppression have also been criticised on grounds of their essentialism. The lack of historical and cultural specificity has been seen to invoke 'an apparently universal and trans-historical category of male dominance, leaving us with little hope for change' (Barrett, 1988, p. 12). Radical feminist theorists have been widely criticised for constructing an account of male dominance which fixes the differences between women and men, if not in biology, in a social system so rigidly patriarchal that it offers little possibility for women to be seen as anything other than passive victims. Their essentialism is perceived in the fixity of their model of patriarchal society, and their classifications of all women as oppressed and all men as oppressive in a way that fails to acknowledge the possibility of diversity and change within these categories. Whilst there is a feeling of the fixity of gender relations within some of this work, there is a troubling tendency to stereotype and caricature radical feminist writing in order to dismiss it. Ironically, some critiques construct a falsely monolithic version of this writing, ignoring important differences between writers.

Within some psychoanalytic theory there are also many questions of essentialism which haunt feminist theory; for example, the assertion of the existence of the libido (the sex drive) with which, according to Freud, we are all born, or the claim that we are all initially bisexual. These general assumptions within psychoanalytic theory are all open to charges of essentialism, since they are assertions about the nature of sexuality and its centrality in all our lives, across time and place. Lacanians have tried to escape the problems of Freudian essentialism by centralising the role of language (a social and changing phenomenon) rather than biology, in the construction of the meaning of sexual difference. However, there remains the tricky problem of the universalism of concepts such as the Oedipus complex, or castration anxiety, which form the basis of so much psychoanalytic theory.

The purpose of including so many different examples of the problems of essentialism within feminist theory is twofold: firstly, it is crucial to highlight the many different meanings which have been given to the term 'essentialism', extending beyond its usual biological connotation; and secondly, to show how the label of 'essentialism' is itself a relative one. In other words, social constructionism and essentialism are not two fixed positions but rather there is a continuum within which all theorists can be labelled by each other in different ways. Whether a particular theorist will be labelled as an essentialist, or a social constructionist, will depend, to some degree, upon the beliefs of the person doing the positioning. The classification may be reasonably straightforward in the cases of those at each end of the continuum, but most feminist theory fits somewhere in the middle and is open to competing classifications. Thus, from a post-structuralist point of view, much Marxist feminist theory using the category 'woman' could be classified as essentialist, whilst the theorists themselves would consider their work to belong to social constructionist traditions. Similarly, much work on patriarchy which considered itself to be producing a social constructionist explanation avoiding biological determinism would be seen as problematically essentialist by many Marxist feminists.

It is thus impossible to escape from the problems of essentialism at some level (Spivak, 1985). All theory which attempts to address questions of political change negotiates some kind of relationship to the questions of essentialism. What seems important, as we move into the 1990s, is to avoid the simple labels and positions that have led to the dismissal of work as essentialist according to stereotypes, and to reframe some key questions outside the rigid dichotomy of essentialism and social constructionism which suggests that these categories are themselves separable, fixed and unified (Fuss, 1990).

Conclusions: thoughts for the future

In this chapter I have outlined a number of key debates within feminist theory which have been important during the last twenty years of feminist thought and political activity. I have attempted to situate these theoretical debates in relation to questions of feminist politics and to show the links between theory and politics wherever possible. For example, theoretical questions about the fragmented meanings of social identities, such as what exactly we understand by the category 'woman', are related to the political conflicts within the women's movement about the lack of recognition of differences between women in terms of ethnicity, sexuality, 'race' and class. The category 'woman' has not simply been deconstructed in Women's Studies' classrooms, but has been struggled over and questioned in all kinds of feminist collectives and feminist political groups. Although they belong to very different discourses, theoretical concerns about the problems of the category 'woman', and political questions about the exclusions of some feminist activism, have coincided historically and have reinforced the doubts and problems raised by much feminist thought and practice in the 1970s and early 1980s.

The question of how closely related to feminist politics Women's Studies should be has become increasingly important in the 1990s, for two reasons. First, the expansion of Women's Studies, especially within higher education, brings with it the troubling question of what some fear to be its increasing institutionalisation, and thus increasing separation from politics. As feminist work becomes more visible and is gradually accepted on to academic syllabuses, which is, after all, what many women have struggled to achieve within the academic world over the years, so it loses its marginal position, and can become part of the mainstream. There is the problem of establishing a feminist canon that centralises key texts and marginalises others. As Lyndie Brimstone has cautioned, within the problematic dichotomy of margin and centre, Women's Studies can only become more mainstream if some parts of it, notably lesbian and Black Women's Studies, remain at the margins to maintain such a distinction (Brimstone, 1991) (see also Chapter 1).

The second reason for the increasing significance of the debate about the relationship between theory and politics in Women's Studies in the 1990s is the changing nature of feminist activism (Christian, 1990). Whilst many forms of feminist politics have survived through the years of Thatcherism and beyond, (Franklin *et al.* (eds), 1991), the disappearance of certain forms of visible activism, such as campaigns and demonstrations, during the late 1980s and early 1990s has produced changes which have crucial implications for Women's Studies courses. This is not to say that we live in a post-feminist age, or to take the gloomy position that feminism has died a death and it is time for new things, for the widespread amount of feminist activity in all areas of social and cultural life attest to the success of feminism in many ways. Rather, the kinds of feminist activity taking place have changed and we have, whether we like it or not, witnessed the gradual disappearance of particular forms of activism that functioned importantly to offer women access to feminism.

Women's Studies has increasingly become *one* way for women to find out about feminism. Rather than many students of Women's Studies coming to the subject with a desire to find out about feminist thought because of their involvement in political campaigns and activism, women are increasingly finding out about feminism through Women's Studies courses in adult and higher education. This tendency will necessarily have implications for Women's Studies in the future: it may mean that some students will have particular expectations of, and probably frustrations with, Women's Studies courses. Educational courses cannot, and indeed should not, replace political activism, but in the absence of visible political alternatives, Women's Studies courses can be seen to 'represent' feminism (McNeil, 1992).

This shift has particular implications for the question of the role of theory within Women's Studies. The anxieties expressed by many about the institutionalisation of Women's Studies and, some would argue, the increasing separation of feminist theory from politics, is likely to increase in the 1990s, as more women look to Women's Studies as a substitute for feminist politics, which exist in very different forms compared with twenty years ago. Unlike certain forms of feminist activism, Women's Studies has been expanding in Europe and the United States and has thus taken on increased significance within feminism. Let us hope that the proliferation of Women's Studies courses provides a suitable forum for the continuation of productive debate about the role of feminist theory and its relationship to a changing feminist politics in the future.[6]

Notes

1. See Chapter 1 in this volume. For the debates about theory, practice and experience, see also: Mary Evans (1982); Sarah Fildes (1983); and Liz Stanley and Sue Wise (1983).
2. Other chapters in this book have offered readers guidance through the selection of Further Reading in their subject areas, I have decided not to make such a selection, for the reasons discussed here.
3. Feminist work does not only include post-1968 writers, or indeed those from first-wave feminism (see Walby, 1990, pp. 191–8), but could also include Mary Wollstonecraft's writing at the end of the eighteenth century, or indeed that of women in the seventeenth century (Graham *et al.* (eds), 1989).
4. For a recent example of the usefulness of the term 'patriarchy', see *Sociology*, 23(2) May 1989.
5. Materialism here refers to a continuing commitment to the analysis of women's oppression as tied to the expropriation of women's activity, defined in the broadest sense, whilst rejecting the class-based focus of the more traditional Marxist analysis.
6. I would very much like to thank Lisa Adkins, Sarah Franklin, Hilary Hinds, Richard Johnson, Celia Lury, Maureen McNeil, Lynne Pearce and Annie Witz for their encouraging and constructive feedback on earlier drafts of this chapter and for helping me to produce this final version. I am also very grateful to Diane Richardson and Vicki Robinson for their patience and excellent editorial guidance.

4

Sexuality and Male Dominance

Diane Richardson

> Sexuality is to feminism what work is to marxism – (MacKinnon, 1982, p. 515)

What is the relationship between sexuality and gender inequality? It is this question which perhaps more than any other has provoked discussion and controversy within feminism. Most feminists would agree that men's power over women, economically and socially, affects sexual relationships; generally speaking, women have less control in sexual encounters than do their male partners, and are subjected to a double standard of sexual conduct which favours men. Where feminists differ is over the importance accorded to sexuality in understanding women's oppression. For many radical feminists, sexuality is at the heart of male domination; it is seen as the primary means by which men control women and maintain their power over women in society generally (Dworkin, 1981; MacKinnon, 1982; Coveney *et al.*, 1984). Others, especially socialist feminists, do not regard sexuality as the fundamental cause of women's oppression, and have criticised this strand of radical feminism for underestimating the significance of other factors, such as women's unequal position in the labour market and their domestic roles within the family (for example Segal, 1987, 1990a; and Rowbotham, 1990a). Some Black feminists have also suggested that other forms of oppression may be experienced as more significant for Black women (see Chapter 2). Women who stress sexuality as a form of social control have also been criticised for neglecting its pleasures (Vance, 1984).

There is also disagreement between feminists – related to differences in the significance attributed to sexuality in the reproduction of patriarchal society – as to the extent to which sexual relations are determined by or are determining other social relations. Socialist feminists who have written about sexuality have tended to emphasise how sexual relations are determined by unequal power relationships in society. Central to most radical feminist accounts, by comparison, is the view that sexual relations are not simply a reflection of the power that men have over women in society generally, but also determine those unequal power relationships. In other words, sexual relations both reflect and serve to maintain women's subordination. From this perspective, the concern is not so much how women's sex lives are affected by gender inequalities but, more generally, how male-dominated sexuality constrains women in virtually all aspects of their lives. It may influence the way we feel about our bodies and our appearance, the clothes we wear, the work we do, our health, the education we receive, and our leisure activities, as well as the relationships we feel able to have with both women and men.

For instance, it is becoming clearer how sexuality affects women's position in the labour market in numerous ways: from being judged by their looks as right (or wrong) for the job, to sexual harassment in the workplace as a common reason for leaving employment (see Chapter 12). Other writers have examined the ways in which girls' educational opportunities are restricted by the exercise of male sexuality. Sue Lees' (1986a) study, for example, shows how boys control girls' behaviour in the classroom through their use of the sexual double standard. Women's social lives and leisure opportunities are also affected by fears of sexual violence, especially around being out alone after dark (Green *et al.*, 1990). Also, when we talk about reproductive rights we are not simply talking about better health service delivery or sex education, we are also talking about the role heterosexuality plays in the oppression of women. As Jalna Hanmer points out in Chapter 10, the focus on the control of women's fertility through contraception, abortion or sterilisation masks the issue of men's assumed 'right' of sexual access to women. Related to this, women's health concerns reflect men's power in sexual encounters. As Holland *et al.*'s (1991) study of young women demonstrates, this is a major constraint on women's ability to protect themselves against AIDS by practising safer sex.

These are some examples of how male sexuality, as it is currently constructed, functions in the social control of women. However, the forms of control of women are likely to be different in different cultures and historical periods. For example, in the past, control over women's sexuality was linked to hereditary rights. If a woman had sex outside marriage there was no way that her husband could be sure that any children she had were his rightful heirs. For the wealthy at least, this was one reason why great emphasis was placed on the need for female chastity.

Nowadays women may no longer be encased in chastity belts, but the notion of women's sexuality as the property of men still underpins many of our laws and social customs. The view that a husband cannot be guilty of raping his wife is a classic example of this. (A view which the English courts upheld until 1991, when rape within marriage became unlawful.) Within marriage, women are expected to be sexually available to men, regardless of their own desires. In a similar vein, we hear about 'wife-swapping' but not 'husband-swapping' parties; we celebrate the father 'giving' away his daughter in marriage; and we expect women to accept a form of sexuality as something they 'give' to the man they love.

This is not to say that sexuality will have the same significance for all women in any given historical period or culture. There may be important differences between women in relation to class, 'race', age, ethnicity, sexual identity and being differently bodied. For example, under slavery in the United States, Black women were generally considered to be the sexual property of white slave owners who were men, and similarly in Australia, Aboriginal women were often sexually exploited and abused by white European 'settlers', as were Black African women (Omolade, 1984). For Black women, therefore, racism informs their experience of male control of women's sexuality; for example when a Black woman is sexually harassed or abused by a white man it is often 'racist sexual violence' (Hall, 1985).

The link between male sexuality and female oppression is not new within feminism. Many nineteenth-century feminists were concerned with the way that women's lives were controlled by 'male lust', and sought to change sexual relations between women and men. They attacked the sexual double standard and drew attention to the ways in which sex was dangerous to women; in particular through the debilitating effect of repeated pregnancies and infection from venereal diseases such as syphilis. The proposed solution was male sexual control; hence the slogan 'Votes for women and chastity for men'. Few feminists at that time demanded a wider knowledge of birth control and the availability of contraceptives, which would have reduced the risk of unwanted pregnancy. On the contrary, many feminists opposed contraception because they feared that it would 'allow men to force even more sex upon their wives and to indulge in extra-marital sex with even greater impunity' (Gordon and DuBois, 1984, p. 40). They were concerned to protect women from the unwanted sexual demands of men and the possible consequences of an increase in extramarital sex, in particular the risk of getting venereal disease and the loss of financial and emotional security if the marriage broke up (Jeffreys, 1985).

Nineteenth-century feminists were more concerned with establishing a woman's right to refuse unwanted sex, including that within marriage, than with the right for women to seek sexual satisfaction on equal terms with men. Celibacy was advocated by some as a positive choice, rather than 'sexual slavery' in marriage. (The affirmation of the right of women to live independently of men was as spinsters, however; lesbian relationships as another form of resistance were rarely mentioned.) In the early twentieth century there were signs of a shift in emphasis; support for contraception grew and there was a greater insistence by some feminists on the importance of sexual pleasure for women. Women, they argued, have as much right to sexual satisfaction as men; although for the most part this was defined in terms of heterosexual relationships. In some cases this led to a critique of spinsterhood as an unnecessary deprivation and the suggestion that celibacy could seriously impair women's health and happiness (Coveney *et al.*, 1984).

Since the nineteenth century, then, divisions have existed between feminists over the issue of sexuality. More recently, feminists have debated the significance given to sexuality in understanding women's oppression, as well as specific issues such as pornography and heterosexuality. However, before examining these debates in more detail, we first need to ask what definitions of sexuality predominate?

What is sexuality?

At first glance, the answer to this question might seem obvious. Sex is often talked about as if it were simply a case of 'just doing what comes naturally'. This is often referred to as an *essentialist* view of sexuality; sex conceptualised as a natural instinct or drive which demands fulfilment through sexual activity (see Chapter 3). It is a 'natural phenomenon', universal and unchanging, something that is part of the biological make up of each individual – although it is assumed that men, in general, have a stronger sexual drive than women. There has also been a division of sexual attributes based on 'race' and class as well as gender. Black women, particularly African and Afro-Caribbean women, are frequently seen as highly sexed, lascivious and promiscuous. Asian women are sexualised as exotic and sexually compliant. Such ideas about Black women's sexuality, and related images of the Black male 'stud', reflect deep-rooted racist notions that Black people are less civilised and closer to nature, having an untamed, animal sexuality. Similarly, it has often been assumed that, like Black people, the working classes are less able to control their sexual 'urges'.

A further assumption within this model of sexuality is that it is 'normal' and 'natural' for this instinctive urge to be directed at the opposite sex. It is, essentially, a heterosexual drive. Sexuality is, ultimately, a reproductive function; with vaginal intercourse being *the* sex act. Society, in so far as it is seen as having an effect, modifies the expression of this natural urge.

This is one way of understanding sexuality. Another approach is social construction theory. To say that sexuality is socially constructed means that our sexual feelings and activities, the ways in which we think about sexuality, and our sexual identities, are not biologically determined but are the product of social and historical forces. Sexuality is shaped by the culture in which we live: religious teachings, laws, psychological theories, medical definitions, social policies, psychiatry and popular culture all inform us of its meanings. Even though our sexual desires may seem to be 'natural', our sexual responses are actually learnt, in the same way as are other likes and dislikes. We learn not just patterns of behaviour, but also the meanings attached to such behaviour.

This is not to say that biology has no influence on sexuality; clearly there are limits imposed by the body. We are, for instance, capable of experiencing different things depending on whether we have a vagina or a penis. The point is that the body, its anatomical structure and physiology, does not directly determine what we do or the meaning this may have. The capacities of the body 'gain their power to shape human sexual behaviour through the meanings given them in a particular cultural context' (Warren, 1986, p. 142).

Consider, for instance, the 'discovery' of the G-spot – a region of the front wall of the vagina which swells during sexual arousal and, it is claimed, is highly sensitive to stimulation. The fact that it is a sensitive part of a woman's body does not, by itself, motivate us to seek it out and touch it. Indeed, many women do not know it exists. That some now spend time searching for their G-spot (and there are books and equipment to help them in their quest), and enjoy being touched there as part of their experience of sexual desire, is a good example of the social construction of sexuality. The G-spot is physiologically the same as it was before it was 'discovered', but it now has a different social significance. By giving sexual meaning to a particular bodily region or function we produce sexuality; we construct desire.

Within the umbrella term 'social constructionist' there are a variety of different perspectives, including discourse analysis (for example, Foucault, 1979); psychoanalytic (for example, Mitchell, 1974); and symbolic interactionist (for example, Gagnon and Simon, 1973; and Plummer, 1975). They all adopt the view that patterns of sexual behaviour may vary over time and between cultures, and that 'physically identical sexual acts may have varying social significance and subjective meaning depending on how they are defined and understood in different cultures and historical periods' (Vance, 1989, p. 19). A kiss is not just a kiss, as time goes by!

Anthropological studies have demonstrated that there are tremendous cultural variations in what is defined as 'sex'; why people have sex; how often they have sex; who they have sex with; and where they have sex. Recognising cultural diversity in the meanings and organisation of sexual behaviour does not, however, necessarily challenge the more fundamental assumptions of the essentialist model. Some social constructionists also believe in the notion of an innate biological drive, albeit a drive that takes different cultural forms. They may also accept the idea that 'heterosexual' and 'homosexual' are natural and universal categories. Others, however, would argue against this, insisting that heterosexuality and homosexuality are social constructions. Work on lesbian and gay history has provided support for this view. Although there is some disagreement between writers as to precisely when the idea of the homosexual person emerged, the general belief is that, in Europe at least, the use of the term 'homosexual' to designate a certain type of person is relatively recent, having its origins in the seventeenth to nineteenth centuries, with the category 'lesbian' emerging somewhat later than that of the male homosexual (Foucault, 1979; Faderman, 1981; McIntosh, 1981; Weeks, 1990; and Baum Duberman *et al.*, 1991).

What is being suggested is that in many historical periods and cultures a woman who has sex with another woman may not think of herself, or be regarded as, a lesbian. Whilst same-sex behaviour may have always existed, it seems that an identity as lesbian or gay or, by implication, heterosexual, is historically and culturally specific.

Within feminist theory, the idea that heterosexuality is a social construction has been further developed. The question, 'Why are people heterosexual?' is central to radical feminist analyses; it is through an examination of this question that we may have a better understanding of the mechanisms by which patriarchy is maintained. For instance, Adrienne Rich (1981) argues that not only is heterosexuality central to the oppression of women, in their roles as wives and mothers especially, but that few women would be heterosexual if it were not for the social and economic compulsions. (This is discussed in more detail later.)

The most radical form of social construction theory suggests that there is no 'natural' sexual drive which it is said we all possess to varying extents as part of our biological make-up. Sexual drive is itself a historical and cultural construction. Symbolic interactionist writers such as William Simon and John Gagnon adopt this position. They argue that not only do we learn what 'sex' means, and who or what is sexually arousing to us, but we also learn to want sex. Whilst they acknowledge that, biologically, the body has a repertoire of gratifications, which includes the capacity to have an orgasm, this does not mean that we will automatically want to engage in them. Certain ones will be selected as 'sexual' through the learning of what Gagnon and Simon call 'sexual scripts'. A particular experience, kissing, say, would not be repeatedly sought after in the absence of any meaningful script. It is the giving of social meaning to a sequence of physiological responses, pursing our lips and moving them about, which creates the motivation to repeat the experience. From this perspective, socialisation is not about learning to control an inborn sexual desire so that it is expressed in socially acceptable ways, but the learning of complex sexual scripts which specify the circumstances which will elicit sexual desire and make us want to do certain things with our bodies. What we call 'sexual drive' is a learnt social goal.

Unlike Sigmund Freud, who claimed the opposite was true, Gagnon and Simon are suggesting that sex is a vehicle for expressing non-sexual 'needs'; in particular, needs that are linked to gender roles. Thus, men express and gratify their 'need' to be masculine – a 'real man' – through sexuality. Feminist theories of sexuality would not disagree with this: they would, however, explain it in the context of a wider understanding of gender inequality. The way men behave sexually is not simply the result of a certain form of upbringing – a certain kind of 'sexual script' learning – it is also partly the result of the power men have over women. In this respect, feminists would criticise Gagnon and Simon and others for relying on socialisation as the explanation of male sexuality, and lacking a concept of power. Another criticism made of symbolic interactionist accounts such as Gagnon and Simon's is that they fail to explain where these scripts come from. In particular, in describing different sexual scripts for women and men, they do not provide an analysis of why they differ and why they take the form they do, as well as the functions this may serve (Faraday, 1981).

Where do these meanings come from? The discursive challenge to essentialist theories of sexuality, characterised by the writings of Michel Foucault and his followers, does engage with this question. Foucault, like symbolic interactionists, argues against the notion of a biological sexual drive. By taking 'the sexual' as their object of study, various discourses, in particular in medicine and psychiatry, have produced an artificial unity from the body and its pleasures: a compilation of bodily sensations, pleasures, feelings, experiences, and actions which we call sexual desire. This fictional unity, which does not exist naturally, is then used to explain sexual behaviour and sexual identity.

Foucault also rejects the idea that this so-called 'essential aspect' of personality has been repressed by various kinds of discourses on sexuality; for example, the law or the Church's teaching on sexuality, or medical and psychiatric accounts. It is not that sexuality has been repressed, he argues, rather it is through discourses on sexuality that sexuality is produced. It is these discourses which shape our sexual values and beliefs. In other words, it is not a case of peeling back the layers of social conditioning to get at our true natures, and of discovering an authentic female (or male) sexuality, but of understanding how the body and its pleasures acquire certain historically and culturally significant meanings. 'Sex' is not some biological entity which is governed by natural laws which scientists may discover, but an *idea* specific to certain cultures and historical periods. Thus, what 'sexuality' is defined as, its importance for society and to us as individuals, may vary from one historical period to the next.

Foucault believes, as do interactionists, that sexuality is controlled not through repression but through definition and regulation, in particular through the creation of sexual categories such as 'heterosexual', 'homosexual', 'lesbian' and so on. In the case of women's sexuality, Foucault argues that it has been controlled not by denying or ignoring its existence, through a 'regime of silence', but by constantly referring to it. He also draws attention to the fact that the history of sexuality is a history of changing forms of regulation and control over sexuality. For example, over the last hundred years there has been a shift away from moral regulation by the Church to increased regulation through medicine, education, psychiatry, psychology, social work, the law and social policy. 'Bad' sex is defined less in terms of immorality than as social deviance or sex we do not enjoy or want. (The latter is clearly evident in much feminist writing.)

A serious criticism of Foucault's work is that he does not examine the relationship between gender inequality and sexuality, nor does his account of the different discourses on sexuality pay much attention to the fact that women and men often 'have different orientations to sexuality, even different discourses' (Walby, 1990, p. 117). In Foucault's work, sexuality is not understood as gendered, it is a unitary concept and that sexuality is male. Feminist theorists have also pointed out how Foucault's account of the construction of the 'homosexual' category similarly ignores lesbianism, implicity encoding homosexuality as male (Fuss, 1990).

The psychoanalytic challenge to essentialism is associated with the reinterpretation of Freud by Jacques Lacan. For Lacan and his followers, sexual desire is not a natural energy which is repressed; and it is language rather than biology which is central to the construction of 'desire'. Lacanian psychoanalysis has had a significant influence on the development of feminist theories of sexuality; in particular on socialist feminist contributions. The work of Juliet Mitchell (1974, 1982), Jane Gallup (1982) and Rosalind Coward (1983) among others, as well as that of French feminist writers such as Julia Kristeva, Hélène Cixous and Luce Irigaray, who have all been influenced by Lacan's work at some stage, even if they have subsequently moved on (see Marks and de Courtivron, 1981).

The view that sexuality is socially constructed is central to most feminist analyses of sexuality. However, even within feminist work, questions of essentialism have arisen. For example, critics have pointed to problems of essentialism within some feminist reworkings of psychoanalytic theory (see Chapter 3). There has also been an unfortunate tendency to misrepresent radical feminist analyses of sexuality as essentialist or biologically determinist. Rosalind Brunt, for example, claims that the radical feminist position 'takes the sexual division between men and women as a permanent and irreversible "given": it is a fact of nature that they are oppressor and oppressed' (Brunt, 1988, p. 57).

Whilst writers such as Mary Daly (1978, 1984) and Kathleen Barry (1979) have alluded to an essential female/male sexuality, they are not typical of radical feminist theories of sexuality. What Brunt and others often choose to ignore is the insistence within most radical feminist writing that sexuality is socially constructed, not biologically deter-

mined. (And if sexuality is socially constructed then it can be recon-
structed in new and different ways; sexuality need not be coercive or
oppressive, it can be changed.) Even where this is recognised, radical
feminists are sometimes accused of a different form of essentialism:
'Though these social constructionist theories may not technically be
biologically essentialist, they are still a form of social essentialism: that
is, they assume a social divide between male and female sexual natures
which is unconvincingly universal, static and ahistorical' (Ferguson,
1989, p. 54). Once again such criticisms seem misplaced; for as Walby
(1990) – who herself adopts a materialist analysis – and others have
pointed out, most radical feminist analyses of sexuality are historically
and culturally sensitive.

What this also highlights is that essentialism and social constructionism
are not two distinct and opposing positions (Fuss, 1990). These are
relative terms and it may be more helpful to think of a social
constructionist/essentialist continuum along which theorists may be placed
(see Chapter 3).

Sexuality and power

Feminist theories of sexuality are not only concerned with describing the
ways in which our sexual desires and relationships are shaped by society;
they are also concerned to identify how sexuality, as it is currently
constructed, relates to women's oppression. As I have already pointed
out, feminists differ on this question. Many radical feminists argue that
the way sexuality is constructed is not merely a reflection of the fact that
men have power over women in other spheres; rather it is constructed the
way it is because it keeps women in their place. It is an important, some
would say *the* most important, means of maintaining male power and
control over women (Jackson, 1984). Others, especially some socialist
feminists, are reluctant to attribute this significance to sexuality (for
example, Segal, 1990a). They prefer to regard the social control of
women through sexuality as the *outcome* of the inequalities of a capitalist society, rather than its purpose.

However, either way, it is clear that a feminist analysis of sexuality
sees gender as central. It is not enough simply to say that sexuality is
socially constructed, we have to decide what it is constructed from? As
part of their socialisation, boys learn that having sex with a woman,
particularly intercourse, is a central aspect of being masculine. It is an

important means of proving themselves as 'real men', with all the privileges, status and rewards that implies (Richardson, 1990). In this sense, power and domination are central to the current construction of male sexuality. By being sexual, a man affirms his status and power over others and his identity as masculine. This is evidenced in the way men often brag about sexuality and talk of sex as if it were about totting-up 'scores'. It also manifests itself in many forms of harassment of women, from wolf whistles to sexual gestures or comments.

Female sexuality has been defined as different from, yet complementary to, male sexuality. Sex is seen as both more important to and uncontrollable for men than it is for women; the result of men's greater sexual urges. It is also suggested that men are naturally the 'dominant' or 'active' partner, whereas women are sexually 'submissive' or 'passive'. Sex is something men do to women; it is they who are expected to 'take the initiative, make things happen, and control the event' (Jackson, 1982). The language used to describe sexual encounters also reflects this; boys and men often talk of 'having' or 'taking' a woman. Such assumptions influence how we define women's sexuality in the broadest sense. For example, the view of sex as something done to a woman by a man implies that lesbianism is not an authentic form of female sexuality. Similarly, the view that women are sexually 'passive' may, for example, result in the sexual desires of women with disabilities being ignored (see Chapter 11).

This is not to suggest that all women and all men unquestioningly accept prevalent notions about female and male sexuality. However, it can be difficult to ignore such pressures, especially when there are negative consequences for doing so. For example, if women do take the sexual initiative they often risk being labelled as 'easy', 'unfeminine' or 'a nymphomaniac'.

The belief in masculine dominance and female submission in sexual activity rests on the assumption that it is a natural expression of sexual difference. There is, within the works of sexologists and sex-advice writers, a tendency to stress that in men the sexual urge manifests itself as a desire to 'conquer', while in women it seeks fulfilment through 'surrender' to the male. Man's power over women turns them both on. Moreover, this relationship between sex and power is assumed to be natural, normal and inevitable; essential to sexual arousal and pleasure. Some feminist writers echo this view, for example Margaret Nichols (1987) argues that if sexual desire requires a 'barrier', some kind of tension, difference, power discrepancy, then lesbians will need to find ways of introducing 'barriers' into their relationships to enhance sexuality and sexual desire (others would question this; see Richardson, 1992b).

Linked with the idea that sex is a natural force, and the concept of sex drive, is the belief that to a certain extent sex is beyond conscious control, more especially for men. The message is that men have powerful sexual urges which they find difficult to control. Women, who are not so troubled, should be aware of this and should not provoke men to a point where they can no longer be held responsible for their actions. This is evidenced in the way that women often get blamed if men sexually harass them, and in the way men's sexual violence against women has often been seen as an understandable, if not acceptable, reaction to female 'provocation'. Common myths are that women provoke men by the way they dress, by leading men on, and by saying 'no' when they really mean 'yes'.

By deflecting responsibility from men, women are placed in the role of 'gatekeepers', with responsibility for both their own and men's sexual behaviour. In much the same way, women have traditionally been expected to take responsibility for birth control, especially since the advent of the contraceptive pill. Similarly, underlying most 'safe sex' campaigns there appears to be tacit acceptance that men are 'naturally' less able to exercise self-control when it comes to sex than are women (Scott, 1987; Richardson, 1990). Such ideas are important in understanding other forms of behaviour. For example, both pornography and prostitution are sometimes regarded as providing 'sexual release' for men who might otherwise be 'driven' to sexually harassing or raping women.

Feminist research has challenged such assumptions, pointing out how these ideas serve to 'naturalise' certain forms of male sexual behaviour that are oppressive to women, and function as a form of social control. They also influence how women 'define, resist, cope with and survive their experiences' (Kelly, 1988, p. 34). For example, it is not uncommon for women who have experienced sexual abuse and/or violence to blame themselves. Feminists have highlighted how the 'commonsense' view that women are responsible for men's violence enables individual men to deny responsibility and insist that they were misled or 'provoked': victims of women, or their own sexual 'natures'.

It is argued by feminists that sexuality has been constructed in the interests of men and, consequently, is defined largely in terms of male experience. For instance, sexual surveys have demonstrated that it is a majority of women who say they do not have orgasms during vaginal intercourse (Kinsey *et al.*, 1953; Hunt, 1975; and Hite, 1976). Sociologically speaking this tells us something about the power relations at play in defining 'good sex'. In a society where there was real equality between women and men, would intercourse still be regarded as 'the Real Thing'? Feminists have also drawn attention to the way language defines sexuality very much in male terms (Spender, 1980).

This was an important aspect of feminist analysis of sexuality in the early 1970s; the main problem with sexuality was that it was 'male-defined'. Women were encouraged to discover their own sexuality for themselves; a sexuality that had been suppressed and denied. (An example of essentialist thinking within feminism.) By exploring their own bodies women would discover how to get what they wanted from sex. As Sheila Jeffreys comments: 'These early feminist thinkers saw sex as something that women had been shut out of. Women had not been allowed the delights that men had taken for granted. Sex was an equal rights issue' (Jeffreys, 1990, p. 236). Men's sexual domination of women was important because it prevented the emergence of 'women's self-defined sexuality'.

Many feminists in the early 1970s also saw a connection between the suppression of women's sexuality and social powerlessness. They believed that discovering one's 'true sexual potential' would empower women, giving them greater confidence and strength to oppose their subordination. With hindsight, many feminists have questioned how beneficial the so-called 'sexual revolution' of the 1960s was for women (Campbell, 1980; and Ehrenreich, Hess and Jacobs, 1987). More fundamentally, some have criticised the association of sexual liberation and women's liberation, asserting that sexual liberation has never been in women's interests (Jeffreys, 1990). Others would claim this is too pessimistic a view, which undervalues the significance for women of certain 'gains' of sexual liberalisation such as changes in the divorce law and attitudes towards lesbianism (Segal, 1987; Walby, 1990).

The end of the 1970s saw a change of emphasis in feminist theory on sexuality; the focus was no longer on women's sexual ignorance and repression, but on male sexuality and its effects on women. Central to this was an analysis of the relationship between sex and power; in particular, how the idea that it is natural for men to dominate women sexually, and that women want and enjoy this, can easily be used to legitimate sexual violence.

Feminists have directly challenged traditional taken-for-granted assumptions about sexuality, whilst acknowledging that a wide range of 'coercive practices' are regarded as normal and natural forms of heterosexual behaviour. For example, the idea that women are not capable of deciding for themselves when they are sexually aroused, but have to be wooed or seduced by a man into wanting sex. Or the assumption that sex is a bargain, where sex is the price women pay for men spending money on them, or a duty, part of what a 'husband' expects of a 'wife' in return for supporting her and any children they might have. (The resistance to making rape in marriage a crime, and the difficulty in enforcing such laws, in part reflects this.)

Feminists have also introduced new terms, such as 'coercive sex' and 'pressurised sex', to describe those situations where women are forced or pressured into having sex they do not particularly want or like (Kelly, 1988a). Such terms challenge the assumption that all sex which is not defined as assault or rape is consensual. There are many reasons why women may engage in sexual activities they do not enjoy or desire. The belief that men have strong sexual desires which women are responsible for controlling or 'provoking', coupled with the expectation that women have an obligation to meet men's sexual 'needs', helps to explain why women can find it difficult to refuse unwanted sex and/or insist on the kind of sex they would like. They may also find it difficult to refuse men because they fear the consequences: for instance, the threat of, or actual, violence or their partner rejecting them. It is for these sorts of reasons that many feminists cannot accept the liberal view that 'anything goes' between consenting adults in private. In the context of unequal power relations between adults in terms of gender, 'race' and class the notion of 'consent' remains problematic.

Heterosexuality

> Should we define heterosexuality as one sexual mode among many, or is it politically important to identify it as a primary institution of women's oppression? (Snitow, Stansell and Thompson, 1984, p. 33)

The view that heterosexuality is central to an understanding of patriarchy is widely accepted within radical feminism; indeed some would want to argue that it is *the* most important institution of patriarchy (Brunet and Turcotte, 1988). Heterosexuality is seen not as an individual preference, something we are born with or fixed as a result of early childhood experiences, but as a socially constructed institution which structures and maintains male domination, in particular through the way it channels women into marriage and motherhood. Similarly, lesbianism has been defined not just as a form of sexual practice, but as a way of life and political struggle; a challenge to the institution of heterosexuality and a form of resistance to patriarchy.

Some feminists have extended this analysis to suggest that far fewer women would be heterosexual were it not 'compulsory'. Adrienne Rich's work has been particularly important in this respect. Rich suggests that heterosexuality may not be a 'preference' at all, but something that 'has had to be imposed, managed, organized, propagandized, and maintained by force' (Rich, 1984, p. 226). She goes on to describe some of the factors which 'force' women into sexual relationships with men rather than women. For example, a sexual ideology which presents hetero-sexuality as 'normal' and lesbianism as 'deviant'; the unequal position of women in the labour market; the idealisation of heterosexual romance and marriage; the threat of male violence which encourages women to seek the 'protection' of a man; and men's legitimising of motherhood.

It is often felt that heterosexual women are being criticised by femin-ists who argue that heterosexuality is oppressive to women; but this is to miss the point. It is the *institution* of heterosexuality, which creates the prescriptions and conditions in which women 'choose' heterosexuality, that is being challenged. (A parallel to this is the labelling of feminists who have criticised the institution of motherhood as 'anti-mothers'; when such criticisms are not directed at mothers themselves, but at the conditions in which women are expected to mother.) Related to this, it is also important to understand that critiques of heterosexuality, particu-larly those by lesbian feminists, are not aimed simply at getting a better deal for lesbians through challenging heterosexual privilege. The argu-ment is that heterosexuality as it is currently constructed restricts *all* women's lives, albeit to varying extents.

Having said this, it is the case that almost all feminist analysis of heterosexuality has been written by lesbians (Douglas, 1990). There has been a distinct lack of heterosexual feminist work on this subject, al-though there are signs that this is changing (*Feminism and Psychology*, 1992). (There are some interesting parallels here between the acknowl-edgment on the part of some heterosexual feminists of the need to problematise heterosexuality and the argument put forward by Black feminists that white people need to deconstruct and problematise the category 'white'.) This is not to ignore the fact that in the early 1970s many heterosexual feminists as well as lesbians voiced criticisms of heterosexuality as a form of sexual practice. In particular, they challenged the centrality of sexual intercourse in heterosexual relations, pointing out that very often this is not the major or only source of sexual arousal for women. Anne Koedt, for example, in a now-famous article, criticised 'the myth of the vaginal orgasm' and stressed the importance of the clitoris for female pleasure (Koedt, 1974). However, despite Koedt's acknowledgment of the implications for lesbianism, such discussions were often focused on how to get men to be better lovers through improving their sexual technique, rather than on any fundamental criticism of heterosexuality. The important concern was establishing women's right to sexual pleasure, primarily within a heterosexual context.

In addition to critiques of heterosexuality as an institution and a form of sexual practice, some feminists have also challenged the heterosexual basis in feminist theory. For example, writers such as Monique Wittig (1981) and Susan Cavin (1985) have criticised many theories about the origins of women's oppression because they assume heterosexuality as being universal. Similarly, much of the work on social policy, including that by feminist writers, can be criticised both for assuming the universality and normality of heterosexuality and for failing to acknowledge the impact this has had on the development and implementation of social policy (Carabine, 1992). Feminist work on the impact on women's lives of providing family and informal care, for instance, can be criticised for its focus on the heterosexual family.

The critique of heterosexuality, and its role in the control and exploitation of women, has been one of the major areas of disagreement and debate between feminists. This was particularly evident during the 1970s when some feminists took the analysis one step further by arguing that, if heterosexuality is the key mechanism which perpetuates male dominance, feminists should reject sexual relationships with men. In the United States, the classic 'Woman-Identified Woman' paper by Radicalesbians, written in 1970, asserted that 'woman-identified lesbianism' was the political strategy necessary for women's liberation and the end to male supremacy. The implication for heterosexual feminists was that they should give up relationships with men and put their commitment, love and emotional support into relationships with women (Radicalesbians, 1973). In Britain, similar ideas were put forward in a paper, first published in 1979, by the Leeds Revolutionary Feminist Group (Onlywomen Press, 1981). The paper proposed 'political lesbianism' as a strategy to resist patriarchy. It stated that all feminists can and should be political lesbians because 'the heterosexual couple is the basic unit of the political structure of male supremacy . . . Any woman who takes part in a heterosexual couple helps to shore up male supremacy by making its foundations stronger' (Onlywomen Press, 1981, p. 6). A political lesbian was defined as 'a woman-identified woman who does not fuck men', it did not necessarily mean having sexual relationships with other women.

Although feminist writers such as Ti-Grace Atkinson (1974) and Catherine MacKinnon (1982) held a similar position to many lesbian feminists in rejecting sex with men, in particular vaginal intercourse, as being oppressive to women, they did not necessarily advocate lesbianism. Atkinson believed, at least in her early writings, that under patriarchy any sexual expression perpetuated women's domination by men and emphasised celibacy. In some ways this compares with the strategy of those nineteenth-century feminists who advocated voluntary celibacy and spinsterhood as a form of resistance to the sexual subjection of women.

Many heterosexual feminists, including some radical feminists, were extremely angry and critical of such analyses of heterosexuality, arguing that they contravened the women's liberation movement's demand for the right to a self-defined sexuality. (An argument that is also used in feminist debates around pornography, and sado-masochism (s/m).) What right had one woman to tell another what to do sexually? Some also argued that heterosexuality could be a political practice or choice, a view which has emerged more recently in attempts by heterosexual feminists to theorise heterosexuality (Robinson, 1993).

Adrienne Rich attempts to bridge this divide through the concept of a 'lesbian continuum' which embraces not only sexual desire for and relationships with other women, but also many forms of bonding among women including female friendship and support for other women (Rich, 1981). This allows women who are in sexual relationships with men to be included as part of the 'lesbian continuum', which Rich suggests is an important form of resistance to patriarchy. While most radical feminists accept Rich's analysis of heterosexuality, her concept of a lesbian continuum has been criticised for, amongst other things, 'shortchanging lesbians' by not recognising lesbianism as a specific experience distinct from being 'woman-identified' (Raymond, 1986). In a similar vein, some lesbian feminists reacted angrily to the arguments for political lesbianism (see Onlywomen Press, 1981). Part of their concern was that lesbianism was becoming associated with a critique of heterosexuality, a rejection of men, and feelings of sisterhood with other women, rather than a 'specific sexual practice between women, with its own history and culture' (Campbell, 1980, p. 1).

Nevertheless, the suggestion that 'any woman can be a lesbian' represented an important challenge to traditional assumptions about lesbianism as an immature or pathological condition of a minority group of women. By providing a political analysis of sexual relationships between women, feminism not only helped to de-stigmatise lesbianism, it also broadened its meaning. In other words, the women's movement not only helped lesbians to feel more positive about themselves and to 'come out', it also 'opened up the possibility for lesbian relationships for many women who had previously considered their heterosexuality a permanent feature' (Stacey, 1991).

Within heterosexual relationships, women service men emotionally and sexually. Men also gain from material servicing; it is women who are primarily responsible for housework and for the work of caring for family members, including male partners. This has implications for women's economic independence, in terms of the relationship between women's unpaid domestic labour and their position in the labour market (see Chapter 12). Clearly, for women to withdraw *en masse* from such relationships *would* be revolutionary, even if some men could afford to pay for such services. It is not a choice that is equally open to all women, however. This is another way of saying that heterosexuality and, by implication, lesbianism is structured by 'race', class, ethnicity, and age. For instance, is it an accident that nineteenth-century spinsters were, in the main, from middle-class backgrounds, or that 'celebrated' lesbians such as Radclyffe Hall and Lady Una Troubridge in the 1920s and 1930s, were women of independent means who could afford such a lifestyle?

In addition to recognising social and economic constraints on 'choice', some writers would argue that there are unconscious factors at work in the construction of sexual identities and desires which can make it hard to change our feelings and relationships (Rowbotham, 1990). Feminists such as Juliet Mitchell, Jacqueline Rose and others using a psychoanalytic perspective have made an important contribution to this debate. However, others have criticised feminist psychoanalysis for privileging heterosexuality and failing to rescue lesbianism from being seen as a pathology. As Diane Hamer (1990) remarks, 'The reluctance to question the status of heterosexuality has led to a frustrating unevenness in feminist psychoanalytic discourse, in which the status quo has been problematized and yet the already existing alternatives to a heterosexual norm are still largely untheorized' (Hamer, 1990, p. 139). Heterosexuality as a form of oppression has also been shaped by the history of racism, and consequently it does not take the same form for both Black and white women. For instance, under slavery, Black women were often forced to have sex with white slave owners; those who resisted risked being tortured and punished. Sexual exploitation was part of their enslavement:

> every part of the black woman was used by him . . . Her back and muscle were pressed into field labor where she was forced to work with men and work like men. Her hands were demanded to nurse and nurture the white man and his family as domestic servant . . . Her vagina, used for his sexual pleasure, was the gateway to the womb, which was his place of capital investment – the capital investment being the sex act and the resulting child the accumulated surplus, worth money on the slave market. (Omolade, 1984, p. 365)

Racist stereotypes of Black people as primordially sexual have provided white men with a way of deflecting responsibility for racial sexual abuse and exploitation on to Black women; white man's desire for Black women has been blamed on her sexuality, her lasciviousness. (This parallels the more general view that women are responsible for men's sexual violence.) They have also fuelled white racism directed at Black men, as well as patriarchal control of women's sexuality. While white men assumed the 'right' to have sex with their Black women slaves, it was considered unthinkable that white women should do the same thing with Black men. Indeed, Black men were likely to be severely punished if it were suspected they had made a sexual advance towards a white woman. For example, in the United States earlier this century, many Black men were lynched and publicly castrated as a way of 'protecting white womanhood' (Simson, 1984). White fascination with and fears about Black male sexuality, although different for white women than for white men, continues to influence social attitudes and practices. For instance, the belief that Black men are more likely to perpetrate sexual assaults or rape.

The fact that sexual ideologies are racialised has different implications for Black women than for Black men. (Having said that, the dominant view of Black sexuality as hyper-*hetero*sexuality helps to render both Black lesbians and Black gay men invisible). The association of 'masculinity' with 'virility', and male sexuality with power and dominance, means that being stereotyped as a 'stud' is likely to have a certain appeal to many Black men, especially when opportunities to achieve social and economic status are restricted. The sexual double standard means that the attraction for Black women of being defined in sexual terms is likely to be more limited; often eliciting contempt and sexual harassment/abuse. Black feminists in particular have addressed these issues, criticising Black men for their deployment of dominant images of Black masculinity. They have pointed out that it is not good enough for Black men to claim they are 'victims' of white racism. Whilst racist imagery has undoubtedly played a significant role in the construction of Black male sexual identities, they argue that this is no excuse for Black men conforming to a male-dominated sexuality which is oppressive to women (Wallace, 1979; Bryan *et al.*, 1985).

Sexuality as pleasure

In recent years there has been a shift in focus in feminist perspectives on sexuality towards greater discussion of sexual pleasure. This is often portrayed as a response to the emphasis on the dangers of sexuality during the 1980s, in particular debates about the meaning and effect of pornography and sexual violence. A number of feminists, for example Carole Vance (1984), claim that the focus on sexuality as a form of social control has led to an 'overemphasis' on the dangers of sexuality and very little feminist discussion of sexual pleasure. Vance believes that 'Feminism must speak to sexual pleasure as a fundamental right' (Vance, 1984, p. 24). There are echoes here of the late 1960s when, as I have already outlined, many feminists saw the search for women's sexual satisfaction as an important feminist goal.

For other feminists, the issue is not finding out how women get sexual pleasure and how to get more of it, but of asking what counts as 'sexual pleasure' and what functions does it serve? Unless we explore these sorts of questions we could be asserting a right to something which is not necessarily in our interests. This is the view taken by writers such as Catherine MacKinnon (1982) and Sheila Jeffreys (1990), who regard 'pleasure' as a problematic concept for women under patriarchy and question the emphasis on the right to sexual pleasure as counter-productive to women's liberation. In brief, MacKinnon (1982) asserts that sexuality constitutes gender. It is not simply that certain forms of sexual practice (such as vaginal intercourse) are important to understanding gender inequality, but that patriarchally-constructed sexuality creates gender. It is through the experience of 'sexuality' that women learn about gender; learn what being 'a woman' means under patriarchy; learn female subordination and male power. 'Specifically, "woman" is defined by what male desire requires for arousal and satisfaction and is socially tautologous with "female sexuality" and the "female sex"' (MacKinnon, 1982).

There has been an unhelpful tendency to stereotype feminists opposed to women's sexual liberation as puritanical or 'anti-sex'. But this is inaccurate: the arguments of writers such as MacKinnon, Jeffreys and Andrea Dworkin are based on the belief that sexual 'liberation' will result in the increased acceptability of beliefs about sexuality, as well as forms of sexual behaviour, which are part of the social control of women and help to maintain their subordination. Also unhelpful is the assumption that feminists interested in expanding the analysis of pleasure within feminist theory will automatically be sexual libertarians. Many of those advocating a woman's right to sexual pleasure are strongly influenced by sexual liberationist arguments, but not all are. Having said this, there are major disagreements within feminism over what a feminist sexual politics should be and nowhere have these been more evident than in the debates over pornography.

Pornography

The anti-pornography movement, which emerged in the United States in the late 1970s, was a dominant issue for feminists in the West during the 1980s. Unlike right-wing opponents of pornography, who object to its sexually explicit nature and its lack of moral values, feminist opponents object to the sexist and misogynist (woman-hating) nature of most pornography, which frequently depicts women as 'commodities' for male consumption, who enjoy being dominated and humiliated. Most feminists would agree on this; where disagreements arise is over how important an issue pornography is for feminism. Opinion differs as to whether pornography is the cause, or one of the causes, of women's oppression, or merely a reflection of men's greater power in society generally. Some feminists, including Andrea Dworkin (1981), believe that pornography is the principal cause of women's oppression. Others regard the significance attached to pornography by feminists such as

Dworkin as misguided; they argue that although pornography may mirror the sexism of society, it does not create it (Rodgerson and Wilson, 1991).

Another long-standing debate within feminism is whether there is a direct link between pornography and men's violence against women. A number of feminist writers have argued that pornography is a direct cause of sexual violence towards women (Brownmiller, 1976; Dworkin, 1981; and see Everywoman, 1988). Others claim that the evidence for this is unclear and unconvincing (Segal, 1990b). Even if it is not easy to prove conclusively a direct connection between the reading or viewing of pornography and specific acts of violence, it can be argued that pornography has an indirect effect by shaping male attitudes towards women and sexuality. Pornography informs men that women are sexually there for them, that they want to be taken and used, that they enjoy being raped, punished, tortured and sometimes killed. Some feminists would also claim that, whether or not it can be proved that there is a connection between pornography and violence, pornography should be opposed on the grounds that it is in itself a form of violence towards women (Dworkin, 1981).

Also hotly debated is the question of what strategies should be used to oppose pornography. Some feminists want to make the production and sale of pornography illegal. In the United States, anti-pornography ordinances (laws which apply only to specific cities) were drawn up in 1983 by Andrea Dworkin and Catherine MacKinnon. The laws were aimed at preventing the distribution of pornography on the grounds that it is a violation of women's civil rights. Although their attempt subsequently failed, it provoked fierce argument between feminists who support the introduction of laws against pornography and those who describe themselves as anti-censorship. The latter believe that the introduction of such laws would be both ineffective and dangerous to women's interests, in so far as they could be used by conservative, right-wing movements to censor feminist opinion and defend traditional family values. Women's health books, for instance, containing information about issues such as birth-control, abortion or lesbianism might be deemed pornographic. They would advocate restricting public access to pornography and increased public discussion to stimulate awareness of why feminists object to it. In reply, anti-pornography feminists would ask why feminists against censorship have not taken a similar stand against laws preventing racial hatred? As Andrea Dworkin comments, 'why they

think race hate laws aren't censorship laws, why it's all right to propa-
gate agitations of hatred against women but not on the basis of race'
(Dworkin, 1991).

There has not been a campaign in Britain on a par with that in the
USA; none the less, a similar division of opinion does exist, though
perhaps not to the same extent as in the United States, between feminists
involved in the Campaign Against Pornography, and Feminists Against
Censorship. For further discussion of the differences amongst feminists
over the issue of pornography, see Kelly, 1985; Chester and Dickey,
1988; and Chapter 5 in this volume.

Other feminists have criticised the focus on pornography as a 'single
issue', and have argued for the need to incorporate feminist action
against pornography into a wider critique of representations of women,
such as in advertising, films and television programmes (Coward, 1982).
More contentious is the suggestion by some that what is needed is more
women 'pornographers'. Providing critiques of the views of women and
sexuality contained within pornography, and their possible effects, is not
enough. It is argued that we need to create a new 'pornographic discourse', in order to produce a feminist pornography/erotica which expresses women's sexuality in words and images of our own choosing,
and transforms the meanings and power relations typically manifested in
pornography and other representations of sex in the process (Myers,
1989; and Smyth, 1990). (The issue of what is pornography and what is
erotica, and whether it is possible to make a distinction between the two,
is another area of debate between feminists.) It is in this context that we
have witnessed the emergence of pornography and erotic fiction by and
for women, but more especially lesbian pornographic/erotic writing
(Califia, 1988; Nestle, 1988; Sheba, 1989, 1990; and Reynolds, 1991).
As with the subject of pornography generally, the question of whether
there can be a feminist erotica or pornography has been hotly contested.
Similarly, where lesbian pornography and erotica are concerned, the
arguments have been deeply divisive (Dunn, 1990; Richardson, 1992b).

Conclusion

In this chapter I have tried to show how over the last twenty years
feminism has politicised sexuality. Feminists have emphasised that sexuality, commonly regarded as something that is private and personal, is a
public and a political issue. They have challenged traditional assump-

tions about sexuality, for instance the notion of sex as equalling intercourse and women as sexually passive, and proposed new ways of understanding sexual relations. In particular, feminist theory has problematised heterosexuality and redefined lesbianism. As well as giving new meaning to these sexual identities, feminists have engaged in a whole variety of debates and campaigns around sexuality. As part of the desire for greater knowledge and control over our own bodies, feminists have campaigned for access to free contraception and abortion, as well as better sex education for women. Sexual violence has been placed on the public agenda largely as a result of the efforts of various feminist groups who have campaigned for changes in the law, over marital rape for example, as well as for changes in policy and practice. Feminist services have been developed: refuges for women who have been sexually abused, rape crisis lines, and self-help groups for women who are survivors of sexual violence. Feminists have also campaigned against pornography, for the rights of lesbians, and for an end to sexual violence, as well as the right to sexual pleasure. They have drawn attention to issues such as sexual harassment at work and in education, and to the fact that many of the health concerns of women are closely connected to sexuality.

Despite these achievements, it is clear that we need to continue to develop feminist critiques of sexuality into the 1990s. Many issues have not been adequately explored or theorised, such as the way in which heterosexuality interacts with 'race', class and age; how sexuality as a form of social control has changed; and the notion of sexual pleasure itself. But most important, we need to continue to emphasise that sexuality is not a private matter, but an 'arena of struggle in which male dominance and women's subordination can either be most powerfully reinforced and maintained, or be fundamentally challenged' (Coveney *et al.*, 1984).

Further reading

Feminist Review (ed.), *Sexuality: A Reader* (London, Virago, 1987). A collection of articles originally published in the British socialist feminist journal, *Feminist Review*. It includes articles on psychoanalysis, pornography and representation, sexual violence and feminism, and the politics of sexuality.

Sheila Jeffreys, *Anticlimax: A Feminist Perspective on the Sexual Revolution*

(London, The Women's Press, 1990). This book concludes that the 'sexual revolution', far from bringing liberation and fulfilment, has actually upheld male power and reinforced women's subordination.

Also useful is the short collection of articles by Lal Coveney, Margaret Jackson, Sheila Jeffreys, Leslie Kaye and Pat Mahony, *The Sexuality Papers: Male sexuality and the social control of women* (London, Hutchinson, 1984).

Carole S. Vance (ed.), *Pleasure and Danger: Exploring Female Sexuality* (London, Routledge & Kegan Paul, 1984). This book brings together papers and talks given at the controversial Scholar and Feminist IX Conference, 'Towards a Politics of Sexuality', held at Barnard College, New York in 1982. It explores sexuality as both pleasure and danger for women, and covers a broad range of topics from a variety of disciplines.

Ann Snitow, Christine Stansell, Sharon Thompson, *Desire: The Politics of Sexuality* (London, Virago, 1984) is another American anthology which explores a wide range of issues, including heterosexuality, pornography, and the connections between power and desire, as well as the relationship between 'race' and class and sexuality.

Carol Anne Douglas, *Love and Politics: Radical Feminist and Lesbian Theories* (San Francisco, Ism Press, 1990). This book provides an overview of radical and lesbian feminist theoretical positions over the past few decades, and looks at ideas on love and sexuality as well as divisions between feminists on these issues.

5

Violence Towards Women
Mary Maynard

This chapter is concerned with a range of different types of violence against women: wife-beating, rape, child sexual abuse, sexual harassment, and pornography. In some of the literature these are considered as separate topics. Here they are treated as part of a spectrum of violence with the aim of demonstrating that our understanding of each form of violence is enhanced by considering them together. This does not mean that we can generalise from one kind of violence to all others without qualification. Rather it is to acknowledge the interrelationship between different kinds of violence, particularly in terms of their impact on and consequences for women's lives.

The chapter also seeks to remind us that, whilst violence against women is a contemporary concern, 'first wave' feminists who campaigned and wrote in the nineteenth century were keenly aware of its existence and significance. Together with the beginnings of a literature about violence against women in other countries and other cultures, this serves to highlight the fact that the abuse of women and children is an issue which spans centuries and continents.

The bulk of the chapter, however, addresses a number of contemporary themes: problems of definition; different approaches to understanding and explaining male violence against women; how the real extent of such violence remains hidden; and how the state and feminists have responded to its existence.

Feminism and violence

The higher profile afforded to the issue of male violence against women in recent years is almost entirely due to the political practice of activists in the women's liberation movement and feminist research deriving from this. Until the early 1970s little was known or written about such violence, and scant attention was paid to it as a social problem. As feminism developed momentum in the late 1960s and early 1970s, the significance of violence in women's lives started to emerge. Feminists began to examine their own experiences of abuse, and provide support for other women who had been victims of violence. As a result, the first rape crisis line was established in the USA in 1971 and the first refuge for battered women opened in England in 1972 (Kelly, 1988a). Subsequently, the issue of violence against women has become an important focus for feminist theory and action. Support groups for women who have been abused now exist in many countries. New issues, particularly those of incest, child sexual abuse and sexual harassment, have been raised. Women from different countries have tackled forms of violence specific to their culture. For example, in India there have been campaigns against 'dowry deaths': women being killed by their husbands and in-laws for not having provided sufficient money or goods on marriage (Kishwar and Vanita (eds), 1984). In Egypt and Africa women have challenged the custom of female circumcision (el Saadawi, 1980). As Liz Kelly has remarked the amount of effort, frequently unpaid, put in by women around the world to counter violence against them has been 'incalculable' (Kelly, 1988a, p. 2).

It is not the case, however, that the extent of violence against women has only recently been discovered. For instance, Elizabeth Pleck (1987) has chartered its significance in America going back over three hundred years, and Anna Clark (1988) describes a similar situation in England for the period 1770–1845. Victorian feminists fought for women's rights to both divorce and legal separation on the grounds of a husband's violence and the successful culmination of this in Britain with the 1878 Matrimonial Causes Act provided an important means of escape for women involved with abusive partners (Walby, 1990). Similarly, many nineteenth-century women, particularly in America, supported the temperance demand for restrictions on alcohol because excessive drinking was seen as contributing to wife-beating (Rendall, 1985). Concern over the sexual abuse of children is also not just a contemporary phenomenon. Research on incest dates back to the late nineteenth century, and public anxiety over child sexual abuse has erupted intermittently ever since (Hooper, 1987).

In many ways, first-wave feminists' analyses of incest and wife-beating are very reminiscent of feminist writing on male violence today.

For instance, they argued that incest was part of a generalized pattern of male violence manifest also in acts such as rape and domestic violence (Hooper, 1987). In an article written in 1878, Frances Power Cobbe referred to wife-beating as 'wife torture'. She derided the fact that it was considered a source of humour and denounced the devalued way with which men regarded their wives. Along with others, she saw violence against women not as the pathological behaviour of a few 'sick' men; rather it was the extension of a system of practices and laws which sanctioned men's rights to regard women as their property and therefore to keep them under their control (Maynard, 1989).

As the public profile of feminism began to focus more and more on the matter of suffrage at the turn of the century, so the interest in violence towards women began to fade. The issue was to remain largely hidden for more than half a century, to re-emerge with the development of the women's movement in the 1970s, as mentioned earlier. It should not be imagined, however, that in the intervening years the abuse of women disappeared or abated. Research has shown that it is not so much the incidence of violence which has changed during the last century, as its perceived significance and visibility (Pleck, 1987; Gordon, 1989). Its persistence as an area of experience in women's lives is one of the reasons why violence is such an important topic for Women's Studies today.

Defining violence

Although common sense might lead us to believe that what comprises violence is fairly self-evident, defining violence, especially in relation to women, is a somewhat contentious affair. Three significant kinds of definition can be identified: legal; professional/expert; and those of women themselves.

Legal definitions

Legal definitions are usually the narrowest ones and they tend to carry a certain authority, since they determine whether agencies such as the police, social services and courts of law are able to intervene or prosecute in particular circumstances. Sylvia Walby (1990) points out that legal definitions tend to omit acts which many women would regard as violent. For example, in Britain until 1990, the law did not recognise that a woman could be raped by her husband, as she was deemed to have consented to sexual intercourse on marriage. This was in contrast to the situation in many states in the United States, some in Australia and most of Scandinavia, where sexual intercourse without a wife's consent *does* constitute rape. Further, the legal definition of rape in most countries is unlawful sexual intercourse, which means that the penis must penetrate the vagina. This excludes forcible penetration by other objects; and other forms of sex, such as anal intercourse.

There are similar problems with legal definitions of sexual abuse against children and of pornography. In Britain, for example, there is no offence called 'child sexual abuse'. Rather it comprises a number of different sexual offences (Viinikka, 1989). Some of these, such as un-lawful sexual intercourse, are age-specific and linked to the legal age of consent for heterosexual sex with girls, which is sixteen years. Others, such as rape, apply to both adults and children. The crime of incest is also defined in heterosexist terms, since it is regarded only as taking place between members of the opposite sex, must involve penetration and is restricted to certain kinds of familial relationships (MacLeod and Saraga, 1988). It is thus confined to what is conventionally seen as 'normal' heterosexual activity. Use of the term 'incest' has been criti-cised by some feminists for focusing attention on *who* is involved rather than upon *what* is happening. They prefer terms such as 'father–daughter rape' instead, since it emphasises that the child is experiencing an act of aggression in which she is denied her self-determination (Ward, 1984). Other feminists employ 'incest' in a wider sense to include all abuse committed within the family or by any relative however distant (Nelson, 1987).

Pornography is also difficult to define legalistically. Carol Smart (1989b) has pointed out that in the UK the law governing pornography has taken the form of restricting the publication of materials deemed to be obscene or indecent. An article can be regarded as obscene if its effect is such as to deprave or corrupt. But, as Smart indicates, the test relates only to the individual consumer of pornography and cannot be used to judge whether the general public as a whole would be depraved or corrupted. The law on indecency prohibits the display of material which would be offensive to the public generally: it was designed to protect people from displays which they would not choose to see. This simply means removing offending items to the top shelves in newsagents, or to sex shops. It does not necessarily involve taking them away completely.

The kinds of legalistic problems which have been described have led feminist researchers to document how the law's definition of violence routinely takes precedence over women's definitions (Brophy and Smart (eds), 1985; Edwards, 1981; Stanko, 1985; Smart, 1989b). They have examined the mechanisms through which the law is able to define the 'truth' of things in rape, child sexual abuse and other cases, in the face of evidence which quite clearly contradicts this understanding. Although the law is supposed to be gender-neutral, its ability to be able to decide what does or does not comprise a violent act gives it tremendous power. The consensus of feminist opinion is that this power works against the interests of women and in the interests of men instead. This is because, by discounting the views and definitions of women, the law is giving legitimacy to those of their male assailants. In failing to challenge the latter, the right of all men to abuse women is upheld.

Professional/expert definitions

A second way of defining violence is one in which the views of professionals and experts are paramount. This involves deciding on the basis of evidence collected, when to define particular acts as violence, regardless of the views of the state or of the women or children involved (Walby, 1990). The work of the feminist social scientist, Diana Russell, who has conducted a number of surveys on violence in America, is an example of someone who uses this approach (Russell, 1982, 1984). For example, Russell defines any act of intercourse where the man has used force as rape, even where the woman concerned does not herself wish to use such an emotive word.

There are a number of professional definitions of child sexual abuse to be found in the literature on the subject and they vary depending on the activities which are included or excluded, and on the relationship of the child to the abuser. Mary MacLeod and Esther Saraga suggest the following as the most widely used: 'The involvement of developmentally immature children and adolescents in sexual actions which they cannot fully comprehend, to which they cannot give informed consent, and which violate the taboos of social roles' (MacLeod and Saraga, 1988, p. 19).

However, as they point out, this definition can be criticised for not including the idea that force or the threat of force may be used. The notion of 'informed consent' is also problematic for feminists since it assumes that the ability to say 'yes' or 'no' in abusive situations is a relatively straightforward affair, when, in fact, it is frequently complicated by relationships of power and emotional blackmail. Additional difficulties with the definition are produced by the terms 'developmentally immature' and 'sexual actions'. The former implies that only younger children can be sexually abused, with the implication of consent and complicity for older ones. There is also a dispute as to what constitutes 'sexual actions'. Whilst professionals tend towards a narrow interpretation of vaginal, oral or anal penetration, feminists adopt a more inclusive stance, including touching parts of the child or requesting the child to touch the assaulter, taking pornographic photographs, and requiring the child to look at parts of the body or at sexual acts or at sexually explicit material (Driver, 1989). Thus, while acknowledging that feminists disagree on the subject, MacLeod and Saraga (1988) suggest that there should be three key elements to defining child sexual abuse. These are the betrayal of trust and responsibility; the abuse of power; and the inability of children to consent.

Professional or expert attempts to define pornography are exemplified in the 1970 North American Presidential Commission on Pornography and, for Britain, in the 1979 Williams Committee on Obscenity and Film Censorship (Smart, 1989b). The latter argued that for material to be pornographic it must have the intention to arouse its audience sexually as well as containing explicit sexual representations. By employing such a definition, Williams intended to differentiate between, for instance, medical textbooks which may be explicit but which are not intentionally designed to arouse, and items produced by the pornography industry. Yet, as Smart argues, the intention of an author or photographer can always be contested and it is impossible to 'measure' the extent of arousal in the consuming public. Degrees of nakedness are more easy to assess, but intention and arousal can only be presumed. In addition, the definition ignores such issues as the objectification, degradation and coercion of women contained in pornography, which have been at the heart of feminist concerns.

Professional or expert definitions can be problematic because they usually involve the imposition of a particular set of meanings upon individuals who may interpret what has happened, been said to them, or what they are seeing, in a different way. For instance, feminist researchers have found that 'flashing' or the constant telling of 'dirty' jokes can be experienced by women as abusive, even though they are commonly held to be rather trivial activities (MacKinnon, 1979; McNeill, 1987). Also included within a feminist analysis of violence are obscene telephone calls, sexual propositioning, and other behaviour which women find sexually harassing (Wise and Stanley, 1987). In addition, women's definitions of violence and what is regarded as serious assault often differ from those held both by the law and by professionals. There is, therefore, a third way of defining violence and that is to adopt the definitions of women themselves. This is the approach taken by many feminists.

Women's definitions

Although violence towards women has been acknowledged as significant by writers from differing feminist standpoints, it is from what is known as the 'radical feminist' perspective that it has been given the most extensive treatment (Stanko, 1985; Hanmer and Maynard (eds), 1987; and Kelly 1988a).[1] Radical feminists argue that, in order to be able to capture the extent of the impact of violence upon women, it is important not to pre-determine the meaning of the term. To do this it is necessary to know about women's experiences of violence and the boundaries which they draw around them. Liz Kelly has extended this argument to child sexual abuse, arguing that: 'if we are to reflect in our definition . . . the range and complexity of what women and girls experience as abusive we must listen to what they have to say' (Kelly, 1988b, p. 71). Kelly (1988a) used accounts of women's own experiences, based on in-depth interviews, to define violence from the women's point of view. She shows how the kinds of abuse which the women described, and which they had experienced both as adults and as children, are neither reflected in legal codes nor in the analytical formulations often used by professionals. Along with other researchers, Kelly points to the wide range of male behaviour which women perceive to be threatening, violent or sexually harassing – many more than are conventionally regarded as abusive (Hanmer and Saunders, 1984; Stanko, 1985). She suggests that our commonsense definitions of what constitutes violence reflect men's ideas and limit the range of male behaviour that is deemed unacceptable to the most extreme, gross and public forms. Thus women often find themselves caught between their own experiences of behaviour as abusive and the dominant beliefs which define such behaviour as normal or inevitable. This leads Kelly to introduce new categories, such as 'pressure to have sex' and 'coercive sex'. Such terms are used to challenge the assumption that all sexual intercourse which is not defined as rape is, therefore, consensual.

One aspect of the feminist definition of violence which should be emphasised is the inclusion of the threat or fear of force as well as its actual use. In her early pioneering article on the subject, Jalna Hanmer argued that the fear of violence both compels and constrains women to behave or not to behave in certain ways (Hanmer, 1978). It affects what they can do, where they can go, and with whom they can go. In other words, both the reality and the threat of violence act as a form of social control. It is therefore necessary to include both in any understanding of what violence is about.

Other writers have also shown how concern about possible abuse or attack can influence women's lives. For instance, Sue Lees has documented how abusive behaviour and language from boys in schools, which often has a sexual connotation, can alienate girls from education and learning (Lees, 1986a). Writing about leisure, Eileen Green *et al.* describe the ways in which concern about violence influences the kinds of activity women choose to engage in. The possibility of attack is taken into account in deciding when to go out and where to go to, particularly in dark areas with poor transport provision (Green *et al.*, 1990). In the area of mental health, writers such as Diane Hudson have shown how professionals are able to use the threat of hospitalisation, electroconvulsive therapy and psychosurgery to control women's behaviour and confine it to channels acceptable to men (Hudson, 1987). Thus it can be seen that the issue of violence is wide-ranging and cuts across a number of others dealt with elsewhere in this book, for example to do with sexuality, the family, education and employment.

With this in mind, radical feminists have attempted to develop a much broader definition of violence which links together a number of different forms through which it occurs and is experienced. The term 'sexual violence' is used to distinguish these on the grounds that they are acts directed at women because their bodies are socially regarded as sexual. Kelly defines sexual violence to include: 'any physical, visual or sexual act that is experienced by the woman or girl, at the time or later, as a threat, invasion or assault, that has the effect of hurting her or degrading her and/or takes away her ability to control intimate contact' (Kelly, 1988a, p. 41).

This definition encompasses a wide spectrum of behaviour including rape, sexual assault, wife-beating, sexual harassment (including flashing and obscene phone calls), incest, child sexual abuse[2] and pornography. They are linked by virtue of the fact that they are overwhelmingly *male* acts of aggression against women and girls, often use *sex* as a means of exercising power and domination, and their effect is to intrude upon and curtail women's activities. Radical feminists argue that they are thus mechanisms through which women are socially controlled.

For example, for feminists, sexual harassment involves a variety of behaviour, some involving physical contact, some of a verbal or psychological kind, ranging from suggestive remarks, looks or joking to unwanted touching or patting, to direct sexual propositioning (Halson, 1989). Some of the more common forms of sexual harassment are often dismissed as trivial or simply 'larking about'. What distinguishes sexual harassment from friendly banter or flirtation is that 'it is not mutual; it is not welcome; it offends; it threatens' (Halson, 1989, p. 132). It may even lead a girl or woman to alter her activities by taking a different route to school, or changing jobs. Because the offensiveness of the act is defined subjectively by the woman involved, it is not possible to draw up objective lines of demarcation between what constitutes serious sexual harassment and what does not (de Lyon, 1989).

Pornography is also included by some feminists in their definition of violence. Andrea Dworkin (1981), for instance, argues that pornography is at the heart of male supremacy. It portrays women's bodies as belonging to men and presents women's sexuality in an objectified, debasing and humiliating way. Dworkin sees this as constituting the foundation of women's oppression, because it legitimates women as the property of men and as subordinate to them. It is a violation of women as human beings and an encouragement to men to treat women as inferior and in abusive ways. For Dworkin, then, it is not just a question of whether pornography contains or causes violence to women, (although she argues both to be the case);[3] rather, she claims that pornography is itself violence to women and that it pervades and distorts every aspect of Western culture.

Hidden violence against women

The extent of male violence against women is not easy to measure. For instance, official statistics record 3305 instances of rape and 15 376 of indecent assault against females in England and Wales in 1989 (Home Office, 1990). Yet it is widely accepted that such figures significantly underestimate the amount of violence that actually occurs. This is because many women do not report their attacks to the police, especially if the attacker is known to them, since they do not expect to be treated either seriously or sensitively, as well as fearing further violence from their abuser as a repercussion. In addition, the police have been very reluctant to intervene in those cases they define as 'domestics'. Evidence from Australia, Britain, Canada and the United States indicates their unwillingness to get involved if violence takes place in the private setting of a woman's home because of a tendency to regard it as simply 'trouble' in a personal relationship (Hanmer, Radford and Stanko (eds), 1989). Even attempts to uncover the 'dark figure' or hidden aspect of crime have had little success in improving our knowledge of the incidence of violence towards women. The British Crime Surveys, for example, are designed to find out how much crime goes unreported and why people choose not to go to the police, by asking individuals directly about their experience of criminal behaviour. So far this has shown a very low rate for rape and other sexual offences, and Home Office researchers involved have readily admitted the difficulties in obtaining information. They explain this in terms of women's shame or embarrassment in talking to an interviewer about such matters and the possibility that the assailant may be in the same room at the time of the interview (Hanmer and Saunders, 1984).

By contrast, feminist researchers have begun to uncover the extent to which violence against women is hidden, by using female interviewers and more sensitive interviewing techniques. For instance, Diana Russell's (1982, 1984) random sample of 930 women in the United States found that 44 per cent of women had been the subject of rape or attempted rape during their lifetime; 21 per cent of women who had ever been married had been beaten by their husbands at some time; and 16 per cent of women had experienced incestuous abuse before the age of 18. Similarly, in Jalna Hanmer and Sheila Saunders' (1984) survey of 129 women in Leeds, 59 per cent reported some form of 'threatening, violent or sexually harassing behaviour' towards them in the previous year. Kelly's in-depth interviews with sixty women found that the majority had experienced violence, the threat of violence, sexual harassment or pressure to have sex. These studies, along with similar research, indicate that violence towards women is far more extensive than official figures might lead us to believe. They demonstrate that, whereas sexual violence is often trivialised and regarded as insignificant it is, in fact, an important, complex and ever-present threat in the lives of many women.

It is especially difficult to provide estimates of child sexual abuse, because very few cases are ever reported to anyone (MacLeod and Saraga, 1988). Children may be too frightened to disclose what has been happening, may not be believed when they do so, or may not have the knowledge and understanding to know that it is abuse. Until the late 1980s, research in this area was very limited. However, there have now been a number of feminist initiatives and several large-scale retrospective surveys have been conducted in Britain and the United States, although their findings are the subject of disagreement. As MacLeod and Saraga point out, the conclusion to be drawn from these studies is that between 1 in 10 and 1 in 3 girls have been incestuously abused, in the wider sense of that term. The proportion of girl to boy 'victims' appears to be about 3 to 2 when all sexual abuse is included, but changes significantly to 5 to 1 when the focus is 'within family abuse'. MacLeod and Saraga state that the majority of respondents revealing child sexual abuse had never reported it to any authority and in many cases it was being disclosed for the first time to the interviewer. 'Race' and class were not significant in affecting incidence, although Russell's study found less incestuous abuse amongst Asian women (Russell, 1986). The research so far undertaken suggests that the prevalence of child sexual abuse is high; much higher than is commonly acknowledged or accepted in Western societies. However, it is difficult to judge whether abuse is actually increasing or whether heightened awareness of its existence is making cases which would previously have been hidden, more visible.

Explaining male violence towards women

Broadly speaking there are three major forms of explanations for violence towards women: the liberal/psychological; the social structural; and feminists explanations (although there may be some overlap between the latter two).

Liberal/psychological explanations

The conventional liberal/psychological view of male violence sees it either as the behaviour of a few 'sick' or psychologically deranged men or as 'invited' by flirtatious or masochistic women. This approach thus focuses on the pathological or deviant characteristics of individuals and tends to ignore social, cultural or contextual facts. For example, men who batter have been presented as mentally ill, neurotic or disturbed (Dobash and Dobash, 1980). Rapists have been described as experiencing sexual frustration in their relationships with women due to problematic childhoods and disrupted family backgrounds (Stanko, 1985). Men guilty of child sexual abuse have been characterised as having suffered a chaotic family life, with resulting emotional deprivation (Driver, 1989). Frequently, it is suggested that men who are abusers have themselves been abused. The problem with such explanations is that they do not hold when more general evidence is taken into account. For instance, as has already been noted, the incidence of violence against women is far greater than most advocates of the liberal/psychological view acknowledge, so that it ends up offering 'an exceptionalist explanation of a universal problem' (Smith, 1989, p. 24). Although it may be useful in understanding a few specific cases, it cannot provide a theory to explain the general phenomenon. Further, such an approach is gender-blind and does not explain why it is primarily men who are violent to women. There also tend to be serious methodological problems with the research upon which such arguments are based. Most of it comprises small, unrepresentative samples and there is little work using control or comparison groups (Walby, 1990). All rapists interviewed in a study conducted by West, Roy and Nichols (1978), for example, were patients in a psychiatric unit and were preselected as having psychological problems. This makes it impossible to evaluate how typical it might be for rapists to have such characteristics. Additionally, there are in any case other empirical studies which challenge the legitimacy of individual explanations. Work by Murray Straus (1980) and by Richard Gelles and Clark Cornell (1985), for instance, shows that men who hit their wives do not exhibit a particularly high degree of psychological disturbance. Nor, as Cathy Waldby *et al.* (1989) indicate, can sexual abusers of children claim to be mentally ill. For all these reasons we need to be wary of accepting explanations which focus on the attributes of individuals alone.

We should also be critical of arguments suggesting that women provoke violent behaviour towards them. It has variously been put forward that women invite rape by deviating from the norm of femininity and acting provocatively (Stanko, 1985); that they incite domestic violence by behaving in such a way (for example, nagging, being too talkative or too extravagant) as to actually cause it (Dobash and Dobash, 1980); that child sexual abuse is the result of children being abnormally seductive (Driver, 1989). Feminist work disputes such accounts, pointing out that 'blaming the victim' in this way serves as a strategy for failing to take the totality of violence towards women seriously, and decreases men's responsibility for it. In this perspective men are regarded either as helplessly driven by their innately aggressive and sexual natures; or as sick, thus requiring treatment; or they themselves become the 'victims' of women and children who invite abuse. Somehow in this analysis the central concerns of the arguments come to focus on the male abuser rather than on the woman or child who has been abused. Such 'victim blaming' must be contested for being both naïve and insidious. It is naïve because it fails to take account of the context in which male violence takes place: that of male domination and power. It is insidious because it appears to accept that violence from men to women is, albeit unfortunately, a likely occurrence.

A particular variant of the liberal/psychological perspective on violence is to be found in a widely accepted explanation for child sexual abuse, which has had an important influence on professional groups such as social workers. Known as the family dysfunction approach, it is in some ways different from that so far discussed in its professed concern for the family rather than for the individuals who may have abused or been abused (MacLeod and Saraga, 1988; Waldby *et al.*, 1989). The argument is that abuse occurs in families which are not operating 'properly' and where the 'normal' family hierarchies based on age and sex have broken down. However, this breakdown is attributed almost solely to the mother, who is regarded as having failed to fulfil her nurturing and protective role. As MacLeod and Saraga comment, 'The extent of mother blaming in the family dysfunction approach is quite breathtaking' (MacLeod and Saraga, 1988, p. 36). Women are blamed for being dysfunctional as wives by failing to meet their husbands' sexual demands, or having too many interests outside the home. They are blamed for being inadequate mothers who have failed to be protective of their children (Waldby *et al.*, 1989). Sometimes it is suggested that mothers collude in child sexual abuse. Here it is assumed that mothers should know if their child is being abused and that they should be responsible for stopping it. The implication of such an approach is clear. It is the woman's fault if sexual abuse is taking place. Once again the responsibility of the man is denied and obscured.

Social structural explanations

The second way of explaining male violence, in terms of social class, regards it as a response to such factors as frustration, stress and blocked goals caused by poor economic conditions, bad housing, relative poverty, lack of job opportunities and unfavourable work conditions (Smith, 1989). On this basis it is claimed that men who are violent towards women are disproportionately drawn from the lower classes, since they are more likely to suffer deprivation. Such a view has been advanced by a number of researchers on domestic violence in the United States. They argue that men resort to violence when aspirations, which they are encouraged to hold regarding work and living standards, fail to be reached (Gelles, 1983). Such arguments have also been put forward as a way of explaining child sexual abuse (MacLeod and Saraga, 1988).

Research on rape has also focused on its supposed prevalence amongst working-class men. For instance, in an early book on the subject, Menachem Amir (1971) discusses how men at the bottom of the social order reject dominant cultural values if they find these difficult to achieve, adopting instead alternative standards which are easier to attain. Amir argues that a deviant subculture of violence then emerges in which attributes such as machismo and physical superiority are particularly valued and where rape is one way of expressing this. Amir's claims that rapists are disproportionately drawn from working-class and Black groups have been challenged as classist and racist by feminists (Walby, 1990). However, some socialist feminists who have written about violence, for example Lynne Segal (1990a) and Elizabeth Wilson (1983), still adhere to the view that the deprivations of class and 'race' positions are responsible for male violence, with its ultimate cause being the inherent inequalities of a capitalist society.

The difficulty with such arguments is that once we look at other evidence, and not just at research based upon violence reported to the authorities, upon which most social class explanations are based, a different picture emerges. Studies of battered women who have sought shelter in refuges indicates that domestic violence occurs in all social classes and groupings (Pahl, 1985). Similarly, community-based studies of rape and child sexual abuse do not indicate any obvious correlation with class position. For instance, Beatrix Campbell, a socialist feminist, writing about child sexual abuse in the county of Cleveland, says that there was no evidence that it was simply an expression of the area's economic deprivation. She concludes that the abusers were: 'the men we all know, not so much the outcasts as the *men in* our lives: respectable dads, neighbours, stockbrokers and shop stewards, judges and jurors' (Campbell, 1988, p. 5). They are men of all ages, 'races', religions and classes. The discrepancy between the two sets of conclusions is likely to be due to the unrepresentativeness of the samples used in that research which advocates a social class position (Smith, 1989). This is due to the under-reporting of the violence which women and children experience, as previously discussed, and to the fact that lower-class and Black men are more likely to be arrested, to appear in criminal statistics and, when convicted, be made available for academics and professionals to study.

An additional problem with the social class approach, as Walby notes, is that little attempt is made to explain why men who are frustrated at their class or 'race' position avenge themselves on women (Walby, 1990). She asks why such men do not attack their more obvious class or 'race' enemies instead, pointing out that it does not even appear to be the case that men attack women of the superordinate class or 'race'. Walby suggests we must find the argument that social deprivation breeds male violence wanting. She concludes that 'its fundamental flaw is that it is unable to deal with the gendered nature of this violence' (Walby, 1990, p. 134).

Feminist explanations

The third way of explaining male violence is that provided by feminists. Feminist research has been able to explode much of the conventionally-held mythology and many of the stereotypes concerning male violence towards women. For example, it is commonly believed that most rapes are committed out of doors by strangers. Feminists have shown that a rapist is more likely to be known by his 'victim'; to attack inside, often in a woman's own home; and to have planned the rape (Stanko, 1985). Domestic violence has been identified not just as the simple 'rough and tumble' of everyday life but to involve serious physical assault and wounding (Dobash and Dobash, 1980). Child sexual abuse has been found to have a profound and lasting significance for adult survivors (Driver, 1989). The work of feminists challenges the notion that violence against women is infrequent, easy to escape and trivial in nature. Instead, it is established as a major social and gender issue of our time.

Although there is no single feminist perspective on male violence, it is in the work of radical feminists that the most detailed analyses are to be found.[4] At the core of their approach is the view that violence is both a reflection of unequal power relationships in society and serves to maintain those unequal power relationships. It reflects and maintains the power that men have over women in society generally and also, there-fore, within their personal relationships. The term 'patriarchy' is usually invoked as a way of conceptualising the oppression of women which results. The exact meaning of the term remains the subject of much debate (see Chapter 3). However, a useful definition, which acknowledges that both the nature and degree of patriarchal control varies with and across societies, is provided by Adrienne Rich:

> Patriarchy is . . . a familial–social, ideological, political system in which men – by force, direct pressure or through ritual, law and language, customs, etiquette, education, and the division of labour, determine what part women shall or shall not play, and in which the female is everywhere subsumed under the male. It does not necessarily imply that no woman has power, or that all women in a given culture may not have certain powers. (Rich, 1977, p. 57)

Broadly speaking, then, radical feminists see male violence as a mechanism through which men as a group, as well as individual men, are able to control women and maintain their supremacy. It is not simply a result of women's subordination in society but also contributes to the construction of that subordination.

Domestic violence, rape, child sexual abuse, sexual harassment, pornography, together with all the other ways in which men are able to abuse women and children, form part of a spectrum of male violence against them. In the 1970s it was usual for feminist analysis and activities to be organised around specific types of violence, which tended to be treated in a discrete fashion. It was commonplace for studies and campaigns to focus upon one particular form of violence. Today, male violence is more often treated as a 'unitary' phenomenon (Edwards, 1987). Particular kinds of violence are regarded as differing in degree rather than kind in the ways in which they contribute to the overall system of male control. Indeed, Kelly has developed the idea of a continuum of violence to emphasise their interconnectedness (Kelly, 1988a).

Feminists argue that men benefit from the existence of such a culture of violence because it means that women live in a constant state of intimidation and fear. This may be the fear engendered by the regular occurrence of beatings or harassment, or a more generalised anxiety about the possibility of rape and sexual attack. In either case women will attempt to modify their behaviour in whatever ways they think fit in order to reduce the possibility of assault. It is not that all men are abusers. Clearly they are not. The problem is, however, that because it is ordinary men who commit sexual violence it is impossible for women to know who are their likely assailants. So, when Susan Brownmiller (1976) suggests that all men are potential rapists she means this to be understood in a specific sense. It is from a woman's stance that her statement should be interpreted and, from that point of view, it is not possible for a woman to know, with any degree of certainty, with which men she is likely to be safe.

There are, however, some differences afforded to this general feminist approach. In particular, there is disagreement as to the degree of significance to be attributed to male violence in the maintenance and reproduction of a patriarchal society. Some radical feminists prioritise it as the basis and very foundation upon which women's subordination is built (Stanko, 1985; Kelly, 1988a). They claim that it is because of the potential for men to act as abusers that they are able to control most aspects of women's lives. Others regard violence as only one of many facets of oppression. They argue that violence cannot be seen apart from other means of controlling women, such as their unequal position within the workplace, their role in servicing the family and their objectification in the media (Barrett, 1980). Further, violence against women has different meanings and different prevalences within different societies at different times. It therefore should be regarded as contributing to, but not as the sole source of, male power.

The response of the state to violence against women

The state's response to feminists' claims about violence towards women always seems to take a similar form. When feminists first tried to put the issues of rape and domestic violence on to the political agenda in the 1970s, the reaction on the part of agencies such as the medical profession, social workers and the police was one of rejection and disbelief as to their significance. Feminists' arguments that the violence which was beginning to surface was but the tip of an iceberg were dismissed, amidst claims of exaggeration, provocation and lying on the part of women. Yet, subsequently, the feminist contentions have been upheld, with the seriousness of rape and domestic violence being increasingly recognised (Dobash and Dobash, 1987). More recently, child sexual abuse has received similar treatment, as illustrated by the 1987 British 'Cleveland Affair' (Campbell, 1988). During the first part of that year paediatricians in the Cleveland area diagnosed an unprecedentedly large number of child sexual abuse cases. The public response was again one of disbelief, with politicians and the media instigating a campaign against the doctors. It later turned out, however, that many of the children so diagnosed had, in fact, been abused. Again the initial position taken by feminists about the extent and severity of this violence was vindicated.

Yet, although violence to women has received an increasingly high public profile, the practical response of state agencies has been very patchy. The recent Home Office report on domestic violence remarks on the lack of help received by battered women from doctors, social workers and the police, with social workers particularly stressing the need for reconciliation between partners and putting the interests of the children first in an effort to keep the family together (Smith, 1989). Such an approach, combined with the economic problems women face in trying to support themselves and their children independently, makes it very difficult for women to leave violent men. A similar attempt to keep a family together at all costs appears to lie behind social-work intervention in child sexual abuse cases. Feminists have been critical of the practice of removing the child from the home rather than removing the abuser, pointing out the implications of apparently punishing the innocent 'victim' rather than the perpetrator of the violence (MacLeod and Saraga, 1988).

There are also problems with the ways in which the legal system deals with violence against women. For instance, Elizabeth Stanko has referred to the police and courts of law as a rape victim's 'second assailant', where women themselves are put on trial (Stanko, 1985). Women are reluctant to report rape because of the ways in which questioning and medical examinations are carried out. In court they have to talk intimately and publicly about parts of their body. Their accusation of rape may well be dismissed if there is no sign of bruising or struggle, even though to resist may put a woman's life in jeopardy. Attempts will be made by the defence to establish that a woman consented to sexual intercourse, that even when she said 'no' she meant 'yes', and that she enjoyed it (Smart, 1989). In other words, women are treated as unreliable witnesses.

This is also largely the case with the way in which the courts treat children who have been sexually abused. Carol Smart (1989) has shown that there is a common belief that children fantasise and lie about sexual abuse and that they are likely to make false allegations. Consequently, the child does not enter the witness box on neutral terms but has already been partly disqualified in terms of the perceived legitimacy of her evidence. Smart argues that the way in which the procedures of the court operate in child sexual abuse cases, as in those of rape, are precisely designed to find ambiguities and flaws in the 'victim's' story. Further, as in rape trials, the child's evidence must be corroborated by independent evidence, from doctors or social workers for example, before a conviction can be secured. The word of the woman or child alone is not sufficient.

It also appears that even those laws passed with the precise aim of assisting women in their fight against male violence have been relatively ineffective. Reporting on the situation with regard to domestic violence legislation in Australia and in Britain respectively, Suzanne Hatty (1989) and Kathy McCann (1985) describe how reactionary judicial interpretations of such laws have limited what can be achieved under them. This is because of the unsympathetic attitudes towards women held by the police and the courts who are the gatekeepers to the legislation. McCann concludes: 'Although the domestic violence legislation improved the formal legal rights of battered women, the real improvement in their position is substantially less' (McCann, 1985, p. 94).

Thus, although the welfare, criminal and judicial agencies of the state have begun to respond to violence against women, the consensus of feminist opinion is that major problems still remain. Feminists played a significant role in raising the profile of sexual violence. They must continue to participate in the dialogue about it and be vigilant in monitoring how it is treated, if their influence is not to be undermined.

What is to be done about violence against women? Feminist responses

One of the most obvious feminist responses to male violence against women has been the establishment of refuges, centres and groups as places where the abused can seek shelter, counselling and support (Dobash and Dobash, 1987). Hostels for battered women, rape crisis centres and telephone lines, incest survivors and self-help groups have been important in providing help in those areas where state agencies have been particularly inadequate. Although frequently underfunded, these developments have constituted an important intervention in dealing with violence practically, suggesting the benefits to be gained from feminist collective work.

Such activities have also led to a change in some aspects of feminist thinking about violence. In the early years, feminist analysis tended to portray women as the passive victims of male abuse. However, the testimony of the women themselves has led to a change in emphasis from woman as 'victim' to woman as 'survivor' (MacLeod and Saraga, 1988). The point of this change is not semantic, nor is it meant to detract from the traumas through which abused women go. Instead, it is a signal that those who have been beaten, raped and sexually assaulted can develop strategies to enable them to cope with their ordeals and that they may be able to devise techniques of resistance. The notion of 'survivor' is much more positive than that of 'victim', asserting as it does women's ability to continue with their lives despite the experience of sexual violence.

Feminists have also been at the forefront of various kinds of campaigning related to sexual violence, arguing for changes in police practice and attitudes, more government funding for anti-violence projects, and a recodification of the relevant laws. One aspect of this has been particularly contentious and involves the issue of feminists, the law and pornography. Two American feminists, Catherine MacKinnon and Andrea Dworkin, attempted to use the legal system to prevent the distribution of pornography, on the grounds that it violated women's civil rights and the right not to be sexually discriminated against (Smart, 1989, see also Chapter 4). Their attempt failed but, none the less, it raised a number of issues amongst feminists. Some have argued that feminism, which emphasises liberation and emancipation, is at odds with censorship, which is designed to limit freedom. They suggest that to support censorship is a hostage to fortune which, in other circumstances, could well lead to the banning of feminist as well as lesbian and gay materials, and also involves an apparent alignment with religious and right-wing movements (Segal, 1990b). Would not a ban on pornography simply push it underground and how far, in any case, does it make sense to use a system which is part of the patriarchal state and which encompasses so many anti-woman values and practices, as we have previously seen? This last question is particularly difficult to resolve. However, although some feminists are sceptical about the gains to be had by working from within the existing system, others argue that it is both possible and necessary to work with and refine the practices of legal and welfare agencies and press for reform in procedures adopted by the police and the judiciary (Kelly, 1985; Hanmer *et al.*, 1989). This is particularly so where the ultimate goal is the protection of women and an increase in their safety. Some signs of progress in this direction in Britain are special rape counselling suites run by female police officers, some police and social-worker consultation with feminist groups (such as Rape Crisis), and government directives to the police that they must regard domestic violence as serious assault.

Conclusion

This chapter has examined various dimensions of men's violence against women. It appears that, although much progress has been made in highlighting the extent and severity of the issue, a lot still remains to be done in terms of how the phenomenon is treated and dealt with. In this context, two specific points need to be made. First, the experiences of Black women and those from different cultural groupings are hidden in the literature. In addition, the violence experienced by lesbians, both as women and as a result of anti-lesbianism, is largely ignored. Most material is overwhelmingly about white, apparently heterosexual women and, where there has been research which includes women from other backgrounds, this tends to ignore issues of racism and heterosexism in analysing its findings. It is thus vital that the parameters of research are broadened in order to be able to include those factors that may effect women's differing experiences of violence.

The second point relates to the kind of focus which has been given when dealing practically with violence against women. Much of this has centred on providing support and help, after the event, for women who have been abused, and it is, of course, quite right that we should be concerned to alleviate their suffering. But should not something also be done about changing men and the boys who grow up to be abusers? Until it is acknowledged that violence towards women is a gender issue and a product of the social construction of masculinity, nothing seems likely to change and we will be unable to prevent violence continually occurring.

An interest in and a concern for understanding masculinity has only recently become part of the intellectual and political agenda as a distinct topic (Hearn and Morgan, 1990). As Arthur Brittan has pointed out, a boy's genitals are the first sign of his potential membership of the category 'male' (Brittan, 1989). However, such categorisation does not just mean the simple acquisition of a label. Rather, it affects the whole way in which a male defines his difference from the category 'female'. In Western societies this notion of difference is heavily charged with symbolic meaning. Thus men are taken to be more aggressive, competitive and sexual than women and, in order to demonstrate the strength of their masculinity, these are the characteristics to which they are encouraged to aspire (Brod, 1987). This means, as Brittan so persuasively argues, that masculinity and power, as presently constructed, are inherently interlinked. In fact, masculinity is a form of power and, to the extent that it is formulated in opposition to femininity, masculinity enables men to act out this power in the subordination and control of women. In one sense, then, to become masculine is to become an oppressor. Yet man as oppressor is not 'born' with his gender characteristics biologically and innately given. Rather, these are socially and culturally 'constructed', since the so-called 'facts' of biology are always interpreted in the context of previously established meanings and beliefs. They are not immutable.

Thus in our anxiety for the 'victims' and 'survivors' of violence we must not allow the question of men and masculinity to disappear off the agenda. We need to think through the strategies for how to get men to change and what are the roles and responsibilities of men themselves in this. A significant part of this process is the necessity for men to take seriously the issues discussed in this book. Politically, feminism has always been concerned with transforming knowledge and with generating alternative practices. Nowhere is this needed so much as in the area of violence to women.

Notes

1.   It is commonplace for differing theoretical and political approaches to be categorised under a number of headings which usually distinguish between liberal, Marxist, radical and, sometimes, socialist feminisms (Jaggar, 1983; Tong, 1989). I am, however, not entirely happy with the practice of assigning feminists to one or other particular group (Maynard, 1990). For one thing, the categories selected tend to be far from homogeneous, often containing writers with differing emphases. For another, not every feminist easily fits into the kinds of classification which are usually constructed. It is also the case that, in the late 1970s and early 1980s, the feminist movement became very factionalised and divided over the existence of the different political camps. More recently, a degree of *rapprochement* seems to have been established. This lends further weight to the argument that any attempt to label feminist positions needs to proceed with extreme caution.

2.   Sexual abuse is included in feminists' definition of violence against women and girls, even though it acknowledged that boys are abused also. This is because boys can also be regarded as the subordinate property of adult

men, who can use their position and power against them as they do against women and girls.

3. The claim that pornography causes violence to women is not uncontentious in both feminist and non-feminist circles. There is disagreement over research findings, with some claiming a direct link between the two, and others claiming that this is not proven. Also, some feminists focus on pornography not as violence in itself but as a mode of representation. The basic point is that nothing is intrinsically pornographic. Rather, the viewer brings various socially-constructed interpretations to images and words so that pornography is that which is defined to be so by social convention.

4. See Note 1 above.

Further reading

Beatrix Campbell, *Unofficial Secrets* (London, Virago, 1988). A good introduction to the issue of child sexual abuse by looking at the Cleveland affair. It traces the way in which abuse was diagnosed, the effect on the children and the role of a variety of professionals, especially social workers, the police and the medical profession, in the context of a particular incident in north-east England. The book also considers the way in which the media took up the issue and how various distortions of detail and information took place.

Jalna Hanmer and Mary Maynard (eds), *Women, Violence and Social Control* (London, Macmillan, 1987). This book collects together a number of articles that illustrate a variety of different kinds of violence and the ways in which this violence can control women. Focus ranges from chapters which introduce new empirical areas for discussion, such as flashing, psychosurgery and language abuse, to those which are more concerned with conceptual and theoretical matters relating to how violence should be defined. Other contributions focus on women's experiences of courts of law; feminist responses to domestic violence; and masculinity and violence.

Liz Kelly, *Surviving Sexual Violence* (Oxford, Polity, 1988). Based on in-depth interviews with sixty women, this book focuses on women's experiences of a whole range of forms of sexual violence over their lifetimes. The book emphasises the importance of allowing women's own views and definitions as to what constitutes violence to have a voice. In it Kelly develops the concept of a continuum of violence to show that women's understanding of what is violent, and the significance of violence in their lives, can differ quite drastically from legal and other professional perspectives. The book concludes with a discussion of the implications of the study for feminist services and political organisations.

Carol Smart, *Feminism and the Power of the Law* (London, Routledge, 1989). This book is concerned with rape, pornography, child sexual abuse and domestic violence. It considers how these issues are defined legalistically and the consequences of such definitions for women's lives. The book also explores what happens to women in courts of law when they have been abused by men. It describes how women's evidence and experiences tend to be marginalised, to the extent that it cannot be said that they get a fair hearing. The author describes how women who have been abused receive a 'second assault' in the courts, because they are frequently subjected to intrusive and unsympathetic questioning. She concludes that the legal system is constructed on heterosexist and patriarchal assumptions which means, certainly in cases involving violence or issues of sexuality, that it is biased in favour of men.

6

The Picture is Political: Representation of Women in Contemporary Popular Culture

Margaret Marshment

> *Represent*, v.t. 1. Call up in the mind by description or portrayal . . .
> 3. Make out to be etc., allege that, describe or depict as . . . 5.
> symbolize, act as embodiment of, stand for, correspond to, be speci-
> men of . . . 6. Fill place of, be substitute or deputy for, be entitled to
> act or speak for, be sent as member to legislature or delegate to
> meeting etc. . . . – *Concise Oxford Dictionary*, 1989

Representation is a political issue. Without the power to define our
interests and to participate in the decisions that affect us, women – like
any other group in society – will be subject to the definitions and
decisions of others. These others (men, in our case) are likely to produce
definitions and decisions that serve their own interests. This need not be
a deliberate process of oppression: it may just seem to be 'common
sense' that women should have babies and cook, that women cannot be
company directors or bricklayers, that they should wish to totter around
on high heels to make themselves attractive to men. This appears to be
the natural order of things. So it just happens, 'naturally', that men are
spared the drudgery of domestic chores, can have most of the best jobs,
and status and wealth that go with them, and can expect women to want
to please and service them.

The apparent naturalness of this social arrangement is evidence of the success of patriarchal ideology. If nineteenth-century feminism may be characterised by the struggle for the vote, for the right to be represented in a legislature that had power to determine so many aspects of women's lives, the 'new-wave' feminism of the later twentieth century can be seen as enlarging the concept of politics to include the personal, the cultural and the ideological (see, for instance, Mitchell, 1971, pp. 99–182; and Rowbotham, 1973, pp. 3–46). This was not just a question of disillusion with the power of Parliament, but an awareness of the 'over-determined' nature of women's oppression in society: the way in which their sub-ordinate position in a multiplicity of structures, institutions and value systems interacted with each other to lock women into an overall sub-ordination. Among these structures are those concerned with producing representations of women: from primary school reading schemes to Hollywood films, from advertising to opera, from game shows to art galleries, women are depicted in ways that define what it means to be a woman in this society: what women are like (naturally), what they ought to be like, what they are capable of, and incapable of, what roles they play in society, and how they differ from men.

If these definitions do not fairly and accurately represent the real lives of women, and the reality of their potential as human beings; if women are being defined, for example, as wives and mothers to the exclusion of their work outside the home; if they are being judged by their sexual attractiveness to the exclusion of their moral and intellectual qualities; if they are being defined as inferior to men; then they are not receiving fair representation in society. So that while, for example, the law may no longer prevent women from entering certain professions, it might still be argued that if women are predominantly defined as naturally belonging to the domestic sphere, this could function just as effectively to prevent them from seriously pursuing careers. Ideology can be a powerful source of inequality as well as a rationalisation of it (see, for instance, Barrett, 1980, pp. 84–113).

This chapter will examine the concern shown by feminists over the past two decades with the issue of how women are represented in the media, and in culture generally. It will suggest that, beginning with critiques of 'images' of women and of the female stereotypes promoted across a range of media, feminist work in this area has developed sophisticated analyses of how representation works, how meanings are created in and for a culture, and how people do or do not accept these meanings.

This is not to say that there is any *one* feminist approach to this question: on the contrary, there has been, and still is, considerable debate and disagreement, not only over how to interpret particular images and texts, but also over such issues as how, for example, to evaluate women's magazines, how feminism has affected the media in the past twenty years, whether women should work for inclusion in mainstream media or should set up autonomous organisations, and, most contentious of all, what links (if any) exist between pornography and male abuse of women.

Because there is a separate chapter in this book on women and literature, this chapter will focus on material that can be described as visual, although because no pictorial text exists separate from language or social institutions, the term 'visual text' will be used broadly to cover, for instance, photography, advertising, film, television and magazines; and, because it has come within the cultural studies' agenda, with some popular women's fiction.

Resistance

The first widely publicised event of the women's liberation movement, at the end of the 1960s, was the 'trashing' of accoutrements of femininity at the Miss America pageant in Atlantic City in 1968 (Coote and Campbell, 1982, p. 11). This was a protest against a particularly demeaning spectacle of women, judged (mostly) by men for their conformity to certain physical criteria of femininity, which women in general were encouraged to aspire to with the aid of the girdles, bras and mascara that were deposited in the rubbish bin. This protest was itself the subject of media representation (again mainly by men) – the mythic 'bra-burning' became for years the dominant cultural signifier of feminism, whereby feminists were accused of being 'unfeminine' – ugly, frustrated, and therefore envious of the truly feminine bathing 'beauties'. This event encapsulated many of the dilemmas women confront in representing their own interests in the context of male domination of the institutions and codes of representation. It was directed at male control of definitions of women, but was interpreted as an attack on other women defining themselves; it aimed to attack ideological stereotypes of female beauty, and was interpreted as an attack on beauty itself; it was a protest against the trivialisation of women, and was itself trivialised; it aimed to challenge the power of men to define women and was itself defined by men.

In patriarchal culture, women are defined by those who subordinate them. It is, for the most part, men who are the photographers, publishers, editors, film directors and so on, who produce the images that define women. And these definitions are ideological: in any situation where a social group has the power to represent another group, it is likely that these representations will serve their own interests rather than those of the group represented. So, it may be argued, for instance, that it is in men's interests, as a group, for women to be confined to the domestic sphere; it reduces competition in the workplace and ensures a servicing for men at home to facilitate their work and leisure activities. Images of women cooing over babies and floor cleaners are not, therefore, necessarily just limiting stereotypes; they may be interpreted as encouraging a division of labour that favours men and disadvantages women.

Women may themselves be seduced into accepting such images, both because patriarchal ideology has achieved a general hegemony, and because, however much they work against women's interests in the long term, in the short term they may offer what benefits are available to women in a patriarchal society. If, for example, single motherhood means poverty, loneliness and exhaustion, women may reasonably decide that marriage is the preferable option; so much so that they will desire marriage before contemplating the alternatives.[1] And if definitions of femininity and heterosexuality demand that women wear make-up and high heels in order to be attractive to men, then not only might women wear them for this purpose, they may well come to feel more confident, more beautiful when wearing them.[2] If, in this way, women come to be subordinated – even in their definitions of themselves and their desires – to the needs of patriarchy, it may be argued that this is because definitions of femininity appear to offer solutions to their material problems. 'Be pretty – get a man – escape poverty' is a crude reduction of what is a very complex process; but what is certain is that representation has an important part to play in it, and needs to be taken very seriously by anyone wishing to analyse, and change, women's subordination to men.

The internalisation of patriarchal values by women is also a reason why it is not necessarily a satisfactory answer for women simply to take control of the means of cultural production. It is obvious that if women are under-represented in professions which produce and reproduce definitions of gender and gender relations, then they are not in a position to speak for themselves and in their own interests. It must therefore be a necessary, if not sufficient, project of feminist politics to work towards proportionate representation of women in the professions of media and cultural production. And, as Anne Ross Muir has shown, much work remains to be done to achieve this (Ross Muir, 1988, p. 143). However, not all women are feminists. Women who accept the ideas and values of what feminists define as patriarchal ideology may be more likely to reproduce it in their work than to challenge it. Women are overwhelmingly responsible for the writing of romance fiction and for editing women's magazines; there are also women editing tabloid newspapers and even pornographic magazines. These are all forms viewed with suspicion by feminists, and with reason. But there is still debate within feminism about the significance of women participating in production regardless of political position: from Rosalind Coward debating with Rebecca O'Rourke over women's fiction (O'Rourke, 1979; and Coward, 1980), to Polly Toynbee asking in 1979 whether women should vote for Margaret Thatcher. The question is whether any woman can represent women's interests by virtue of being a woman, or whether a feminist analysis is essential, and, if so, whether men who espouse a feminist politics can represent women with this same analysis.

Reflecting reality

Early feminist critiques of representations of women were often concerned with 'representativeness' in another sense: if most women were not like the stereotypes of femininity available in the media, then they were not being accurately depicted. Critiques by, for example, Mary Ellman on 'feminine stereotypes' (Ellman, 1968, ch. III) and Sue Sharpe on the media (Sharpe, 1976, ch. 3), compared media stereotypes of women as sex symbols, domestic drudges or virulent harridans with the real lives of real women and concluded that the misrepresentations amounted to an injustice that needed to be redressed by more 'realistic' representations. Elena Gianini Belotti, for example, sets a content analysis finding of gender roles in children's books against a sociological finding on women's work outside the home: 'In the 144 reading texts for elementary schools, mothers are seen in the kitchen; in reality 40% of American mothers work in factories and offices' (Belotti, 1975, p. 90). Sharpe also implies the desirability of accurately reflecting social reality in her critique of children's readers:

> It is not only this portrayal which is wrong, but also the way that the conditions and standard of living are represented. Most children are

where near the upper middle-class world in which Peter and Jane live. Some primers have started to try to correct this fault, by recognising the modern world of tower blocks and supermarkets . . . However, the basic parts played by girls and women are little altered by their change in surroundings. Their place is still a domestic one. (Sharpe, 1976, p. 95)

This reflective model of representation has often been employed by social movements demanding more democratic regimes of representation. What is demanded is representations that show life 'as it really is', providing an accurate reflection of society and its people, including portrayals of members of dominated groups showing their position within the whole society, and their 'real' individual natures, as opposed to reproducing myths and stereotypes. This would mean, for example, not always depicting authority figures as white and male; not always showing *women* doing the housework, and not always showing them as happy and glamorous when they do. It would mean including in mainstream representation the whole range of roles and experiences of women – of whatever age, size, sexuality, class, 'race' or ethnic group; and portraying them as important in their own right, not just for their role in relation to the dominant group. The assumption behind this demand is that truth and justice are inseparable: only by accurately reflecting the shape of society and its members can the arts be seen as serving the needs of the whole society.

Women have always been faced with a peculiar problem in this respect. For, whereas it could be claimed that, say, working-class and Black people were under-represented in the works of upper-class white artists, the same could hardly be said of women. Women have never been absent from the range of representations produced by men. The question was, rather, how well women were represented by them – and the answer was 'not at all well'.

Liberal liberation

What then was to be done? The obvious answer was that: (a) women ought to be portrayed 'as they really were'; and (b) such portrayals ought to promote the interests of women – that is, they should expose the oppression experienced by women under patriarchal capitalism, encourage social equality between the sexes, provide women and girls with positive role models and question ideological notions of sexual difference.

This may be described as the liberal approach to representation. The reflective model it employs has, as we shall see, been subject to considerable criticism in the light of more complex theoretical formulations of the relationships between representations and reality. However, we should perhaps not be too quick to dismiss its usefulness as a starting point for the analysis of these relationships. For, despite its complexity, there always *is* a relationship between representation and reality, and, even at the simplest reflective level, where this 'reflection' is felt to be accurate, the recognition involved can be a considerable source of pleasure: we all seem to enjoy the sense that an artist, in whatever medium, has 'got it right' in capturing the texture of real-life experience.

However, the liberal approach is flawed in its analysis and contradictory in its demands. First, how do we measure accuracy in representation? If particular images are accused of inaccuracy, by what standard are they measured – by the critic's own experience, or by other representations, such as sociological reports, history or journalism? If so, what makes these sources more reliable as an account of reality than the particular material under review?

Second, what is meant by accuracy? Are photographs not accurate representations? Yes, but they can be set up, cropped, retouched. And if they are still *fairly* accurate, does it not matter *who* is photographed? Margaret Thatcher, Joan Collins or a *Vogue* model cannot be said to represent the majority of women. Are we then asking that the experience of the majority of women should be represented? Yes . . . but, obviously not to the exclusion of minorities: women who are socially disadvantaged by, for example, class, 'race', disablement, sexuality or old age have a right to be represented. And so too do those atypical by virtue of their achievements in public life, the arts, sports and so on. In fact, we can legitimately ask for *all* women to receive due representation as regards whatever social groupings they may fall into.

However, numbers are not the only issue. Some women and groups of women are inherently more interesting to us: exceptional achievement, skill, courage or influence, merit our attention, so that while we may be critical of particular criteria of, say, newsworthiness used by the media (the tabloids' excessive attention to entertainers, for example), we must also concede that a complete democracy of the image is extremely unlikely.

Third, it is not necessarily the isolated image or characterisation that is important. What is more significant is the regime of representation as it concerns gender in our society: the range and frequency of particular types of representation, the extent and nature of omissions, the meanings attached to particular types of representation (for example, slim women are desirable, fat women are funny), the way these meanings are produced and reproduced in specific contexts, how context and assumed (and actual) audience contribute to the determination of meaning, and how representations of women compare and relate to representations of men.

In theory, the problem of establishing a 'truth' against which representations can be judged is an insuperable one. In practice, we accept that we must make judgements about how accurate and fair representations are. This does not mean accepting that 'reality' can ever be simply or fully 'reflected': all representation requires principles of selection; omission, emphasis, explanation, context – these are all processes that produce meaning, and it is not always of primary importance whether the end result accurately reflects reality or not (advertisements and pop videos, for instance, are not usually judged for their realistic appearance). What matters is to recognise that understanding the meanings that are produced, understanding what 'woman', 'femininity' and 'gender' (and indeed, 'man' and 'masculinity') mean in our culture, will require an analysis that acknowledges these as complex constructions rather than more-or-less accurate reflections of some given 'reality'.

The double-bind

Liberalism's adherence to realist criteria produces a dilemma for itself. Asking for representations that are faithful to the reality of women's position in patriarchal society may risk demanding representations that show women predominantly in subordinate roles, as oppressed, as victims. Replacing stereotypic images of women with images of them as, for example, underpaid workers, bored housewives, battered wives, put-upon mothers, rape victims, may be more 'realistic' as evidence of the oppression of women under patriarchy, but they are not, in themselves, empowering images – less so, perhaps, even than patriarchy's stereotypes of women as desirable sex objects or all-nurturing mothers. The latter at least grant women a compensatory power.

Indeed, a contrary demand from a similarly liberal perspective is quite the opposite: this is the call for 'positive' images of women, showing what women *can* do, to act as role models to empower women in their sense of themselves and perhaps even in the conduct of their lives. But a constant stream of images of women as tycoons or professionals can hardly be said to be 'realistic' in the sense of being typical of women's experience: not only are such images unrepresentative of the majority of women's lives under patriarchy, they may be accused of glossing over the grimmer reality of these lives by presenting a deceptively comforting image of how wonderfully women are doing. The spate of television advertisements in the late 1980s showing glossy professional women driving company cars attracted feminist criticism on precisely these grounds, although it could equally be argued that these ads were doing what earlier feminists had complained they were not doing – showing women succeeding in the world of work, on men's terms. The question is, whether the token woman, even the token image of woman, functions as a trail-blazer, a thin edge of the wedge, or as a diversion from issues that affect the generality of women, a co-option of feminist values for commercial ends.

Whose values?

This brings us to another problem. A patriarchal society is one in which masculinist values have become general values. For women to be shown 'proving' themselves by these criteria is to confirm the validity of the very values which a feminist critique of patriarchy may be concerned to question; thus rather than challenging patriarchy, such representations may contribute to its validation. If a strong woman is one who is strong within patriarchal terms – a rich and powerful tycoon, say, or a gun-toting cop – this denies the strength of those women (and those men) who are poor, compassionate and gentle.

A contrary feminist position would ask for a redefinition of the values of patriarchy: to redefine, for example, 'positive' and 'powerful' in feminist terms. This is a logical, and valid answer to what I have called the liberal dilemma: representations that demonstrate the causes of women's subordination and the strength of women in enduring, subverting and challenging oppression may be seen as both 'realistic' and 'positive'. But they are still struggling against the signifying codes of power in our culture which have defined strength as those qualities possessed predominantly by men (physical prowess, institutional power, wealth, for instance) and then defined masculinity as connoting these qualities. This struggle for the redefinition of the meanings of words and the values of meanings (in so far as they can be distinguished) is a political one. To some extent we may claim, I think, that feminism has produced some significant shifts over the past two decades in both meanings and values attached to gender.

It has done so both by laying claim to those qualities and values defined as masculine, and by questioning their worth. If the latter may appear the more radical strategy, the appropriation of 'masculinity' for women should not be underestimated in terms of its effectiveness. Because women's subordination is overdetermined, a multiplicity of strategies is required to challenge its representational forms. We must remember that many of the more appropriative strategies, showing women succeeding in men's terms, occur in extremely popular forms (*Dynasty* or *Alien*, for example), so that simply in terms of audience size their effect may be considerably more widespread than more radical and challenging forms which reach limited audiences. In any case, we cannot be sure that, however carefully and critically we may analyse the co-optive elements of a representation such as Joan Collins' Alexis Carrington or Sigourney Weaver's Ripley, these are more important than the em-powering quality they represent for notions of femininity as powerful and victorious. Equally, of course, we cannot be sure that the reverse does not occur. It is, however, arguably impossible to represent certain aspects of, say, power outside the context within which the culture has defined them. If definitions of 'woman' are to acquire a heterogeneity comparable to definitions of 'man', then representing women in con-ventionally masculine roles, with masculine qualities (positive *and* negative) can be welcomed as contributing to this process. The represen-tations may not themselves qualify as 'feminist', but in extending de-finitions of femininity to include conventionally masculine qualities they may serve to break down gender stereotyping.

Substitution

But, as Griselda Pollock argues (Pollock, 1977, p. 44), substituting male for female (or vice versa) within a text does not necessarily shift the meanings attached to one gender over to the other. As she demonstrates, a naked male in a woody glade does not have the same meaning as a naked female in the same scene – the culture's regimes of representation inform the latter in ways they do not inform the former: the image of the naked woman is not an arbitrary element in the whole, it shares meanings of beauty, romance and naturalness with elements such as grass, flowers and sunshine that the image of the naked man does not possess: to simply replace female with male will not imbue the image of naked man instantly with these meanings – it might; but equally it might appear incongruous, even comic. The total image may acquire a quite different meaning as a result of substituting the one, crucial, element of gender.

Consider, for example, the different meanings of Alexis Carrington and JR as scheming tycoons; or of 'I am what I am' ('and what I am needs no excuses') sung by a Black woman (Gloria Gaynor) or by a gay drag artist (as in *La Cage aux Folles*). Lorraine Gamman argues that, while substituting female for male buddies in the television police series, *Cagney and Lacey*, does endow the women characters with the power associated with these authority roles, at the same time their femaleness alters the shape and concerns of the series, so that, not only does it deal more with 'feminine' issues like domestic violence and child pornography, in addition the interactions between the private and professional lives of the characters are dealt with in more depth, thus adding a dimension of soap opera to the genre (Gamman, 1988, p. 15). What happens, therefore, is that *both* the police series genre *and* definitions of femininity undergo some shifts as a result of the gender substitution of the leading protagonists. So that, however powerful social definitions of gender may be in determining the meanings of images/narratives, nevertheless, they are not themselves unalterable.

Film forms

This optimistic conclusion would seem to run counter, however, to the implications of an influential strand of feminist film theory. While earlier feminist approaches to film, especially in the United States, adopted a liberal model that critiqued images of women in films, some British feminists drew upon French post-structuralist thought and psychoanalytic theory, as these applied to literature and film, and developed a theoretical approach which saw the relationship between form and content in film as so closely interlocked as to require a more radical strategy than merely calling for more 'positive' images of women.

The key article in this approach was Laura Mulvey's 'Visual Pleasure and Narrative Cinema' (Mulvey, 1975), in which she claimed that the cinematic forms of dominant Hollywood cinema reproduce unequal gender relations through their construction of narratives based on an active male protagonist. The audience are invited to view the action through the point of view of this male protagonist, and – crucially – also to view the woman in the film, who is erotically coded for 'to-be-looked-at-ness', from this male perspective. The pleasures of this structure for the male spectator are divided between identification with the controlling gaze of the male character and the visual pleasure of looking at the body of the female character – a concept known, in Freudian psychoanalytic theory, as scopophilia. Through this organisation of looking in film, women's activity and subjectivity are denied: instead, they are subordinated to the look and the needs of the male. Film thus represents and reproduces the patriarchal power relations of society, in which men act and women are, men look and women are looked at, men's pleasures are served and women's are ignored (Mulvey, 1975, p. 20).

Mulvey concluded that it was necessary not only to destroy the pleasures of mainstream forms through analysis, but also to construct alternative film languages which would deny audiences the familiar pleasures of narrative and scopophilia which depended on, and reproduced, patriarchal power relations (Mulvey, 1975, p. 26). Because these pleasures could not be separated from the artistic forms of patriarchal production processes, these forms could not be utilised for the creation of alternative meanings. In her own film-making practice – in works like *Amy* and *Riddles of the Sphinx*, Mulvey, and others, such as Sally Potter with *Thriller* and *The Gold Diggers* and Lizzie Borden with *Born in Flames*, produced challenging work that aimed to fulfil this brief.

One problem is, predictably, the audience. Distribution of films outside the mainstream commercial cinema circuits severely restricts the size of the potential audience. In addition, most people watch films for pleasure. An aesthetic that deliberately sets out to deny audiences pleasure is likely to confront difficulties. Feminist theory and practice in this respect was part of a general cultural debate in the mid-1970s that questioned the radical possibilities of realism – the most familiar and popular form for dramatised narratives – and recommended an *avant garde* practice in line with Bertolt Brecht's concept of 'alienation', whereby audiences were distanced from the spectacle and action, and required, not to identify *with* it, but to think *about* it. Using also Roland Barthes' distinction between *plaisir* (comfortable pleasure) and *jouissance* (ecstasy that disturbs), (Barthes, 1975, p. 14), radical critics called for texts to be 'open' rather than 'closed', to reject what Colin MacCabe called the 'hierarchy of discourses' whereby audiences are directed towards understanding a text to have one, unambiguous, meaning (MacCabe, 1976, p. 34). The 'closed' text is one which, by means of its consistent characterisation and/or realist *mise-en-scène*, and its coherent narrative, which is resolved at the end, directs the audience towards one particular meaning. This, it was alleged, was inherently conservative; a genuinely progressive text would discomfort the audience by requiring them to confront contradiction and irresolution, rather than fulfilling their expectations regarding narrative coherence and resolution. In so far as gender definitions are embodied in narrative forms and aesthetic regimes, it was therefore necessary for feminist work to reject these forms and regimes in order to destabilise cultural definitions of masculinity and femininity. A new, non-sexist society would require a new non-sexist conceptual order of meaning, value and aesthetics; this could not be created within the forms which embodied patriarchal meanings, values and pleasures: a new language was needed.

The resulting deliberate denial of familiar sources of pleasure in these *avant garde* feminist works meant that even among the minority who saw them, there would be many who were frustrated and/or bewildered by a novelty of form which made them difficult to understand. In so far as the aim was to challenge and redefine the ways in which gender is represented, its radical impact could be seen as limited, not only by the size of the audience, but also by its necessarily elite nature.

However, the development of alternative, feminist, venues for exhibiting these films – at women's events; in educational contexts; on Channel 4 – has secured a significant and growing audience for these and other feminist films. But it is important to note that alternative feminist film practice has not been confined to the *avant garde*. The past twenty years in Britain, and more especially in North America, Europe and Australia, has seen a burgeoning of women's films in a variety of forms – documentaries, cartoons, educational and full-length feature films – which are neither mainstream entertainment nor *avant garde*. The development of video has been of great significance, not only in facilitating the production of films relatively cheaply, but also in enabling them to be used in community and educational contexts. This has increased many women's awareness of what film can achieve as a medium, and of the narrowness of the codes and conventions within which mainstream cinema functions. It is also a powerful demonstration of how a range of approaches can interact to effect significant change: the political activism of women's groups, the establishment of Women's Studies, the exploration of theories of representation, the utilisation of new technology – all may be seen to be involved in this particular development.

Moving in on the mainstream

Meanwhile, mainstream cinema has itself extended the scope of its representations of women. Perhaps our perspective on film's portrayal of women has been skewed by the powerful stereotyping of the 1950s, for, as Molly Haskell (1973) and others have demonstrated, there were many strong, independent female stars and roles in movies up to and including the 1940s (Joan Crawford, Bette Davis, Katharine Hepburn, Marlene Dietrich, Barbara Stanwyck). However, even where the narrative did focus on the powerful woman, this was too rarely in a positive sense; most often she was morally flawed in ways that led to her death or defeat. Even rarer was the portrayal of female solidarity: except occasionally in melodrama (*Imitation of Life*) and comedy (*Stage Door*), women were shown as relating predominantly to men, or, if to each other, as rivals.

Perhaps in response to feminist pressure from within the industry, perhaps sensing a new demand from women audiences, commercial cinema, like television, now includes a significant minority of works which treat women and women's issues seriously. Notable among developments in the past decade and a half has been the serious cinematic treatment of strong women and of friendship between women. Sigourney Weaver in *Alien* and *Aliens*, Meryl Streep in *A Cry in the Dark*, and Jamie Lee Curtis in *Blue Steel* are just a tiny sample which may indicate the range of genres featuring central female protagonists. And from *Turning Point* and *Julia* in the 1970s to *Desperately Seeking Susan* and *Beaches* in the 1980s, and *Thelma and Louise* in the 1990s, we can now see portrayals of women as committed to and supportive of each other. Nor has this excluded sympathetic portrayals of lesbian relationships, as in *Desert Hearts* and *Lianna*, and, on television, the adaptation of Jeanette Winterson's novel, *Oranges are not the Only Fruit*. Perhaps the most remarkable instance was Steven Spielberg's adaptation of Alice Walker's *The Color Purple*. Here was a film centred predominantly and sympathetically on relationships between Black women, produced by a white man, which attained huge box office success – if also considerable critical controversy.

None of these mainstream works, in fact, was received by feminists without reservation. Many were seen as sanitising or glamorising feminist issues; of having had to compromise too much with the commercialism of the project. Intervention in popular cultural production has continued to be a matter of debate within feminist criticism. Whether workers within the representational arts should strive for inclusion within the mainstream and risk compromising their principles, or should risk marginalisation by pursuing their artistic consciences, is a common dilemma for those excluded from mainstream cultural production. Rozsika Parker and Griselda Pollock's summing up of the problem for visual artists could apply to all women working in cultural production: 'Should women artists' energies be directed towards gaining access to the art establishment, demanding full and equal participation in its evident benefits, exhibitions, critical recognition, status – a living? Or, instead, should their efforts be channelled into their independent and alternative systems of galleries, exhibitions, educational programmes?' (Parker and Pollock, 1981, p. 135). Their conclusion is that these are 'differing strategies' rather than oppositions. Globally, this is clearly true: a multi-faceted oppression requires a multi-faceted response. But for individual women, the choice and the judgement still remain to be made on an ongoing basis, in the context of their specific financial and other resources.

The problem is not fully solved in those cases where minority culture succeeds in entering the mainstream. Rather, new problems arise around issues of context and commercialism. Texts change their meaning according to context, so that when, for example, dungarees were taken up as High Street fashion for all women, they ceased to be able to signify a feminist resistance to feminine dressing. Commercial success may similarly affect a work's political meaning. Photographer Cindy Sherman, for example, has expressed dismay at the popularity of her work: '"The more horrific works came out of a feeling that everyone accepted my stuff too easily. I was deliberately trying to be antagonistic towards collectors and critics. I thought, right, let's see if they want to shell out money for *this*" . . . As it turned out, all of New York wanted to shell out and cash in on Cindy Sherman' (Rumbold, 1991, p. 28).

The commercial success of some feminist fiction has raised similar problems. Angela Carter and Alice Walker are avowedly feminist writers whose work asks awkward questions within feminist debates. Carter tackles the dangerous ground of female desire in her fiction, so what happens when a male film director adapts a short story for a commercial film? Maggie Anwell has argued that the film of *Company of Wolves* distorts the delicacy of Carter's challenge to feminist debates around female sexuality (Anwell, 1988, p. 81). Walker's challenge, in showing Black women oppressed by Black men, has been to the male-dominated Black politics of the 1960s that subordinated Black women's struggle to Black struggle; but in representing the Black woman's experience, she was also participating in the debate within feminism about the dominance of white women in defining issues concerning women. Whether or not the complexities of this debate were faithfully reproduced in Spielberg's film of *The Color Purple* (and this is much debated), there is no doubt that a mass audience that is uninformed about and insensitive to what is at issue, would be less likely to understand Walker's message in the way that one familiar with its nuances might. Andrea Stuart, for instance, has expressed a Black woman's relief that Spielberg did *not* make too explicit the lesbian relationship between its leading characters, Celie and Shug, because of the way this might be viewed by audiences that are not predominantly Black and female (Stuart, 1988, p. 73), and Jacqueline Bobo has investigated Black women's positive responses to the film in the face of Black male disapproval (Bobo, 1988).

Feminist critics, then, are far from agreeing about particular texts or strategies. While some welcome evidence of feminist influence in the representations of women as being powerful and independent in television series such as *Cagney and Lacey*, *Widows* and *Dynasty*, or blockbuster fiction such as *Lace*, *Princess Daisy* and *A Woman of Substance*, these works can alternatively be accused of having co-opted elements of feminism and harnessed them to a non-feminist message of competitiveness. Not only might the sympathetic portrayal in fiction of a female cop or business tycoon be seen to validate the patriarchal hierarchies within which they operate, it can also be argued that the heterosexual glamour of the cop or tycoon reinforces women's need to be glamorous – and now, in addition, to be competent and clever. Moreover, such images of superwomen do little to shift regimes of representation which exclude categories of women from being defined positively within the culture – old, poor or lesbian women, for example, receive no validation from images such as these.

It may sometimes seem that, in maintaining a necessary alertness to the possibilities of co-option by the dominant ideology, feminist criticism is bent on driving all cultural production into a no-win corner: damned if you do enter the mainstream, damned if you don't; damned if you show women succeeding, damned if you don't; damned if you show women as victims, damned if you don't.

Not that staying *out* of the mainstream solves the problem: Judith Williamson's criticism of Mulvey's film, *Riddle of the Sphinx* – a decidedly *avant garde* work (Williamson, 1986b, pp. 131–44), and the fairly widespread criticism of Judy Chicago's *The Dinner Table* – consisting of a huge triangular dinner table with place settings representing famous women throughout history – is evidence enough that, however consciously feminist in intention and uncompromisingly 'alternative' in form, no work can be guaranteed to deliver an acceptably feminist message to all feminists.

All for love

Similar debates have informed discussions of feminine cultural forms and female spectatorship. Feminist criticism has demonstrated a particular interest in forms and genres specifically directed at a female audience. Genres such as soap opera, melodrama and romance fiction not only foreground the experience of women as their subject-matter, but also address women as readers/spectators. This is clearly of significance in a culture which assumes maleness as a norm, for in these works femaleness is the norm: heroines dominate the narratives, which deal with issues defined as feminine ones – romance and relationships, family and community, while men and their concerns are relegated to the margins. But romance fiction, in particular, poses a problem for feminism (see also Chapter 7). On the one hand, it is not only extremely popular among women readers, it is also largely produced, if not actually owned, by women. On the other hand, this fiction can certainly be accused of promoting stereotypical definitions of women as primarily concerned with emotional relationships, confined to romance and the family; and of doing so in terms which show women as subordinate to men socially and emotionally.

As long ago as 1971, Germaine Greer in her critique of the hero of romance fiction in *The Female Eunuch*, held women responsible for their own oppression in this respect: 'This is the hero that women have chosen for themselves. The traits invented for him have been invented by women cherishing the chains of their bondage. It is a male commonplace that women love rotters but in fact women are hypnotized by the successful man who appears to master his fate; they long to give their responsibility for themselves into the keeping of one who can administer it in their best interests' (Greer, 1971, p. 180). That the message of romance fiction appears to recommend marriage to a domineering man as the pinnacle of women's fulfilment, and that women, far from rejecting this message as so much sexist rubbish, consume such fiction in its hundreds of thousands, can lead to the conclusion that women are their own worst enemies. Critiques by, for example, Margolies (1982) (romance fiction is a plot to keep women unaware of their economic class oppression) or Snitow (1983) (romance fiction is pornography for women) also suggest (if they don't actually say it) that women readers, in their enthusiasm for such fiction, are colluding in their own oppression. 'Collusion' in domestic violence, 'contributory negligence' in rape: these are concepts feminism has reason to reject; must it not equally reject a cultural criticism that appears to write off millions of women as 'cultural dopes'?

Later feminist work on romance fiction has attempted to explain its appeal to women in terms of its, albeit utopian, engagement with real dilemmas faced by women in patriarchal society. Notable among these are the analyses of Tania Modleski and Janice Radway. Modleski suggests that the narrative of formulaic romance fiction negotiates women's fears of men by interpreting the hero's indifference or hostility towards the heroine as motivated by overwhelming love for her, and that his ultimate submission to her may be read as a fantasy of revenge upon men for their treatment of women (Modleski, 1982, pp. 45–8). Radway's ethnographic study of women readers of romance fiction focuses also on the uses to which women put the practice of reading: these, she suggests, include having time for themselves away from the responsibilities of domestic routines that service men and children, and supplying a basis for a community of women exchanging and discussing the novels (Radway, 1987, pp. 86–7). Ann Gray's research on video-recorders in the home suggested that these functions were similarly served by women hiring 'women's' films to watch together, in a context where male choices dominated video viewing within the family and excluded genres considered to be 'feminine' (Gray, 1987, pp. 48–9). It has also been suggested that romance makes available to women the pleasures of the erotic in a socially acceptable form – a narrative of sentiment expressed in sensual language (Snitow, 1983, p. 249). This is an erotic, however, which is not only exclusively heterosexual, but is also frequently informed with disturbingly masochistic implications. In more recent years some genres of romance fiction have become more sexually explicit, and the emergence of blockbuster fiction such as Shirley Conran's *Lace* make a more direct address to women readers' desires for sexual fantasy (Lewallen, 1988, p. 101).

Street cred

It would seem that genres assumed to be addressed to women audiences – such as romance fiction, melodrama or soap opera – have long served as measures of awfulness, with men (for the most part) deriding them, and women often admitting to liking them (when they do) rather apologetically. Interest in soap operas, however, has not been confined to female critics; the peculiar characteristics of this form (its endlessness, multiple plots, lack of a central protagonist) and its immense popularity (top of the TV ratings almost every week) have attracted interest in cultural studies generally (see, for example, Dyer *et al.*, 1981). But, while 'soap' audiences have become less gendered, with the inclusion of business plots in American prime time soaps such as *Dallas* and *Dynasty* and the cult-like following among young people (female and male) for daytime Australian soaps such as *Neighbours* – phenomena which may be linked to changing norms of masculinity – nevertheless, women have traditionally constituted the majority audience for soap opera, and perhaps continue to be considered as such.

Its appeal for women has been explained both in terms of its focus on family, friends and relationships, and its variety of strong female characters. Tania Modleski also sees parallels between the disjointed, repetitive form of 'soap' and women's domestic work (Modleski, 1982, p. 101), while Ien Ang conducted a study of European fans of *Dallas* in a sympathetic attempt to understand its phenomenal international appeal, especially to women (Ang, 1985, pp. 1–12). What these studies have raised are questions both about the criteria for analysing popular texts, and about the pleasures and purposes of those who read/watch them. The criteria traditionally employed for evaluating the products of 'high' culture have proved inappropriate for analysing popular culture and its audiences. From assuming a coherently meaningful text which readers must strive to appreciate for their own moral and aesthetic enrichment, attention has shifted to analysing the ways in which, on the one hand, texts may rework ideological positions around, say, gender and gender relations, and, on the other, how readers/audiences may negotiate their own understandings of these reworkings in deriving their own meanings and pleasures from them. Thus, for example, just as gay male culture appropriated the star image of Judy Garland in defiance of her hetero-sexual appeal, so Australian schoolgirls saw in *Cell Block H* a parallel with their own educational institutions and women may perhaps derive pleasure from representations analysable as sexist, showing women as 'evilly' exploiting their sexual power over men, for example, or simper-ingly snaring the most eligible bachelor.

Women's own culture

Women's magazines too are open to opposing interpretations. Here the work of Marjorie Ferguson and Janice Winship may serve as examples. Ferguson defines femininity as a cult, which is preached to women by its high-priestesses, the women's magazine editors. This is a cult which keeps women subordinate to men through its insistence on the sexual/domestic roles of women promulgated everywhere in the magazines from fashion and beauty to cooking and home décor to problem pages and features (Ferguson, 1983, pp. 11–12). Winship's study shows more awareness of the differences between the magazines (Winship, 1987, p. 148). Their historical development demonstrates that ideals of femin-inity change, though not necessarily entirely to women's benefit, unless it is assumed that pressures to be 'superwoman' in the 1980s are clearly less oppressive than those restricting women's role to wife and mother in the 1950s. Differences between magazines in their address to women on the basis of age, class, wealth or (feminist) politics, may be seen either as demonstrating a media response to the heterogeneity of female experience, or, alternatively, as showing the extent of the media's co-option of that experience into a more flexible, but no less powerful, ideology of femininity; though one that, on the whole, omits the experi-ence of women who are, for example, Black, lesbian and/or old.

Informing Winship's analysis of the contradictions of this popular feminine genre is the issue of pleasure: 'I felt that to simply dismiss women's magazines was also to dismiss the lives of millions of women who read and enjoyed them each week. More than that, *I* still enjoyed them, found them useful and escaped with them . . . That didn't mean I wasn't critical of them. I was (and am) but it was just that double edge – my simultaneous attraction and rejection – which seemed to me to be a real nub of feminist concern' (Winship, 1987, p. xiii). It is a 'double edge' that plagues feminist analysis of popular culture, as perhaps of popular culture analyses generally. Our own pleasures, and those of others, constitute a perennial thorn in the flesh of political critique. How are we to explain the pleasures derived from texts that are at best ambiguous, at worst downright reactionary, in respect of their representation of gender? Should we aim to destroy the pleasure because of the politics? Or rescue the politics because of the pleasure?

Dressing down

Comparable problems arise in relation to the politics of appearance. Men wear clothes, adhere to fashion and construct their appearance quite as much as women do,[3] but an *interest* in appearance has become defined as a specifically feminine one. Cultural definitions identifying femininity with physical 'attractiveness' compound this identification. An early, and continuing, feminist response to this has been a rejection of traditionally 'feminine' modes of dressing: the trashing of bras and girdles, for instance, in the first women's liberation media event, and the related development of feminists adopting a mode of visual self-presentation that resisted the feminisation of women – flat shoes, trousers, short hair, no make-up, for example. These could be justified on practical grounds (one cannot run in high heels) or on ideological ones (make-up pandered to the sexual desires of men), although in the end these rationales could probably not withstand logic much better than fashion itself.[4] Feminist challenges to dress codes, from the nineteenth-century 'rational dress' movement onwards, have been subject both to co-option by mainstream culture (dungarees in Miss Selfridge) and to marginalisation through derogatory stereotyping (the tabloids' characterisation of feminists as 'dungareed dykes'). But there are problems from within feminism too: feminist dress can be criticised for aping masculine dress, and/or for establishing an alternative puritanical orthodoxy (see Young, 1988, pp. 178–9). As responses to the fashion industry's dominance in defining femininity through clothes, therefore, feminists have also shown interest in practices such as 'post-modern punk' (Wilson, 1985) and 'retro' fashion (McRobbie, 1989).

The importance of dress as a feminist issue is that it is the one area of representation in which *all* women participate. We are all obliged, constantly, to represent ourselves by the way we dress. We have to wear clothes, and clothes (whether we wish them to or not) always convey a meaning to others, which is socially constructed and understood, about

such factors as age, class, fashionability and so on, and about our attitudes towards these factors. We cannot escape these meanings. At the
same time, however, within constraints such as money, availability or
workplace rules, we can choose what to wear – we decide how to
represent ourselves. We are all, therefore, practically and intimately
involved in debates about the relations between ideology and pleasure,
about defining sexuality, about the ethics of consumerism, and, above all
perhaps, about whether, and how, to reject or re-evaluate the 'feminine'.

Post-modern Madonna?

One strategy for negotiating this impasse might be identified in the
concept of post-modernism, which has proved to be of particular interest
to feminist cultural criticism – though, again, not without reservations.
Because post-modernist works are characterised by irony, pastiche and
excess, they offer the pleasures of the 'popular' while simultaneously
undermining the ideologies embedded in it by virtue of not taking them
seriously. Linda Hutcheon sees post-modernism as characterised by both
critique and complicity, and therefore as facilitating a feminist critique
of male-defined traditions of representation from within those traditions
themselves (Hutcheon, 1989, p. 11). Post-modernist artistic production
uses pastiche and plagiarism to undermine the stability of meanings in
cultural texts and practices. In so far as this stability underpins society's
definitions of gender, any post-modernist destabilisation may be seen as
contributing to an undermining of the patriarchal world order of meaning
that oppresses women (see Chapter 3).

Thus, for example, the star image of Madonna can be seen as a post-
modern text, analysed as a play upon cultural definitions of femininity,
combining in her attire such disparate signifiers as lace gloves (gentil-
ity), leather jacket (butchness), beribboned untidy hair (child or tart?); or
masquerading as a pantheon of Hollywood stars; or performing in under-
wear that resembles armour (the male reviewer of her Blonde Ambition
tour who complained that he didn't find this attractive would seem rather
to have missed the point!). The frequency with which Madonna changes
her 'image' might itself be read as an ironic comment on a society that
focuses so much on 'image', or as depicting the unstable and fragmented
identity of contemporary life, or as mocking social constructions of
femininity. If Madonna's images, like her performances, are tongue-in-
cheek, then we can enjoy her display of sexuality because its very

outrageousness is evidence of its irony: if this is woman displaying her sexuality for the delight of men, it is simultaneously mocking that display.

Or is it? Might it not equally be interpreted as an excuse for reproducing, and enjoying, the same old sexist stereotypes? What model of female identity is offered the young teenage girls who have constituted her keenest fans? Do they enjoy the ironic mockery of conventional femininity? Or, in emulating her style, do they transform it into yet another way of being fashionable and 'sexy'? How are we to understand these fans following both Madonna *and* Kylie Minogue? Can we read Kylie Minogue's image for similar tensions – girlish curls/garage mechanic, girl-next-door turned 'sexy' megastar – or would this be pushing it?

Since post-modernism is both a cultural practice and a critical approach, it is possible to re-read any number of texts within its terms. If Madonna's pastiche of Marilyn Monroe in her 'Material Girl' video is post-modern irony, what of Monroe's original performance in *Gentlemen Prefer Blondes*? Is this not also ironic about female sexuality in its display of a glamour addressed to men combined with a somewhat cynical piece of advice addressed to women?

Polysemy rules OK?

This raises an interesting problem as to whether it is the 'text' that is post-modern, or the 'reading' of it. Certainly, developments in cultural studies have demonstrated that no text, however apparently simple, really is simple; there is always some degree of polysemy – some room for disagreement about meaning, some potential for an interpretation that goes against the grain of the apparently intended meaning. Monroe, for example, may have been sold as a sex symbol for male consumption, but has been appropriated both as a symbol of male exploitation of women and as a symbol of capitalist exploitation of the individual.

Where earlier feminist analysis concentrated on identifying the reproduction of gender ideologies in representations of women, later work has also been concerned to reveal the contradictions in these representations, to demonstrate that, however sexist a text may appear to be, it cannot conceal *all* the contradictions of sexism as an ideology. To take an extreme example: a pornographic magazine will present images of naked women as available for male readers to gaze at, with the implication that the women are available for sex; but the models are precisely *not* available for these male readers physically, and if the women's implied availability suggests a compliment to male sexual power, then we have to ask why these same magazines carry so many advertisements (for fancy condoms, plastic vaginas, devices to enlarge the penis) that suggest their readers are extremely unsure of their sexual prowess.

Janey Place, in her discussion of *film noir* heroines, concludes that, while the narratives often destroy the sexually aggressive woman, the films' visual style reinforces an image of the women characters as 'deadly but sexy, exciting and strong' (Place, 1980, p. 54). Similarly, it has been argued that it was the resistance of, say, a Doris Day role to the machinations of the predatory male, or, as in *Calamity Jane*, to the social demands of femininity, that characterised her stage image rather than the 'happy ending' in which she submits to marriage and femininity (Clarke *et al.*, 1982, p. 36).

Is there, in fact, any text that is proof against a post-modernist reading? Inasmuch as narrative, for example, depends on conflict, or the rectification of a disruption in order, knowledge or control, then the mere *fact* of this conflict or disruption puts in question the values that the ending will resolve; that the resolution is necessary at all is presumably because the values *are*, or are felt to be, in question. If the hero has to prove his masculinity through victory of some sort, then his masculinity cannot be taken for granted. If the romance heroine has to work, through the narrative, to get her man, then it cannot be assumed that heroines automatically do get 'their' men. Underlying the simplest narratives, then, such as an adventure story or a romance, is an unspoken insecurity: there would be no story if there were no doubt about the outcome. Perhaps in some genres there appears to be no doubt, even from the beginning (we know the detective or the romantic heroine will 'get his/ her man'); and in less formulaic works there can be no doubt by the end of the narrative, once the hero or heroine has triumphed or failed. But narrative forms work precisely to conceal the doubt that men are necessarily masculine and heroic, or that women are necessarily feminine and desirable, and to affirm a *natural* connection between biological sex and cultural constructions of gender.

Or consider Mulvey's point about the controlling male gaze: in analysing the structure of looking in mainstream cinema, she demonstrates how women may be seen as *subjected* to the male gaze (Mulvey, 1975, p. 19); but may we not also read this relation of looking as one where the woman simultaneously controls the desire of the man, so that what we are dealing with here is less simple than a one-way power relationship? And what about the many narratives with central female protagonists? Should we not regard these as examples of the controlling female gaze? (see, for example, Gamman and Marshment, 1988, Introduction). But finally we have to question whether control of the gaze necessarily amounts to control of the situation. Are gazes – even male ones – always, as Mulvey assumes, 'controlling'? After all, if a cat may look at a king, that presumably is *all* the power the cat has in that relationship.

What is to be done?

Sexism is everywhere in society. So we are likely to find it everywhere in representation. But if this means that we can never find an instance of *totally* feminist representation – by which I mean one that is not only not sexist, but also counters all forms of oppression of women, omitting no women's plight – then we would be in danger of feeling that feminism confronted an impossible task. But if we recognise that sexism itself, however ubiquitous, is also a leaky system, then we can admit that its contradictions give rise to some privileges for some women: queens, prime ministers, film stars, heiresses, leisured upper-class wives; and, at more mundane and ambiguous levels, women's greater rights to custody of children, their greater choice of dress styles, their lower incidence as prisoners, their greater facility for forming expressive relationships and freedom to express their emotions. Such 'privileges' do not come without a price, nor, usually, without a struggle; but the possibility of struggle, the mere existence – let alone the achievements – of feminism, demonstrates the 'leakiness' of patriarchy.

At the representational level too, women are not without their 'privileges'. The tradition of using women as symbols of nations, virtues, trades; fictional heroines from Shakespeare's Rosalind to Tolstoy's Anna Karenina; the mythic status of stars such as Garbo, Callas or Monroe. Feminist appropriation of the culture's language and images about women has not had to rely entirely on reversing negative meanings. There has always been sufficient ambiguity in the culture's regime of representations overall to enable feminism to find ammunition within them that can be turned against the patriarchal system of meanings – these reversals may constitute very small victories, or ones liable to further co-option, but they are victories nevertheless, interventions in what is not, in effect, a totally closed system.

This is not to deny that feminists still have far too much to be angry about: racism in its myriad manifestations continues to inform too many mainstream representations of Black women; 'serious' news and current affairs is still predominantly presented by men (witness media coverage of the Gulf War); 'page 3' is still a feature of the nation's most popular daily newspaper; the pornography industry has grown massively in recent years; and the women who campaigned for peace at Greenham are still a cultural sign of all that's wrong with feminism, while 'our boys' are hailed as heroes. It is often difficult to find post-modern irony an adequate response to such outrages. Feminism is about finding adequate responses on the political level, whereas, as Linda Hutcheon, (1989) has pointed out, post-modernism is not a political project. If it has, nevertheless, political implications, this may be because all aesthetic forms – realism, modernism, surrealism, dadaism, futurism, for instance – cannot escape such implications, and have all been appropriated to, not always consistent, political programmes.

There are risks inherent for feminism in utilising any of the aesthetic regimes which have emerged within patriarchy; and there are risks inherent in trying to forge an alternative aesthetic. But then, would we be content to hope for a feminist culture which doesn't take risks? Much of the most challenging work which has engaged with gender issues, whether avowedly feminist or not, is that which has taken the greatest risks and has attracted criticism, including from feminists; contradictions produce controversy. And without contradictions, without debate and difference, feminism, like any other movement, would die. The Greenham women took risks: when they left homes and jobs and children and braved the wrath of patriarchy; when they braved the weather and the law at the base; and too when they wove spider webs and doves and children's clothes into the perimeter fence and angered those feminists who were convinced that women should reject such mystical and domestic identifications. Writers like Angela Carter, exploring women's sexuality, taking the risk of confirming myths about female masochism; Fay Weldon not allowing her 'She-Devil' a wholesome recovery from her husband's betrayal, driving her instead to an agonising pursuit of physical beauty and a deplorable revenge; Alice Walker taking the risk of feeding racist myths by writing about Black men's abuse of Black women. Photographers such as Jo Spence and Cindy Sherman, using themselves as models in images that can be accused of being narcissistic, embarrassing, ugly, offensive, to challenge our conceptions of what a photograph is or should be. Judy Chicago using a plethora of vaginal imagery and the traditionally feminine 'crafts' of embroidery and pottery and (it seems) other women's labour: is this celebratory of female identity, or a reduction of women's experience to the genital, or – in the hushed environment of a gallery – an ironic comment on the masculine norms of the art establishment?

Do we feel our lives more justly represented here than by a Renoir or a Degas, a Flaubert or a Lawrence? Maybe, and maybe not; but these feminist artists – and there are many more – do not offer us easy answers; rather, they challenge us to confront the difficult questions that feminism itself presents us with; they force us to think about what it means to be a woman in our society, whether we want to change that meaning, and if so how. And this, I think, is how we would wish to be represented, to ourselves and to others – as fully conscious human beings, struggling with the contradictions of our existence. This is, in fact, who we are, and it is in our interests that feminist culture should represent us as such.

If this article has seemed to contradict itself, to double back on its own arguments, to 'if' and 'but' about the effectiveness of various feminist positions and strategies, this is not because feminists are unclear in their perspectives on the representation of women in our culture. Nor is it just that, there being many feminisms, feminists disagree with each other; it is also because, on the one hand, feminist analyses have acknowledged the complexity and contradictoriness inherent in issues about representation; and, on the other, because so has patriachal capitalism (let us not underestimate the enemy – it has been watching us and responding!). If it was relatively easy, in the 1960s, to protest against the insultingly stereotypical characterisation of women as domestic morons in Persil ads; it is perhaps not quite so easy, in the 1990s, to know how to respond to the strong and beautiful woman in the Volkswagen ad who throws away everything her lover gave her, except the keys to her car – her means to freedom.

Notes

1. This is not intended to imply that women are always somehow coerced into relationships with men; only that even our most intimate decisions may not be quite as 'free' from social forces as we might assume.
2. See, for instance, Sheila Rowbotham on her relationship to mascara, in Rowbotham, 1973, pp. 44–5.
3. Consider, for example, the daily construction of men's faces through shaving.

4.   It is not, for instance, self-evident that trousers are always more comfort-
      able than skirts, and dungarees in particular are decidedly inconvenient
      for going to the toilet!

Further reading

Rosemary Betterton (ed.), *Looking On: Images of Femininity in the Visual Arts and Media* (London, Pandora, 1987). A collection of key feminist essays on issues of representation in the arts and the media.

Charlotte Brunsdon (ed.), *Films for Women* (London, British Film Institute, 1986). A collection of essays on films made by and for women.

Lorraine Gamman and Margaret Marshment (eds), *The Female Gaze: Women as Viewers of Popular Culture* (London, The Women's Press, 1988). A collection of essays produced in response to Mulvey's argument about the 'male gaze', examining popular film and television texts.

Tania Modleski, *Loving with a Vengeance: Mass-produced fantasies for women* (London, Methuen, 1982). A book examining popular fictional forms produced for women, including romance fiction, gothic novels and soap opera.

7

Women, Writing and Language: Making the Silences Speak

Gill Frith

This chapter looks at women and words: at women's writing and women's relationship to language, and at what contemporary feminist theory has had to say about these issues.

Why should we look at literature in terms of feminist politics? When I studied English Literature at university in the 1960s, the literary 'canon' (that selective list of texts considered worthy of academic study) consisted almost entirely of work by white men. My course included a tiny handful of books by women (Jane Austen, the Brontës, George Eliot), but we did not study these writers *as* women. Great Literature, we were told, was about 'universal truths'. Gender was irrelevant.

This picture was challenged by the emergence, in the late 1960s, of the contemporary women's movement. Feminist researchers began to uncover the vast body of neglected women's writing: forgotten reputations were retrieved, and long-out-of-print texts republished by feminist publishing houses such as Virago and The Women's Press. But redressing the balance, proving that women's writing was 'as good as' men's, was not the only issue. The reconstruction of women's history has been a central concern for contemporary feminism, and the study of women's writing has played a vital part in that process. The rediscovery of pioneering feminist texts such as Virginia Woolf's *A Room of One's Own* (1929/1977) led to the realisation that much of what contemporary feminists were saying had been said before. The area of fiction, in which women have been actively engaged, in large numbers, since the eighteenth century (Spencer, 1986; and Spender, 1986a), provided a particularly rich source of material about women's lives. Fiction, paradoxically, precisely because it is not 'true', provides a space for the writer to explore ambiguities, contradictions and dissatisfactions which cannot be expressed openly. 'Classic' texts, as I shall be demonstrating, suddenly looked different when read from a feminist perspective.

But even as the process of recovery and re-reading got under way, new questions emerged. Can literature tell 'the truth' about women's lives? Is it the case, as Virginia Woolf suggested, that the 'man's sentence' is 'unsuited for a woman's use' (Woolf, 1977, p. 73)? Is it possible to identify or devise an alternative, 'female language'? Don't generalised terms such as 'the woman writer' and 'the female imagination' effectively marginalise Black and lesbian writers? Shouldn't we be challenging traditional modes of literary judgement, and looking at texts outside the canon: romantic novels, science fiction, thrillers, for example? And what of the 'woman reader'? What do books mean in women's lives? What about the reader's 'race', class, sexuality – aren't these also important elements in her response?

We may all look at the same words on the same page, but what we make of them depends upon what questions we ask. My aim in this chapter is to introduce the different questions which feminist critics have raised, and to show how changing the terms of the question affects the 'reading', or interpretation, of the text. Each section deals with a different strand within feminist criticism, but the approaches identified are not mutually exclusive. Most individual critics, in fact, 'belong' within at least two sections: there are Black lesbian critics, socialist feminist critics influenced by French feminism, and so on. Feminist criticism has become increasingly 'pluralist' in its nature, moving from an initial suspicion of 'theory' towards what is, in my view, a productive, but undoubtedly also sometimes bewildering, cross-fertilisation of ideas.

In the interests of clarification, I shall be focusing on a single text, Charlotte Brontë's *Jane Eyre*,[1] chosen partly because it is well-known and easily available, but primarily because it has been discussed by so many feminist critics from diverse perspectives and can therefore highlight differences between feminists. Upon its first publication in 1847, *Jane Eyre* was perceived as a dangerously subversive text (Gilbert and Gubar, 1979, pp. 337–8), and the novel was still 'banned' in girls' schools in the late nineteenth century. Contemporary feminist critics have rediscovered those subversive qualities, but while most feminist readings of *Jane Eyre* identify a secret or 'repressed' text buried beneath the surface of the apparently simple tale of the governess who gets her man, the nature and significance of that hidden text is seen in very different ways.

I have concentrated upon feminist literary theory because this is often regarded as the most challenging and difficult area for the student new to Women's Studies, but I do not want to neglect the wealth of writing which is being produced by women today. At the end of the chapter, I shall move beyond *Jane Eyre* to indicate some recent trends and developments in contemporary feminist fiction.

Declaring it aloud: images and experience

'Wicked and cruel boy!' I said. 'You are like a murderer – you are like a slave-driver – you are like the Roman emperors!'

I had read Goldsmith's *History of Rome*, and had formed my opinion of Nero, Caligula, &c. Also I had drawn parallels in silence, which I never thought thus to have declared aloud. (*Jane Eyre*, p. 43)

Jane Eyre begins with an assault upon a girl by a male text, or, more correctly, by a male *armed* with a text. Jane's pleasurable retreat into the world of books is disrupted by the male heir of the household, who dispossesses her of her book, flings it at her, and causes her to fall, wounding her head. Pain displaces terror: in the outburst quoted above, Jane breaks her silence and gives voice to her long-nurtured resentment and rage. The two interlinked events – male assault and female response – may be seen as representative of the two feminist approaches to literature which were dominant in the early 1970s: the analysis of 'images' and the appeal to 'experience'. Here, similar questions are asked in two rather different ways.

'*Images of Women*' criticism asks: what have men's texts, and male mastery over the text, done to women's heads? Kate Millett's *Sexual Politics* (1970), with its witty exposure of the misogyny endemic in the novels of D. H. Lawrence, Norman Mailer and Henry Miller, paved the way for many later studies which looked at the books which have been 'flung' at women. Feminist critics dissected the sexual stereotyping pervasive in male-authored texts in the literary 'canon', in children's literature, magazines and popular fiction. In contrast to the dominant, negative images – such as passive woman and active man, self-sacrificing virgin and predatory whore – feminists sought to identify and encourage alternative, positive images of women (see, for example, Cornillon, 1972).

'*Authority of Experience*' criticism asks: what happens when a woman speaks out, gives *her* interpretation of the text on the basis of a woman's experience? In her 1977 essay on *Jane Eyre*, Maurianne Adams emphasised the cohesiveness of women's experience, and the reader's identification with the novel's heroine. Adams makes little distinction between author and character, critic and reader: when 'we' read *Jane Eyre*, memories of our girlhood reading, 'when we saw in Jane's dreadful childhood the image of our own fantasies of feeling unloved and forever unloveable' interact with 'our more mature understanding' of the complexity of Jane's journey from childhood to womanhood (Adams, 1977, p. 137). Jane is split: torn between the need to love and be loved, and the desire for autonomy, 'to be somebody in her own right' (p. 139). She is torn, also, between two unsatisfactory images of women, as either spiritual and asexual, or furious, passionate and mad. Jane is, according to Adams, an instinctive feminist who suppresses her feminist awareness, only to have it surface in her turbulent dreams.

As we shall see later, subsequent feminist theorists have questioned some of the assumptions behind these approaches, notably the idea that oppressive and 'false' images and readings can be replaced by an alternative, universal, woman-friendly 'truth'. But 'Images' and 'Experience' criticism reflected the two pressing needs of an emergent women's movement: to identify the sources of oppression, and to assert female collectivity. Together, they represented a radical challenge to the way in which English Literature, conventionally a 'woman's subject', was taught in schools, colleges, and universities. By exposing the distortions and preconceptions which underpin the portrayal of women in literature, and by asserting a woman's right to speak about her reading as a woman, they questioned the assertion that the male-dominated literary canon offered a universal 'truth', transmitted by the (usually male) tutor to the compliant female student.

Opening the chamber: gynocriticism

The red-room was a spare chamber, very seldom slept in. . . . (*Jane Eyre*, p. 45)

What happens to Jane in the red-room, that 'haunted' chamber to which the fiercely resistant Jane is conveyed by women, and where the sight of her own face in the mirror terrifies her into insensibility? According to Elaine Showalter in *A Literature of Their Own* (1978), Jane's ritualised imprisonment is both a punishment for 'the crime of growing up' (Showalter, 1978, p. 114) and an 'adolescent rite of passage' (p. 115), in which entry into womanhood is characterised by Victorian vigilance and control over female sexuality. The 'bondage' of the frenzied Jane in a chamber dominated by vibrantly contrasting reds and whites echoes Victorian fears of and fantasies about 'the lethal and fleshly aspects of adult female sexuality' (p. 115). Noting the recurrence of enclosed and secret rooms in the novels of women writers, Showalter suggests that the red-room, 'with its deadly and bloody connotations, its Freudian wealth of secret compartments, wardrobes, drawers and jewel chest' may be seen as 'a paradigm of female inner space' (pp. 114–15).

A Literature of Their Own is one of the 'classics' of feminist 'gynocriticism', a term coined by Showalter herself to define an approach concerned with the woman as writer, and including 'the psychodynamics of female creativity; linguistics and the problem of a female language; the trajectory of the individual or collective female literary career; literary history; and of course, studies of particular writers and works' (Showalter, 1979, p. 25). It is a broad definition which could encompass much of contemporary feminist criticism. In practice, however, 'gynocriticism' has come to be associated with the quest to identify a specifically female literary tradition. 'We think back through our mothers,' said Virginia Woolf in *A Room of One's Own* (Woolf, 1977, pp. 72–3), a book which anticipated many of the questions asked by contemporary gynocritics. In the late 1970s, pioneering texts such as Showalter's book and Ellen Moers' *Literary Women* (1976) reopened the 'spare chamber', and set out to provide a map of women's literary history, by rediscovering neglected texts and reinterpreting familiar ones, by analysing the lives of and connections between 'literary women', and by identifying shared themes, tropes (figures of speech), and plot-devices.

The value of gynocriticism should not be underestimated. By uncovering the rich legacy of a neglected female 'subculture' and emphasising its thematic coherence, it provided ammunition and substance for establishing the study of women's writing, not only in higher education, but in schools, extramural classes and informal reading groups. Gynocriticism has been much criticised for its 'essentialism' (Moi, 1985;

and Mills *et al.*, 1989), but it is notable that both Showalter and Moers question the idea of a 'female imagination', seeing the female tradition rather as a 'delicate network of . . . influences and conventions, including the operations of the market-place' (Showalter, 1978, p. 12). Showalter emphasises the conditions in which women's writing has been produced and received, placing *Jane Eyre* historically, within what she sees as a unified but 'disrupted', and specifically British, female literary tradition. *Jane Eyre* belongs to what Showalter calls the 'Feminine' phase of British women's writing, in which the female 'subculture' is secret, ritualised, characterised by internalisation and self-censorship; women, united by the physical facts of the female life-cycle (menstruation, child-birth) but unable to express them openly, developed a covert symbolic language to explore the range of female experience.

Gynocriticism opens the secret chamber, but does not tell us how to arrange the furniture. Resistant to 'theory', preferring to rely on 'evid-ence', it provides no coherent framework for interpreting the rich and suggestive material it uncovers about women's lives and work. Showalter and Moers both draw upon Freud in interpreting the recurrent motifs in women's writing, but such psychoanalytic borrowings are random rather than systematic. While the idea of a female literary tradition can be a fruitful basis from which to research and study women's writing, it carries the risk both of perpetuating the traditional marginalisation of women's literary production, and of assuming that, at any point in time, a unified female subculture can be satisfactorily identified. The position of the writer or reader outside the white, heterosexual, middle-class 'mainstream' can too easily be ignored or subsumed under the envelop-ing banner of 'female experience'.

Secrets of nature discovered: radical feminist criticism

> They conversed of things I had never heard of; of nations and times past; of countries far away; of secrets of nature discovered or guessed at; they spoke of books; how many they had read! What stores of knowledge they possessed! (*Jane Eyre*, p. 105)

Radical feminism has been summarised as founded in the belief that 'the original and basic class division is between the sexes, and that the motive force of history is the striving of men for power and domination over women, the dialectic of sex' (Heidi Hartmann, quoted in Palmer, 1989, p. 43). Radical feminist literary criticism prioritises female experience and solidarity, by validating autobiographical and subjective responses and foregrounding the issues of 'woman-identification, feminist community, lesbian relations and relations between mothers and daughters' (Palmer, 1989, p. 160). 'Woman-identification' is central to Adrienne Rich's essay on *Jane Eyre*, written in 1973 before Rich identified herself as a radical feminist. Rich's analysis of Jane's relationships with women is framed within a 'humanist' reading of the novel: Jane journeys towards self-discovery, independence and equal marriage (Rich, 1980c). Nevertheless, Rich's reading stands in striking contrast to Elaine Showalter's, and illustrates how differently the novel may read when relationships between women are foregrounded.

Showalter interprets *Jane Eyre* as reflecting the impossibility of female solidarity when women are powerless; Brontë's women, she argues, 'police' one another as agents of patriarchal control. Rich sees Jane as encountering a succession of traditional female temptations, each of which is placed against an alternative: a positive female role model who offers Jane nurturing and support. At Lowood, Miss Temple (substitute mother) and Helen Burns (substitute sister) are protective figures who encourage Jane's moral development and intellectual growth. But for Rich, the key moment in the novel comes when Jane dreams of a visitation from the moon, who tells her 'My daughter, flee temptation' (*Jane Eyre*, p. 346). Now in touch with the matriarchal aspect of her psyche, Jane is able to resist the temptation to become Rochester's concubine, just as, later in the novel, she is saved from 'passive suicide' by Diana and Mary Rivers – maternal role-models whose names represent, between them, the pagan and the Christian aspects of the Great Goddess.

Although not presented as a lesbian reading, the essay anticipates Rich's later idea of the 'lesbian continuum' (Rich, 1984, p. 227), which does not limit lesbianism to the experience of or desire for genital sexual experience, but encompasses a range of 'woman-identified' experience, including the sharing of a rich inner life, bonding against male tyranny, and practical support. According to this (controversial) definition, Jane's relationships with women at Lowood and Moor House could be seen as representing a 'lesbian' impetus in the novel which is repressed in the conclusion.

Rich's essay also illustrates two concerns central to her later work and to radical feminist criticism in general: the reclamation and reworking of female myth, and mother–daughter relationships (such as Demeter and Persephone, mythical mother and daughter). In *Of Woman Born* (1976), Rich sees motherhood (once separated from its restrictive institutionalisation under patriarchy) as the primary source of female power and creativity. The celebration of motherhood is interlinked with the rediscovery of matriarchal myths, a project shared with Mary Daly (1978) and other radical feminist critics who see male violence as the chief instrument of patriarchy, to be countered by the establishment of a separate women's culture and the assertion of specifically female creative powers. 'Myth criticism' sets out to decode the myths selected and passed on by patriarchy, to expose their subtexts of male aggression and violence, and to reclaim myths for women both by reversing male stories and recuperating earlier, female-centred mythologies (Humm, 1986). Myth criticism is appealing for the same reasons as it is problematic: it offers a romantic, celebratory vision of a lost tradition of female goddesses and woman-bonding which conflates female 'nurture', female 'nature' and female creativity, and depends upon the assumption that women are naturally and uniformly *good*.

Perhaps the most significant contribution made by radical feminism has been on the question of language. In *Man-Made Language* (1980), Dale Spender argues that women constitute a 'muted group' in society because meaning has been controlled by men (but see Cameron, 1985). Language reflects male experience and perpetuates male power; 'feminine' words are negatively marked (think of the different connotations carried by dog/bitch, master/mistress, bachelor/spinster). Mary Daly and Adrienne Rich both experiment inventively with ways of wresting linguistic domination from patriarchal control. In *Gyn/Ecology* (1978), Mary Daly sets out to create a language which will serve the interests of women, by changing the syntax, reclaiming obsolete or pejorative words (Hag, Spinster, Harpy) and restructuring familiar ones (as in 'Croneology'). Rich's methods are less drastic, but she too aims to repossess meaning for women by creating a language of the collective 'female body', by defining 'a female consciousness which is political, aesthetic and erotic' (Rich, 1980a, p. 18) and finding ways of 'converting our physicality into both knowledge and power' (Rich, 1977, p. 284). Such an unashamed affirmation of the links between female biology and female creativity contrasts interestingly with the work of Sandra Gilbert and Susan Gubar, for whom the female body is a haunted house.

Echoes in the chamber: *The Madman in the Attic*

> While I paced softly on, the last sound I expected to hear in so still a region, a laugh, struck my ears. It was a curious laugh – distinct, formal, mirthless. I stopped. The sound ceased, only for an instant. It began again, louder – for at first, though very distinct, it was very low. It passed off in a clamorous peal that seemed to echo in every lonely chamber. . . . (*Jane Eyre*, p. 138)

The source of the laughter is Bertha, Rochester's mad wife, who is confined to an attic from which she occasionally, and dangerously, escapes. As the title of their book implies, Bertha is a central figure in Sandra Gilbert and Susan Gubar's *The Madwoman in the Attic* (1979). The book is 'gynocriticism', in the sense that it traces a female literary tradition, but I have considered it separately, both because it gives a very distinctive interpretation of that tradition, and because it is perhaps the most frequently cited text produced by contemporary feminist criticism.

It could be said that Gilbert and Gubar ask a single question: who is Bertha? The answer is that Bertha is Jane's 'truest and darkest double', her 'ferocious secret self' (Gilbert and Gubar, 1979, p. 360). Gilbert and Gubar point out that each one of Bertha's appearances in the novel is associated with an experience (or repression) of anger on Jane's part, and that the text draws a number of parallels between them. They suggest that Bertha is not only *like* Jane, but acts *for* Jane: when she attacks Rochester, tears the wedding veil, burns down Thornfield, she is acting as the agent of Jane's secret desires. The idea that Bertha is Jane's *alter ego* was not new: all of the readings discussed so far see Bertha as an expression of Jane's repressed passion and anger. The difference is that Gilbert and Gubar see Bertha as representative of the restrictions experienced by the woman *writer*. Their famous opening sentence – 'Is a pen a metaphorical penis?' (p. 3) – sets the terms of their argument. Creativity has traditionally been defined not only as male, but as generated by the male body. Women have been 'framed' by male texts which represent the creative woman as a monstrous transgression of biology, and thus suffer from a debilitating 'anxiety of authorship'. Like Showalter, Gilbert and Gubar see the house as a trope for the female body, but argue that it represents women's anxiety about enclosure within the patriarchal text: the 'house' of literature is a prison, 'womb' is a metaphor for tomb. Trapped by biology and ideology, ill-at-ease in the patriarchal literary tradition but unable to speak directly as women, female authors resort to covert strategies. They come to terms with their feelings of fragmentation by conjuring up the figure of the mad or monstrous woman who, acting as 'the *author's* double, an image of her own anxiety and rage' (p. 78) seeks the power of self-articulation. *Jane Eyre* is an exemplary text, not only for the figure of Bertha, but also because of its recurrent motifs of enclosure and escape, first established when Jane is confined within the red-room. In this 'patriarchal death-chamber' (p. 340) – a placed tended by women, but presided over by the spirit of a dead man – Jane sees in the mirror the trapped image of herself.

Gilbert and Gubar have been criticised, with some justification, for their representation of the woman writer as a spellbound victim. Paradoxically, though, the appeal of their argument is that, despite the emphasis on stifled creativity, the story they tell is an oddly comforting one. Women have been put down, but they have fought back. The writer–heroine, tied to the railway track, is crushed in body, constrained in mind, but free in spirit: she escapes the chugging wheels of patriarchal tyranny by declaring her resistance, if not exactly aloud, at least in ways that the reader can decode. Although the dazzling virtuosity of Gilbert and Gubar's readings is hard to imitate, they do offer a mode of reading which can be applied to almost any novel by a woman writer: any text is potentially a feminist text. The problem is that there is only *one* text, and only one female author who, whatever her name, tells much the same secret story of repression and rebellion (Jacobus, 1981). There is, indeed, only one woman: in Gilbert and Gubar's reading of *Jane Eyre*, every woman becomes an aspect of Jane's rage; even Miss Temple and Helen Burns are seen as concealing, beneath their calm surface, 'sewers' of resentment and rebellion.

Madwoman deals with nineteenth-century British and American writers. Gilbert and Gubar's more recent, three-volume project on twentieth-century writing, *No Man's Land*, (vol. 1, 1988; vol. 2, 1989) shows some interesting shifts of emphasis. The pen is now a metaphorical pistol, signalling the battle between the sexes which the authors see as characteristic of the modernist period. *Jane Eyre* remains a key text, but it now reads differently: Bertha's echoing laughter expresses 'the alien urgency of female desire, with its threat to male potency' (1988, p. 137) and her attack on her husband is 'a kind of primal scene of sexual battle' (1988, p. 69). As Toril Moi has commented, Gilbert and Gubar's pervasive use of the term 'female' throughout *Madwoman* implicitly fuses the biological and the social (Moi, 1985, p. 65). So far in this chapter, I too have not distinguished between 'female' and 'feminine' (or 'male' and 'masculine'), because much early feminist criticism is hazy about the relationship between the two. In more recent feminist work, the distinction between the biologically 'female' and the socially constructed 'feminine' is crucial. In *No Man's Land*, Gilbert and Gubar define their project as an attempt to collate the individual narratives produced by 'a gendered human being whose text reflects key cultural conditions' into 'one possible metastory' (Gilbert and Gubar, 1988, p. xiv). In the sense that they now see the writer as a 'gendered being', whose writing reflects 'key cultural conditions' rather than the author's own experience, Gilbert and Gubar are speaking the language of post-structuralism.

Truth and the author: post-structuralism

I am merely telling the truth. (*Jane Eyre*, p. 140)

Jane's claim to be telling 'the truth' is linked to some caustic comments about the supposedly angelic nature of children, but its position in the novel is interesting. It comes just before the famous 'feminist manifesto' in Chapter 12, in which Jane declares that:

women feel just as men feel . . . they suffer from too rigid a restraint, too absolute a stagnation, precisely as men would suffer; and it is narrow-minded in their more privileged fellow-creatures to say that they ought to confine themselves to making puddings and knitting stockings, to playing on the piano and embroidering bags. (p. 141)

Part of the attraction of *Jane Eyre* is its 'autobiographical' narrative, which leads the reader to feel that she is sharing Jane's experiences and that Jane is telling her 'the truth'. But Jane is a fictional character. Whose 'truth' does the novel represent? One answer is to see it as Charlotte Brontë's truth, rooted in her own experience, and to celebrate Brontë as a feminist heroine for telling it.

Such deference to the authority of the writer has been placed in question by what is called 'The Death of the Author'. In an influential 1968 essay of that title, Roland Barthes argued that 'To give a text an Author is to impose a limit on that text, to furnish it with a final signified, to close the writing' (Barthes, 1977, p. 147). The idea that the author's intention is an unreliable and inappropriate basis for interpreting the meaning of a text was not in itself new; it is central to that influential and long-established branch of literary criticism known as 'New' Criticism. But Barthes' essay went further, questioning the idea that *any* final meaning can be allocated to the text: a productive and revolutionary reading will, rather, refuse to assign 'a "secret", an ultimate meaning, to the text' (p. 147) and will aim to disentangle its codes rather than decipher its message.

Such an argument challenges the validity of two of the central pre-occupations of the 'Anglo-American' approaches discussed so far in this chapter: to research the lives and works of individual authors, and to uncover the 'secrets' of female experience which lie beneath the surface of the text. The idea of 'the death of the author' has had an ambiguous impact upon feminist criticism, which, having laboured to find and restore the female author, has felt a less pressing need to kill her off. Taken to its logical conclusion, Barthes' essay renders the author's gender irrelevant. Feminist critics have continued, for the most part, to focus upon writing by women and to see the writer's gender as significant, but the influence of 'post-structuralism' has resulted in a new kind of analysis, which sees the text not as an authentic expression of experience, but as a site for 'the discursive construction of the meaning of gender' (Weedon, 1987, p. 138).

'Post-structuralism' is an umbrella term which encompasses most recent developments within literary criticism, including work influenced by such diverse thinkers as Michel Foucault, Jacques Lacan, Jacques Derrida and Julia Kristeva. A central influence is 'semiotics': the study of discourse as a system of 'signs' which have no direct correspondence with the real world. The implication for the analysis of literary texts is that the meaning of terms is not derived from external reality, but is determined by the place of those terms within the structure of the text and by their relationship to other signs. (For example, 'female' takes on its meaning through the ways in which it is played against the term 'male' within a specific text).

Post-structuralism develops these ideas to argue that: (i) meaning is neither fixed nor controlled by individual readers or writers: it is culturally defined, learned, and plural; and (ii) human subjectivity is shifting and fragmented; the idea of the subject as a unified and free whole is the product of liberal–humanist ideology. For feminists, perhaps the most important point is that subjectivity is seen as changing and contradictory: gendered identity is not static and natural, but formed within language and open to change. Post-structuralist feminist analyses reject the idea of an authentic female voice or experience, but see the study of women's writing as a means of understanding patriarchy, mapping 'the possible subject positions open to women' (Weedon, 1987, p. 157). Meaning and culture, precisely because they are unstable and cannot be finally 'owned', are the site of political struggle and potential resistance.

As Elizabeth Wilson has warned, there is a danger that the post-structuralist flux of identity can become a modish, alternative 'higher truth' (Wilson, 1988, p. 42). How exactly feminism as a political practice is to survive the deconstruction of 'woman' as a unitary category in favour of 'a multiple, shifting, and often self-contradictory identity . . . made up of heterogeneous and heteronomous representations of gender, race, and class' (Teresa de Lauretis, quoted in Wall, 1990, p. 10), is currently the subject of much debate. Will it dilute feminist politics? (see Chapter 3 for a fuller discussion of this question). But the challenge to the idea of a unitary 'woman's truth' has clearly been a necessary one, both fuelled by, and opening up a space for, the approaches I discuss in the next three sections.

Splitting the subject: socialist feminist criticism

> Before I left my bed in the morning, little Adèle came running in to tell me that the great horse-chestnut at the bottom of the orchard had been struck by lightning in the night, and half of it split away. (*Jane Eyre*, p. 285)

For the Anglo-American critics of the 1970s, the 'truth' of *Jane Eyre* lies in its expression of feminist rage. Jane represents 'everywoman', homeless, oppressed and searching for autonomy, a quest finally rewarded by independence and equal marriage. Penny Boumelha (1990) questions such a 'heroinisation' of Jane, arguing that her movement from oppressed child to keeper of the patriarchal keys in fact confirms and reinstates the social institutions of class. Jane is always 'naturally' a lady, a displaced spiritual aristocrat whose apparent rise in social status only confirms what the reader knows to be already there. For Boumelha, the 'dark' secret of the novel, represented by Bertha, madwoman and creole, is the 'maddening burden of imperialism concealed in the heart of every English gentleman's house of the time' (Boumelha, 1990, p. 61; see also Politi, 1982).

While Anglo-American criticism emphasises the cohesiveness of female experience, socialist feminist criticism foregrounds contradiction, in the interests of identifying the complex ways in which gender intersects with class and 'race' within the literary text. Methods of maintaining the connection between the 'double trunk' of Marxism and feminism vary, but a characteristic mode of analysis may be seen in a groundbreaking essay by the Marxist Feminist Literature Collective (1978). The Collective follow the model of the Marxist theorist Pierre Macherey – focusing on the gaps, ambiguities, incoherences and evasions within the text – to locate the feminism of *Jane Eyre* in the novel's 'not-said'. What was most significant and controversial about the essay was the way in which it challenged Marxism's 'not-said', its silence about gender, by using Lacanian psychoanalytic theory. Psychoanalysis is not famous for its sensitivity to class or historical change, and may seem an odd instrument for socialist feminist analysis, but psychoanalytic theory has been attractive to socialist feminists (and others) because it provides a way of theorising gendered subjectivity as socially constructed, precarious, contradictory and capable of change.

The case for a synthesis between psychoanalysis, semiotics, and a materialistic feminist attention to class and 'race' is persuasively argued by Cora Kaplan (1986b), one of the original members of the Collective. Such a synthesis, Kaplan argues, offers a way of analysing both the splits within the individual female psyche, and 'the splitting of women's subjectivity, especially her sexuality, into class and race categories' ('Pandora's Box', 1986, p. 162). In her analysis of the 'feminist manifesto' in *Jane Eyre*, Kaplan points out that the language of the 'manifesto' defiantly links political and sexual rebellion even while distinguishing between them. But this temporary recognition of the congruence between women's subordination and the class struggle threatens to break up the class politics of the novel as a whole; Bertha's mocking laughter follows, warning us that to associate feminism with the class struggle leads to madness. This may sound like an 'Awful Warning', but Kaplan's point is that we need to remain alert to the social and ideological constraints which lie behind a particular text, while also recognising the instability of class and gender categories, and the fragmented character of the female psyche.

Socialist feminism's central contribution has been to emphasise that both fiction and its readers are the products of specific social structures. This emphasis on the material conditions in which culture is produced and received has led in two significant directions. Firstly, towards the investigation of popular culture, questioning the division between 'high' and 'low' art, and analysing the relationship between gender and genre, a subject to which I shall return later. Secondly, towards challenging gynocriticism's picture of the marginalised and silenced woman writer. Nancy Armstrong's *Desire and Domestic Fiction* (1987) and Terry Lovell's *Consuming Fiction* (1987) both present important correctives to the influential arguments of *The Madwoman in the Attic*, by emphasising the ways in which bourgeois domestic ideology facilitated the emergence of the middle-class woman writer. Armstrong sees the history of the novel as one in which competing class interests have continually been mapped on to the more containable, 'apolitical' arena of the struggle between the sexes. In *Jane Eyre*, she argues, the threat of social disruption is contained by being located on to the body of Bertha: political resistance is gendered, neutralised and reconceived as aberrant sexual desire through the spectre of the 'monstrous female'. Lovell emphasises the unevenness of literary history and the ways in which ideologies of domesticity have been simultaneously enabling and disabling. On the one hand, women have consistently played a central part in the production and reception of literary culture; on the other, they have been systematically reduced to the position of transmitters, rather than producers, of bourgeois culture. Women have been allowed to 'speak' but only on certain terms; a small number of female-authored texts have survived the process of literary 'canonisation', but, Lovell suggests, 'woman-to-woman' fiction has consistently been filtered out.

Listening alternately: lesbian feminist criticism

> I was fain to sit on a stool at Diana's feet, to rest my head on her knee, and listen alternately to her and Mary, while they sounded thoroughly the topic on which I had but touched. (*Jane Eyre*, p. 377)

Is *Jane Eyre* a lesbian text? As I have already noted, Jane's female friendships could be placed within Adrienne Rich's definition of the 'lesbian continuum'. Arguably, too, there is an erotic component in Jane's attraction to the dynamic Diana, and the pleasure she feels in yielding to her will. There has, however, been much debate within lesbian feminism about how exactly lesbianism is to be defined. Is it a question of political commitment or sexual desire? Does Rich's emphasis on 'woman-identification' eliminate lesbianism as a meaningful category? Does the lesbian challenge patriarchy precisely because she is *not* a woman according to heterosexist definitions of the term? (Zimmermann, 1981; Jay and Glasgow, 1990). Opinion over what constitutes a 'lesbian text' is similarly divided, but three main strands within lesbian feminist literary criticism may be identified here.

In '*Images of Lesbianism*' criticism (Rule, 1975; Faderman, 1981), homophobic and voyeuristic stereotypes are identified and representations of lesbianism evaluated against the touchstone of contemporary lesbian feminist politics and experience. '*Sapphocritics*' represents the quest to identify a lesbian literary tradition. Whereas Faderman argues for a *political* rather than *sexual* definition of lesbianism which can embrace the passionate friendships of women in earlier eras, Sapphocritics focuses on recovering and re-evaluating writing by women identifiable as lesbian or bisexual. While Sapphocritics has uncovered much rich and illuminating material, it is inevitably a limited enterprise, since biographical evidence of the writer's sexuality is often hard to come by. '*Lesbian Stylistics*' shifts attention from the lesbian *author* to the lesbian *text*, by decoding the codes and covert strategies characteristic of lesbian writing. The question of how far specific tropes or formal experiments can be clearly identified as 'lesbian' has been much debated, but such an approach has the advantage of extending the field to writers whose sexual identity cannot be known, and of opening up the possibility of a lesbian reading.[2]

Is *Jane Eyre*, then, open to such a reading? I have been unable to uncover a lesbian–feminist reading of Brontë's novel, but a recent essay by Marilyn Farwell (1990) suggests one direction which it might take. Farwell argues that the 'lesbian text' does not depend on the author's sexuality. Even a basically heterosexual novel may contain 'lesbian narrative space' if it includes an episode with erotic overtones in which the two women relate to one another in terms of 'sameness', defined by 'fluid instead of rigid boundaries', and in which the divisions between self and other, lover and beloved, subject and object, dissolve. Such episodes provide a critique of heterosexual norms by disrupting the conventional, male-centred dualities of 'difference': active/passive, mind/body, male/female.

Brontë, it could be argued, offers just such a dissolution in Jane's relationship with the Rivers sisters. Diana teaches Jane German: 'I liked to learn of her; I saw the part of instructress pleased and suited her; that of scholar pleased and suited me no less. Our natures dovetailed: mutual affection – of the strongest kind – was the result' (p. 377). Jane teaches

Mary to draw: 'Thus occupied, and mutually entertained, days passed like hours, and weeks like days' (p. 377). In this three-way relationship, Jane shifts between the position of teacher and pupil, subject and object; the fluid boundaries here not only imply a critique of the heterosexual relationships in the novel, but also prefigure the final form of Jane's relationship with Rochester. Jane's friendship with the Rivers sisters is founded upon free and animated talk: 'Thought fitted thought: opinion met opinion: we coincided, in short, perfectly' (p. 377). Jane's life with Rochester is described in this way: 'We talk, I believe, all day long: to talk to each other is but a more animated and an audible thinking . . . perfect concord is the result' (p. 476). The master–servant relationship of Thornfield is revised, at Ferndean, into a marriage founded upon the principles of female friendship.

It is arguable that such an analysis blurs the line between a 'lesbian' and a 'feminist' reading, but Farwell's essay reflects a significant shift within some recent lesbian feminist criticism, away from the idea of a unitary lesbian identity towards the concept of lesbianism as 'a position from which to speak', and away from the quest for 'authentic' representations of lesbianism towards the idea of the 'lesbian text' as one which challenges heterosexist structures and stereotypes. Lesbian feminist criticism at present employs a wide range of approaches: experiential, biographical, psychoanalytic, deconstructionist, semiotic and French feminist (Jay and Glasgow, 1990; see also Lilly, 1990). Its field of study has been much enriched by the proliferation and diversity of contemporary lesbian writing (Palmer, 1990). Currently, Jeanette Winterson's *Oranges Are Not the Only Fruit* (1985) looks likely to overtake Radclyffe Hall's *The Well of Loneliness* (1928) as the most-discussed novel in the lesbian literary canon.

Freedom for bondage: Black feminist criticism

> My hopes of being numbered in the band who have merged all ambitions in the glorious one of bettering their race – of carrying knowledge into the realms of ignorance – of substituting peace for war, freedom for bondage, religion for superstition, the hope of heaven for the fear of hell? Must I relinquish that? (*Jane Eyre*, p. 400)

Is *Jane Eyre* a racist text? In her analysis of the imperialist discourse which underpins *Jane Eyre*, Gayatri Spivak scrupulously avoids posing this question, directing her rage, rather, at the 'imperialist narrativisation of history, that it should provide so abject a script' for Charlotte Brontë (Spivak, 1989, p. 176). Spivak uses the techniques of 'deconstruction'[3] to draw out the connections between imperialism's 'civilising' mission, as described by St. John in the quotation above, and the portrayal of Bertha – identified in the novel with the world of the West Indies – who is represented as subhuman and beyond the law. How, Spivak asks, does Jane move from her position as 'outsider' to acceptance and self-realisation? Her answer is that Jane's achievement of feminist-individualism depends upon the exclusion of the native female: she gets there over the body of Bertha, the 'woman from the colonies' who is sacrificed 'for her sister's consolidation' (p. 185).[4] Spivak's essay demonstrates the blind-spots in feminist 'heroinisation' of *Jane Eyre*, but it also provides an implicit commentary on more far-reaching omissions. In the 'classics' of gynocriticism, the writing of Black women, like the question of lesbianism, was conspicuous by its absence.

In a pioneering essay published in 1977, Barbara Smith challenged that exclusion, arguing simultaneously for the establishment of a Black feminist criticism and a Black lesbian feminist criticism. Smith's reading of Toni Morrison's (1973) *Sula* has affinities with the essay by Marilyn Farwell discussed previously: *Sula*, she suggests, despite its apparent heterosexuality, works as a lesbian novel because of its critical stance towards heterosexual institutions. But Smith also emphasises the communality and specificity of Black women's writing, pointing to the recurrence of 'traditional Black female activities of rootworking, herbal medicine, conjure, and midwifery' and the use of 'specifically Black female language' (Smith, 1986, p. 174).

The history of the quest for a Black female literary tradition is comparable with that of Sapphocritics. On the one hand, the reclamation of 'literary foremothers' like Zora Neale Hurston, Nella Larsen and Gwendolyn Brooks has been paralleled and fuelled by the rich material provided by contemporary Black women writers such as Toni Morrison, Alice Walker, Maya Angelou and Audre Lorde. On the other hand, the viability of identifying a unitary Black female tradition has increasingly been questioned by those who emphasise the discontinuities, diversities and historical shifts within that 'tradition' (Carby, 1987; and Wall, 1990). For some Black feminist critics, the influence of post-structuralism has resulted in a new emphasis on 'positionality' rather than 'experience', seeing theory as 'a way of reading inscriptions' of 'race', gender and class 'in modes of cultural expression . . . in order to raise questions about the way "the other" is represented in oppositional discourse' (Valerie Smith, 1990, p. 39).

Since its inception, Black feminist criticism has questioned the distinction between 'high' and 'low' forms of art. Alice Walker (1984) echoes and extends Barbara Smith's emphasis on communal activity, to argue that the Black female creative tradition includes quilting, gardening and singing the blues. SDiane Bogus (1990) takes the argument a stage further by identifying the 'Queen B' – the female blues singer who bonds with women – as a recurrent figure in Black women's writing, including Shug Avery in Walker's *The Color Purple* (1982). Charlotte Pierce-Baker (1990) takes up the quilting metaphor and applies it to the literary curriculum. Demonstrating the connections between *Jane Eyre* and Harriet Jacobs' slave narrative, *Incidents in the Life of a Slave Girl* (1861; reprinted 1988), she argues that studying the two rebellious, 'confessional' texts together creates a 'quilting of voices' which highlights the similarities and differences between two women from very different cultural backgrounds.

Another central concern in Black feminist criticism, the identification and validation of a Black female language, has been placed in question by post-structuralist critics, who see such a quest as essentialist and ahistorical. Mae Gwendolyn Henderson (1990) has inventively turned this argument on its head: what distinguishes Black women's discourse, she argues, is its heterogeneity and multiplicity. Black women's multiple and complex cultural position – simultaneously aligned with and competing with, Black men, white women and other Black women – produces the ability to speak in diverse languages, which Henderson calls 'speaking in tongues'.

Taking up French: women, language and French feminism

'Jane, what are you doing?'
'Learning German.'
'I want you to give up German and learn Hindustani.'
'You are not in earnest?'
'In such earnest that I must have it so: and I will tell you why.'
(*Jane Eyre*, p. 423)

St. John's words may be seen as exemplifying both patriarchal domination over language and the displacement of a shared women's discourse:

German is the new 'tongue' which Jane studies with Diana and Mary, and St. John's inflexible imposition of *his* chosen language upon Jane contrasts with the fluid and generous interchange which, as already noted, characterises her relationship with his sisters.

The relationship between language and gender has been much discussed by feminist theorists; I have already mentioned the ways in which radical feminists have set out to challenge patriarchal control over meaning. Here, I want to look at the influential school of thought known as 'French feminism'. While there are some interesting overlaps between the two approaches, there is a central difference between the radical feminist vision of an oppositional, authentic language of female experience, and French feminist theory, which, drawing on the psychoanalytic model given by Jacques Lacan, sees 'woman' as unrepresentable within existing linguistic structures.

Within Lacanian theory the acquisition of gendered identity corresponds with, and is inseparable from, the acquisition of language. Entry into the 'symbolic order' of language and culture is an essential precondition of becoming 'human', able to communicate with other humans, but the symbolic order is a gendered order, which inscribes and confirms male dominance. Women remain marginal within culture, placed 'in a special relation to language which becomes theirs as a consequence of becoming human, and at the same time not theirs as a consequence of becoming female' (Kaplan, 1986a, p. 82). French feminism extends and revises this model to identify 'feminine' writing – '*l'écriture féminine*' – with what is repressed or rechannelled upon entry to the symbolic order, when the all-encompassing union between mother and child is broken. *L'écriture féminine* expresses both the free-floating pleasures of prelinguistic, ungendered infancy, and the multiple, diffuse nature of female 'jouissance' (orgasmic pleasure). Whereas 'masculine' language is linear, finite, structured, rational and unified, 'feminine' language is fluid, decentred, playful, fragmented and open-ended. *L'écriture féminine* is seen as revolutionary because it poses a potential challenge to the patriarchal order by subverting masculine logic and disrupting dominant linguistic structures. I say a 'potential' challenge because, after early childhood, the feminine is located in the unconscious; it cannot be fully expressed, only glimpsed, occasionally, in certain texts.

French feminist theory has been attractive to feminists because it offers a celebratory and inspirational vision of what might be, the subversive potential of women's words. There are, however, important differences between the three theorists who have had most influence upon English-speaking writers. Julia Kristeva (1986) sees 'semiotic' language (the rhythms, intonations and erotic energies characteristic of the prelinguistic stage) as equally accessible to both women and men, since both have to repress the feminine upon entry to the 'symbolic'. For Hélène Cixous, 'writing the body' is an expression of what women have been forced to suppress, through a 'return to the body which has been more than confiscated from her, which has been turned into the uncanny stranger on display' (Cixous, 1981, p. 250). For Luce Irigaray (1985a), 'parler femme' expresses the 'doubleness' of female physiology: the two lips of the vulva speak a language more complex, subtle and diversified than that of male desire. British critics have tended to prefer Kristeva's separation of feminine language from female bodies, but it is arguable that women *do* after all have bodies, and that Cixous and Irigaray offer ways of representing (and challenging) the experience of the female body as socially and culturally mediated, rather than innate.

The impact of French feminism has been controversial (Moi, 1985; and Jones, 1986). One problem is that to identify a particular kind of language with the 'feminine' is to risk perpetuating patriarchal notions of gender difference: order, logic, and control over language are 'masculine'; the irrational, the marginal, the contradictory are 'feminine'. As Deborah Cameron comments, both radical feminism and French feminism 'stress the basic inauthenticity of women's language at present' (Cameron, 1985, p. 133). As a feminist linguist, Cameron questions whether contemporary feminism has attributed too much importance to language; whether (either by developing a form of linguistic determinism which sees women as inescapably formed and trapped by language, or by prioritising language as the site of revolution) we are deflecting our attention from the real issue: the power structures which lie behind, and are reproduced in, language.

French feminism privileges a particular style and form of writing, the *avant-garde*; it is the experimental, fragmented, open-ended text which approximates most closely to *l' écriture féminine*. While traces of *l' écriture féminine* might be found in *Jane Eyre* (the red-room scene is ripe for such an analysis), such a reading works effectively by discarding the 'realist' elements of the text – the lucid, the orderly, the linear – in favour of its 'modernist' moments of fracture and rupture. The idea that the modernist text (in its refusal of linearity and closure) is intrinsically more subversive than the realist narrative has had much currency among feminist critics, but as Rita Felski comments, multiplicity and indeterminacy are not necessarily feminist (1989, p. 7). To reject the realist text as colluding with the phallocentric order is to relegate much of what women have written – and, equally importantly, much of what women *read* – to the realms of the 'inauthentic'.

Reader, I married him: gender and genre

Reader, I married him. (*Jane Eyre*, p. 474)

So far I have been focusing on *Jane Eyre* as a 'feminist text'. But Brontë's novel is also a romance, the 'mother-text' of all those novels – written, and read, primarily by women – in which innocent heroine meets brooding hero and lives happily ever after. Is it the case, as Germaine Greer once suggested, that romantic fiction is 'the opiate of the supermenial' (Greer, 1970, p. 188) and the romantic hero the invention of 'women cherishing the chains of their bondage' (p. 180)? More recent feminist studies have argued that romantic novels offer women readers a way of dealing with real anxieties and difficulties (male power and aggression, female dependence and confinement within the home) and a chance to fantasise alternatives: masculine tenderness, female power (Radway, 1984; Modleski, 1982; see also Chapter 6). (When reading *Jane Eyre*, for example, we know that no matter how cold and aloof Rochester may seem, he *needs* Jane). Romance 'addicts', Radway emphasises, read selectively, not passively: their reading gives them 'space' for themselves and entry into a shared female subculture (see also Light, 1984).

This reassessment of romance is related to the current feminist interest in the relationship between gender and 'genre' (literary form), and in popular fiction by women (see for example Radstone, 1988; Carr, 1989; and Cranny-Francis, 1990). Do certain genres offer particular possibilities for the woman writer? Violence, vulnerability, conflict and fear are central issues in the thriller, a field in which women have long been prominent (Coward and Semple, 1989); science fiction, while often regarded as a 'male' form, offers opportunities, which women writers have seized, for fantasising alternative worlds, whether terrifying or desirable (Lefanu, 1988; and Armitt, 1991). Popular genres may be used for radical ends, which is not to say that they are necessarily progressive. As Light (1984) shows, subversive explorations of female desire may be underpinned by conservative assumptions about class. But taking the 'bestseller' seriously challenges conventional assumptions about the inferiority of popular culture, and focuses attention upon the way in which culture is produced and received. Socialist feminists have been particularly active in this area; it is noticeable that several of the original members of the Marxist Feminist Literature Collective have turned their attention to the analysis of the bestsellers written and read by women (Kaplan, 1986c; and Taylor, 1989), to the meaning which books actually have in women's lives and to the ways in which those meanings may differ, at different times or from within different cultural contexts (O'Rourke, 1989; and Taylor, 1989). We need more work on the female reader, which remains an under-researched area. But for now, I want to return to the woman writer, leaving *Jane Eyre* in order to look, necessarily briefly, at the impact of feminism upon contemporary women's fiction.

Writing as revision: contemporary women's fiction

In the early 1970s, the dominant feminist form was the 'consciousness-raising' novel: typically, a 'confessional' first-person narrative which traced the protagonist's movement from self-deluded dependence to autonomy and self-discovery. Novels such as Marilyn French's *The Women's Room* (1977) – the 'novel which changes lives' – clearly met an important need, but the 'consciousness-raising' novel's claim to be 'telling the truth' for 'everywoman' and its focus on independent self-realisation have been criticised by some feminists (Coward, 1989; and Gerrard, 1989; but see Felski, 1989). Gritty realism has increasingly given way to novels which draw attention to their own fictionality, a path pioneered by Angela Carter's 'magic realist' novels and the slippery, fragmented narratives of Doris Lessing and Fay Weldon.

Weldon's *Female Friends* (1975), like Michèle Robert's *A Piece of the Night* (1978), exemplifies another characteristic feminist form: the 'patchwork' novel, which pieces together the lives of three or four women to uncover the hidden patterns of women's oppression across time and place. In these novels, 'fact' and 'fantasy' are often mixed. The continuity and cohesiveness of female experience is emphasised through the appropriation and reworking of myth and folklore, and through the stories passed on by mothers to daughters, as in two novels by Chinese–American writers, Maxine Hong Kingston's *The Woman Warrior* (1976) and Amy Tan's *The Joy Luck Club* (1989).

The retelling of old tales has been a favourite enterprise: Angela Carter's *The Bloody Chamber* (1979) is a feminist revision of traditional fairy tales; Suniti Namjoshi's *The Conversations of Cow* (1985) is a lesbian reworking of Hindu myth, and the novels of Michèle Roberts inventively transform biblical legend and Roman Catholic iconography. Another dominant trend is the appropriation of popular genres. Feminist science fiction – such as Joanna Russ's *The Female Man* (1975) or Margaret Atwood's *The Handmaid's Tale* (1985) – comments on the present by envisaging alternatives, through utopian or dystopian visions of future possibilities for women; Barbara Wilson's *Sisters of the Road* (1986), and *She Came Too Late* (1986) by Mary Wings are lesbian-feminist thrillers which use the murder mystery formula to explore debates within contemporary feminist politics.

In the past decade, lesbian-feminist fiction has proliferated and diversified. There has been a noticeable shift away from sombre realism and the 'politically correct' celebrations of sisterhood which were prevalent in the early 1980s towards more questioning, playful and erotic fictions in a variety of different genres (Hennegan, 1988; and Palmer, 1990). Fiona Cooper's *Rotary Spokes* (1988), an exuberantly rip-roaring tale of lesbian self-discovery in a fantasised American mid-West, and Jeanette Winterson's unique blend of comedy, fantasy and confessional coming-out story, *Oranges Are Not the Only Fruit* (1985) demonstrate a more recent shift, towards a 'post-modernist' parodying and crossing of genres.

The post-modernist novel, as neatly summarised by Leslie Dick, 'uses strategies of plunder and purloinment, plagiarism, replication and simulation . . . to challenge the category of what an art work is' (Dick, 1989, p. 206). Dick's own post-modernist/feminist novel, *Without Falling* (1987) was explicitly conceived as 'a challenge to the genre of the feminist novel . . . the novel of positive role models and peppermint tea' (Dick, 1989, p. 212) and illustrates another (controversial) current trend: the questioning, from within, of some of feminism's own cherished 'truths'. Novels such as Margaret Atwood's *Cat's Eye* (1989) and Sarah Schulman's *After Delores* (1988), for example, set out to challenge earlier feminist sentimentalisation of 'woman-bonding'.

But perhaps the most dramatic development on the contemporary scene has been the achievement, and recognition, of Black women writers such as Alice Walker, Toni Morrison, Paule Marshall and Toni Cade Bambara. I end with their work because, while it exemplifies the process of 'writing as revision'[5] – retrieving, re-imagining, redefining – which is at the heart of contemporary feminist literature, it also demonstrates the importance of cultural specificity. History and culture are central preoccupations in Afro-American women's fiction (Willis, 1987), from Alice Walker's exuberant rewriting of the past in *The Color Purple* (1982) to Toni Morrison's haunting and powerful reclamation of the history of slavery in *Beloved* (1987). These novels foreground women's lives, tribulations and pleasures, but they do not claim to speak of all women, or even of all Black women.

The complex positions from which women may 'speak' are delicately and humorously explored in the poetry[6] of Grace Nichols (born in Guyana and living in Britain). I shall conclude with her short poem, 'Epilogue', which speaks of a particular woman's experience, but also encapsulates the story I have been recounting in this chapter:[7]

> I have crossed an ocean
> I have lost my tongue
> from the root of the old one
> a new one has sprung
> (Nichols, 1984, p. 64).

Notes

1. Numerous editions of *Jane Eyre* are available. Page references in the text of this chapter are to Charlotte Brontë, *Jane Eyre*, edited by Q. D. Leavis (Harmondsworth, Penguin, 1966).
2. For an interesting example of 'lesbian stylistics', see Paula Bennett's analysis of the clitoral imagery in the poetry of Emily Dickinson, 'The Pea That Duty Locks: Lesbian and Feminist-Heterosexual Readings of Emily Dickinson's Poetry', pp. 104–25 in *Lesbian Texts and Contexts: Radical Revisions*, edited by Karla Jay and Joanne Glasgow (New York and London; New York University Press, 1990). This collection also includes a useful bibliography of work on lesbian writing.
3. The central technique of deconstruction is to expose and undo the 'binary oppositions' (two apparently opposite terms of which one is, in fact, dominant) at work in the text. As Hélène Cixous has demonstrated, the binary system is not only hierarchical, but often privileges the term culturally associated with masculinity. Among the examples she gives are: Activity/Passivity; Sun/Moon; Culture/Nature; Father/Mother; Head/Heart (see Cixous, 'Sorties', pp. 101–16 (Catherine Belsey and Jane Moore) (eds), in *The Feminist Reader: Essays in Gender and the Politics of Literary Criticism* (London, Macmillan, 1989).
4. Bertha's story is the central theme of Jean Rhys's novel *Wide Sargasso Sea* (1966), a fascinating 'rewriting' of *Jane Eyre* which Spivak also discusses in her essay.

5. I have borrowed this term from Adrienne Rich's 1971 essay, 'When We Dead Awaken: Writing as Re-Vision'. The essay also contains Rich's inspirational definition of the task of feminist criticism: to provide 'a clue to how we live, how we have been living, how we have been led to imagine ourselves, how our language has trapped as well as liberated us, how the very act of naming has been till now a male prerogative, and how we can begin to see and name – and therefore live – afresh' (Rich, 1980d, p. 35).
6. I am conscious that poetry and drama have been neglected in this short essay. For introductions to contemporary feminist work in these areas, see Jan Montefiore, *Feminism and Poetry* (London and New York, Pandora, 1987) and Hélène Keyssar, *Feminist Theatre* (London, Macmillan, 1984).
7. I would like to thank Paulina Palmer for her helpful comments on an earlier draft of this chapter.

Further reading

Catherine Belsey and Jane Moore (eds), *The Feminist Reader: Essays in Gender and the Politics of Literary Criticism* (London, Macmillan, 1989). Excellent collection, primarily post-structuralist; includes important essays by Cixous, Kristeva and Spivak. Lucid introductory overview. For a fuller overview with useful chapters on French feminist theory, see Toril Moi, *Sexual/Textual Politics: Feminist Literary Theory* (London and New York, Methuen, 1985).

Deborah Cameron, *Feminism and Linguistic Theory*, 2nd edn (London, Macmillan, 1992). First published in 1985. Refreshingly down-to-earth guide to the complex field of contemporary linguistic theory.

Sara Mills, Lynne Pearce, Sue Spaull and Elaine Millard, *Feminist Readings/ Feminists Reading* (Hemel Hempstead, Harvester Wheatsheaf, 1989). Distinctive for being a collective venture, and for its practical application of theory to specific texts. Post-structuralist Marxist-feminism is the preferred approach. Helpful glossary.

Elaine Showalter (ed.), *The New Feminist Criticism: Essays on Women, Literature and Theory* (London: Virago, 1986). Primarily, but not exclusively, 'Anglo-American' in emphasis. Contains pioneering essays by Bonnie Zimmermann (lesbian feminist criticism) and Barbara Smith (Black feminist criticism). For more recent developments in these areas, see Karla Jay and Joanne Glasgow (eds), *Lesbian Texts and Contexts: Radical Revisions* (New York and London, New York University Press, 1990) and Cheryl A. Wall (ed.), *Changing Our Own Words: Essays on Criticism, Theory, and Writing by Black Women* (London, Routledge, 1990).

8

Women and the Family
Stevi Jackson

Given the importance of family relationships in most women's lives it is not surprising that 'the family' has occupied a central place in feminist theory and research. Various aspects of family life have been identified as crucial to an understanding of women's subordination. Some feminists have emphasised male violence and men's control over women's sexuality and reproduction; others have looked at the economics of domestic labour and have discussed the contribution it makes to capitalism or the extent to which men benefit from it; still others have concentrated on the familial relationships which shape the construction of masculinity and femininity; many more have examined the state regulation of family life. These issues have proved highly contentious. Indeed, the major debates between feminists on the interrelationship between patriarchy and capitalism have often been fought on the terrain of 'the family'. Recent discussions of differences among women in terms of class, 'race', ethnicity and sexuality have raised new questions for feminist analyses of family life.

Until the 1980s many theorists sought to locate the cause of women's subordination in the family, but it is now widely recognised that women's position within families is itself something which needs to be explained in terms of wider social processes and structures. This has resulted in a change of emphasis in feminist thinking. For example, where women's disadvantage in the labour market was (and sometimes still is) attributed to the burden of their domestic responsibilities, now women's domesticity is often seen as a result of gender segregation in waged work (Walby, 1986, 1990).

It has also become clear that the term 'the family' is itself problematic since it glosses over the historical and cultural variability of family forms and the many different forms of family life that women today experi-

177

ence. The 'cereal packet' image of the supposedly 'normal' family –
white and middle-class with a breadwinning husband, domesticated dependent wife and two children – does not, in fact, represent the normal
or the typical. Married couples with dependent children account for only
28 per cent of British households and 44 per cent of the total population.
Over half of these nuclear families have two breadwinners and only
about one in five adult women under retirement age are full-time
houseworkers. Although over 80 per cent of women can still expect to
marry, cohabitation and divorce are both on the increase, and 36 per cent
of marriages are remarriages. Growing numbers of women are living
alone or rearing children independently; 16 per cent of families with
children are headed by single parents and 22 per cent of children are not
living with both of their natural parents. One quarter of children are now
being born to unmarried women, just over half of whom are cohabiting
with a man, and 20 per cent of children can expect to experience parental
divorce before they reach the age of sixteen (Central Statistical Office
(CSO), 1990; Kiernan and Wicks, 1990).

Underlying these statistics is the varied and complex reality of women's family lives, the choices we make about the form of family life we
enter into and the many economic, social and cultural constraints on
those choices. Understanding this diversity, and especially the impact of
class, ethnicity, racism and sexuality on family life, is essential to a
feminist analysis. If we theorise women's subordination in terms of 'the
family' as if it had only one form, we are in danger of perpetuating a
version of the white heterosexual middle-class myth of the 'typical'
nuclear family.

This is one of the grounds on which Black feminists have been critical
of white feminists' preoccupation with the family as a basis of women's
oppression (Carby, 1982a; hooks, 1982; and Bhavnani and Coulson,
1986). Black and white women's experience of family life are not the
same, and there are differences between the various Black communities
in Britain. For example, over 10 per cent of Asian households contain
more than one family with children, compared with only 2 per cent of
Afro-Caribbean households and 1 per cent of white households. Afro-
Caribbean women, on the other hand, are more than five times more
likely to head single parent households than white or Asian women
(CSO, 1989). This is not just a matter of ethnic diversity, but also of the
impact of institutionalised racism. Slavery, colonisation and, more recently, immigration and citizenship laws have had profound effects on
Black families. Moreover, familial ideology has been central to racism,

with Black families branded as pathological because they do not match white definitions of normality. Here racism and sexism converge in particularly damaging definitions of Black womanhood:

> the Afro-Caribbean family is seen as being too fragmented and weak and the Asian family seems to be unhealthily strong, cohesive and controlling of its members . . . Afro-Caribbean women are stereotyped matriarchs, or seen as single mothers who expose their children to a stream of different men while Asian women are construed as faithful and passive victims . . . identified as failures because of their lack of English and refusal to integrate. (Parmar, 1988, p. 199)

Black feminists have also challenged white feminist perspectives on the grounds that many Black women see their families as a base for protection from and resistance to racism rather than the cause of their oppression. This highlights a more general point, that in identifying the family as a site of women's subordination, the ambivalence of women's feelings and the contradictory nature of our experience of families should not be ignored. Patriarchal family structures may be oppressive for both white *and* Black women, but families may also supply women with their closest and most supportive relationships, not least in relationships between female kin.

Feminist criticism of the family, then, should not be read as a blanket condemnation of all aspects of family life, nor as an attack on those women who live in families. Some feminists have experimented with alternative forms of domestic life, such as communal living, and with patterns of child-rearing which challenge conventional sexist assumptions about girls and boys. In so doing we learnt about the limitations of individualistic efforts to change social and cultural structures, but also about some of the possibilities for choice and resistance.

Even if many of us do not live in 'normal' families, certain conceptions of normality predominate within our culture and inform the framing of much state policy. Awareness of the diversity of family forms existing today, and sensitivity to women's ambivalent feelings about their families, do not invalidate feminist analyses of the inequality and exploitation structured into family relationships. What is clear, however, is that we cannot treat 'the family' as an isolated 'cause' of women's oppression, but need to relate family relationships to other aspects of society.

It is also important to challenge the commonly-held assumption that families are natural units, an assumption that is often used to justify women's subordination and which has informed functionalist socio-logical analyses of the family as serving universal human and social needs (Gittins, 1985; and Morgan, 1985). An appeal to 'naturalness' is often made as part of the Right's political defence of patriarchal family structures. For example, early in 1990 the then British Prime Minister, Margaret Thatcher, spoke of 'the right of a child to be brought up in a real family' (Family Policy Studies Centre, 1990, p. 5). A 'real' family is one based on a heterosexual couple. This is made explicit in Section 28 of the 1988 Local Government Act which stipulates that local author-ities should not 'promote the teaching in any maintained school of the acceptability of homosexuality as a pretended family relationship'. Lesbians (and gay men), it seems, can form only 'pretend', not 'real', families. Such narrow definitions of 'normal' family life treat as natural, universal and transhistorical something which is, in fact, culturally and historically specific.

Cross-cultural and historical perspectives

If family forms vary in contemporary Western society, then we can expect much greater diversity to have existed historically on a world scale. There is no simple, single entity that can be defined as 'the family' and compared across cultures. What we are dealing with is not a fixed structure but a complex set of relationships and practices, each element of which can vary cross-culturally (Edholm, 1982).

Ties of kinship, which we usually think of as biological, are, in fact, social: 'relatives are not born but made' (ibid., p. 167). The way Europe-ans classify kin relationships is only one of many possible ways of deciding who is related to whom (Keesing, 1975; and Harris, 1990). The precise configuration of kin and non-kin who live together and co-operate economically varies greatly, as does the extent to which house-holds are recognisable as distinct units within a society (Harris, 1990). Husbands and wives do not always live together, nor are children neces-sarily reared by either of their biological parents (Mair, 1972; Edholm, 1982; and Moore, 1988). Marriage can be monogamous or polygamous, it may be an enduring relationship entered into after much negotiation or it may be a relatively informal arrangement (Mair, 1972).

Marriage usually confers some sort of legitimacy on a woman's children, but her husband need not necessarily be the father of those children. Fatherhood is culturally defined (Keesing, 1975; and Harris, 1990). Motherhood is often regarded as a more natural role, but there are great differences in the meaning of motherhood from one society to another; in ideas about conception, birth and child-rearing; and in the relationship between mothers and their children, particularly the extent to which mothers are solely responsible for the care of their own off-spring (Edholm, 1982; and Moore, 1988). Women as wives and mothers are not generally wholly dependent on men. One of the most pervasive myths about gender relations in Western society is that men are natural breadwinners and have provided for women since the dawn of human history. In most non-industrial societies, however, women make a sub-stantial contribution to subsistence, and in many they are the main food providers (Rogers, 1980; Moore, 1988).

Colonialism and world capitalism have had a major, and sometimes devastating, impact on the domestic structures of non-European societies (see, for example, Rogers, 1980; Moore, 1988). Such changes, however, should not be understood as a result of capitalism alone, or simply as social structures responding to the 'needs' of capital: 'These processes of transformation have been equally determined . . . by the existing forms of kinship and gender relations' (Moore, 1988, p. 116).

This is also true of the transition to capitalism in Europe. In under-standing how modern family forms emerged it is necessary to keep in mind that they developed in a society which was already patriarchal. Women's family lives today have been shaped by the interrelationship between patriarchy and capitalism. The history of that interrelation-ship reveals both continuities and discontinuities in European patterns of family life.

Until the industrial phase of capitalism, most production, whether agricultural, craft or domestic industry, was centred on households. Everyone – men, women and children – contributed to the household economy. There was, however, a distinct sexual division of labour, and generally men controlled productive resources, including the labour of their wives (Middleton, 1983 and 1988). With industrialisation the re-moval of commodity production from households reduced most of the population to wage labour, and separated family life from paid work. Among the bourgeoisie in the early nineteenth century these changes were associated with a new 'domestic ideology' which defined the home as women's 'natural' sphere (Hall, 1982 and 1989; and Davidoff and Hall, 1987). This ideology was subsequently adopted by sections of the working class. Male-dominated labour organisations sought to exclude women from many forms of paid work and to establish the principle of the male breadwinner earning a 'family wage' (Barrett and McIntosh, 1980; Walby, 1986; and Jackson, 1991).

By the twentieth century, normal family life had come to be defined in terms of a breadwinning husband and domesticated wife, although this was not a pattern that many poorer members of the working class could afford to adopt. Even today, when the majority of married women are employed and women spend a far smaller proportion of their lives rearing children than they did a century ago, the idea persists that a woman's purpose in life is to care for home, husband and children.

There have been intense debates among feminists as to whether this ideal of family life serves the interests of capitalism, patriarchy or both. I hope to demonstrate that, while male-dominated families may be functional for capital through producing labour power and providing a basis for social stability, men themselves are the direct beneficiaries. I will concentrate my analysis on marriage, since other aspects of family life are covered elsewhere in this book. Moreover, it is marriage which binds many women into unequal relationships with men. This inequality is not intrinsic to relations between women and men in themselves, but is linked to wider social and economic structures and is sanctioned by the power of the state.

The economics of domestic life

The distribution of resources and the organisation of labour within families are interconnected, and are related to unequal access to paid work. These economic processes are crucial determinants of women's subordination within families. Family ties are ties of economic co-operation, of support and dependency, but also of inequality and exploitation. In exploring these economic relations I will begin by looking at the income coming into families and how it is allocated.

The increasing number of female-headed households and the rising proportion of women in paid work has led feminists to question the myth of the male breadwinner. In Britain, only one in five women is wholly dependent on a male breadwinner, and women's earnings make a vital contribution to the economic survival of many households and families (Land, 1983; Millar and Glendenning, 1987; and Morris, 1990). It should not be forgotten, however, that women's work is generally lower paid and less secure than men's work, and that many women work part-time (see Chapter 12). Hence women are likely to be at least partly financially dependent for most of their married lives. A number of studies have found that even where women make a substantial contribution to household income, the importance of their earnings may be played down so that the man is still defined as the breadwinner. Women's wages, however essential, are often seen as covering 'extras' (Hunt, 1980; Brannen and Moss, 1987, 1991; Mansfield and Collard, 1988; and Pahl, 1989). There are potent ideological forces at work here whereby the financial role of women is downgraded and women's domesticity is reaffirmed.

Feminist researchers and theorists have challenged the assumption that families are units in which all resources are distributed equally (Delphy, 1979; and Brannen and Wilson, 1987). There is growing evidence that 'while sharing a common address, family members do not necessarily share a common standard of living' (Graham 1987a, p. 221). Since husbands generally earn considerably more than their wives, they have potentially greater power in determining how family income should be allocated. Among married couples the degree to which men exercise direct control over domestic expenditure varies depending on the strategy adopted for apportioning that money. Whether women control the bulk of domestic finances, have a housekeeping allowance, draw from a common pool, or cover certain costs from their own wages, they generally keep little money for themselves. Men almost always have personal spending money (Hunt, 1980; Morris, 1984; Graham, 1987a, 1987b; Wilson, 1987 and Pahl, 1989). Men and children have pocket money; women have housekeeping money.

This pattern is attributable both to men's greater economic power and to ideas about men's rights and needs. A couple may talk of the husband's wages as 'ours' rather than 'his', but in practice wives often do not see themselves as having an equal right to spend it, especially on themselves. One of the major attractions of paid work for married women is that it provides them with money over which they have direct control (Comer, 1974; Hunt, 1980; Wilson, 1987; and Pahl, 1989). The 'extras' they spend their earnings on, however, are usually for their children or the family as a whole rather than for themselves. Hence women generally contribute a higher proportion of their wages to housekeeping than do men (Hunt, 1980; Westwood, 1984; Brannen and Moss, 1987, 1991; and Pahl, 1989).

There is now considerable evidence of hidden poverty in families dependent on men. One telling indicator of this is that a number of studies have found that a substantial proportion, sometimes as many as half, of previously married single mothers feel that they are as well off or better off financially than they were when with their partners (Marsden, 1973; Evanson, 1980; and Graham, 1987a, 1987b). This is surprising given that nearly two out of three lone mothers live on state benefits and that households headed by lone mothers are three times as likely to be poor than are two-parent households (Millar and Glendenning, 1987).

It is not only men's spending on personal consumption that accounts for this, but also the greater degree of control lone mothers have over the total family budget (Graham, 1987a, 1987b). They can plan their expenditure, decide their priorities and make economies in the interests of their children and themselves without having to take a man's desires and demands into account. In part this is simply a freedom to go without, since women are often prepared to make personal sacrifices that men are not, but lone mothers can find that exercising their own preferences leads to a more economical lifestyle (Graham, 1987a, 1987b).

The domestic distribution of money demonstrates a more general point: that consumption within families rarely takes place on the basis of fair shares for all. The same can also be said of patterns of work and leisure. Modern families are often seen as sites of consumption and leisure (Berger and Berger, 1983), but for women home is also a place of work. Whether they are in waged work or not women carry most of the burden of domestic labour (see, for example, Witherspoon, 1988).

It is still taken for granted, as an implicit element of the marriage contract, that women take primary responsibility for domestic work (Leonard, 1980; Delphy, 1984; and Gittins, 1985). This is evident from the beginning of married life. Among newly-wed couples interviewed by Penny Mansfield and Jean Collard (1988), women did most of the chores, even if they were employed full-time. They saw themselves as overburdened 'because of their working role and not because of their husbands' lack of domestic involvement' (pp. 135–6). Being viewed as secondary breadwinners means that it is women who must make the adjustments necessary to ensure that both partners can go out to work and cope with domestic work (Hunt, 1980; Yeandle, 1984; Westwood, 1984; and Brannen and Moss, 1991). Men may be more inclined to 'help' around the house when their wives are employed, but their contribution is generally limited.

The work women do constrains their own leisure while making that of others possible. Men are able to go out more because of their greater financial independence and because of freedom from domestic responsibilities: they do not have to consider who is taking care of the children or whether there are clean clothes ready for the next day. Someone else is doing the work and taking the responsibility. Women's work creates men's leisure. Women not only have less leisure time than men, but they are more likely to spend it at home so that they are constantly 'on call' even when not actually working (Chambers, 1986). Women's time is a household resource drawn upon by other family members (Seymour, 1990). The consequent lack of segregation between work and leisure is one of the key features that differentiates housework from waged work.

Domestic labour

Feminists have sought to establish that housework is work. In the 1970s, for example, there was considerable discussion around the issue of wages for housework (see Malos, 1980). There are, however, a number of ways in which domestic labour differs from waged work (Malos, 1980; and Oakley, 1984). No other occupation is not only exclusively allocated to one gender, but includes almost all adults of that gender among its practitioners. No other job is so intimately bound up with personal ties or so grounded in an ethic of personal service. There is no fixed job description for a domestic labourer, no agreed hours and conditions of work and no trade unions. Housework is work without boundaries or limits, with no clear beginning and end points, with no guaranteed space or time for leisure.

Research on housework has shown that women's feelings about it are profoundly ambivalent. Women commonly express dissatisfaction with the content, quantity and conditions of domestic labour. They frequently find it monotonous, repetitive, unstimulating, isolating, tiring and never-ending. They may resent the low status of housework within society at large, or feel that their work passes unnoticed and is taken for granted by other household members. They are often well aware that they carry an unfair burden, especially when they also engage in wage labour. These sources of discontent have been well documented (Oakley, 1984; Hunt, 1980; and Westwood, 1984). Yet despite their willingness to state these grievances, women usually stop short of an overall critique of their situation, will rarely dismiss housework as a whole as unrewarding, and are even less likely to challenge the sexual division of labour which makes housework their responsibility (Oakley, 1984; Hunt, 1980; and Westwood, 1984).

Housework is not merely a set of chores, it is also work which is given meaning through ideas of home and family. Because it is a personal service which involves caring for those a woman cares most about, she is unlikely to see it as just a job and to judge it accordingly (Hunt, 1980; and Westwood, 1984). Not only is it difficult to dissociate feelings about the work of caring from feelings about the recipients of that care, but women may also derive considerable satisfaction and a sense of pride from doing this work well, work which is essential to the well-being of all household members. Ann Oakley (1984) suggests that the contradictions and ambivalences in women's attitudes to housework can be clarified by distinguishing between feelings about housework (as work) and their orientation to 'the housewife role'. It is the work itself which is the focus of declared dissatisfactions, whereas 'the housewife role' is more often understood in terms of caring for others and creating a home and is viewed far more positively.

It is sometimes thought that feminist critiques of housework hold true only for white middle-class women. In terms of 'orientation to the housewife role', as opposed to feelings about the work itself, this may be the case. For women workers in a Leicester factory, housework was:

> their *proper* work which offered them a place at the centre of family life, and, through that, status and power which work outside the home did not offer . . . it was invested with a special status because it was work done for love and was part of the way that women cared for their families. Boring, manual work was, therefore, transformed into satisfying, caring work which required both an emotional and an intellectual commitment. (Westwood, 1984, p. 170)

In a society which is both racist and patriarchal, where Black women are likely to have the worst-paid and least-satisfying jobs, family life may be particularly highly valued as a source of more positive identities and relationships. It is often argued that Black women do not experience domesticity as oppressive to the same degree that white women do (Carby, 1982a; hooks, 1982; and Parmar, 1982). None the less, housework itself was still disliked by the Asian women in Sallie Westwood's sample. Nicki Thorogood (1987) found a high degree of dissatisfaction with domestic chores among Afro-Caribbean women, and those of them living independently of men felt a major advantage of this arrangement was that it reduced the amount of housework they had to do. All the research I have cited indicates that dislike of housework as work is widespread and is experienced by women irrespective of class, 'race', ethnicity, education or paid occupation – albeit to varying degrees. For those who are full-time houseworkers, isolation and loneliness are an added problem (Comer, 1974; Hobson, 1978; and Hunt, 1980).

Housework is also, of course, unpaid; it is not part of the wage economy but takes place within private households. This is related to other specific features of domestic labour. It lacks clear temporal defini-tion because, unlike most paid work, it does not involve the sale of labour power for a set number of hours in return for a given wage. The goods and services which a housewife produces are consumed by her immediate family rather then being destined for the commodity market. The peculiarities of domestic labour arise from these socioeconomic relations rather than being intrinsic to the tasks housewives perform. Such tasks can be undertaken as paid jobs and the services housewives provide can be purchased on the market. Only when performed within households where it is unpaid and where its products have no monetary value does such work become subject to the specific conditions of housework.

It is clear that housework takes place within social relations very different from those of capitalist production, and I would suggest that these relations are patriarchal. The work accomplished within house-holds does, however, connect with the capitalist economy. One aspect of this connection which has been the subject of much discussion is the production of labour power. Women do the work which maintains their own and their husbands' capacity to work and they rear the future workforce. This was the central focus of the 'domestic labour debate' through which feminists sought to understand the specific location of women within capitalist society (for summaries see Kaluzynska, 1980; Malos, 1980; and Walby, 1986).

A major limitation of this debate was that it concentrated on the contribution of domestic labour to capitalism and did not consider the extent to which men benefit from it. Some writers did point out that housework took place within relations of production distinct from those of capitalism (Gardiner *et al.*, 1976; and Smith, 1978), but Marxists and Marxist feminists were unwilling to see these distinctive productive relations as patriarchal. This line of enquiry has subsequently been pursued by Christine Delphy (1977, 1984) and Sylvia Walby (1986, 1989, 1990). Both these theorists argue that housework takes place within a domestic or patriarchal mode of production in which men exploit women's labour. This has proved very contentious, and Delphy's work in particular has been subjected to fierce criticism by Marxist feminists (see, for example, Barrett and McIntosh, 1979; Barrett, 1980; and Delphy, 1980).

At the heart of the objection to the concept of the patriarchal mode of production is a refusal to accept that men benefit directly from women's domestic labour (see, for example, Barrett 1980, pp. 216–17). It is clear from the evidence that I have cited on consumption and leisure that men do gain a great deal from women's household work. Men do not only 'evade' their share of housework and child-care, as Michèle Barrett puts it, they also have their share done for them. They thus receive services for which they do not have to pay, beyond contributing to their wives' maintenance. Moreover, a woman is not simply a dependant whom her male partner's wage must support: she contributes to his capacity to earn that wage. She produces his labour power which he exchanges for a wage which he controls (Walby, 1986, 1989). It is in this sense that a man may be said to exploit his wife's labour within a patriarchal mode of production.

The patriarchal mode of production is not a fixed, inflexible structure and has developed in 'dynamic articulation' with capitalism (Walby, 1986, p. 55). Patriarchal production has also been shaped by the history of colonial exploitation and racism. It does not, therefore, take exactly the same form in Black and white households. For example, the particular niche in the British imperialist structure occupied by Asian peoples dispersed from their country of origin has produced a strong tradition of family-based enterprise. Within Britain today this form of entrepreneurship provides an alternative to competing for jobs in the face of racist discrimination (Wilson, 1978; Westwood and Bachu, 1988; and Afshar, 1989). The descendants of Africans enslaved in the Americas have experienced a different history. The brutal conditions of slavery has had profound consequences for family life (hooks, 1982). Racism and the economic insecurity consequent on it continue to ensure that few Afro-Caribbean and Afro-American women have the chance to be full-time, economically-dependant housewives (Carby, 1982; hooks, 1982; and Coonz, 1988). Moreover, Black women have historically often worked within the patriarchal mode of production as other women's servants. This has historically been more common in the USA than in Britain (Nain, 1991), but it was also a feature of societies under British and European colonial rule.

It remains the case that across the diverse range of ethnic groups which make up British society, it is commonly accepted that housework is women's work. There are, however, ethnic variations in the degree to which women live independently of men. There are a higher proportion of female-headed households among Afro-Caribbeans than among those of white European origin, and more among Europeans than among Asians. This does suggest that there are differing degrees to which women are likely to be subject to patriarchal exploitation within households among different ethnic groups. Many Asian women, from a variety of ethnic backgrounds, work within a family business. Their work within the patriarchal mode of production thus involves more than just housework. This can intensify the degree of patriarchal exploitation occurring within households, since kinship obligations can mean women working for little or no wages within such family enterprises (Afshar, 1989; Bhachu, 1988; and Baxter and Raw, 1988).

This is not a situation peculiar to Asian women. The wives of self-employed men, Black or white, from chimney sweeps to lawyers, may provide free labour to their husbands' businesses. There are also grey areas where housework shades into work connected to a husband's business or employment such as, for example, entertaining his colleagues, clients or contacts. Women can, in many ways, find themselves married to their husband's job (Finch, 1983). All these situations are characteristic of the patriarchal mode of production in which women's unpaid work is expropriated by their husbands (or other male kin). A woman's labour is exploited whether she is the wife of a poor working-class man and her life is one of unremitting toil, or the wife of a prosperous businessman who is freed from physical drudgery in order to concentrate on such wifely duties as planning elaborate dinner parties. Few wives, even among the upper classes, are exempt from providing some form of domestic service (including sexual services) to their husbands. The conditions under which wives labour and their standard of living vary enormously, but they share a similar relation to the means of production within the patriarchal mode of production.

Over the last two decades domestic productive relations have undergone considerable change:

> Women are no longer necessarily bound to an individual husband who expropriates their labour till death do them part. Instead, increasing numbers of women change husbands, have children without husbands and engage in work for an employer other than their husband. Women spend a smaller proportion of their life-time's labour under patriarchal relations of production. (Walby, 1990, p. 89)

Walby sees these changes as part of a shift from private to public patriarchy, with male control of individual women in families and households giving way to public patriarchal control through the state, the labour market and so on. If Walby is correct, this means that the patriarchal mode of production may be declining in relative importance within the social structure as a whole. The decline, however, is far from terminal. Most women still marry or cohabit with men, most still spend much of their adult lives performing housework for men.

Why do women enter into a relationship in which they are exploited? Somewhat paradoxically, it is likely to be in their immediate material interests to do so. Because women have been marginalised in the labour market, with adverse effects on their capacity to earn, entering upon the labour contract of marriage may offer them a better chance of economic security than does remaining single. This is particularly the case for working-class women or those with few qualifications. The choice of marrying cannot, however, be explained only in economic terms. Marriage may be a labour relationship, but that is not all it is. Neither women nor men enter into it motivated entirely by economics, and both expect rewards other than material ones from it. It is to these other expectations and desires that I will now turn my attention.

Marriage as a personal relationship

The vast majority of women marry at least once, but over the last twenty years there have been distinct changes in patterns of marriage. In 1971 nearly a third of first-time brides in Britain were under twenty, but by 1987 the figure had dropped to 13 per cent. At the same time the median age of first marriages for women rose from 21.4 to 23.3. Two decades ago only 4 per cent of women would still be single when they were fifty, but now 17 per cent can expect to reach that age without having ever married. More women are staying single and more are living with men without formalising their relationship in marriage (Kiernan and Wicks, 1990). Cohabiting prior to marriage is increasingly becoming the norm (ibid.; and Wallace, 1987).

It may be that some women are able to exercise more real choice over whether they marry, as a result of greater financial independence. Conversely, it may be that for others high male unemployment has made marriage less economically viable and therefore less attractive (Beuret and Makings, 1987; and Hutson and Jenkins, 1989). There have also been changes in sexual mores over this period, but older attitudes to courtship, love and marriage persist and coexist with newer ideas (Mansfield and Collard, 1988; and Hutson and Jenkins, 1989). The degree to which things have changed can be overemphasised. Cohabitation may be little different in practice from formal marriage, and most of those who cohabit later marry. Over two-thirds of British women enter their first marriage by the time they are thirty (Kiernan and Wicks, 1990).

Despite increasing numbers opting to delay or eschew marriage, it is still taken for granted by most young women as a normal and inevitable part of their lives (Leonard, 1980; Lees, 1986a; Griffiths, 1987; and Mansfield and Collard, 1988). This expectation is part of the way in which 'compulsory heterosexuality' (Rich, 1980) is maintained, making lesbianism appear to be a deviant, unnatural choice. While marriage is generally regarded as desirable there is some ambivalence here, a recognition that 'settling down' might mean losing out on freedom and independence (Lees, 1986; Griffiths, 1987; and Beuret and Makings, 1987). 'Settling down' also has its positive aspects, admitting young people to full adult status and the possibility of a home life independent of their parents (Mansfield and Collard, 1988). Although the decision to marry is based upon realistic choices and mundane aspirations, within the Western cultural tradition being 'in love' is seen as an essential basis of marriage.

Marrying other than on the basis of free choice and romantic love, particularly the forms of arranged marriage practised by many Asian people in Britain, are judged very negatively from the standpoint of the dominant white culture. The popular image of arranged marriage is informed by racist stereotypes of Asian women as passive victims forced by unscrupulous parents into marriages of convenience (Parmar, 1982, 1988). In fact, Asian parents usually select their daughter's husband with considerable care, and young women have varying degrees of choice in the matter (Wilson, 1978; Westwood, 1984; and Afshar, 1989). The ideal is that love should develop within marriage.

There are no logical or empirical grounds for arguing that choosing a spouse on the basis of romantic love offers any greater guarantee of marital happiness than does having one's marriage arranged. Many a white woman who has married for love can find herself feeling vulnerable, powerless and restricted within marriage. Tales of male violence and exploitation could be told about love matches as well as arranged matches (Dobash and Dobash, 1980). Asian women themselves do not usually attribute unhappy marriages to the fact that they are arranged, but to women's lack of status and power within families (Wilson, 1978; and Sharan-Shan, 1985). It is mistaken, and indeed arrogant, for white women to assume that young Asian women necessarily want to emulate their white contemporaries. Haleh Afshar, for example, found that the younger generation of British Pakistani women 'felt strongly that they should be consulted about the choice of future husbands' but still accepted the arranged marriage system and 'were somewhat sceptical about romantic love and Western style marriages' (1989, p. 216).

Most research on marital relationships deals with white couples. It is clear from this that marriage on the basis of romantic love does not deliver what it promises. While women do not expect to live out their lives in a state of romantic passion, they do hope for affection and companionship (Leonard, 1980; and Mansfield and Collard, 1988). 'Togetherness' is central to the modern Western ideal of marriage, but it is often one-sided. The unity which marriage is supposed to create disguises the two marriages which exist within each marital union (Bernard, 1982): 'his' and 'her' marriages are not merely different, but fundamentally unequal.

Penny Mansfield and Jean Collard's study of newly-weds paints a poignant picture of the disillusionment which can be experienced by wives. Although still in the 'honeymoon' period of the first six months of marriage, many of the women felt abandoned by husbands who left them alone too often, and let down by the lack of affection the men demonstrated. Husbands and wives defined the ideal of 'togetherness' differently. The men wanted a home and wife, a secure physical and emotional base, something and someone to come home to. The women desired 'a close exchange of intimacy which would make them feel valued as a person and not just a wife'. They 'expected more of their husbands emotionally than these men were prepared, or felt able, to give' (ibid., pp. 179 and 192). In general the men were unaware of this divergence of expectation and far more content with marriage; where they complained about their wives it was often because they saw them as being too emotionally demanding. The only other major source of dissatisfaction was with wives' housekeeping skills. This research suggests that it is the emotional divide which is the most keenly felt source of dissatisfaction among women in the early days of marriage. The women seemed, on the whole, willing to accept the inequitable distribution of work and resources in marriage: they asked only to be loved and valued.

These findings are not unique. In a large-scale American study of women's experience of love, the majority of heterosexual respondents felt that their emotional needs were not being met by their partners, that men failed to demonstrate affection while relying on women for emotional support (Hite, 1988). Janice Radway's (1987) account of avid romance readers in a Mid-Western town is suggestive of a similar pattern. It would seem that women put a great deal of emotional labour, as well as domestic labour, into maintaining marital relationships. Here, as well as in the economic aspects of marriage, they give more than they receive. Women are not totally powerless within marriage, but structurally and culturally marriage favours men.

One indicator of this, and of women's refusal to accept economic and emotional deprivation within marriage, is divorce. Since divorce was made more widely available in Britain in 1969, increasing numbers of women have availed themselves of the opportunity to escape from unsatisfactory marriages. Not only have divorce rates risen, but so have the proportion of divorces initiated by women as it has become easier for them to leave and survive outside unsatisfactory marriages. For most of the post-war period more women have sued for divorce than men, but since 1970 the percentage of divorce petitions filed by wives has risen from 63 per cent to 73 per cent (Coleman, 1988). During the 1970s divorce rates doubled, but have since remained constant. If current rates continue, then 37 per cent of marriages are likely to end in divorce. Divorce, however, only ends a particular marital relationship. It does not necessarily undermine the institution of marriage itself. Most of those who divorce subsequently remarry, many only to divorce again. Women's discontent with marriage does not seem to be experienced as disillusionment with the institution, but rather with a particular relationship.

The legal regulation of marriage and divorce

Marriage in Western society is regarded as the most intimate and private of all relationships, but the fact that it is controlled by the state indicates that it is not just a personal relationship: it is of wider social and political significance. The state does not merely regulate family life; it helps to constitute it by defining what counts as a family (Barrett and McIntosh, 1982). It does so through such provisions as Section 28 of the 1988 Local

Government Act and Section 13 of the Human Fertilization and Embryology Act 1990, which states that a woman should not have access to
certain treatments for infertility 'unless account has been taken of the
welfare of the child who may be born as a result of the treatment
(including the need of that child for a father)'. It has been suggested,
during the controversy over 'virgin births' early in 1991, that this condition should be extended also to donor insemination, thus preventing
single women from being able to conceive except through vaginal intercourse. Single women and lesbians are thus not regarded as having the
same rights to motherhood as women involved in a heterosexual relationship. Marriage, then, is central to this definition of heterosexual
family life and establishes patterns of rights and dependencies around
which much state policy revolves. Not only are the processes whereby
we enter into or terminate a marriage legally prescribed, but the state also
defines who may marry whom.

Marriage institutionalises heterosexual monogamy, and privileges
only one form of sexuality as a socially and legally valid foundation for
family life. A lesbian couple, however long established, have no recognised relationship to each other. For example, they will not be defined as
each other's next of kin as a heterosexual married couple would, and
have no automatic rights in relation to each other. A lesbian mother can
lose custody of her children and her partner has no legally-sanctioned
relationship to the children they have helped to rear unless they have
formally been appointed as the children's legal guardian (Rights of
Women, 1984). Lesbians may escape the constraints of patriarchal
marriage, but they are also denied its privileges.

The reasons why marriage is by definition heterosexual lie in its
history as a patriarchal institution: a sexual relationship whereby a man
established rights in the person and property of his wife (Leonard, 1978).
Under English common law the rights a man acquired through marriage
were extensive. Until the nineteenth century a wife's property became
her husband's and she effectively became his property. He had near
absolute claims to her labour, her children and her body, and the authority to chastise her if she did not fulfil her obligations. This patriarchal
power has only very slowly been eroded (Leonard, 1978; Sachs and
Wilson, 1978; and Brophy and Smart, 1981).

In 1839 men lost their absolute right to their children and subsequent
legislative change and judicial decisions gradually gave women more
chance of keeping their children when a marriage ended. It was not until
1973, however, that both parents became equal in law, and recent cus-

tody decisions threaten once more to empower fathers at the expense of mothers (Lowe, 1982; Smart, 1984, 1989a; and Brophy, 1989). Married women gained rights to their earnings in 1870 and the right to own property in 1882. Equal divorce rights have existed only since 1923 (Brophy and Smart, 1981; Smart, 1984; and Burgoyne *et al.*, 1987). Family law has moved towards the idea of marriage as a partnership and the establishment of formal equal rights even to the extent that since 1990 the existence of rape in marriage has been recognised in British courts, thus challenging men's ancient rights over their wives' sexuality. Yet while men's power within marriage has been reduced, it has not been totally undermined. The partnership of marriage is, as we have seen, far from being an equal one (Sachs and Wilson, 1978; and Brophy and Smart, 1981).

Formal equality before the law is meaningless in a society where women are economically unequal and where other state agencies enforce that inequality. Indeed, the idea of equality founded on an essentially masculine conception of legal subjects, abstractly equal before the law, can erode those rights: for example, custody of children, that women have won by virtue of recognition of their specific place within families, particularly as mothers (Smart, 1984, 1989). In practice, women's rights within marriage have always been conditional, bound up with the interests of their children and dependent on their being defined as 'good' mothers (Brophy and Smart, 1981; and Smart, 1984).

Custody of children has, during the twentieth century, increasingly been awarded to mothers 'in the best interests of the child'. If a mother is deemed 'unfit', however, she may lose her children. Such women are often those who challenge patriarchal relations – in the 1950s the adulteress, today the lesbian (Brophy and Smart, 1981; and Smart, 1984, 1989a). Here, there has been a backlash against women in the name of fathers' rights. Mothers are still being awarded care and control, but courts are moving towards granting joint custody and greater access to children for fathers. This renders a woman subject to surveillance and possible harassment by her former husband, and can mean that she is effectively rearing the children under his supervision (see Brophy, 1989; and Smart, 1989a).

British law on marriage and divorce, then, has developed in the direction of greater formal equality, but this has not always been in women's interests. Although the absolute control of individual women in marriage characteristic of the nineteenth century has gone, legal processes continue to reproduce patriarchal relations. The limited ways in which violence within marriage is subject to legal regulation is a further example: here the state has historically condoned male violence and still fails to provide adequate protection for women (see Chapter 5).

The state, welfare and the family

The regulation of marriage is one of the ways in which the state can be seen as constitutive of the family. Other aspects of state regulation contribute to this process: welfare provision, through defining women as men's dependants; and immigration policy, through determining which of a person's relatives be allowed into the country and under what conditions. Other areas of policy such as housing, health, education and so on are informed by assumptions about 'normal' family life.

The state, however, is not a monolithic entity which has consistent effects. It is made up of a number of agencies and apparatuses which do not always work in harmony. There are differences, for example, in the degree to which family law, taxation and the social security system define wives as dependent upon their husbands. Moreover, state policy is only rarely formulated purposefully to impose a particular form of family life on the populace. More commonly it is underpinned by commonsense ideas about family life which give rise to an implicit family policy (Land, 1979). During the 1980s, however, Britain's Conservative government was more explicit in identifying the family as a target for policy, in seeking to promote and defend traditional patriarchal structures (David, 1986; and Abbot and Wallace, 1989). These concerns were evident, for example, in the speech by Margaret Thatcher quoted at the beginning of this chapter.

During the last decade cuts in public expenditure have threatened the welfare state which, in its modern form, developed in post-war Britain in a climate of greater consensus between the two major political parties. The growth of welfarism has usually been seen by Marxists as functional for capital, ensuring the efficient reproduction of labour power and a degree of social stability. Support for a particular family form is held to follow from this (Barrett, 1980). Such a view ignores the possibility that patriarchal interests are served by the state. As is recognised by many Marxists, the welfare state is in part a response to struggle and represents concessions won by the working class (Urry, 1981). These struggles were dominated by organised male labour, who shared certain patriarchal concerns with bourgeois men. The former's demands for recognition as family breadwinners were ultimately incorporated into modern welfare legislation. In its welfare provision, as elsewhere, the state is patriarchal as well as capitalist in that it supports family structures which benefit men (Walby, 1990).

The ways in which welfare policy has defined women as family carers and dependants is well established (Land, 1983; and Ungerson, 1990). Unlike children, who are treated as dependants because they need care, women are regarded as dependants because they provide care. Yet, as Land (1979) points out, the assumption of dependency applies to women as wives rather than as mothers. This underlines the patriarchal interests and assumptions which inform the formulation of state policy.

Child benefit is one area where the British state defines women as mothers rather than as wives and pays *them*, rather than their husbands, a benefit. It is not such a contradiction as it might seem that the 1980s British Conservative administration, ostensibly committed to 'family values', should freeze child benefit for four years. The form of family they have sought to promote is a patriarchal one, hence the recent emphasis on paternal responsibilities. It is quite in keeping with this to refuse to acknowledge the economic inequalities that exist within families and therefore claim that only poor families require benefits for children. This view also happens to coincide with other political aims, notably the reduction of public expenditure and 'welfare dependency'.

The patriarchal and capitalist aspects of New Right philosophy do not always fit together so neatly. The two facets of 'Thatcherite' ideology – aggressive, individualistic economic liberalism and pro-family moral authoritarianism – have sometimes conflicted. In particular, women's dependence contradicts the principle of individual self-reliance. The resolution usually attempted emphasises an ideal of self-reliant families rather than individuals.

The general trend of recent British welfare legislation has been to increase the dependence of women on men (and also young people on parents). Cuts in non-means-tested benefits paid to women, such as the freezing of child benefit and the abolition of universal maternity benefit, are examples of measures which have reduced women's access to independent income and which particularly affect those who are not employed. While stressing the importance of women staying at home to care for young children, the government penalises those who do.

Gestures towards equality have been made by treating women in employment as individuals rather than as dependants for some purposes, for example by taxing husbands and wives separately. Other areas of policy, however, assume women's availability for unpaid work in the home. Child-care provision in Britain is appallingly inadequate, with less than half of the parents who would like places for their children able to find them, and most relying on the private sector (Cohen, 1988). The emphasis on 'community care' means more women shouldering the burden of care for sick or elderly relatives, with little support. Here 'the family' (meaning women) is explicitly invoked as an instrument of policy (Deakin and Wicks, 1988). It is estimated that more than one in five of women between the ages of 40 and 60 provide such care (Martin and Roberts, 1984).

While stressing the importance of family responsibility for care, especially that of mothers of young children, the government has sought to attract some of those women working at home back into the paid labour force. Such conflicts of demand for women's labour both inside and outside the home has sometimes been seen as resulting from contradictions within capitalism, but can also be conceptualised as a tension between patriarchy and capitalism (Walby, 1986, 1990). This tension is at its most acute and obvious in the conundrum presented to British Conservative policy makers by the situation of lone mothers, most of whom live on state benefits. On the one hand there is the stated aim of reducing what the Conservatives call the 'dependency culture' and the need for the labour of some of these women. On the other is the patriarchal ideal which holds that mothers should stay at home to look after their children. This makes the government unwilling to create conditions, particularly with regard to child-care, which would make it possible for these women to go out to work.

The solution has been to plump for the patriarchal option, replacing dependency on the state by dependency on men, by introducing in 1990 provisions to force fathers, whether married or not, to maintain their children. Most of the women affected will be no better off, since what they gain in maintenance will be lost in benefit. While some women will welcome the prospect of men being made to take some responsibility for their offspring, enforced dependency on a former partner is something many women would wish to avoid, particularly where it makes them vulnerable to harassment or violence.

The pro-family stance adopted by the British government in the last decade, and indeed the familial ideology underpinning state policy in general, is not applied universally. The family which successive governments have wished to promote and protect is the white, heterosexual family. This 'family' has long been one of the focal points around which ideas of 'Britishness' have been constructed, so that families of 'others' are seen as suspect and pathological (see Lawrence, 1982). That the welfare state has been, from its inception, racist as well as patriarchal is exemplified in Lord Beveridge's famous pronouncement made in 1942 on the role of British women: 'In the next thirty years housewives as mothers have vital work to do in ensuring the adequate continuance of the British race and of British ideals in the world' (quoted in Deakin and Wicks, 1988, p. 20).

In the post-war era, immigration legislation has consistently threatened the unity of Black families. The Thatcher administration, supposedly committed to the defence of family life, introduced the Nationality Act, the 'primary purposes' rule[1] and tighter visa restrictions for people from specified African and Asian countries. As a result, many families have been split up through deportation. The primary purposes rule, for example, places the onus on a couple to prove that their marriage is not a marriage of convenience and results in many being subjected to intrusive and humiliating vetting (Jacobs, 1988). These changes in immigration law have had particularly negative consequences for young Asian women and their families. Those who had promised their daughters in marriage prior to these new restrictions, in the expectation that their sons-in-law would move to Britain, found themselves in the situation of their daughters having to leave the country (Afshar, 1989).

The racism which results in families being divided cannot be reduced to a side-effect of capitalism. State policy on the family has been shaped by a complex interplay between capitalist, patriarchal and racist interests.

Conclusion

Women are differently located within a patriarchal, racist and capitalist society and thus have varying experiences of family life. Some of us are freer to make choices and experience less contradictions than others (Ramazanoglu, 1986, 1989). All, however, make choices – albeit within given limits: we are not simply passive victims ensnared into oppressive marriages. It may be that it is becoming easier for some women to live independently of men, and it is certainly the case that marriage no longer ties us to an individual man for life. Given other constraints on women's lives, however, marriage will still seem to many to be an attractive option.

Neither the differences among women in our experience of family life, nor our ambivalent feelings about it, should blind us to the fact that gender divisions remain a ubiquitous and pervasive feature of families, affecting all of us irrespective of class, sexuality, 'race' or ethnicity. Families can be the basis of political solidarity in Black and working-class communities, but they are also central to the reproduction of patriarchal relations and the perpetuation of women's subordination (Lees, 1986b; and Nain, 1991).

Note

1. The primary purposes rule, introduced in 1983, gave immigration officials the power to refuse the foreign spouse of someone living in Britain entry to the country, or to deport them, if it was judged that the 'primary purpose' of the marriage was to secure residence in Britain.

Further reading

Michèle Barrett and Mary McIntosh, *The Anti-social Family*, 2nd edn (London, Verso, 1991) first published 1982. The first edition of this book was much criticised for its implicit racism. It could also be seen as unduly moralistic in tone. None the less, it does provide a useful overview of key areas of Marxist and feminist debate.

Diana Gittins, *The Family in Question* (London, Macmillan, 1985). An accessible introduction to women and family life with a strong historical emphasis and an explicitly feminist stance.

Stevi Jackson, *Family Lives: A Feminist Sociology* (Oxford, Blackwell, 1993). Deals in detail with the issues covered in this chapter, as well as other aspects of family life such as parenthood and childhood, violence and sexuality.

Lydia Morris, *The Workings of the Household* (London, Polity, 1989). A summary of British and American research on the effects of economic change on households.

9

Motherhood and Women's Lives

Paula Nicolson

Introduction

Motherhood and womanhood stand in a complex and contradictory relationship with one another. Under patriarchy, mothers appear to have a mythological, mysterious and powerful status. Only women are granted this status, and it is one to which all women are expected to aspire. The reality of mothers' lives, however, often fails to match these aspirations. Motherhood is a challenge; although potentially enjoyable, it is also hard work and routinely stressful (Richardson, 1992). It is central to women's lives whether or not they become mothers, and constrains their available choices. Becoming a mother often means economic dependence on another person or the state, and frequently reduces women's income. It affects relationships with men and other women, and changes occupational, domestic and sexual arrangements. Being a mother influences social and personal identity, and has implications for women's health (Nicolson, 1988).

Feminist analyses of the conditions surrounding motherhood have identified its socially prescribed conditions: as an accompaniment to marriage, heterosexuality, monogamy and economic viability (Macintyre, 1976; and Gittins, 1985). It is further argued, particularly by radical feminists, that motherhood is the key means of women's oppression in patriarchal societies (Bleier, 1984), but despite this, many young women see it as a means of 'liberation' from the prospect of dreary paid employment (Griffin, 1989).

Despite the prominence of motherhood as a social institution, and the almost universal expectation that women will become mothers, the everyday reality of mothering is frequently invisible. For women caught up in the myths that accompany motherhood, failure to achieve that imaginary status is frequently a 'shock' (Antonis, 1981). Women who do not have children are also caught in these contradictions and constraints. Women who are not mothers are seen as failed and unfeminine women, and achievements and pleasures gained outside motherhood are condemned within patriarchy as substitutes for 'normal' femininity (Woollett, 1991). In this chapter the consequences of the contradictions surrounding motherhood are explored, with particular emphasis on the ways in which the conditions of motherhood, both social and psychological, have been socially constructed within patriarchy and capitalism.

What is motherhood?

Perceptions of mothers as powerful and influential (Kitzinger, 1978) and the romanticisation and idealisation of the mothering role (Ussher, 1990) need to be qualified in the context of women's everyday experiences. Motherhood as an institution includes certain responsibilities and duties, but women's power is limited. Women's power in both the public and private/domestic spheres is subject to the rule of men – both as individuals and as represented by patriarchy. Psychologists have traditionally claimed priority for mothers' power over children, through emphasising the importance of mother–child relationships (Walkerdine, 1984) and through the debate on mothers' responsibilities to their children (Riley, 1983). However, legal and traditional power over women and children is held by men (Lummis, 1982).

Matriarchy (defined as a society with matriarchal government and descent reckoned through female lineage), is not recognised in most societies and is certainly not an influential means of social organisation. Claims from community and anthropological studies, that matriarchies prevail in certain subcultures, for example among Black urban American groups (Kitzinger, 1978) or among traditional white working-class communities in British cities (Young and Wilmott, 1966), cannot be upheld in terms of true power. Ruth Bleier (1984), reviewing anthropological studies of a large number of cultures, argues that women's roles are always of a lower status to those of men. In some small, non-industrial societies where men have primary responsibility for aspects of child-care, 'mothering' is taken very seriously and given high status, which is not the case when women do it.

Most mothers in industrial and non-industrial, urban and rural, societies are oppressed. They may have particular responsibilities, but not the accompanying rights to choose how they mother or whether to mother at all. The popular perceptions of maternal influence and power are mythological and the origins of this myth lie within patriarchy. The repercussions of this have had a powerful psychological effect on relationships between mothers and daughters, and affect expectations of mothering from generation to generation.

It is through the everyday experience of the mother–daughter relationship that the contradictions in the myth become clear: 'Belief in the all powerful mother spawns a recurrent tendency to blame the mother on the one hand, and a fantasy of maternal perfectability on the other' (Chodorow and Contratto, 1982, p. 55). The romanticised and idealised woman, full of love, forgiveness and selflessness does not and cannot exist, so that all mothers are destined to disappoint their children and themselves.

Mother-blaming occurs on a number of levels, from individual attributions to mothers as the cause of psychological insecurities, to the portrayal of the cold, rejecting, neurotic or inadequate mother in popular culture (Dowling, 1981; and Sayers, 1988). The patriarchal myth of maternal power renders women culpable, and thus in reality deprives them of effective social influence. Women are consequently perceived as imperfect in their central role, while men as fathers can maintain their own mythological status and claim the admiration of their sons and daughters.

Science and motherhood

How is it, then, that mothers are 'blamed' and seen as both powerful and destructive? These contradictory images of motherhood are constructed and exploited within patriarchy through the medium of 'scientific knowledge', and operate to ensure that many aspects of motherhood are rendered invisible, and that women as mothers are denied the power to change this within existing social structures. The mechanisms through which the status of motherhood are controlled are both social and psychological. Motherhood is often idealised and some argue that men experience 'womb envy', that is, they envy women's ability to become pregnant and give birth. The image of the idealised mother, however, exists in stark contrast to men's apparent unwillingness to become involved in the aspects of infant care that are available to them (Nicolson, 1990) and with the daily lives of the women attempting to mother (Gavron, 1966; Wearing, 1984).

The role of 'mother' has not evolved in a 'natural' way, outside culture and free from ideology. It has been socially constructed within patriarchy through a complex set of power relations which ensure that women become mothers, and practice motherhood, in narrowly-defined ways. This is achieved in part through the mechanism of 'science', which attends to and bolsters existing power relations. Contemporary motherhood is the product of (at least) nineteenth- and twentieth-century medical/biological and psychological/social science, and this can be seen in a number of ways.

Social prescriptions for contemporary motherhood are constantly offered, reinforced and embellished by 'experts' with recourse to 'science', and their versions of what constitutes good mothering practice is the socially received 'wisdom'. Certain kinds of claims to knowledge are given priority over others, and it is those which serve the needs of the socially-powerful (that is, in this case, men) (Foucault, 1973; and Philp, 1985), that pass into popular discourse and come to represent our everyday understanding of what we all take for granted as 'truth' or 'facts' (see Antaki, 1988).

In the case of motherhood, while there are potentially a myriad of dimensions which could be studied to explain and determine mothering practice (that is, the nature of the role itself, what behaviour is appropriate and so on) only a small proportion of what constitutes motherhood has been identified and described. In other words, *normative* behaviour associated with mothering has emerged from the power of the knowledge-claims of scientists which suit the needs of patriarchy (Foucault, 1973). These knowledge claims have not only informed the ideology of mainstream social and psychological science, but more importantly, the everyday understanding of women themselves. This means that the accompanying stresses of motherhood may be experienced by women as their own 'inadequacies' (Boulton, 1983; and Brown *et al.*, 1986).

I shall briefly explore some of these knowledge-claims and normative prescriptions, before identifying their manifestations in the social and psychological conditions of contemporary motherhood.

Experts and child-rearing: how to become a good mother

The focus of 'experts' on motherhood has been upon the effects of mothering on children, and the marital relationship, and clearly reflects the ideology underlying their claims to scientific knowledge. They have suggested a number of ways in which maternal behaviour can have potentially dire consequences for children, not only in their infancy and pre-school years, but also through adolescence and into adulthood. John Bowlby's assertions about the mothering role is a good example of this. Mother love in infancy, he claimed, is as important for mental health as vitamins and proteins are for physical health (Bowlby, 1951). Above all else, infants need mothers, and those mothers have to love them. This love, by implication, needs to be ever-available and offered without qualification, regardless of the mother's own needs and circumstances.

The consequent development of the 'maternal deprivation thesis' redefined the responsibilities of women towards their children, although the implications for women's lives were largely ignored. The emphasis in all this work was on the dependency needs of infants, and the psychological implications of separation traumas for the remainder of life. Mothers themselves were invisible.

This thesis not only informed popular ideas about child-care, but also set the parameters for subsequent psychological research on infant/child development, adopting the notion of the 'secure base' as an ideal context for human development. This paradigm emerged as a moral as well as psychological prescription for mental health. The burden for providing the secure base fell upon mothers, regardless of circumstances and abilities (Ainsworth, 1992).

Evidence of the interconnection between science and politics can be seen in Denise Riley's (1983) study of women's work and day-care in the immediate post-war/post-Bowlby period: 'The reproductive woman at the heart of family policy was surrounded by the language of pronatalism. By pronatalism, I mean that despondency and alarm over the low birth rate, both past and as anticipated by demographers, which took the solution to the problem to be encouraging women to have more children; four per family was a widely agreed target' (Riley, 1983, p. 151).

Riley paints a complex picture, contrasting with some popular contemporary feminist images of women's post-war resistance to leaving the labour market (for example, as in the film *The Life and Times of Rosie the Riveter*). Many women, exhausted by the multiple burdens of child-care, domestic responsibility and work outside the home, appeared to welcome the pronatalist direction of government policy, which included ideas about the dangers for children of anything less than maternal dedication and constant availability. This was accomplished, at least in part, through direct information on film and in child-care manuals, for the specific consumption of women (Ehrenreich and English, 1979; and Richardson, 1992), making it clear that experts know best, but also helping to ensure that women focused their major efforts upon mothering, or the management of mothering.

More recently, attention has been paid to the role of the father; however, the treatment of fatherhood by experts has been explained differently from the motherhood role. In clear contrast to mothers, fathers are represented as adding positive ingredients to the beleagured and insufficient mother–child relationship. Fathers' involvement is seen as improving children's intellectual and social capacities (Parke, 1981). Mothers, it seems, are seen primarily as supplying the basic conditions for survival and maintenance, while experiencing a decline in their own wider capacities. Feminist studies of motherhood clearly show the ways in which the mothering role operates to exclude women's own development; for example, sometimes resulting in a self-defined sense of being unfit for tasks demanding intellectual skills (Gavron, 1966; and Nicolson, 1988).

Interest in fathers has led to a further strand of expert concern: the 'family'. Functionalist sociologists have in the past been concerned to divide and stratify family roles/functions in terms of gender and generation; portraying the family as a social microcosm, where women were seen as both dependent and nurturant in the home in relation to men and children, and nurturant and dependent in society (Parsons and Bales, 1953). Subsequent sociological studies, as with mainstream psychology, focused upon motherhood as a role or as a variable in predicting marital satisfaction, and it was not until the publication of Hannah Gavron's *The Captive Wife* in 1966 that contemporary sociologists attempted to take seriously women as mothers. Even Elizabeth Bott's (1957) sensitive and influential study, which took class and gender into account, failed to identify and challenge the conditions surrounding women's role in the family and in relation to child-care.

Feminist analysis of the family has redefined the context within which domestic relationships are enacted, dispelling the myth of the traditional nuclear family unit. Single parenthood, domestic violence, divorce and lesbian parenting, all indicate the need to re-evaluate the way 'experts' define and prescribe women's lives (Gittins, 1985).

In contemporary mainstream psychology, expert attention to the family has focused upon the transition to motherhood, and the consequences of becoming a mother for reducing marital intimacy (Moss *et al.*, 1983), for women's impaired physical attractiveness, and for women's rejection of what had been 'normal' pre-pregnancy sexual relations (Reamy and White, 1987; and Nicolson, 1991), and for precipitating postnatal or maternal depression which is detrimental to child-rearing (Puckering, 1989). These issues have all been taken as indices through which good motherhood/wifehood might be assessed.

Within the social sciences and medicine, mainstream patriarchal values are given the status of knowledge. Feminist analyses, or woman-focused studies (such as Gavron, 1966), are less often adopted into the mainstream and so have less impact on popular ideas and beliefs. However, patriarchal frameworks alone do not fully account for women's thinking about their own experience of motherhood. Women draw upon personal experience as well as popular discourses, and this often sets up the contradictions that potentially lead to feminist consciousness.

Becoming a mother

Motherhood is *not* a unitary experience, nor is it a simple one. To be a mother demands that a woman takes on a complex identity (Richardson, 1992). She is still herself but she is also a mother, with the encumbant roles, responsibilities and relationships which this entails. Becoming a mother has been part of most women's identities since childhood and although many accept that they did not really know what motherhood was like until they experienced it, the fact of becoming a mother is no surprise in itself.

Why do women become mothers, or at least take the option of becoming a mother so seriously? On an individual level, women recognise their biological capacity to have children, and through socialisation into the female role, come to equate femininity with marriage and motherhood, often seeing women who do not do this as 'inadequate' (Woollett, 1992). Motherhood potentially provides girls/women with 'entry' into womanhood:

One of the attractions of motherhood is its normative quality. Motherhood is an expected and normal role for all women. To become a mother is to do what women and those around them expect and want them to do. It is to be the same as other women and not stand out as different. In this ideological context, women's decisions about motherhood are not so much about when to have children, but how many to have, or increasingly, in which social context to have them. The mandate for motherhood, as it has been called, means that women opt out of motherhood rather than opting in to it. (Woollett, 1987, p. 1)

Many women believe, then, that they can only achieve adult, feminine status through becoming mothers. Ann Phoenix's (1991) research with teenage mothers supports this view, in that their desire for motherhood as entry to womanhood is not so much a biological desire to become pregnant and nurture a child, but an implicit recognition of apparent privilege unavailable to childless women. This system of beliefs is related to the patriarchal idealisation of women as mothers, which is part of women's subordination. It has traditionally been 'the special contribution . . . of western state ideologies, to elaborate, ritualise, mystify, and institutionalise motherhood as the core element in the enforcement of patriarchal relationships of power. Motherhood became the means and metaphor for women's subordination' (Bleier, 1984, p. 159). In other words, the romanticisation of motherhood, and the sets of relationships which accompany it, are dictated by patriarchical power relations. It suits men for women to mother.

The motherhood 'mandate' is 'serviced' by the popular and powerful belief system surrounding the notion of a 'maternal instinct'. This 'instinct' is characterised by two desires – to have children, and to care for them: 'In the common view, every woman fulfils her destiny once she becomes a mother, finding within herself all the required responses, as if they were automatic and inevitable, held in reserve to await the right moment' (Badinter, 1981, p. xx). Women's destiny, we are also told, is subject to 'inner promptings which induce women to care for their offspring' (Whitbeck, 1984, p. 186).

The notion of the maternal instinct underpins the contemporary construction of motherhood. It underlies notions of femininity and required maternal behaviour, and its 'absence' is used to explain women's maternal 'failures' such as not protecting children from or perpetrating child abuse or neglect. It is also used, in conjunction with theories of attachment, to explain childhood anxieties, subsequent problems in adulthood and in developing childbirth and day-care policies.

The myth of femininity encapsulated by this notion of the 'maternal instinct' is the one through which women's psychology and social role are determined 'scientifically'. This myth may be summarised thus:

1. All women have a biological drive towards conceiving and bearing children.
2. This is a precursor to the drive to *nurture* those children.
3. The skills/capacities required to care for infants/children emerge or evolve immediately after the birth without the need for training.

The logical consequence of this 'instinct' would be the knowledge that all women want to (and thus should be enabled to) have children, and are capable of looking after them without training. The 'maternal instinct' cuts across ideas that women are *socialised* into wanting children – it is a biological imperative (Wilson, 1978).

Feminist research has challenged such myths by showing contradictions within the idea of a 'maternal instinct'. For example, by observing that doctors differentiate between 'possessors' of the maternal instinct (married women) and those who do not (unmarried women). Married women are encouraged to seek fertility counselling if necessary, and condemned for wanting abortions. Unmarried women (especially lesbians; see Burns, 1992) are challenged for wanting children (Macintyre, 1976; and Boyle, 1992).

There certainly appears to be little historical or psychological evidence for an innate desire either to bear or nurture children (Dally, 1982; and Whitbeck, 1984). Elisabeth Badinter (1981), for example, distinguished maternal 'instinct' from 'love' in her historically grounded critique of motherhood: 'Maternal love is a human feeling. And like any feelings, it is uncertain, fragile and imperfect. Contrary to many assumptions, it is not a deeply rooted given in women's natures' (Badinter, 1981, p. xxiii). She provides evidence of historical variations in maternal behaviour which sometimes reflect interest in and devotion to the child, and sometimes not (Riley, 1983). Research on women's responses to their newborn infants further challenges the belief about instinctual maternal love (Sluckin *et al.*, 1983), but does identify the influence of the scientific experts' advice, through the fact that women expect to feel this and experience guilt and distress when they do not (Nicolson, 1988).

What is apparent is that when women have children (whether or not the children are planned) they usually try their best to care for them and often grow to love them. Many evaluate their personal worth through this relationship and discharge their responsibilities as well as they are able.

The motherhood role, contrary to the ideology of the maternal instinct, appears to be one for which most women are ill-prepared. However, it is an experience which seems to be reproduced from generation to generation of women, and women continue to mother. Why should this be the case? Nancy Chodorow (1978) has suggested that this 'reproduction' of mothering within the context of patriarchy, although not a biological imperative, is in one sense both 'natural' and 'inevitable' for women, given the dominant social structures. Women's mothering is not only a product of biology, but also causally related to historical conditions and the way that child-care and the division of labour have evolved. She argues that girls/women and boys/men develop in a context which encourages the psychological capacities and commitments to participate in the existing social relations and structures. The dominant structures, whereby women mother and men work outside the home, are accompanied by appropriate psychological capacities which underlie these tasks, and these are reproduced at both conscious and unconscious levels: 'Women as mothers, produce daughters with mothering capacities and the desire to mother. These capacities and needs are built into and grow out of the mother–daughter relationship itself. By contrast, women as mothers (and men as not-mothers) produce sons whose nurturant capacities and needs have been systematically curtailed and suppressed' (Chodorow, 1978, p. 7).

Many radical feminists would challenge this view, proposing that men avoid sharing child-care because they do not want to, not because they are incapable of it. Further, by focusing upon the personality dimension, Nancy Chodorow fails to explore social, economic and other psychological aspects of parenting which might be changed to make shared parenting more of a reality (Richardson, 1992). Chodorow's analysis implies a determinism, with an emphasis on childhood socialisation, which potentially enables men themselves to employ the 'excuse' that they have not been brought up to be good at child-care! Child-care is not mysterious or part of early developmental psychology. It is learnt in adulthood, often following childbirth (Sluckin *et al.*, 1983). Also, as Lynne Segal points out in her discussion of Chodorow's work, such a view ignores the stability of power relations which privileges men over women (Segal, 1987).

Sue Sharpe (1976) proposed a very different view of how girls choose and learn to mother, and adopt the accompanying behaviour and beliefs associated with being a woman. Her study, which focused on white, Afro-Caribbean and Asian girls living in London, identified ways in which cultural stereotyping was used to represent the typical or ideal characteristics of women and men so that, despite class differences and changes over time, certain fundamental qualities and beliefs are pervasive and represented as feminine or masculine 'natures'.

School, family and the media all act to reinforce these images of the norm which, on the whole, designate men to have the more socially desirable traits. Even so, 75 per cent of the girls in Sue Sharpe's study said they would have chosen to have been girls, and part of their choice was 'the anticipated joys and satisfactions of becoming wives and mothers and caring for homes and children' (Sharpe, 1976, p. 206). She suggests that all the girls had been presented with an idealised image of motherhood and many appeared unaware of the oppressive conditions so that 'motherhood remains one of the most positive aspects of the feminine role for many girls'. Any conflicts between their futures as housewives and mothers, and the low social status of this role did not seem to arise. Some clue to this might be their perceived potential of life as a worker outside the home. The limited possibilities in employment, particularly for working-class girls and, because of racism, Black girls, contrasted with the possible fulfilment, satisfaction and apparent relative freedom and adult status which comes with the housewife/ mother role. So, despite the struggles the girls in this study witnessed in their own mothers' lives, the perceived satisfaction from mothering potentially outweighed the lack of satisfaction they saw in paid employment or unemployment.

More recent studies of adolescent girls bear this out. Hazel Beckett (1986) and Chris Griffin (1986, 1989) both observed the impact of gender socialisation on school leavers. Hazel Beckett suggests that marriage and motherhood were part of almost all her respondents' eventual aims. However, 'The question of motherhood versus career seems, for the majority, to have been stably resolved in the direction of combining them. They seem to have made a unanimous and unconflicted choice to experience occupational involvement, marriage and motherhood' (Beckett, 1986, p. 47). From this, she argues that female gender identity contains a flexibility that traditional theorists have ignored.

Chris Griffin's (1986) study of young women from a variety of backgrounds leaving school indicates similarly that 'Marriage and motherhood were seen as distant events which might occur some ten years in the future, but they were also seen as inevitable for most young women. Few financially feasible or socially acceptable alternatives were available, particularly for young working class women' (1986, p. 181).

Women mother, on the whole, because the motherhood 'parcel' is the one most open to them; other ways of life for women are not as well rewarded. Women are often (unless, for example, they are lesbian or single women) made to feel that there must be something wrong with them if they do not choose to be a mother. Men, on the other hand, although encouraged into a particularly well-defined masculine role which precludes 'mothering' (Archer, 1989), remain more able to choose whether, or how far, to involve themselves in child-rearing (O'Brien, 1984).

The experience of motherhood

Early sociological studies in the 1960s and 1970s indicated that the mother/housewife role (more common then) was not the ideal that women had been led to believe awaited them (Friedan, 1963). Gavron's (1966) study suggested that this cuts across social class groups. She found that expectations of marriage and motherhood contradicted the actual experience, which led to confusion surrounding women's roles. This affected her respondents' attitudes to marriage: 'For some wives of both classes marriage was seen as a kind of freedom; yet when it was combined with motherhood it became a kind of prison and they felt their freedom had been restricted before they had really been free at all' (Gavron, 1966/77 edn, p. 136).

Ann Oakley (1976) found a similar pattern of disillusion and suggested that while marriage and motherhood are seen as potentially providing the greatest life satisfaction for women, in reality they provide disappointment: 'Before they become mothers, women have a highly romanticised picture of what motherhood is . . . before motherhood is experienced they want more children than they do later' (Oakley, 1976a, p. 189).

What makes images of marriage and motherhood so appealing while remaining problematic in reality? Each step in women's 'normal' lives – finding a male partner, marriage and having children – increases the disappointment. The more women fulfil their destiny the more pernicious, it seems, is the trap. Why do women appear not to learn the lessons of their foremothers?

It is difficult for us to believe that our biological 'destiny' and 'instinctual drives' lead us to such a confusing end! It is often not until we come face to face with motherhood itself that we realise, through experience, that this idealised image is a patriarchal myth. What is it that causes this confusion? If motherhood is so bad, why do women not just opt out?

To understand this it is necessary to look in more detail at what mothering entails. Some studies have focused upon changes in role and social status following childbirth which demonstrate the reorientation of women's domestic and working lives once they have had a baby (Oakley, 1989); others focus on more psychological dimensions, examining it as a life transition which requires psychological adjustment in identity (Breen, 1975; and Nicolson, 1990). Although arguably a woman's identity as a mother starts in childhood, the process of actually giving birth to and caring for a baby changes most women's sense of themselves and also their values and beliefs. Many women report that it is not until they do become mothers that this change becomes a reality (Nicolson, 1988). The initial transition to motherhood is a shock in a number of ways – physically and emotionally (Oakley, 1980) and this does not appear to diminish with second or subsequent births (Nicolson, 1988). Each time the pressures, hard work and need to relearn child-care skills, confronts each woman anew. With each child, women are expected, and expect themselves to take primary child-care responsibility regardless of their other responsibilities or their specific abilities.

The practice of mothering (that is, the day-to-day experience of child-care and associated tasks) can be difficult and may lead to depression and unhappiness (Gavron, 1966; Oakley, 1980). However, motherhood is not always a negative, stressful, tiring, depressing experience brought about through an oppressive set of social structures. It can also be an exciting, rewarding and emotionally stimulating one. It is inherent paradoxes such as these that produce what Adrienne Rich describes as 'the suffering of ambivalence: the murderous alternation between bitter resentment and raw-edged nerves and blissful gratification and tenderness. Sometimes I seem to myself, in my feelings towards these tiny guiltless beings, a monster of selfishness and intolerance' (Rich, 1984, p. 21).

It is the children themselves who produce rewards, and the motherhood role includes the power, responsibility, satisfaction and independence that child-rearing brings, as well as the boredom, hard work and pain. Motherhood can introduce meaning and purpose into life as well as bring new opportunities for exploring a woman's own capacities, and forming relationships: 'Having children can bring greater vitality, fun and humour into our lives, as well as providing us with a different insight into the world' (Richardson, 1992, p. 1). Supporting this view, Mary Boulton (1983) found that several mothers reported their children to be rewarding companions, and that this overcame much of the negative experiences of routine child-care. Also, two-thirds of the women she interviewed found that motherhood gave them a sense of meaning and purpose, and they invested hopes and dreams in their children.

Motherhood certainly does qualitatively change women's lives, for better and worse. Even so, motherhood remains a low-status role in patriarchal society. Further, the image of the 'mother', things that mothers do, qualities they are perceived to have, and their additional strengths and achievements are often treated with a degree of disdain.

While there is no evidence that women are innately endowed with special maternal qualities, the experience of mothering does enable women (and men) to develop skills and capacities which can be gener-alised to other activities. Also, being a mother may stimulate particular ways of perceiving and explaining the world. This is what Sarah Ruddick has called 'maternal thinking' which, she claims, evolves through the very experience of being a mother who of necessity engages in the universal and culturally prescribed practices needed to maintain a child's life and nurture it. Socially and psychologically, women develop a distinctive way of seeing and being in the world in order to accomplish this, and mothers frequently adopt a style of 'humility' and 'cheerful-ness' to cope with their priority activities. However, 'Because in the dominant society "humility" and "cheerfulness" name virtues of sub-ordinates, and because these virtues have in fact developed in conditions of subordination, it is difficult to credit them, and easy to confuse them with self-effacement and cheery denial that are degenerative forms' (Ruddick, 1982, p. 81).

In fact, Ruddick argues, far from motherhood being a humble activ-ity, 'maternal thinking' demonstrates resilience and strength. Mothers need to be strong to cope with mothering and with the social conditions surrounding that role: child-rearing; running the home; managing com-plementary child-care arrangements; and maintaining relationships with their partners, family, friends and others. They have to be strong in order to maintain a sense of their own identity and fulfil some of their own needs and negotiate their way through the associated social subordina-tion. A feminist consciousness and feminist analysis of motherhood helps to enable this to happen, and makes women's strengths explicit.

The social conditions of contemporary motherhood

Contemporary motherhood, as argued above, exists within a clearly prescribed social context: 'Heterosexuality, marriage and having children are . . . all part of the western patriarchal parcel of rules for appropriate sexual relations and behaviour between men and women. Indulging in one without accepting the rest of the 'parcel' has been, and still is, widely condemned' (Gittins, 1985, p. 92). Each one of these conditions – heterosexuality, marriage, motherhood – entails a form of oppression. Social class, 'race', ethnicity, sexuality and economic status further impinge upon the social conditions of mothering for individual women and differentially influence their experiences. For example, the experience of some Asian women in Britain includes arranged marriages and different expectations and experiences in relation to their husbands, children and extended families, than that of many white middle-class women (Dosanj-Matwala *et al.*, 1990).

However, women who are married are expected to have children (Gittins, 1985) and most fulfil, or want to fulfil, this expectation. Women who do not have children may be seen as odd or abnormal, whether they fail to conceive by choice or through infertility (Woollett, 1992), as are married women seeking abortion (Macintyre, 1976; and Boyle, 1992). Although it has been argued that voluntary childlessness among married women has begun to carry less stigma than before (Campbell, 1985) motherhood is still the most popular option (Woollett, 1992).

Lesbians do not manage to escape male power over their fertility, and along with other unmarried women seeking fertility counselling, are often assessed as 'sick' or abnormal. Such women who succeed in becoming pregnant are treated with official caution (Burns, 1992), and attempts at targeting policy towards preventing pregnancy among this group are applied enthusiastically. For example, the case of the so-called 'virgin births' (reported widely in Britain during March 1991) illustrated the vehemence of professional and popular opinion towards those who choose to seek maternity without having sex with a man and without the intention of marriage (Nicolson, 1991).

There is no evidence, however, that women who *do* fulfil the obligations in this 'patriarchal parcel' necessarily live 'happily ever after'. Indeed, although the 'dream' has been accomplished, the experience frequently fails in its promise. Betty Friedan (1963), describing the experience of primarily white, married, middle-class, non-working mothers, expressed this as the 'problem with no name':

It was a strange stirring, a sense of dissatisfaction, a yearning that women suffered in the middle of the twentieth century in the United States. Each suburban wife struggled with it alone. As she made the beds, shopped for groceries, matched slip cover material, ate peanut butter sandwiches with her children, chauffeured Cub Scouts and Brownies, lay beside her husband at night, she was afraid to ask, even of herself, the silent question: 'is this all?' (Friedan, 1963, p. 13)

It was this feeling that began to awaken a feminist consciousness among some American women. How far, though, are such feelings representative of all mothers? What of other social groups: single parents, Black mothers, working mothers, lesbians, the poor and the working class? In what ways do they experience motherhood? The model of the married heterosexual two-parent, 2.4 children household is no longer the norm, although it is still the most powerful *image* of the family.

In the United States since the 1970s, the number of lone parent families has increased (Clarke-Stewart, 1982). Similarly, in England and Wales there was a sharp increase in the number of one-parent families, from 8 per cent in 1971 to 14 per cent in 1983 (OPCS, 1988). In 1988, 16 per cent of families in England and Wales were headed by lone mothers, of which the majority were single or divorced rather than widowed, which would have been more likely to have been the case during the 1970s. These lone mothers are more likely to have no academic or professional qualifications (48 per cent had none at all) and less than women who were married or cohabiting. Lone mothers are also more likely to have dependent children under school age and younger than those in the care of a lone father. All lone parents are more likely to live in rented rather than owner-occupied accommodation (OPCS, 1988). This suggests that lone mothers (a substantial and increasing number of mothers) are likely to be suffering economic hardship, poor housing and are unlikely to be able to exercise much choice over employment – because they are poorly qualified and because they are more likely to have young children dependent on them. Further, as Brown and Harris's (1978) large-scale study of depression in London clearly demonstrated, such conditions are all factors associated with long-term depression.

The divorce rates in the UK, Europe and the USA have also been steadily increasing over the past two decades. During the 1970s, the rate of divorce doubled in the UK, from 6 per 1000 to 12 per 1000 of the population. During the 1980s about 150 000 couples a year divorced compared with 51 000 in the 1960s. If these trends continue into the 1990s, the Office of Population Censuses and Surveys (OPCS) estimates that 37 per cent of marriages in the 1990s will end in divorce, with one in four children suffering parental divorce before they themselves reach the age of sixteen. So for an increasing number of mothers and their children, the married, heterosexual parenthood dream is a myth!

Further, for an increasing number of women, parenthood does not necessarily mean marriage. During the 1980s in the UK there was a marked rise in children born outside marriage – from 77 000 in 1980 to 177 000 in 1988. (Most were born to women under 25.) In fact, 28.9 per cent of births in England and Wales in 1989 were outside marriage (Birth Statistics, 1989). For married women, the mean age for having children increased to 28.4 years during 1989, which was the highest mean age since 1952 (calculated for all births not just first children), although most births still occur to married women between the ages of 25 and 34 years (Birth Statistics, 1989).

Another dramatic change has been an increase in childlessness; for women born in 1946, 11 per cent were childless in 1989; and for those born in 1951, 18 per cent were childless in 1989 (Birth Statistics, 1989). This may be because of later marriage and a high level of marital breakdown as well as reasons of infertility and decisions not to have children. The fact that, of women with 'O' Levels in England and Wales, more than 10 per cent said they did not want children, and 5 per cent of those without such qualifications, said the same, also adds an interesting dimension, indicating that motherhood now has some limits to its appeal.

Finally, the model nuclear family with the husband as breadwinner is challenged by the large number of women with dependent children who are also working outside the home in the UK, a trend mirrored in the USA (Clarke-Stewart, 1982). Between 1973 and 1988 in England and Wales there was an increase of 47–56 per cent, which was characterised by an increase in part-time working. Before 1986, lone mothers were less likely to be working outside the home, but since that time they too have been more frequently involved in part-time employment (OPCS, 1988).

The reasons women gave for wanting to remain at work were: liking their jobs; enjoying getting out of the house; and avoiding the boredom and frustration of the daily housework–child-care routine – reasons which emerge time and again in other studies (Hughes *et al.*, 1980; Sharpe, 1984; Brown *et al.*, 1986; and Nicolson, 1988).

However, working mothers do not experience comparable conditions to those experienced by working men. They are not nurtured or 'serviced' in the way the 'traditional' breadwinner expects to be. To be a working mother produces a range of additional stresses and problems for women. For instance, it is still primarily women who shop, cook, clean and manage the house, as well as child-care arrangements (Lewis, 1986; and Nicolson, 1990). Delivering and collecting children from childminders and nurseries still falls mainly to women, often because they work fewer hours outside the home, or do shift work to fit in with child-care arrangements. They manage to combine their roles as mothers, housewives and workers, but often at a cost to their health and the quality of their own lives.

Working mothers need good and adequate day-care provision for their children. This means that not only should the quality of the provision in relation to the children's care be stimulating and appropriate, but it should be available when needed and physically accessible. Many women need to leave their children with a substitute carer early in the morning, or until late at night, because they have shift work, or cleaning or factory jobs. Council and private day-care facilities are not normally flexible in this way. Even if they were to be, their availability is severely limited both by the number of places and by cost. One survey showed that of the two-thirds of pre-school children requiring day-care, only 40 per cent were catered for and a significant proportion of these places were part-time (Sharpe, 1984). Another limiting factor is the cost. State-run nurseries in Britain have strict criteria for allocating places, normally related to the interests of the child, so that mothers who do not have acute social or psychological problems will not qualify. In 1988, day-nursery places were available for only 2 per cent of children under five in England and Wales (Equal Opportunities Commission, 1990). Between the mid-1970s and mid-1980s, there was an increase in births and the number of women with dependent children who were working. Alongside this has been the continued cuts in public spending during the 1980s, suggesting that pressure on day-care places is still acute. More recently, though, the birthrate in England and Wales has fallen by 6000 between 1988 and 1989, to 6 877 000 (Birth Statistics, 1989).

Informal reliance on the extended family and friends, or upon childminders (approved or unapproved) is common, and although studies have shown that most mothers would prefer good-quality nursery provision (Tizard *et al.*, 1976), child-minders and informal arrangements are often more flexible. Women wanting to work 'unconventional' hours, who cannot afford day-nursery fees, are thus more likely to use child-minders. Child-minders themselves are usually mothers of pre-school children who thus work long, extended hours, often for low pay. It is a complex and vicious cycle. Nannies, au-pairs and nanny-shares are normally confined to more affluent mothers, as they not only require a salary or 'pocket money' but also accommodation and food. However, such child-care arrangements may carry their own problems: ill-trained, homesick teenage 'nannies' often needing mothering themselves.

Even if the provision for child-care were adequate, it would not be the end of the organisational problem for mothers. Working mothers consistently experience pressure from almost every sphere of their lives. Firstly, there is the difficulty of dealing with their own emotional reactions to working. Despite the financial/emotional/psychological need to work, and the satisfaction that working might bring, many mothers who do paid work suffer from guilt prompted by the continued claims that maternal deprivation arises when mothers go to work (Sharpe, 1984).

Another pressure is that the worlds of work and home are often in conflict. Where do priorities lie? Can mothers afford to spend extra hours doing overtime, attending union meetings or other extra work-related activities? There is often pressure from employers on women, to convince them that their loyalties lie at work and not at home (Wearing, 1984).

Mothers' relationships with partners (or attempts to find a new partner) are also likely to suffer because of the overall increase in workload, and the inherent conflicts often do not leave much energy for social or emotional life (Rapoport and Rapoport, 1976; and Wearing, 1984). There is also the question of division of labour in the home, particularly in relation to women living with male partners. The 'new man' has been demonstrated to be a myth (Lewis and O'Brien, 1987; and Nicolson, 1990), and though there is some evidence of an increase in fathers' interest and involvement in parenting, it seems this does not stretch to the daily child-care routine, or equal participation in activities such as nappy changing or taking time off work when a child is ill (Lewis, 1986).

Men are selective about what they will do and it is often middle-class men, who demonstrated the greatest 'promise' prior to becoming fathers, who are most likely to let their partners' down, with their reluctant or non-existent participation in domestic and child-care activities (Nicolson, 1990). In single-parent male households, most of the men appear to seek female support in order to limit their domestic roles. This varies from female friends and relatives to housekeepers, depending upon financial resources (O'Brien, 1984). While women are more likely to have to cope alone, there is some evidence that lone mothers may be less stressed than unhappily-married ones, and that they experience greater autonomy and satisfaction from coping alone (Brown *et al.*, 1986), although this may depend on their economic situation.

Feminism and motherhood: towards the future

> . . . the aim of feminism is not to free women from motherhood but from the conditions in which they find motherhood oppressive. (Richardson, 1992, p. 124)

Despite the research by sociologists, psychologists and other 'experts', it has been primarily through the effects of feminist writers that the reality of mothers lives, and the impact of the idealisation of motherhood and the family upon girls'/women's experience, that the conditions of motherhood were made explicit.

Feminist writers have paid sustained attention to the experience of being a woman and the ways in which motherhood impinges upon women's lives. Accounts of childbirth prior to the work of Ann Oakley tended to be either 'medical' or to extol the joys and fulfilment of childbirth for the truly 'feminine' woman. Feminist writers, while not denying the pleasures of children and the various experiences of child-birth, explored the medicalisation of birth and the ways in which wo-men's control (both as professionals and mothers) had been eroded (Oakley, 1980; and Nicolson, 1988). Recognition of patriarchal control of women's bodies inspired women's action in a number of ways over childbirth, for instance the 'right' to homebirths and the challenge to routine induced deliveries, fashionable in the mid-1970s.

Understanding the daily lives of mothers with young children was first made explicit by Hannah Gavron (1966), and was followed by other writers who have made further contributions towards explaining the conditions of motherhood (Boulton, 1983; and Sharpe, 1984). Gavron specifically explored issues of class and motherhood, and noted the way that for both working- and middle-class women, becoming a mother changed their lives as they lost their independence. However, her work also clarified the ways in which social class differences are exacerbated with the transition to motherhood, as social class is, in part, determined through men's levels of income and, as mothers, married and cohabiting women are more likely to be dependent on men.

Over ten years later, May Boulton's (1983) study supported the view that experiences of motherhood are to some extent class-related. Although all the mothers in her study reported positive and negative aspects of mothering: 'A large house and domestic conveniences . . . can lighten the burden of child care and give a woman the time and space for her interests apart from the children; a car and telephone can also help her maintain these interests as well as reduce her sense of isolation at home' (Boulton, 1983, p. 205). For the vast majority of women, these may only be obtained with the help of a partner and even then are clearly subject to social and economic status. Lone mothers, as argued above, are more likely to be poor, in bad housing and not well educated, so for them the oppressive conditions of motherhood remain unalleviated.

The married woman, however, despite the possibility of greater affluence, does not avoid oppression. Similarly to Friedan (1963), there are still issues about the lack of satisfaction in her relationship with her partner and the sense of pointlessness in her life when she realises she has been pursuing a myth. This myth has been sustained despite some changes in domestic roles. Since the 1960s and 1970s much attention has been paid to men's fathering. The representations by experts of the benefits to men and their children of being an active father were discussed earlier, along with the evidence that men's fathering is usually on their own terms. Popular ideas about the fatherhood role have changed so that men are expected to, and expect themselves to, enjoy children. The idea that particularly the middle-class men would take an equal part in domestic activities after becoming parents has, however, been challenged by a number of studies. For example, Charlie Lewis's (1986) study of fathers, which also demonstrated class differences in child-care involvement among men. Although all men in the study failed to achieve the mythical 'new man' status, working-class men tended to do less housework and less routine child-care than middle-class men.

Despite the centrality of motherhood in women's lives, and the contributions of feminist writers to challenging the invisibility of women's own experience as mothers, feminist analysis has had an ambivalent relationship with motherhood. This may be due in part to the overemphasis upon middle-class white women which emerged from work such as Friedan's, and perhaps a failure to understand the covert pressures towards maternity. Perhaps many feminist writers lost patience with the problems faced by 'comfortable' mothers when there were potentially more pressing political issues.

But women do still opt for motherhood and feminism has made the experience of lone mothers, lesbians, Black and working-class mothers more visible. It is the influence of these groups that has clarified the conditions under which motherhood exists and also the ways in which, paradoxically, motherhood may still be the best option for many (Griffin, 1989). Consciousness of feminism may not necessarily change potential choices, but it can make women from all groups aware of discrimination at work, and the lack of domestic equality in the home, as well as the added discrimination experienced by Black women and lesbians.

Conclusion

The influence of feminism has meant that women no longer have to see motherhood, heterosexuality and marriage as the only possible lifestyle, and myths portraying women's happiness as being confined within these parameters have now been exploded. This is not to say that issues of inequality have been removed from women's lives, but through analysis of the motherhood role and its consequences, women and men have access to feminist ideas as dynamic forces of social criticism and change.

Investigations by feminists of mothering in the 1960s identified the hard work and isolated conditions characteristic of most women's lives, in contrast to traditional studies which ignored women in favour of the 'family' and child development. The impact of scientific ideas about child-care and the 'maternal deprivation thesis' had meant that women not only struggled in their tasks individually, but also felt guilty for wanting anything for themselves beyond the home, and inevitably 'failed' as mothers. However, gradually these negative individualistic images of motherhood, which presented a sense of hopelessness, were replaced through a focus upon the social and economic conditions of mothering. This served to unite women in an awareness that the 'failure' was not personal but was a consequence of capitalism and gender inequalities. Also, women began to identify the special and important qualities associated with the motherhood role, which strengthened their ability to cope in a number of spheres.

Such confidence has led to feminist campaigns for change, including ones for better and more flexible day-care, maternity benefits, equal opportunities and improved employment conditions for women generally. Women now feel they have greater choice as to whether or not to have children, or marry, or to opt out of heterosexual relationships altogether. Motherhood and womanhood, although still linked, no longer prescribe women's lives as they did in the 1950s.

Further reading

Paula Nicolson and Jane Ussher, *The Psychology of Women's Health and Health Care* (London, Macmillan, 1992). This volume, with essays by feminist psychologists, focuses specifically upon the ways in which mainstream psychology seeks to pathologise women's health and health care, particularly in relation to sexuality and reproduction. It includes chapters on infertility, pregnancy, abortion and health-care provision in relation to childbirth and early motherhood. It also explores the ways in which traditional psychological images of femininity equate with expectations of women's mothering.

Adrienne Rich, *Of Woman Born* (London, Virago, 1985). This extremely readable book provides a touching and powerful personal account of motherhood combined with rigorous feminist analysis of the experience of being a mother.

Diane Richardson, *Women, Motherhood and Childrearing* (London, Macmillan, 1992). This provides a lucid account of all aspects of mothering from a feminist perspective, drawing upon sociological, historical and psychological ideas. Like Adrienne Rich's book, it identifies the complex and often contradictory emotions surrounding the experience of mothering. It is also useful in clarifying the different ways in which feminists have conceptualised motherhood and the changes that the women's movement has brought about in women's lives.

Ann Phoenix, Anne Woollett and Eva Lloyd (eds), *Motherhood: Meaning, Practices and Ideologies* (London, Sage, 1991). This collection of essays focuses on particular aspects of mothering practice, concentrating upon the ways in which motherhood is socially constructed and how that construction effects the ways in which women become mothers. Chapters include an analysis of childcare manuals, and the messages that those convey, as well as exploring infertility, the experience of teenage motherhood and becoming a mother later in life. The influence of developmental psychology on the expectations about motherhood practice is also discussed.

10

Women and Reproduction
Jalna Hanmer

Early women's liberation movement theory on reproduction

This chapter is about biological reproduction; how it has and is being theorised and why it is central to some strands of feminist theory. The initial questions and issues of concern to women since the 1960s are discussed first. Scientific developments and medical technologies currently restructuring biological reproduction are described next, followed by a description of how this is impacting on rights, choice and self-determination for women. This chapter concludes with crucial issues for an agenda to secure a better future for women in the 1990s.

Feminists in the early 1970s were concerned with basic questions. Why are women oppressed? Who or what is oppressing women? Have women always been oppressed? How can our oppression be overcome? Feminists identified family, marriage, child-bearing, children, capitalism and men as basic causes of women's oppression, and biological reproduction was occasionally prioritised (Rose and Hanmer, 1976).

In the early 1970s in Britain, women formed groups around reproductive issues in order to provide advice and practical services in relation to pregnancy testing, contraception, abortion and childbirth. The aim was to gain control over our bodies. But during the 1970s this broad focus on reproduction was overtaken by political actions to retain the provisions of the 1967 Abortion Act. Throughout the 1970s feminist and Left political groups participated actively, as abortion was accepted as a major means of obtaining women's social equality with men, and much of women's political action on reproduction was redirected to retaining our limited right to abortion. From time to time, however, other major single issue campaigns arose, such as the attempt to retain London's women-only hospital, the Elizabeth Garrett Anderson; and the demon-

224

strations on the management of birthing at the Royal Free Hospital.

The demand to take up broader concerns, including those of Black women, and for a women-only organisation eventually led to a political split within the National Abortion Campaign in 1981. Upon the creation of the Reproductive Rights Campaign with its separate Information Centre, a broader focus on reproduction again became a dominant theme of practical political work: for example, objections to the testing and introduction of Depo-Provera, the long-term contraceptive injectable, was the focus of a sustained campaign. The National Abortion Campaign continued as a single-issue mixed organisation.

Over this period the political emphasis on reproduction shifted from women's liberation to women's rights, but, based on a more critical approach to science and technology, a strand of thought and action rooted in the concepts of oppression and imperialism began to re-emerge in the mid-1980s. The women's liberation movement was initially largely uncritical of science and technology, although the medical establishment received substantial criticism (Ehrenreich and English, 1979). Scientific and medical interventions in conception (for example, the hormonal contraceptive pill) had been welcomed, with few dissenting voices. Women gradually became more critical throughout the 1970s, however, as the immediate and long-term adverse health implications of developments such as the contraceptive pill, and medication prescribed during pregnancy such as DES (diethylstilbestrol), began to surface. Also, it became clearer how science and technology were being used to disempower growing numbers of women by extending interventions initially justified in exceptional circumstances only to routine use. Specific techniques identified from pregnancy and the birthing process include fetal monitoring, hormonal drips, ultrasound, inductions, episiotomies and amniocentesis (Rakusen and Davidson, 1982). Women found they could directly use some very low-tech interventions, such as self-insemination, or pregnancy-testing kits, but as the technology became more developed control passed increasingly into the hands of professionals, as, for example, with *in vitro* fertilisation (IVF), or the genetic testing of embryos.

Although these types of intervention were yet to be successfully used on women, in 1971 Shulamith Firestone in the *Dialectic of Sex* precipitated a debate on artificial reproduction. Her view is that because women bear children it has been possible for men to gain ascendancy over them. The reason she gives for this is that the subjugation of women is rooted in the division of labour which begins with the differing roles males and females have in the reproduction of the species. This division of labour is institutionalised in the family, therefore to free women it is necessary to eradicate the family. A transitional stage in the elimination of the family is to develop alternative life-styles and social institutions. Eventually science will enable the full realisation of this project by reproducing people artificially, thus eliminating the female reproductive function.

Firestone wanted to sketch a future in which women and men could live in harmony with full equality between the sexes. In her theory, science and technology ensure the new utopia by stripping the division of labour at the root of the family (that is the differential parts played by women and men in human reproduction) of any remaining practical value. The transitional phase includes strategies that are shared by feminist theorists from other perspectives, for example to open up jobs to satisfy individual social and emotional needs so that the pressure on women to establish family units is not so great, and to encourage alternative life-styles which imply non-fertility, such as lesbian mothers living on their own or in groups; and gay fathers, as well as collectives. Firestone believed that adopting new forms of living will, over several generations, lead to the obsolescence of the monogamous couple and family.

Her clearly-articulated analysis of reproduction both as the cause of and the solution to women's oppression has been criticised for biological reductionism and for her assumption that science, technology and the state are neutral institutions. Historically, her work is important to the feminist process of clarifying what and who is oppressing women, but unfortunately for an understanding of feminist theory, her work continues to be used negatively to caricature all radical feminism as essentialist or biologically determinist.

Other theorists were less centrally committed to a single strand of analysis. Juliet Mitchell (1966), a Marxist feminist, sought to specify the separate structures that form the complex total of women's oppression. She identified production, reproduction, sex and socialisation as the four structures. Each of these is to some considerable extent autonomous of the others, and each has its own momentum.

Maria Rosa Dalla Costa (1972) moved the analysis of reproduction in another direction, one that had immense influence in the development of Marxist feminist analyses in Britain. She argues that women are engaged in social production through housework, including child-bearing and child-rearing. Dalla Costa expands the concept of reproduction to include the social reproduction of the paid industrial worker through housework, and of the next generation of workers. She argued that these forms of reproduction are not just private, but create labour power and therefore value, which makes women part of the working class.

Although written around the same time, the work of the French radical feminist Christine Delphy (1970) was not translated into English until 1974. She too argues that housework creates value, and that it does not seem to be so because women do not receive a wage for their work because they are trapped in a non-capitalist form of production more closely approximating that of master and slave. Delphy is not concerned with biological reproduction as a form of labour power, while Dalla Costa sees it as intimately linked with domestic work generally, although she makes only a brief reference to the need for women to control reproductive science and technology. Dalla Costa and Delphy are highly critical works within a Marxist framework, but it was left to Mary O'Brien some years later to develop a materialistic analysis based on biological reproduction (1981, 1989).

Carla Lonzi of the Italian group Rivolta Feminile (1972) is another radical feminist profoundly influenced by Marxist analysis, and quite unlike Firestone, who ignored power in analysing the role of science and technology. Like Mitchell, she separates reproduction from sexuality, but unlike Mitchell she does not regard the split between sex and reproduction to be impossible for the dominant social class to accept. Rivolta Feminile argued that a male world is able to turn the separation of reproduction and sexuality to a male and ruling-class advantage. They describe men as 'colonizing women through the penis culture', and that while the split between sexuality and reproduction made possible by contraception and abortion tends at present to aid women, it also increases male power over women. Men obtain sexual satisfaction, and their dominant status is amplified by permissiveness. This issue began to be raised with the development of birth-control and continues to be important for radical feminist writing on sexuality today (Coveney *et al.*, 1984; and Jeffreys, 1985, 1990). The conclusion that Rivolta Feminile draw is that women should only consort with men to conceive while real sexuality and tenderness can be obtained with other women.

While the women's movement all over the world seeks in some general sense to increase women's control over our own bodies as part of the wish to control our own lives, the theoretical analyses of the early 1970s which focused on reproduction were concerned to identify and reorganise the oppressive conditions under which women live in relation to men. These early feminists were writing at a time when fundamentally reshaping women's role in biological reproduction was understood to be utopian, although research and experimentation was rapidly developing and the first IVF conception and birth, in 1978, of Louise Brown was only a few years away. The themes they explored – women's relation to reproductive science and technology and how its use may alter gender relations – retain their relevance for feminist theory. Not only are we rapidly entering an era when a technological reorganisation of human reproduction is partially and may become fully possible, but the issues raised by early feminists have not been resolved.

Before going further it is necessary to describe the new reproductive technologies, including recent contraceptive developments.

Scientific developments and medical technologies

To look first at contraception, there are a number of new developments that are based on hormonal interventions as well as inter uterine devices (IUDs), barrier methods such as the diaphragm, and sterilisation.

- The hormonal contraceptive pill is taken for a number of days each month. It ensures that the embryo does not attach to the lining of the womb and was developed through experimentation on Black women, particularly in Puerto Rico.
- Long-acting hormonal injections that last for three to six months are licensed in Britain and tend to be used on the most vulnerable women, that is, those deemed not sufficiently reliable to use other contraceptives. Working-class and Black women are more likely to be prescribed injections with Depo-Provera, which works by ensuring that the embryo does not attach to the lining of the womb (see Chapter 11).
- Hormonal implants that last up to five years are currently being tested on women in Latin America and Asia, and have been accepted for use in the United States, but not yet Britain. The implants are surgically placed, usually in the upper arm, and cannot be removed without surgical intervention. These small hormonal rods slowly release hormones that stop the embryo from implanting in the womb. There is concern that if licensed in Britain, it will be used on socially-vulnerable women.
- Hormonal abortifacients such as the 'morning after' pill which is taken after unprotected sexual intercourse; (RU486) are being

developed. There are also various methods of surgical abortion involving both abdominal and vaginal interventions.

As well as for contraception, there is a growing market for hormonal products and services to increase conception. Britain set up the first governmental committee world-wide to consider the new developments in conception and how they might be regulated. The UK Report on Human Fertilisation and Embryology (Warnock Report, 1984) focused on the following techniques and processes:

- Insemination by donor (AID) is a simple procedure in which sperm is introduced into a woman's vagina as close to her cervix as possible. This can easily be performed by a woman herself without a doctor or medical agency/clinic.
- *In vitro* fertilisation (IVF) involves a number of procedures. First, hormones are administered to the woman to induce superovulation so that more than one ovum (or egg) is produced during the monthly cycle. The ova (eggs) are removed surgically by one of several egg-collection procedures. The ova are then fertilised in a laboratory dish and reimplanted in the woman's body. Gamete intrafallopian tube transfer (GIFT) is a variation of IVF, with the eggs replaced in the Fallopian tube with sperm so that fertilisation takes place there rather than in a laboratory dish.
- Egg or embryo transfer occurs when a woman receiving the ova or the embryo is not the same woman who provided them.
- Egg, sperm and embryo freezing are procedures for saving human genetic material that is surplus to immediate requirements.
- Embryo flushing or lavage is a procedure for washing out a woman's fertilised egg, or embryo, for diagnostic assessment or implantation in another woman, or for experimentation.
- Embryo experimentation involves using 'spare' embryos for research purposes legally, in Britain, for up to 14 days after fertilisation.
- Surrogacy involves a woman entering a contract to produce a child for someone else. She may be subjected to a number of interventions, such as artificial insemination, superovulation and IVF, and may use her own egg(s) or those of another woman.

The only technique discussed above that is unproblematic for women's health is artificial insemination (provided, of course, that the sperm used is not infected with HIV or sexually transmitted diseases). Hormonal stimulation and surgical interventions, including embryo flushing, involve both immediate and long-term health risks to the woman and/or her embryo/child (Holmes, 1989; Klein and Rowland, 1988; and Rosier, 1989).

- Sex selection involves the identification of the sex of an already-existing embryo. There are two basic processes to determine the sex of the embryo; as it develops in a woman's body through amniocentesis, a test of the fluid around the embryo in the sixteenth week, or a less-reliable test earlier on; or by screening an IVF embryo prior to entry into the women's body. Abortion, or implanting the desired sex only, achieves sex selection. This is happening in Britain and is justified as medically necessary to eliminate certain genetic conditions. In India, amniocentesis followed by selective abortion is widely practised for social reasons in order to achieve the birth of sons, not daughters (Kishwar, 1987).

Other potential interventions that as yet have not received approval in the UK for their use with humans are:

- Transgenic species involves mixing the genetic material of different species, including potentially that of human and other animal life.
- Cloning involves splitting the early embryo into separate cells so that genetically identical individuals are produced.

These techniques are currently being used on life forms other than the human. It takes little imagination to understand, for example, the commercial profit to be made by producing via cloning and sex selection high-milk-producing female calves for dairy and quality-meat-producing male calves for beef herds.

Other developments yet to be achieved are:

- Sex predetermination is an attempt to obtain the desired sex prior to fertilisation of the egg. As the sex of the human species is determined by sperm, various methods of as yet dubious reliability for identifying X- and Y-carrying sperm are being used or are being developed in Britain and elsewhere.

- Ectogenesis will involve conception and pregnancy outside a woman's body in an artificial womb.
- Genetic counselling of adults and diagnosis of embryos are practices involving the identification of chromosomes or genes believed to be defective, and assessment, advice or selection based on the eugenic principle of reproducing genetically 'desirable' traits/individuals. The possibilities for the genetic manipulation of embryos are increasing and we should anticipate that the Human Genome Project also will be of direct relevance in the transformation of human reproduction (Ewing, 1988, 1990a). This is a multinational, multibillion, multiyear project to record the chemical composition of the 100 000 or so genes that make up each individual.

To sum up, the techniques and processes of concern to the first governmental committee to consider these issues, the UK Report on Human Fertilisation and Embryology (Warnock Report, 1984), are those that alter human conception through insemination by donor (AID) and *in vitro* fertilisation and related procedures, or genetic continuity through egg or embryo transfer; embryo, egg and semen freezing and storage; embryo experimentation; embryo flushing; sex selection; so-called surrogacy; and potential practices such as the creation of transgenic species, cloning and sex predetermination. It is essential to look at the developments in genetics to fully understand the future potential of these technologies.

Feminist critiques of the new technologies and genetics

In the West, the birth-control movement was influenced by eugenic ideas and their political expression, as well as being a grass-roots movement to help women space their children in order to protect their health (Gordon, 1977). This double edge of control by women and of women by the state remains an unresolved issue today. Feminist critiques of contraceptive techniques, especially hormonal methods and IUDs, abortifacients, sterilisation, new reproductive technologies and genetic engineering increased during the 1980s.[1] Critical arguments centre on the social experiences of women and the social structures in which gender relations are embedded, contesting the truthfulness of claims of safety for both contraceptives and interventions in conception and, even more basic, of reproductive science as infertility treatment. These arguments offer an alternative analysis that links the technologies of contraception with those of conception on both a practical and a theoretical basis. The same hormonal products in differing combinations are used both to create and to eliminate pregnancy, and the power relations promoting pronatalism mirror those that deliver population control. This developing international analysis challenges the positive claims made by reproductive science and medicine, and the ideological justifications and social forces through which the technologies are directed at women's bodies.

One critique of these technologies challenges the notion of choice for women by arguing that the pressures on women to have children, but only when it is socially acceptable to do so, are so great that it is ridiculous to speak of choice. Women are seen as having no option about whether or not to have babies. They must be prepared to go through any emotional and physical pain, distress and effort to achieve a successful pregnancy. Motherhood is socially compulsory, even in countries with coercive population control policies. This is not the same as arguing that women are passive robots who do not know their own minds, but rather that their 'choices' are highly circumscribed.

The new reproductive technologies are used to uphold traditional notions of motherhood and femininity via the selection of those who should or should not be mothers. While contraception and abortion can be seen to play the same social role, until the recent advent of fully-medically-controlled contraceptives, many women in the West and North felt they were largely in charge of reproductive decisions. Women in the South and East have been subjected to contraception, including sterilisation, for some years, in conditions that cannot be described as free choice. As in the West, the social factors of class, 'race' and ethnicity, and male domination determine differential treatment of women.

In Britain, we see these social forces at play with the new reproductive technologies; women who are not dependent on men are largely deemed to be unacceptable for motherhood by the medical gatekeepers and the state: that is, lesbians, virgins, and women not in stable cohabiting relations with men. Also, the technologies tend to be expensive, with access usually limited to those who can afford to pay. Restricted access is damaging to women as a group, as it creates divisions between women and reaffirms the patriarchal rule that husbands or male partners and fathers have unrestricted authority over women and children. But in terms of individual experiences, limiting access can be a protection against psychological and physical abuse as the documenting of women's experiences of IVF programmes demonstrate (Crowe, 1985; Fleischer, 1990; Klein, 1989, 1990; Koch, 1990; and Williams, 1988, 1990, 1991).

Women's 'choices' to pursue IVF and related technologies are shaped by a variety of factors, including the expectations and demands of others amongst women's families and friends; the presentation of the technologies by medical staff as unproblematic; and, by implication, likely to lead to a child. Clinics, particularly commercial clinics, use a variety of techniques to encourage women to enter programmes (for example, open days) and to continue with programmes, such as newsletters organised by patients in which women tell their stories of repeated attempts and determination to not give up, or support groups with similar aims. Women rarely receive counselling on how women may have a fulfilling life without producing their own biological child.

While hormonal conception contains health risks for women, it is largely reliable. But the new reproductive technologies do not offer as effective a means of having babies as is implied in the media and claimed by medical teams. In the first investigation of success rates Gena Corea and Susan Ince (1987) found that clinics in the United States (as elsewhere) were including chemical pregnancies, that is, a rise in a woman's blood levels of certain hormones for several days only; pregnancies that spontaneously abort; and still births, as well as living babies. Because the latter is the way in which people in general understand, and therefore interpret, claims of success, the charge is misrepresentation (Klein, 1989).

Registers of children conceived by IVF and associated techniques are being set up in a number of countries, but the National Perinatal Statistics Unit in Australia is the first to report on the worse health outcomes for children born by IVF (Batman, 1988). These include prematurity (26.9 per cent in 1986); delivery by caesarian section (43.9 per cent compared with 15–18 per cent of pregnancies generally); an increase in multiple births and medical problems associated with low birth weight and prematurity; a higher percentage of babies with major abnormalities, primarily neural tube (spina bifida) and cardiac problems (transposition of the great vessels) (2.2 per cent rather than 1.5 per cent of births generally). The Australian Report concludes that the success rate for an unproblematic live birth is 4.8 per cent: that is, fewer than 5 women from each 100 who undergo IVF will have a completely healthy baby, while another 3 women will have a child with health problems. The remaining

92 per cent will not have a child. Even these success rates are open to challenge, as cases have been reported of women who conceive naturally before their turn for IVF treatment arrives, and even of a child being born who was conceived naturally along with two others inserted through IVF techniques.

The British 'success' rates are very similar. The Voluntary Licensing Authority For Human In Vitro Fertilisation and Embryology in 1989 cites the live birth rate per treatment cycle in 1987 as 10.1 per cent; in 1986 8.6 per cent and 1985 also 8.6 per cent (VLA, 1989, p. 19). Small centres in the UK are identified as achieving 3.1 per cent live births per treatment cycle (VLA, 1989, p. 19), and some clinics have never produced an IVF baby. Their success rate is zero, yet they continue to advertise their services to the public and to intervene in women's bodies as if this is not the case. Described as failed technology, there are demands for its cessation (Klein, 1989), but in Britain the state has responded by setting up a licensing authority for IVF centres and research.

Another line of attack criticises the new reproductive technologies for being about something very different from what is claimed; not about helping women to have children, but rather being an aspect of genetic engineering closely associated with new developments in biotechnology (Bartels, 1988; Hynes, 1989a, 1989b, 1989c; Kollek, 1990; and Shiva, 1988). This includes the attempt to map the entire gene pool, beginning with the Human Genome Project, to 'improve' human embryos through genetic testing and ultimately adding and subtracting genetic material (Kaufmann, 1988; and Leuzinger and Rambert, 1988). Modifying and eliminating people before birth gives a new twist to eugenics (Bridenthal, Grossman and Kaplan, 1984; Degener, 1990; Ewing, 1988; Kaupen-Haus, 1988; Schleiermacher, 1990; and Zimmermann, 1990). It can also be seen to be about men as a class taking control of women's reproductive activities as husbands/male partners/fathers; scientists/medical practitioners; businessmen; and governmental leaders (Hanmer, 1981, 1983, 1985; and Hanmer and Allen, 1980). For example, in India there is growing resistance by women to the expanding use of amniocentesis to detect female foetuses, followed by abortion (Lingam, 1990; Patel, 1989).

These critiques also analyse the differential interventions into the bodies of women in the South and East, and the North and West, and find common ground. An analysis of the ways in which governments, aid agencies to the so-called Third World and multinational pharmaceutical companies are intermeshed is slowly gaining momentum, particularly in relation to population-control activities (UBINIG, 1991a; Gupta, 1991; International Solidarity for Safe Contraception, 1990; McDonnell, 1986; and Nair, 1989). In Britain, the provision of IVF and other new reproductive technologies are dominated by commercial interests. Bourn Hallam, the largest reproductive technology centre in the world, is owned by the multinational pharmaceutical company, Ares Serono. Ares Serono manufactures, wholesales and, with Bourn Hallam, retails, hormonal and other products to women. Bourn Hallam also serves as a research and development centre for Ares Serono.

Conceptualising science, ethics and a woman-centred analysis

Robert Edwards, a key figure in the development of the new reproductive technologies, argues in his popularising work on IVF after the birth of the world's first 'test-tube' baby, Louise Brown, that IVF is medical treatment for infertility (Edwards and Steptoe, 1980). In his later popular work he defends the social desirability of surrogacy and embryo experimentation (Edwards, 1989). These issues may at first sight appear unrelated, but what they have in common is the redefinition of motherhood (Bartels *et al.*, 1990; Chesler, 1990; and Rothman, 1989).

Many women are afraid to object to embryo experimentation, whatever their private misgivings, as their greater fear is that to do so will endanger the 'rights' of women to abortion. The reasoning is that if embryos and foetuses up to 20 weeks can be aborted, then there is no logical reason why embryos cannot be experimented upon. From this perspective, to protect embryos from experimentation necessitates protecting embryos and foetuses from abortion. The argument is framed around the concept of 'right to life'.

Edwards too makes these connections, but in a different way. He justifies embryo experimentation because experimentation on foetal material obtained through abortion is routine, and has been for many years (Edwards, 1989, p. 148). With regulatory guidelines introduced by the state he sees no difficulty in obtaining the full range of foetal material for experimentation, as 'Most studies in vitro can be completed by day 25, and after that the current rules for using tissues from aborted foetuses will suffice. So the time of research in dispute is really very small indeed' (1989, p. 173). As he points out, the time in dispute is becoming smaller as the new abortive drug, RU486, will enable embryonic tissue to become available at 18 to 20 days.

Edwards also dismisses criticisms of embryo experimentation as a new form for the expression of eugenics, or selective breeding. Edwards distinguishes between negative and positive eugenics, defining negative eugenics as avoiding the birth of children with defects while positive eugenics is making children superior by changing their characteristics. Eugenics embody value judgements about which types of people and which characteristics are to be preserved and promoted, and which are to be eliminated. In societies dominated by social inequalities, such as our own, it is inevitable that women, Black people, the disabled, and the poor will be less valued, and that certain physical, mental, personal or social characteristics will be classified as undesirable. Given the implementation of eugenics in Western history it is foolish to imagine that in medicine the line between what is ethical and what is not is clearly demarcated (Klein, 1989b).

There are ethically dubious practices taking place in medicine today. IVF is a painful and stressful procedure with low success rates that is applied to fertile as well as infertile women. Male fertility problems are routinely being dealt with by submitting fertile women to these procedures as well as women whose condition remains undiagnosed. Women with children who have undergone sterilisation and later remarry are viewed as appropriate candidates for IVF. There is a tendency within society generally to dismiss the vulnerability of women to men, as biological reproduction becomes progressively under their control, as being negative, or pessimistic, or 'science fiction'. But given these practices we can deduce a social belief that men own women's reproductive function. The social rule is that each woman must produce biological children for a particular man should he so wish it.

But control of women's reproductive processes can be exercised in other ways. The most extreme scenario that has been considered is to phase out women altogether or to keep just a few as 'queen bees' for their eggs. Women will become redundant to the process of creating new life once immature eggs, for example foetal eggs, can be matured, and ectogensis becomes a reality. Less extreme future visions retain women in more-or-less their present numbers to caretake the results of the biological manufacture of human beings to exact specification. Science and technology are systems of social relations resonating with power differentials. We must face the fact that, given the power and interests of men in science and society, those who decide on what is desirable in relation to human reproduction are unlikely to be those most affected, that is, women.

The central contradiction of these developments is that the new reproductive technologies are presented as a return to the natural, while replacing a biological activity with technology. Doing this challenges the naturalness of biological processes while claiming to restore to every woman her natural nature. The Warnock Report, for example, does this by justifying the technologies as a response to infertility, even though the report does not consider the causes of infertility, nor available and needed infertility services (Humm, 1988; Pfeffer and Quick, 1988; and Solomon, 1988).

Rights, choice and self-determination for women

The struggle of women to claim a personhood that is more than 'nature' or 'natural' pre-dates the French Revolution, with its demands for individual rights. Rights, nature and the natural are shifting terrain in relation to the definition of woman; in particular, in relation to women as wives/heterosexual partners, mothers and sexual beings. More recently these issues have been expressed as a central demand of the post-1968 wave of feminism for control over our bodies through the prescient slogan 'Our Bodies – Ourselves'.

Being a wife, heterosexual and a mother are relational statuses to men. The socially validated uses of the new reproductive technologies illustrate that our relation to men is more fundamental to society than women's relation to the future generation and their specific biological children. The primacy of the relation of these statuses to men surfaces in the re-emergence of demands and legislation around 'fathers' rights' (Stolcke, 1988), in the ways in which women become invisible or are reduced to body parts when the state considers the new reproductive technologies; by the dissociation of embryos and foetuses from women's bodies through so-called 'foetal rights'; in the demands for embryos for experimentation; and in the social opposition to so-called virgin births or lesbian motherhood.

While 'wifehood' as a biological need, that is, to ensure mental and physical healthy functioning, is being denied, and heterosexuality as a natural system is being questioned by feminists, to do so can be seen as leaving women vulnerable. Andrea Dworkin (1987) argues that Right-wing women understand only too well that to challenge wifehood is to make women vulnerable to servicing not just one man but many, and to economic poverty. Feminists resist these vulnerabilities by demanding a better position for women in the labour market and in society generally, rather than strengthening the idea that being a wife is a natural facet of being female.

But with motherhood, the issues are not so simple or so well worked out. Not having children was a feminist political issue in the 1970s that led to accusations that feminists were anti-mothers. The so-called need to mother can be more complicated for women to confront than any other aspect of life. As with being a wife, it is constructed through hetero-sexuality as a system of social relations. Within heterosexuality, the issue is seen as contraception, abortion, the sterilisation of women with learning difficulties, or spacing children so that 'every child is a wanted child'; the 'problem' is to control the fertility of women, not men. The hidden agenda is that women remain sexually available to men at all times through the regulation of their fertility and its outcome: pregnancy and birth. Women's fertility is seen as a problem to be addressed through international population control policies – sometimes urging women to have children and sometimes denying women the ability to have children – and not the difficulties women have in controlling the access of men to their bodies. The 'need' to mother and the heterosexuality on which it is based is rarely challenged, but only when, where, how and with whom, as not only are women the biology to be controlled, we are also believed simply to *be* our biology, and therefore we must have children. The media hype is of perfect babies for perfect, and grateful, heterosexual couples.

It is because of the general acceptance of women as their biology, and as the biology to be controlled, that the new reproductive technologies can be presented successfully as a choice for women. The political position that centres on rights is not unlike that of the mainstream because of the strength of the heterosexual belief that women must be available to men, and the pronatalism that permeates all our Western societies, although the arguments take a different form. Surrogacy, for example, can be seen as a way of strengthening women's rights, includ-ing the rights of the gestational mother. The view is that surrogacy contracts should be legally enforceable, even if the gestating mother changes her mind, because these contracts recognise legal parenthood as a matter of autonomous decision-making before conception. Money payments should be permitted to gestating mothers because in the result-ing transformation of reproductive consciousness male–female biolo-gical differences will be transcended and women can reclaim their pro-creative power (Shalev, 1989; and Cohen and Taub, 1989). All the technologies can be seen as unproblematic if the issue of power is not acknowledged; for example, Singer and Wells (1984) argue for new ways of making babies as an unqualified benefit, as choice is being extended. They define any curtailment of access and future developments, for example of ectogenesis, as an act of paternalism. The degree of criticism of science and technology in human reproduction also affects feminist views on the new developments and leads to more positive assessments, albeit with reservations (Birke, Himmelweit and Vines, 1990; and Stanworth, 1987).

Mothers' rights and fathers' rights

The respective 'rights' of women and men in relation to biological reproduction is under constant dispute, and the new reproductive technologies offer opportunities for significant changes. In human reproduction the interests of women and men are not identical, nor do the physical processes of conception, gestation and birth affect women and men in the same way. But how are these differences to be understood? There are two strands to consider. The first is the denaturalising of motherhood through increased medical and scientific intervention into the processes of conception, pregnancy and birth, while utilising an ideology of women's nature as justification for these interventions. Naturalising fatherhood through these same interventions, utilising the ideology of the central importance of the male genetic contribution, is the second.

Mary O'Brien has developed a theoretical explanation around these issues by reinterpreting the work of G. W. F. Hegel and Karl Marx on the natural and nature (O'Brien, 1981, 1989). She argues that in childbirth women labour, transforming biological reproduction (the natural) into a human activity. Men do not labour in the same way, as the ejaculation of sperm is the sole contribution to biological reproduction. Mary O'Brien argues that they are alienated at the point of biological reproduction because they do not labour. If we accept this as a premise, it is logical to argue that science and medical technology can become the social process by which men attempt to overcome their alienation. As men labour through science and technology with biological reproduction, of necessity they conflate nature and the natural with women's bodies. The outcome of this fusion is that it is women who are to be transformed as they become the 'natural nature' on which men work. The new reproductive technologies do not alienate men, but overcome their alienation by enabling them to control 'natural nature', while the new reproductive technologies increase women's alienation by intervening with the work process in which women are engaged, as they turn a natural biological process into a social activity, the production of new life. In the shift in alienation from men to women, social power between men and women also shifts. Men gain, women lose.

Mary O'Brien has been criticised by some feminists for producing theory rooted in biology, but the commodifying of things and life processes is structurally related to capitalism and the societies in which it has developed. It is logical in a capitalist economic system that human reproduction and all life processes should be turned into commodities, as ownership is the highest social goal of the individual. However, these same social relations of science and medical technology were being developed in previous socialist societies in relation to women's bodies and life processes generally. This is because any economic system can restructure its ideology in order to serve its economy and power structures. Gender domination varies its forms as societies alter over time, and it is only now, in the latter part of the twentieth century, becoming possible to intensify control over women through highly-developed technologies based on reproductive biology.

Denaturalising motherhood while naturalising fatherhood begins with the discourse on the new reproductive technologies. This is so powerfully organised that oppositional views are marginalised or totally excluded from public debate. In Britain, it has been particularly difficult to gain popular media attention for viewpoints that challenge the new reproductive technologies as infertility interventions. The media exposure can only be described as free advertising, as smiling IVF doctors and couples with babies, and heart-rendering stories of surrogacy, epitomise the coverage. These representations draw primary strength from a particular view of women, whose need to mother is unquestionable.

Reducing women to biology facilitates our social disappearance. These basic assumptions enable government reports, beginning with the Warnock Report in the UK (Warnock Report, 1984), to not mention women, but to write of disembodied parts of women's bodies or of couples. The discourse is of technical processes, in which the differences between the contribution to and impact upon women and men inherent in the new reproductive technologies is absent. When bodies appear it is as couples who make equal contributions to biological reproduction. It is becoming common parlance, for example, to hear of 'pregnant couples'.

Dismembering bodies and reconstituting them in new forms enable embryos to be seen as separate from the women in whose bodies they thrive. Embryo research can then be presented as not affecting women differently from men. The foetus becomes an independent subject whose interests can be defined as in opposition to that of its mother and further, it may become necessary to protect the foetus from a hostile maternal environment. The arguments can then rage on when embryos become sufficiently human to be legally granted an independent existence. The embryo as part of the mother, subjectively and objectively, is disengaged and mothers' rights and fathers' rights cannot be differentiated. (These points also apply to the abortion debate.)

Another form of supposed biological equality between women and men is to equate sperm collection for donor insemination with egg retrieval. The very obvious difference in the methods of obtaining eggs and sperm, however, make it less easy to obscure their different meanings for women and men in terms of health outcomes, bodily interventions, and the commitment of time, energy and psychological resources. Equating selling eggs with selling sperm is less likely to gain social acceptability, as the unsuccessful libel action brought by an IVF doctor in Austria against women who objected to his egg-buying illustrates (Riegler and Weikert, 1988, 1989).

The rights of individual men as well as men as a social group are also being strengthened through legal actions brought by individual men, and through legislation arising out of government reports and European agreements. Individual men are demanding more 'rights' to 'their' children generally; for example, custody and control of children who have been born; bringing actions to require women to carry foetuses to full term (*Observer*, 30 July 1989). They also are demanding more control over whether or not 'their' children can be born. A custody action in the USA over frozen embryos, which the woman wanted to use and the estranged husband refused on the grounds that his wife wanted to make him a father against his will, illustrates the extension of legal control in disputes between women and men over children (*The Daily Telegraph*, 8 August 1989).

The competing claims in the American case turned on the physical and social impact on women and men of the new technologies, while the lawyers appealed to existing law. The woman argued that the embryos represented more than eight years of tests and surgery, and a test-tube baby was her only chance of having a child. The man said that it would be 'very unsettling' to bump into his child without knowing it in ten years' time. His lawyer argued that the embryos are joint property to be disposed of like any other assets in a divorce, while hers appealed to tradition based on biology: 'It has never been within the man's power to cancel a pregnancy once an egg has been fertilised' (*The Daily Telegraph*, 8 August 1989). Expert witness and law professor comment was that the husband would be the most hurt by losing, and therefore the case should be decided in his favour. The ultimate judgement turned on a principle that disempowers women even though she won the case and was allowed to implant the embryos, that of embryo rights, that is, the right-to-life argument. This disempowers women because embryos are given an existence independent of the maternal environment, even though they cannot at the present time become a child without it.

These individual legal actions are being located within the law relating to disputes between women and men over children. For example, when divorce is legally contested, men are likely to extinguish a mother's 'natural' rights, even to very young children. The 'rights' of unmarried men, sperm donors even, are beginning to be established and a women's 'right' to abortion without the man's permission is beginning to be contested (*Observer*, 30 July 1989). These new 'rights' are being gained in a social situation where it is extremely difficult to extinguish a man's rights of access to 'his' children. Men are not expected to take responsibility for the day-to-day care of children. Theirs is a right based on authority, so even a man who kills his wife may be given custody of her children once out of prison. As the exposure of male abuse in families grows, so too does the counter-attack. In Britain, 'Families Need Fathers', and similar organisations of men, vociferously argue that harm is being done to men and to children by the 'unfair' treatment men receive in courts. The attack is on women's 'privileged' position in relation to children.

Law and legislative issues include the development of contract law to severely limit or extinguish women's rights to their biological children, particularly in US surrogacy cases (Raymond, 1988a, 1988b). The contract takes precedence over a woman's wishes: so if a woman, prior to artificial insemination, has agreed to hand over the child she will gestate, courts will not subsequently allow her to keep the child. The rights of women to their illegitimate children is also changing in Britain. In the past, the threat of non-recognition of the child by the father was an important social and economic control regulating biological reproduction through marriage. As this status becomes less stigmatised, and as the proportion of illegitimate births continues to rise, unmarried men are being given the same rights to children that married men have. This is being legally codified within Europe as a result of a Council of Europe agreement, and in Britain via the Children Act 1991.

Spain was the first European country to legislate on the new reproductive technologies, with the Law on Technologies for Assisted Reproduction, 1988 (Varela and Stolcke, 1989). This law substantially implements the recommendations of the UK Warnock Report, although discriminatory treatment of single women was modified so that any woman able to work independently of her marital status and her life-style is deemed to be suitable for IVF and other interventions. But, if married, the consent of her husband is required.

In Britain legislation arising out of the Warnock Report, the 1990 Human Fertilisation and Embryology Act, means that the consent of husbands and cohabitees is necessary for women to have access to IVF and other treatments, and effectively limits IVF, artificial insemination, and other interventions in conception to married or stable cohabiting heterosexual couples. Fathers' rights are clearly specified in the Act.[2] The legislative attempt to criminalise the use of AID for single and lesbian women, however, failed, possibly because of feminist opposition, the difficulty in implementing any such law and the likelihood of its challenge in the European Court of Human Rights.

International feminism: an agenda for the 1990s

We are living in a time of increasing scientific and medical intervention in women's bodies. Today, so-called Third-World women are sterilised and given contraceptives dangerous to their health, while 'First-World' women are expected to have babies (Parsons, 1990). The Norplant trials in Bangladesh provide one of many examples of coercive population policy activities, in which women are used for experimental purposes without their consent, and 'motivated' to accept the five-year hormonal implants without basic knowledge of the problems that may result and, once these are evident, requests to remove the implants have been refused (Akhter, 1988; UBINIG, 1990, 1991a; and Reis, 1990). Within 'First World' countries, the same pattern exists between ethnic and racial groups. Thus in Britain, for example, it is easier to get a free NHS abortion if a woman is Black and working-class, and much more difficult if white and middle-class, although for any individual, sufficient funds to obtain a private-sector abortion is likely to override this problem. Today, skin colour, sexuality, social class, disability and age converge to weight women's chances of being selected as a 'fit' or 'unfit' reproducer, and a range of techniques are being utilised to ensure the appropriate outcome (Wichterich, 1988).

Surrogacy provides another way in which working-class women serve higher social classes and men (Arditti, 1990; Ewing, 1990; Kane, 1988, 1989; and Rowland, 1990). The well-reported Mary Beth Whitehead case in the United States, was of a working-class woman who entered a surrogacy contract for altruistic reasons. As her pregnancy advanced and with the birth of her daughter, she resolved to keep the child, but lost her legal case to the middle-class professional man who provided the sperm. Mary Beth Whitehead gave birth to an illegitimate child, but the use of contract law enabled her position as a mother to be largely denied.

Now that it is possible to implant an embryo genetically unrelated to the mother who gives birth, her claims upon the child are likely to be further eroded. In the United States, surrogacy agencies speak of the reproductive use of Black and 'Third-World' women as surrogates by economically and socially dominant white people (Raymond, 1989). The lower fees needed for the reproductive use (abuse) of women from countries of the South and East will spur on this development. In Australia, surrogacy is being publicly opposed by women, including feminists (Ewing, 1990b). In Britain, commercial surrogacy is not legally permitted, but expenses can be paid. Contracts are not legally enforceable, but the Human Fertilisation and Embryology Act 1990 makes it possible to treat a child born as a result of a surrogacy arrangement as the child of the commissioning parents, even though the surrogate mother is the legal mother at birth. In Britain, IVF clinics engage in surrogacy, in secrecy protected by the courts (Re W (Minors) (Surrogacy), 1991).

Women contribute more biologically and socially to the origin and care of children than do men. It is a false equality to attempt to eradicate these physiological and social differences by ideological fiat. Any discussion of ethics which does not recognise these basic factors can only be experienced by women as negative – as denying the basis from which ethical choices are made. But the recognition of difference is not to collapse women into the category of the natural or nature. With respect to the sperm-providing male, a woman's interests may be interlinked with his, but different. Her immediate task is the protection and creation of new life within her body. The male cannot do this and therefore the interests of women and men are different. Mary O'Brien (1981) argues that this is why genetic lineage matters so significantly for the Western male, and was in the past so important in regulating women's sexuality. Ideologically, for a woman-centred perspective to be taken seriously, the masculinist discourse of the various national reports on the new reproductive technologies and embryology must be seen as one-sided, and not representing the interests of women/mothers.

For women to control their reproductive processes, the importance of the power difference between women and men needs to be recognised. For women, choice can only have meaning if women are able to control the access of men to their bodies – and I mean this in a very general sense. This is a general point that arises out of the subordination of women so that, for example, in many countries the law decrees that rape in marriage is not a crime. Ideologically and legally, a woman cannot restrict her husband's access to her body. He can take that which the law defines as rightfully his by force if the woman attempts to deny him. Even in those countries and states where rape in marriage is now recognised as a crime, the prosecution of offenders and the success of these prosecutions is greatly reduced in comparison with stranger rape, because socially it is not fully accepted as crime. Translated into reproductive technology, this difficulty in denying men access to women's bodies is illustrated powerfully through the progressive utilisation of the bodies of fertile women to enable male subfertility to be overcome through IVF.

Women in Europe have shown that it is possible to confront the development of surrogacy and win. In Britain, legislation defines the mother as the woman who gestates the child; and a leading North American surrogacy agency was driven out of Germany (Winkler, 1988), but what of embryo research? To resolve how to defend abortion while opposing embryo research is a central issue. Holding both positions at the same time only makes sense when the relationship between the growing cells that will become a child, and the woman who will become a mother is acknowledged, and neither mother nor embryo is objectified.

While not all feminists object to embryo experimentation and demand that abortion be fully available to all women at any time during pregnancy, the objectification of the embryo/foetus that is implicitly involved in this position is damaging to women's civil status. Roe vs. Wade, the US Supreme Court decision that gave women an unrestricted right to abortion in the first three months, lesser rights in the next three, and no right to abortion in the last three, was hailed a victory by both pro-

and anti-abortionists, as it gave women limited rights to abortion as well as establishing the foetus as a person. Legal cases, including that of the frozen embryos described earlier, are now being decided on a principle that disempowers women; that is, that the embryo equals a child. While this can mean that women are allowed to gestate their embryos, the woman becomes an incubator: the subject is the embryo. The principle of foetal personhood is being used to legally legitimate the artificial split between the woman and her body part, the embryo. The frozen embryo case, for example, could have turned on the principle that the embryo is a part of the mother's body, and therefore hers to gestate or not as the case may be, while a child is a person viable in the environment and separate from the woman's body.

The defence of safe, legal abortion under women's control turns on the same principle. It is not sufficient to reverse the argument defining the embryo as object and woman as subject as this implicitly accepts the split between us. The dynamic relationship between embryo and woman, and her responsibility for the interior growth of the resulting child and, more likely than not, her continued responsibility for its survival and development once born, must be acknowledged. It is these responsibilities that should determine her sole authority to continue or not with the pregnancy. That the state should legally sever women's control over her embryonic material by legally granting the right to others to experiment upon it, should be a matter of concern to women. Legislation that protects embryos, degrading women to the status of foetal environment, as in Germany in 1991, is one possible way to further women's social subordination (Roach, 1989; Sadrozinski, 1989; and Waldschmidt, 1991).

Women who seek to challenge this dismembering discourse are trying to enter a game with three players; scientists/doctors; theologians; and lawyers. A feminist, woman-centred perspective is excluded rigorously, as it demands a fundamental reordering of knowledge, an epistemology in which woman is subject, her body whole, in one piece with the growing cells that will become a child. Ethical choice can have no meaning for women if our subjectivity is not recognised. The ethical issue for women is how to transform the dominant ethical discourse and practice in order to regain our bodies for ourselves. It can be argued that to control the access of men and their so-called ethics to our bodies is the central problem for women today. The major issue is the dissection of the female body into discrete parts, ideologically and literally, and specifically the severing of the relationship between the embryo and the womb (Mies, 1988). This is central for yet another reason: the social acceptance of the severing of the embryo from the woman is necessary for the next stages of scientific endeavour – genetic manipulation and ectogenesis. Once achieved, new possibilities for reshaping gendered dominance will then be fully realisable and, while the precise form this will take is not predetermined, we have no grounds for thinking women will be responding to events other than from a continuing position of social subordination.

The Feminist International Network of Resistance to Reproductive and Genetic Engineering (FINRRAGE) emerged in 1984, with growing awareness among some feminists that it was time to question the assumption that older and newer forms of contraceptives, the new reproductive technologies, and genetic engineering, are neutral or even benign (Hanmer and Powell-Jones, 1984; and Wichterich, 1988). FINRRAGE links women with common concerns and viewpoints from thirty-four countries. Women work within their countries choosing priorities for issues and activities suited to their specific situations, such as critical grass-roots investigation or academic research; providing information to women and the general public; lobbying; promoting cultural and political forms of opposition; and establishing alternatives for women, for example, counselling or self-help groups.

FINRRAGE seeks to develop a global movement of feminist resistance to population control policies and reproductive and genetic engineering, while confronting the issues that divide women because of differences in their social, economic, political and cultural situations. As with women from the North and West, women from the South and East also have differing politics on population control and the new reproductive technologies. Women's international meetings are important occasions for both dissent and agreement. Women's experiences of (and attitudes towards) reproductive technologies differ between as well as within countries, and sharing knowledge and participating in confrontations between opposing viewpoints can increase consciousness and move theory and politics forward. These occasions can result in the development of common strategies and analyses with women world-wide (Salomone, 1991; and UBINIG, 1991b).

Crucial issues for the 1990s include women continuing to organise themselves to refuse the new eugenics and the racism, anti-Semitism, heterosexism and ablebodiedism on which it is built; to resist the extension of the division of women into body parts, objectified, reduced to the carriers of male genetic material, the beneficiaries of the smiling, white-coated 'fathers' of hundreds of IVF babies that we see in newspapers and on television; and to build a responsive politics by listening to those whose bodies constitute the prime experimental matter for the control and replication of life processes.

Notes

1.   Arditti, Klein and Minden, 1984; Baruch, D'Adamo and Seager, 1988; Conseil Du Statut de la Femme, 1988; Corea, 1985; Corea *et al.*, 1985; Hanmer, 1981, 1983, 1985; Hanmer and Allen, 1980; Hartmann, 1987; Homans, 1985; Holmes, Hoskins and Gross, 1981; Hubbard, 1990; IRAGE and RAGE, all issues; Kirejczyk, 1990; McNeil, Varcoe and Yearley, 1990; Overall, 1987; Spallone, 1988; Spallone and Steinberg, 1987; Scutt, 1988; and Stanworth, 1987.
2.   The Human Fertilisation and Embryology Act 1990 specifies in Section 1.3.5., 'Conditions of licences for treatment', that 'A woman shall not be provided with treatment services unless account has been taken of the welfare of any child who may be born as a result of the treatment (including the need of that child for a father), and of any other child who may be affected by the birth'; and in Section 1.3.6., women being treated with men may not receive services involving sperm, egg or embryo donation unless the man (but not the woman) has been 'given a suitable opportunity to receive proper counselling about the implications of taking the proposed steps, and have been provided with such relevant information as is proper'.

Further reading

Jocelynne A. Scutt (ed.), *The Baby Machine: Reproductive Technology and the Commercialisation of Motherhood* (London, Greenprint, 1990). A collection of articles on IVF, surrogacy, biotechnology, genetic manipulations, interventions in conception, embryo research, eugenics, infertility, pregnancy, childbirth, motherhood, fathers' rights, women's reproductive choice and rights, law and commerce, and the relation between science, technology and society. This volume offers a view from women, both as objects of these interventions and as critical protagonists. This largely Australian collection exposes the international character of medical, scientific and commercial developments in reproduction.

Renate D. Klein (ed.), *Infertility: Women Speak Out About Their Experiences of Reproductive Medicine* (London, Pandora, 1989). The focus in this collection is on women's experiences of conventional infertility treatment, IVF procedures, the use of fertile women through surrogacy, dealing constructively with infertility without using reproductive medicine, the connection between reproductive technology and genetic engineering, and the impact on and resistance of women in the North and South. The aim is to present the experiences of women, and to offer alternatives that can work for individual women. The contributors are from the countries of the West, and Europe is well represented.

Gena Corea *et al.*, *Man-Made Women: How the New Reproductive Technologies Affect Women* (London, Hutchinson, 1985). Sex predetermination and sex selection is an age-old dream of mankind and this collection explores the current technologies and their use, gender preference internationally, the issue of 'choice' or voluntarism in sex selection, the concept of reproductive consciousness, and its transformation through the medicalisation of biological reproduction more generally. There are articles from women in the West and from India, the country with the most developed use of amniocentesis for aborting female foetuses. The extension of existing practices to a farming model applied to motherhood, the reproductive brothel, is explored. While sex predetermination techniques have not developed scientifically as quickly as anticipated due to technical problems, this remains on the commercial, medical and scientific agenda.

Michelle Stanworth (ed.), *Reproductive Technologies: Gender, Motherhood and Medicine* (Cambridge, Polity, 1987). This largely British collection proceeds from the view that technologies draw their meaning from the cultural and political climate in which they are embedded. The question is, can the cultural and political conditions be created so that reproductive technologies can be employed by women to shape the experience of reproduction according to their own definitions? The authors explore the relation of women to science and medicine; infertility and infertility services in the National Health Service; the restructuring of motherhood and paternal authority; the social and legal redefinition of the foetus; eugenics; surrogacy; and the various forms taken by technology in human reproduction.

11

Women and Health
Jenny Hockey

Feminist research and writing of the past twenty years has shown how the conditions of women's lives affect their health; for example, material conditions such as poverty, and ideological conditions such as constraining notions of femininity. Indeed, the dominant conceptions of health, which underly the theory and practice of medicine, can themselves be seen as one of the constraining conditions of women's lives. Both the medical view of what constitutes women's 'health', and medical responses to ill-health, help shape women's bodily and emotional experience.

A focus on women's health calls for an examination of aspects of their lives which make them vulnerable to illness. Questions must be asked about how social institutions, such as medicine, frame women's experience of health and illness and help to maintain their social subordination. In asking these questions, Women's Studies participates in women's struggles to redefine the term 'health' and take control of their own needs. It offers both a critique of existing health-related conditions and a commentary on the changes being made by women in these areas.

The conditions of women's health

Women are the major consumers of health care, and appear to suffer more ill-health than men. While they live longer, women's health none the less appears to be inferior to that of men. Why might this be the case?

Constance Nathanson's review of research explores the relationship between illness and the feminine role (1975). Many of the studies reviewed had difficulty in defining what was meant by 'illness'. Were they interpreting the relationship between gender and the degree and nature of illness actually experienced, or were they looking at women's behaviour associated with illness, such as seeking medical help? Given these difficulties the studies none the less introduce a series of important questions. In Western Europe and North America, women have been living longer than men since at least the eighteenth century. In 1989, British women's life expectancy at birth was 78.4 years, compared to 72.8 years for men (Social Trends, 1991). Nathanson argues that this shows that women are naturally more resistant to infectious and degenerative diseases. Survey data from Britain and North America, however, shows that both women's morbidity (ill-health) and their utilisation of health services between the 1950s and the 1970s exceeded that of men's. Three explanations for these differences can be considered. First, that women report more illness than men because it is culturally more acceptable for women to be ill; second, that women's flexible domestic timetables more easily embrace visits to the doctor and periods of ill-health; and third, that women's social roles are more demanding and therefore more likely to produce ill-health. Nathanson argues that these explanatory models are useful to the extent that they account for variation between women of different social class, 'race', sexuality and age, as well as between women and men.

Exploring the third explanation – that women's ascribed social roles are particularly demanding, she highlights Walter Gove and Jeannette Tudor's work on the relationship between marital status and mental health (1973). Comparisons between married women and men show women experiencing more mental illness, a difference which Gove suggests may be grounded in the lack of alternative gratification available to housewives; the low status of housework; the unstructured and invisible nature of housework; the poor conditions experienced by women in paid employment; and the conflicting role expectations faced by women. Whilst arguing that marriage appears to exert a protective influence upon men's health and an undermining one upon women's, Nathanson presents studies to show that levels of morbidity, and rates of mortality, are even higher for single women than for married women. Within a patriarchal society women can assume a privileged status through links with individual men, a status which would seem to be reflected in married women's correspondingly better health and increased longevity. (Having said this, there are other issues which may mitigate against married women having better health and longevity than single women, for example the risk of domestic violence and the stress of women's traditional caring roles within the family.)

Research also shows links between both paid employment and the presence of pre-school children and less reported illness, while poor housing was linked to an increase in mental illness, particularly for women living in high rise flats. Nathanson usefully introduces debates about gender-based differences in health, but encounters problems when seeking distinctions between illness itself and behaviour associated with illness. This exemplifies the social role of medicine in shaping the concepts of health and illness. Visiting the doctor may not necessarily reflect disease but rather the medicalisation of stresses women experience as a result of poor housing or unemployment. Similarly, failure to use health services may reflect the sense of powerlessness experienced particularly keenly by working-class or Black women in interactions with white, male doctors.

Hilary Graham (1987) develops these debates, again stressing the need to account for differences between women as well as those between women and men. She highlights the issues of class and 'race', taking as an indicator of women's health experiences the example of the perinatal death rate (number of babies stillborn or dying in the first week of life per 1000 births). She points out that in 1984 the perinatal mortality rate was twice as high among lower-working-class women as it was for the upper social classes. Similarly, among babies born to women whose birthplace was the Caribbean or Asia the rate was 50 per cent to 70 per cent higher than for those born to women whose birthplace was Britain. Differences between women in terms of their sexuality are a similarly important aspect of their health-related experience. For example, in seeking advice for gynaecological problems, lesbians who use conventional health services may fail to have their needs addressed by doctors who assume heterosexuality.

Drawing on gender- and class-based differences in illness reported in response to the 1984 General Household Survey, Graham confirms Nathanson's point that while women live longer than men, they also suffer more illness. Furthermore, while 47 per cent of lower-working-class women are suffering from a long-standing illness, less than half this proportion are to be found in the upper social classes.

Gender strongly influences the distribution of disability within the population – two-thirds of the 4 million people who are disabled in Britain are estimated to be women. (This, in part, is related to the predominance of women among the section of the population who are very elderly (Graham, 1987c).) Similarly, in the area of mental health, women are more likely than men to either diagnose themselves (or be diagnosed) as having a mental-health problem. Hospital admission and the prescription of mood-altering drugs is also more common among women than among men. Before we look more closely at the diversity of women's experiences of disability and mental illness, we can compare Graham's and Nathanson's discussion of how differences between women's and men's health can be accounted for. Graham notes physiological reasons why women may be more vulnerable to ill-health, in that they have the additional biological role of child-bearing, and that more of them survive into their eighties and nineties. However, studies cited by Nathanson excluded health care associated with female reproduction – and still found women experiencing more illness and making more use of health services. The cultural explanation, referred to by Nathanson, which suggests that the sick role is more compatible with a feminine than a masculine social role, is challenged in Graham's discussion of studies such as Cornwell (1984) and Pill and Stott (1982). Their work suggests that working-class women in particular are more likely to normalise and accommodate symptoms of ill-health, giving priority to the needs of their families. Ruth Cooperstock and Henry Leonard's study (1979) of the meaning of tranquillisers shows that, particularly for white women, their use is justified as a way of remaining calm whilst caring for a family.

Nathanson's third explanatory model, that women are assigned less satisfying and less healthy social roles than men, is echoed in Graham's assertion that the material circumstances of women's lives may strongly affect their health. For example, women are more vulnerable than men to poverty. Moreover, women experience forms of poverty which have gender-specific implications. Not only are they discriminated against in employment, they are also expected to act as the primary carers of dependent relatives throughout their lives. Economic disadvantage inevitably follows, women in manual work earning on average only 70 per cent of the hourly pay of male manual workers; and women in non-manual work earning on average only 62 per cent of their male equivalents' hourly wage (Equal Opportunities Commission, 1990). In the absence of effective child-care provision, female single parents may find it difficult to enter paid employment. In 1988, day-nursery places were available for only 2 per cent of children under five in England and Wales (Equal Opportunities Commission, 1990). Furthermore, as Jan Pahl's (1983) study of household income decision-making shows, as the partners of men, women's control over family financial resources may be limited. Both women and men with very low incomes will be likely to live in poor-quality housing in areas more vulnerable to airborne pollution. However, women's commitment to domestic and care work means they are likely to spend far more time in the home, suffering both material deprivation and social isolation.

Material conditions such as these – poor housing, diet, environment and social support – can produce emotional and bodily stresses. Furthermore, as shown in an extensive feminist literature of domestic violence, men, and male partners in particular, can endanger women's physical and mental health (Hanmer and Maynard, 1987; Yllo and Bograd, 1988; and Hanmer, Radford and Stanko, 1989). Health is in part constituted out of the way bodily or emotional changes are perceived and categorised, and how, if at all, they are treated. By exploring two aspects of women's health: mental health and disability, the effects of women's material circumstances and the cultural and social responses to these effects can be demonstrated. Both the material circumstances and the social responses to them reflect the workings of patriarchal and capitalist forms of power.

Women and mental health

In 1972, Phyllis Chesler opened debates about the medicalisation of mental health. She argued that medicine, in the form of psychiatry, has been able to control and shape both the nature of masculinity and femininity, and also the relations of power through which they are linked. Chesler's work prepared the ground for a radical feminist reading of madness which developed within feminist theory during the 1970s and 1980s. She argues that madness is a category which encompasses all women, rather than just a particularly troubled minority. The apparently ungendered profile of madness – passivity, emotionality, irrationality, dependency, lack of initiative, and need for support – is, she argues, also a profile of a 'normal' woman. (Chesler's point is echoed by Ehrenreich and English (1979) and Doyal and Elston (1986), who link nineteenth-century notions of femininity, constructed around women's fragile reproductive nature during the nineteenth century, with a 'cult of invalidism' during this period.) Thus, women are socialised into behaviour which, in men, would be categorised as mental illness. In effect, women are placed in a double bind in relation to psychiatry. Not only is madness a particularly extreme manifestation of the behaviour expected of a 'normal' woman, but women who display independence or an aggressive resistance to their social roles also risk receiving a psychiatric label. As Chesler argues, 'Women who reject or are ambivalent about the female role frighten both themselves and society so much that their ostracism and self-destructiveness probably begin very early. Such women are also assured of a psychiatric label and, if they are hospitalized, it is for less "female" behaviours, such as "schizophrenia", "lesbianism", or "promiscuity"' (Chesler, 1971, p. 56).

Women who appear before a criminal court are twice as likely as men to be sent for psychiatric treatment, and seven times as likely to be sent to maximum-security hospitals. Unlike men receiving a fixed-term prison sentence, women sent to hospital may have their liberty denied for an indefinite period. The 'moral enterprise' of psychiatry would, therefore, in Chesler's view, be the maintenance of women's subordination to men through the pathologising and subsequent medicalising of the 'natural' attributes of femininity; and the labelling as deviant those women whose behaviour contradicts such attributes.

Nearly twenty years later, psychiatry retains its power and Chesler's view remains radical. Dale Spender (1986b) suggests that more criticism is heard of the use of psychiatry for political purposes within the Soviet Union than within the West, for the political ends of patriarchy. Feminist theory has none the less continued to document the hidden dangers for women of an apparently benign system of mental health care, and to debate the sources of women's apparently greater incidence of mental health problems.

Edwin Schur (1984) argues that psychiatry operates within a medical framework which locates disorder or disease within the patient, rather than within the relationship between the patient and the surrounding world. Emotional distress therefore fails to be categorised as a rational response to the oppressive circumstances of women within society. This raises one of feminism's fundamental questions about mental health. Is women's mental illness a rational response to their own subordination, one which is subsequently controlled through a set of psychiatric labels? Or, alternatively, is it the behaviour into which women are socialised, in that it often represents the opposite of men's required behaviour, which is inevitably liable to be categorised as pathological. Women in Mind (1986), a group of Black and white women from Africa and Europe, take the former view: that women are driven mad by the circumstances of their lives. However, they also highlight the capacity of madness to disrupt and reveal the workings of a system of power which then controls and mutes their responses through psychosurgery, electroconvulsive therapy and drug therapy.

Joan Busfield (1989) discusses the view that Chesler gives no clear account of how psychiatry and sexism are linked (Allen, 1986). Furthermore, Chesler's position means the abandonment of psychiatry as being inherently oppressive to women, and a fruitless context for feminist intervention. Chesler, in describing mental illness as the sexist social construction of psychiatry, also fails to acknowledge the very real mental suffering experienced by women. Busfield seeks a reconciliation between the apparently conflicting views that mental illness is either the construction of the psychiatrist, or the product of the conditions of women's lives. She argues that women do indeed experience mental suffering as an outcome of their circumstances. However, psychiatry's responses to disorders of this kind, in terms of both their constructs and their judgements, help to reproduce women's subordination.

There are parallel issues to be considered in the case of Black women. Among Black, particularly Afro-Caribbean people admitted to mental hospitals in Britain, 50 per cent are diagnosed as schizophrenic compared with only 20 per cent of white people admitted (Sashidharan, 1989). Research has also indicated that British-born Afro-Caribbean women are thirteen times more likely to be admitted to mental hospitals with a diagnosis of schizophrenia than white women, while Afro-Caribbean men are seven times more likely than white men to receive this diagnosis (Littlewood and Lipsedge, 1988). Philip Rack (1982) argues that a Western psychiatric model of schizophrenia pathologises Asian and Afro-Caribbean reactions to stress. Paranoid delusions, hallucinations, fragmentation of thought, incongruity of mood and strange or unpredictable behaviour are the expected responses to stressful events which might lead a white Westerner into reactive depression. Again, a rational response to external demands is being constructed as pathological according to the theories and practices of a predominantly white male body of knowledge, psychiatry.

Women and disability

Oppression is experienced by both women and men with disabilities. Not only are their material needs often unmet, but they also suffer as a result of negative social attitudes. However, Susan Lonsdale (1990) highlights a range of gender-specific issues associated with disability. She provides another example of how women's experience is shaped and controlled by medical expertise. Without medical certification, necessary benefits and services cannot be obtained.

Disability can therefore be seen as a social role and one which is particularly oppressive for women in that a visibly imperfect body particularly disadvantages them. As Rosalind Coward (1984) has argued, for a woman, a socially-desirable bodily appearance is seen as a prerequisite for finding a sexual partner, and for maintaining individual self-esteem. Contrary to stereotypical images, many women with disabilities do enjoy satisfying sexual relationships; exclusion from mainstream education, public transport, work and leisure, together with the resulting poverty and social isolation, can be far more of a hurdle to creating such relationships than any bodily limitation. None the less, women with a male sexual partner may feel themselves to be second-best to an able-bodied woman, and be particularly vulnerable to sexual abuse. While social and economic dependency prevent many women from escaping an abusing partner, women with disabilities may risk institutionalisation if they leave a partner who is their primary care-giver. Bullard and Knight (1981) describe lesbianism as an important option for women with disabilities, in that women offer one another potentially more supportive and less threatening relationships than they may find with men.

Lonsdale highlights the invisibility of women with disabilities. Femininity is associated with passivity and the enforced passivity of disability may therefore seem less problematic for women than for men. Their probable exclusion from the labour market is similarly seen as a less catastrophic event than if they were men. As a result, research, policy-making and public opinion in general focus less on the needs of women with disabilities. For example, the belief that men require penetrative sex is expressed in a considerable amount of literature about the sexual needs of men with disabilities. By contrast, the view that women are sexually passive has meant that little has been written about the sexual needs of women with disabilities. Similarly, their loss of privacy through being institutionalised and through constant bodily exposure to doctors and carers effectively desexualises them, given that the covering-up of women's bodies is customarily an acknowledgement of their sexuality.

As Lonsdale explains, physical or mental impairment can mean that an individual becomes disabled. Acknowledging the problems of measurement, she none the less argues that it is more common among both Black and female populations. Reasons for this are complex. The rate of disability within British Afro-Caribbean households is 151 per 1000 adults, as opposed to 137 per 1000 white adults. Social, economic and occupational factors are all thought to play a part in this disparity, as can health problems specific to the Afro-Caribbean population such as thassalaemia and sickle cell anaemia. Among women over the age of sixteen in Britain in 1988, 161 per 1000 were disabled, as compared with only 121 per 1000 men (Office of Population Censuses and Surveys, 1988). Reasons for this include women's greater longevity, and, as in the case of Black people, poverty and poor housing.

Defining health – providing health care

Western medical knowledge and practice has been understood as the outcome of a male appropriation of the expertise and skills of both middle-class and working-class women from the thirteenth century on-wards (O'Connor, 1987). While women have always been concerned with health care, men's emergence as high-status, highly-paid medical experts is a recent phenomenon, a rising above the ranks of female carers. Previously, women had cared for their families and communities as wives, mothers, midwives and healers, using an holistic, intuitive approach which contrasts with recent more intrusive, curative regimes (O'Connor, 1987). Women of all social classes were involved. Some worked as priestess-physicians, taking responsibility for public health, hospital administration and medical education as well as individual health care (O'Connor, 1987).

A new wealthy middle class in eighteenth-century England provided a market for medical remedies, formerly used only as aids for dying people (Illich, 1975). Medical knowledge and skill acquired a new value in terms of wealth and status. Health care ceased to be largely a domestic concern, and instead became a focus within the marketplace. With lifting of religious prohibitions on dissection in the eighteenth century, male doctors could refine their new scientific approach by studying disease directly. Women had been excluded from universities since the estab-lishment of these in the thirteenth century, and the transmission of developing scientific medical knowledge through university education secured it as the property of the male medical profession. Additionally, medical guilds, the precursors of the Royal Colleges, helped define health-care practices as medical skills; activities which were reserved for qualified men.

Other important elements within the loss of women's control of health care are the role of the Church and the murder of women as witches. Women's exclusion from a university education became grounds for the Church to disqualify them from medical practice, 'If a woman dare to cure without having studied she is a witch and must die' (Ehrenreich and English, 1979, p. 35).

Margaret Versluysen (1981) contributes to debates about a takeover by a male medical profession through a study of childbirth in Britain. The growth of 'lying-in' (maternity) hospitals during the eighteenth century meant that childbirth came under medical control for the first time. The growth of such hospitals did not reflect the development of medical techniques, but rather the creation by male doctors of a site within which to extend their sphere of expertise. Before the eighteenth century, male participation in birth had been taboo; working-class births were the province of the female midwife. Lying-in hospitals allowed male doctors to restrict the amount of work available to female mid-wives; to exercise greater control over their patients; to increase the number and range of births they had attended; and to promote the idea that childbirth was a dangerous venture requiring medical attendance.

The example of childbirth shows the expansion of medical models of health through male medical professionals' efforts to develop their practice and thereby their income. Such was their social and professional status that their female patients were under pressure to accept as 'natural' a narrow, medicalised view of their bodies and minds. This theme is addressed by Lesley Doyal and Mary Ann Elston (1986, pp. 178–9), who argue that the effectiveness of curative medicine increases the status of the doctor. Once the subordinates of their wealthy, upper-class patients, doctors are now accustomed to treating people from lower social classes. Doctor–patient interaction can therefore reinforce a patient's more general sense of powerlessness within society. Women, Doyal and Elston suggest, are particularly susceptible in that men constitute the majority of doctors, their relationship with female patients mirroring gender-based power imbalances within the wider society. The more serious a woman's illness, the more likely she is to be offered treatment by a male doctor, men predominating in the higher-status roles of Consultant and Registrar.

Within the medical profession, the majority of women have found only the subordinate role of nurse open to them. The figure of Florence Nightingale embodies a number of paradoxes associated with women's role in health care during the second half of the nineteenth century.

Doyal and Elston (1986, pp. 196–7) note that while Nightingale is remembered as a ministering angel, her work and writings reveal a shrewd politician rather than a figure of gentleness and compassion. However, while she sought to reorganise the nursing profession under female control, she none the less promoted a notion of the nurse as subordinate to the doctor, a naturally quiet, forbearing servant who faithfully fulfilled her male superiors' orders.

Contemporary women's roles within the formal provision of health care continue to reflect nineteenth-century concepts of masculinity and femininity, despite the fact that in 1988 women represented 43–44 per cent of the workforce (Equal Opportunities Commission, 1990). Indeed, if anything, the female-controlled nursing hierarchies which Florence Nightingale worked to construct have, since the mid-1960s, become increasingly male-controlled. Not only have men's nursing roles ceased to be restricted largely to psychiatry, in addition, the 1960s marked the abolition of the female role of Matron. It has been suggested that the Salmon Committee, which recommended replacing the matron system with a hierarchy of administrative grades, carried an implicit critique of female authority, suggesting a lack of management and decision-making skills among women (Carpenter, 1977). Doyal (1985) examines the distribution of gender across different nursing positions to reveal a predominance of women in lower-status jobs. In 1988, the ratio of men to women employed as State Registered Nurses in England was 1:5.7 as opposed to 1:11.6 among less-qualified State Enrolled Nurses (Department of Health, 1990). Furthermore, among the total of 367 891 women employed as nursing and midwifery staff, well over a third (144 485) were women with part-time contracts. By contrast, among the 43 682 men employed as nursing and midwifery staff, only 2465 had part-time contracts (Department of Health, 1990). This suggests that, for many women, nursing as a career is constrained by the demands of partners, children and other dependents. In addition, 72.3 per cent of ancillary workers, those who perform the lowest-status work within the hospital system, are women. Again, many of them have part-time contracts, these women making up 56.1 per cent of all ancillary workers (Department of Health, 1991). Among the women who fill lower-grade nursing or ancillary posts, many are Black women. Subject to regional variation, research in 1971 suggested that 21 per cent of all female ancillary staff were born overseas, this figure rising to over 80 per cent of the domestic and catering workers of a London general hospital. Similarly, in nursing, research in 1977 showed that 12 per cent of all student nurses were born overseas, though only a small percentage of these were accepted by higher-status London teaching hospitals. Many were recruited directly into less-popular psychiatric and geriatric hospitals, and their final qualification was more likely to be a 2-year State Enrolled Nurse certificate rather than a 3-year State Registered Nurse certificate. Doyal points out that despite British immigration policies designed to restrict entry to overseas workers from the 1960s onwards, qualified doctors and nurses received employment vouchers under the 1962 Commonwealth Immigration Act. She argues that overseas nurses were more likely to accept the poor conditions, low pay and rigid discipline traditional to the nursing profession at a time when British-born women were becoming more resistant. For Black women, however, gaining medical qualifications in British medical schools and subsequently developing a career in medicine are goals fraught with obstacles erected by what Tandon (1987) sees as the racist and sexist attitudes endemic to the profession. As an applicant for medical training she needed higher grades than her white male counterparts; as a qualified doctor she found herself confined to short-term contracts. Overall statistics for the distribution of NHS employment according to 'race' and ethnicity remain unavailable in 1991, ethnic monitoring as yet being conducted by only a limited number of health authorities.

Tandon's experience is shared by the 30 per cent of qualified female doctors working low-visibility NHS community health services, where they make up over half the overall number of doctors employed. Similarly, another 30 per cent of qualified female doctors are to be found in general practice, where they make up a fifth of the total number of general practitioners. The remaining 40 per cent of female doctors find employment in the NHS hospital service. However, while an equal number of women and men entered medical school in 1990, only 14 per cent of the consultants in this country are female. The male appropriation of women's traditional midwifery roles during the eighteenth century continues to be evident. The small proportion of obstetricians and gynaecologists who are women (12 per cent) has remained unchanged for the last twenty-five years (Doyal and Elston, 1986; and Montague, 1991).

In addition, women are grossly under-represented on the councils of the Royal Colleges and as British Medical Association negotiators, positions from which they could influence medical training. A 1988 report argued that the career structure of the medical profession severely disadvantaged women wishing to pursue a family life. Career counselling, part-time opportunities and a review of the 'old boy network' were essential if discrimination against women was to be effectively countered (Allen, 1988). The drop-out rate of female doctors persists, despite consumer pressure for their services.

Excluded from positions of responsibility within the NHS, women none the less find themselves pressured into taking responsibility when it comes to informal health care. The shift away from institutional health care during the 1960s and early 1970s led originally to the provision of care in the community. That is to say, within small homes and hostels, staffed by paid workers. Inadequate public expenditure has since produced a subtle shift in policy away from care *within* the community, to care *by* the community. Indeed, the 1981 White Paper 'Growing Older' makes the explicit statement, 'Care in the community must increasingly mean care by the community' (Department of Health and Social Security, 1981). As authors such as Janet Finch and Dulcie Groves (1983) and Gillian Dalley (1988) have made abundantly clear, the 'community' is in many cases a euphemism for 'a female relative'.

Care of this kind takes place within the domestic sphere and not the community, a context difficult to document accurately. Hilary Graham (1987) reports that an estimated 1.3 million people act as principal unpaid carer to a disabled child or adult, of whom 1.2 million actually live with the dependent person. As regards the gender and the nature of the relationship which links those involved, it is estimated that where an adult or elderly person is in need of care, the carer will, in 75 per cent of cases, be a female relative. Where it is a child who is disabled or chronically ill, the carer in nearly 100 per cent of cases will be their mother. Similarly, the carer for an adult with learning difficulties will, in 80 per cent of cases, be their mother. Within the domestic sphere women are therefore providing health care in much the same way that they have done since medieval times. Moreover, care work often means not only the physical, emotional and financial dependency of cared-for upon carer, but also the financial dependency of the carer upon either another family member, such as a male partner, or upon the state.

Gillian Dalley (1988) argues that if women resist the dependency brought on by unpaid care work, they must also resist being labelled as uncaring. Men, she points out, show themselves to be caring through financing the provision of care. Women can only show that they care sufficiently about someone by caring for them emotionally and practically. Change, both for women and for those whom they care about, requires that the individualist bias within Western society be replaced by a collectivist approach. In other words, a culture which values the rights of the individual over those of the collectivity, or community, needs to give way to one in which both decision-making and action are undertaken on a shared basis. (An example of the latter would be the emergence of Women's Aid in the 1970s in Britain.) If a collectivist approach to care is not adopted, women will continue to care for dependent people on an individual basis, a system which assures men's individual freedom to pursue their own ends, unconstrained by the needs of their relatives.

Graham (1985) highlights three aspects of the long-term care of dependent relatives. These include providing for health, teaching for health and mediating professional health care. Graham criticises feminism's focus on illness, healing and the low status of women's paid health-care work. She argues that women's labour in creating good health is being made invisible: 'The routine business of keeping individuals alive and functioning has gone uncharted. We still know little about the ways in which women have provided, negotiated, and mediated health throughout history; we can only guess at the division of resources and responsibilities within the community on which this health work rested' (Graham, 1985, p. 29).

Documentary evidence from the nineteenth century, and more recent studies such as that by Mildred Blaxter and Elizabeth Paterson (1982), show women securing their family's health by sacrificing their own interests and welfare in times of hardship, when resources are low. Moreover, the site of women's informal health work, the family, is isolated from the public world. Women hide whatever deprivations occur within it in order to protect other family members and safeguard their own reputations as effective guardians of family health. As teachers of health, women are often expected to set a good example by not smoking, and by planning healthy menus. As mediators of professional health care, women can become vulnerable, encountering medical professionals at a point when they failed to maintain the good health of their relatives.

However effectively a woman performs a protective role by consuming only the minimum of available resources, the lack of adequate housing or a pollution-free environment are ills which no amount of sacrifice can remedy. The orientation of health education projects towards women effectively masks the major source of ill-health, which Doyal (1979) argues to be the public domain. Breast-feeding, attendance at antenatal and child-welfare clinics, and the eradication of unhealthy forms of personal support such as drinking and smoking are all demands made upon women. All can be seen as examples of the state situating responsibility for health within the community, an apparently ungendered policy which in practice has a highly gendered focus. As Doyal and Elston (1986) remind us, the high infant mortality rate in nineteenth- and early-twentieth-century Britain was similarly attributed to poor mothering. Reformers highlighted the 'ignorance' and 'fecklessness' of mothers, thereby playing down the social and economic context of poverty and insanitary housing.

Reclaiming women's health

Versluysen (1981), Ehrenreich and English (1979), and Oakley (1976b) describe the appropriation of women's knowledge and skills as healers by Western male medical professionals. Helen Roberts (1981b) describes the contemptuous way with which male doctors now refer to women's lack of knowledge about their own bodies. This lack of knowledge has become a focus within the women's movement, generating handbooks such as *The New Woman's Survival Catalog* (Grimstad and Rennie, 1973), *Our Bodies, Ourselves* (Phillips and Rakusen, 1978, 1989) and *The New Women's Health Handbook* (MacKeith, 1978). Anne Williams (1987) argues that these handbooks, together with feminist health-related research, seek first to redefine women's health by listening to women's accounts of their own experiences; and second, to facilitate women in taking control of their own health. In the example of the Boston Women's Health Collective's *Our Bodies, Ourselves*, Williams shows how a small discussion group at a Boston Women's Conference in 1969 chose to research health issues relevant to themselves as women from existing medical sources, bringing this material together with accounts offered by women attending talks given by the group. Working with the mismatch between medical opinion and women's experience, the outcome of this 'never-ending' learning process was the publication of *Our Bodies, Ourselves*. Such books were read predominantly by white, middle-class Western women during the 1970s, therefore contributing little to the well-being of Black and working-class women who were most vulnerable to ill-health and discriminatory health-care practices. (Since then, handbooks have been published which do address the needs of women other than white, middle-class and heterosexual, for example, *Alive and Well: A Lesbian Health Guide* (Hepburn and Gutierrez, 1988) and *The Black Women's Health Book* (White, 1990)). However, traditional women's magazines also offer health-related information, albeit under headings such as 'Ask the Doctor', where the focus is as much family health as women's health matters. Gardner (1981) suggests that women often seek medical advice because of their responsibility for contraception and child-care, in their role as guardians of family health, as already discussed. Williams (1987) argues that for women in the ambiguous role of consumer/provider of health-care, support rather than medical advice is often what is needed, and indeed what would empower them. As it stands, the requirement that female carers should submit to the advice of a medical professional in order to gain any form of 'support' can result either in avoidance, and therefore a deepening of the carer's social isolation, or a series of medical interactions which can reinforce their sense of dependency.

Handbooks such as *Our Bodies, Ourselves* urge women to take control their own health. Susan Sontag (1983), however, criticises concepts of illness which focus on the sufferer as the source of healing, which demand that the sufferer take back responsibility for their own health. She argues that they are not only punitive in the sense of being victim-blaming, but also misleading in that they deflect attention away from the state's responsibility for health care. Until recently the growing medicalisation of human experience has deflected attention away from environmental sources of illness. For example, the celebration of Robert Koch's discovery of the tubercle bacillus in 1882 as the first stage in a medical triumph over tuberculosis, masked the way that improved living conditions were to lead to a steep decline in the occurrence of the disease by 1900. However the accepted authority of medical models narrows the field of discourses to one in which the patient and the doctor dispute their relative spheres of responsibility for health care. Thus, while doctors may argue that if young women refuse to be bound to one male sexual partner they irresponsibly court cervical cancer, women themselves may feel they have a right to sophisticated laser treatment for this form of cancer. It is in this area that a feminist demand that women take back responsibility for their own health must beware of echoing the demands of health 'educationalists' who urge changes of individual lifestyle as the remedy for poor health. Indeed, it is women's efforts to develop their own definitions of what 'taking responsibility for health' means which have led feminists to involve themselves actively in areas ranging from Green politics and the peace movement, to feminist therapy.

This raises the question of the appropriate siting of women's health care. If Women's Studies has unmasked the hidden political agenda of conventional medicine then, as Chesler's case demands, should conventional health care be abandoned in favour of feminist-conceived and controlled women-centred forms of care? Well Women Clinics and breast, ovarian and cervical screening are services made available only in limited ways within the NHS, yet these are key forms of preventive health care for women. Within feminist health care such services would play a central role, alongside widely available feminist therapy and counselling around, for example, issues such as AIDS and abortion. It would need to take account of differing values and needs of different groups of women, for example lesbians, disabled women and Black women, unlike the present health care system which is generated from within a society which believes itself to consist primarily of white, heterosexual, able-bodied individuals, supported in ill health and old age by their 'families'.

Doyal (1985) reviews the way in which women have addressed the shortcomings of the National Health Service in Britain by working within rather than outside the dominant system of health care. She notes that if women not only use the NHS more than men but also find employment within it (women make up 70 per cent of health service workers), then they stand to suffer most if the service is reduced. Referring to National Health Service cut-backs since the 1979 British election of a Conservative government, she argues that reductions in staffing levels among lower-grade workers and in services to the community are particularly likely to affect women and those they care for.

As a result, women working within the National Health Service have joined trade unions, and women's health groups have been supported by feminist health workers such as the radical nurses group, the radical midwives group, the radical health visitors group and a national group for feminist doctors and medical students. Similarly, women performing unpaid care work have sought to overcome their isolation, banding together in support of women's issues within the Association of Carers. While women from a variety of backgrounds are finding a common cause as NHS cuts take hold, they all none the less face the paradox that they are working to support a system which research over more than twenty years has been shown to be instrumental in reproducing their subordination. Nevertheless, they have campaigned both for changes within the existing service, for example in areas such as Well-Woman Clinics and woman-centred childbirth, as well as against cuts such as the threatened closure of the female-staffed Elizabeth Garrett Anderson Hospital for women in London in 1974 and 1992. Rather than entirely eschewing a currently male-dominated system in the belief that it must inevitably operate in ways which are oppressive to women, many feminists argue that responsibility for the provision of health care for people of all classes, both women and men, must lie with the state rather than with any one group within society. Their perspective is important, given the unwillingness of the state to make apparent the class-based nature of inequalities in health. Awareness of class-based differences in health in Britain was only raised effectively in 1982 when Peter Townsend and Nick Davidson published the Black Report. This account of the persistence of class-based inequalities in life-expectancy despite the introduction of the Welfare State was virtually suppressed by its government sponsors when it first appeared in xerox form in 1980.

While most feminists might be wary of removing responsibility for health care from the state, and, for example, risking the development of class-based inequalities in women's access to 'private' forms of feminist health care such as women's therapy, it remains clear that the NHS itself does not benefit women equally. Doyal (1985) shows that while women in lower social classes make more use of their GPs, their needs so far exceed those of women in higher social classes that merely counting the number of visits to a general practitioner does not indicate the proportion of resources received by working-class women in relation to their needs. She adds that the distribution of resources available to general practitioners also varies in a way which privileges more affluent regions of Britain. Finally, she refers to the many studies of doctor–patient interaction which show middle-class patients receiving longer consultations during which far more information is exchanged (Cartwright and Anderson, 1981). Again women's need for support in their role as guardians of family health care increases their likelihood of experiencing awkward or undermining interactions with GPs when compared with their male counterparts. In the areas of cervical cancer screening, birth control and abortion the needs of working-class women are being met less effectively than those of middle-class women. Sterilisation operations are, however, offered far more readily to both working-class and Black women, Doyal argues, on the basis of a medical perception of them as being 'ignorant' or 'feckless'. For women lacking alternative resources, abortions are sometimes offered only if they agree to simultaneous sterilisation. Similarly, in Doyal's view, Black women's 'needs, desires and life-styles' remain unaddressed and are sometimes attacked within the NHS. Language difficulties can result in a poorer service, particularly in the area of obstetric care. Failure to meet the specific needs of Black women is compounded by the more direct expression of

institutional racism in instances such as the use of the injectable contraceptive drug, Depo-Provera, at times without the knowledge or consent
of the woman herself. Research by Brent Community Health Council
(1981) suggested that half the prescriptions for Depo-Provera were made
out for Black women, a bias which the Council saw as reflecting a
perception of Black women as ignorant and unreliable. Institutional
racism also manifests itself in the role of NHS staff during the immigration process, vaginal examinations and X-rays being used to verify the
age and marital status of immigrant women. Indeed the withholding of
health care from individuals who have not proved themselves to be
'ordinarily resident' in the UK is a practice which is particularly likely
to undermine the health of Black people.

Debates persist as to whether real change can come from within
existing systems or whether alternative forms of woman-centred health
care are the only viable way forward. A broad survey of forms of health
care which have grown up outside the NHS – for example, homeopathy,
massage, and hospice care for people who are terminally ill – shows that
they are now beginning to be available within the system itself, or at
least to influence the nature of available medical care. This choice then
opens up the possibility of redirecting the focus of the National Health
Service, based on knowledge and experience developed in contexts
which are free from its more oppressive assumptions and practices.
Doyal (1985) charts the changing focus of a feminist critique of women's health care provision. While early research focused on the inequalities to be found within and perpetuated by the National Health
Service, the material conditions of women's lives and their role and
position within society as a whole have come more and more under
scrutiny (see Graham, 1987). For example, links have been made between women's health, their roles as informal carers and their poverty.
Feminist research into the gendered nature of work and leisure provides
additional insight into the ways women's health is subject to different
influences from that of men. These include the ideological and material
constraints which endanger women's access to leisure (Green, Hebron
and Woodward, 1990); the reproduction of women's subordination
through physical activities such as sport (Hargreaves, 1985; and Boutilier
and San Giovanni, 1985), and the health risks associated with the use of
new technology for women in clerical work (Downing, 1983; and Lewin
and Olesen, 1985). The Women and Work Hazards Group (1987), in
their account of the risks women face in the workplace, point out that
official records carry no information about married workers. Women's

occupations may not even be mentioned on their death certificate. In addition, the belief that the home is a safe, healthy place for women ignores the volume of rape, violence and accidental injury suffered by women confined within domestic space (O'Connor, 1987). Feminists have therefore highlighted the wider cultural and social context of women's health, as well as specific areas of concern for women which are not being addressed adequately within the existing system of health care. These range from the provision for need in the areas of contraception and abortion, through to slimming and eating disorders. For example, Ann Oakley (1989) offers a critique of health professionals' response to women's smoking. She points out that prominence is given to female smokers' production of low-birth-weight babies rather than to women's health itself. Furthermore, in that the remedy put forward is individual lifestyle change, women who continue to smoke are perceived to be morally at fault. As Oakley stresses, clear links have been identified between women's smoking, their social class position and the demands placed upon them as carers, yet medical responses to smoking continue to ignore these aspects of women's lives. Michelle Stanworth highlights the political implications of new reproductive technologies, and argues that such technologies are 'demanding human decision where previously there was biological destiny' (Stanworth, 1987, p. 2). She urges women to inform themselves about the range of reproductive technologies, their application and wider social context, as well as their varying implications for women of different backgrounds (see Chapter 10). In particular, she warns against polarised positions which see reproductive technologies as either an attempt by men to appropriate women's reproductive power, or as an unproblematic enhancement of women's reproductive potential. The need for women to exercise control is therefore central to developments in this area. Feminist research has therefore not only questioned the male appropriation of women's roles as healers, but also challenged the 'medical' assumptions which underly contemporary definitions of health and health care. If women are to 'care' for their own and each other's health, then the broader material and ideological conditions of their subordination must be given priority as the sources of their ill-health.

When the challenges of the 1990s are considered, one area of growing concern is women's encounter with AIDS. Here the need for a feminist perspective is paramount, as numbers of AIDS deaths are predicted to rise more rapidly for women than men in the next decade. Moreover, the syndrome has a wide range of implications for women in the area of reproductive rights, sexuality and informal care. Thus, for example, with the spread of AIDS, the right of HIV-infected women to become pregnant may come under state surveillance. Campbell (1990) reports that the care of a gay son with AIDS often falls to his mother, given fathers' and brothers' more frequent negative reactions. As carers, such women may be deprived of the informal support of other women, owing to the stigma attached to the syndrome, yet women do seek out therapy and support groups more readily than men. None the less, middle-class women predominate when it comes to finding relief through such groups. Indeed, as stressed in other areas of women's health-related experience, the incidence of AIDS reflects the diverse forms of women's oppression. Predicted to become the main cause of death for women under forty in the West in the next decade, it is not, however, distributed evenly. In the United States, for example, for every white woman who contracts AIDS there are 13.2 Black women and 8.1 Hispanic women (Women and AIDS Project, 1991). In the Caribbean, young women and children are becoming the most endangered of the population as a result of AIDS. Therefore, whether as someone who has AIDS or as the carers of people with AIDS, women's experience not only differs from that of men and reflects the diversity of women's social position; it also reflects their vulnerability within patriarchal and capitalist systems of power (Richardson, 1989).

Working from a feminist perspective, Women's Studies has researched and documented women's health-related experiences, stressing their material and ideological oppression. Much of this material has addressed the experience of Western women, yet the male appropriation of women's healing roles in the West from the thirteenth century onwards has its contemporary counterpart in developing countries. Carol MacCormack (1989) reminds us that outside the West women retain their roles as midwives and paramedics, as well as contributing significantly to production. None the less, ill-informed planners frequently fail to provide them with access to and control over medical technology, often as a result of established publishers' exclusion of research in the area of women and health.

In this, as in other areas discussed in this chapter, recommendations for the future include monitoring of women's health-related employment; of work experience generally; and of actual choices in the area of medical technology. It is through information gained in this way that the possibility of critically evaluating and transforming women's health can be fostered.

Further reading

Emily Martin, *The Woman in the Body: A cultural analysis of reproduction* (Milton Keynes, Open University Press, 1987). The framing of women's reproductive processes in terms of medical models is compared with the models used by women themselves. Implicit metaphors of production are seen to alienate women from the experiences of menstruation, childbirth and menopause.

Helen Roberts (ed.), *Women's Health Matters* (London, Routledge, 1992). This collection offers accounts of research into Black and white women's health which address funding issues, the role of qualitative methods, and women's own accounts. Childbirth, food and prostitution are central areas covered.

Penny Kane, *Women's Health: from womb to tomb* (London, Macmillan, 1991). A useful resource book which provides extensive quantitative data covering every aspect of women's health, thereby complementing the more qualitatively-derived insights of work such as Emily Martin's *The Woman in the Body*.

A number of books highlight both the diversity of women's health-related experience and a feminist commitment to women's empowerment. Several have been mentioned in the text, and in addition to these, Jean Shapiro, *Ourselves, Growing Older* (London, Fontana, 1987), sister volume to Angela Phillips and Jill Rakusen's *Our Bodies, Ourselves* (Harmondsworth, Penguin, updated 1989).

12

Women at Work

Anne Witz

In what ways is waged work gendered? Why has waged work become gendered? To what extent is women's oppression in the home and in the workplace interrelated? These questions have preoccupied feminists and are the central concerns of this chapter. The study of women's employment has been and continues to be of crucial importance to feminists, because they are concerned not only to identify the processes and structures which generate gender inequalities and gender segregation, but also to devise appropriate strategies for equalising the position of women and men in paid work. The study of paid work also provides feminists with the opportunity to understand better how gender divisions intersect with class and 'race' inequalities, for the fortunes and fates of working-class women in employment differ from those of middle-class women, just as those of Black working-class women differ in turn from those of white working-class women. The labour market, then, is a site of complex and interrelated inequalities. In addition, gender inequalities in the labour market are linked to and reinforced by those in other areas, such as, for example, women's and girls' unequal access to education and training which, in turn, has important ramifications for the terms on which women participate in paid employment, affecting their choice of jobs and their opportunities for advancement. Gender segregation in employment is further reinforced by media stereotypes of women in certain kinds of paid employment, such as secretarial and clerical work or the health professions, where they are largely represented in subordinate work roles, usually assisting or caring for others.

Women engage not only in paid work but also in unpaid work in the household, where they are responsible for the bulk of housework, childcare and other forms of physical and emotional labour. In addition, women perform a whole variety of unpaid caring activities in the neighbourhood and the community, as well as for family members and kin. Many feminists now refer to this as caring *work*, emphasising how it is usually women's work and may be performed on a paid or an unpaid basis. However, just because it may be done for family, friends or neighbours for no payment this does not make it any the less 'work'. Some sociologists have captured the complex reality of women's work which spans the divide between the public and private spheres with the term 'women's dual role'. Feminists prefer to see this more in terms of the double-edged nature of women's oppression; of the way in which women are allocated the bulk of unpaid household and child-care work and, in the sphere of waged work, are segregated into low-paid and low-status jobs, many of which replicate the functions they perform on an unpaid basis within the household. Because of the way in which women's 'work' spans both the private and the public domains, feminists exploring and explaining the complexity of women's participation in waged work have redefined the concept of 'work' in such a way as to dissolve the distinction between the 'private' sphere of unpaid and the 'public' sphere of paid work. It is no longer assumed that work is something you go 'out' to do, nor is it assumed that work is necessarily producing things or moving bits of paper around offices. There are clearly links and interconnections between women's work in the 'private' sphere of the household and the 'public' sphere of paid work. The work which women perform within the private sphere of the household is discussed in Chapter 8. This chapter will focus on women's paid work, although I will also consider the different ways in which feminists have sought to understand the interconnections between women's oppression in the two spheres of the family and employment.

First, changes in women's working lives that have occurred as a result of industrialisation and throughout the twentieth century will be examined. The nature and extent of gender segregation in the labour market will be established before moving on to consider feminist attempts to explore and explain gender segregation at work. I will discuss recent studies of women in the workplace which illustrate different feminist theories, and then look at feminist explanations of gender inequalities in paid work.

Women and paid work: a shifting reality

Women's working lives, like men's, have been fundamentally shaped by the development of industrial capitalism. The pre-industrial family system of labour, which involved the contribution of men, women and children in the household towards its economic survival, was a casualty of the Industrial Revolution and the development of capitalism.[1] Although working-class women provided the first industrial workforce in cotton textiles, the development of industrial capitalism in the nineteenth century progressively restricted women's participation in all forms of paid work, whilst the ideology of domesticity increasingly defined a woman's place as a full-time wife and mother in the private sphere of the family, dependent upon a husband's wage. This became the ideal, if not the reality for many working-class women. The ideology of domesticity had a much greater and earlier impact on the lives of middle-class and upper-middle-class women, and by the mid-nineteenth century it was virtually impossible for a middle-class woman to support herself outside marriage. Indeed, one of the earliest concerns of middle-class feminists was to open up the professions such as medicine, and crafts, shop work and clerical work to women (Holcombe, 1973). In the mid-nineteenth century, as middle-class women began agitating for wider employment opportunities, the state was intervening to restrict the hours and nature of working-class women's employment in the form of 'protective legislation', and the growing trade union movement was hostile to working women, affording them virtually no representation or protection. None the less, working women have always been a significant part of the industrial labour force, accounting for about a quarter of all waged workers between 1851 and 1951, although female participation rates have varied considerably by region (McDowell, 1989).

By the beginning of the twentieth century, the typical lifetime pattern of employment for women was employment for young single women followed by withdrawal (whether voluntary or compulsory) from the labour force on marriage. This has been described as the 'marriage career' (Hakim, 1979). The twentieth century has witnessed many changes in the social role of women. In particular, there has been considerable change in women's participation in paid employment, so much so that we may speak of the 'feminization of the labour force' (Hagen and Jenson, 1988), which describes the fact that women have made up a steadily increasing proportion of the total labour force over the past fifty or sixty years in most industrial capitalist societies (see Table 12.1). The feminisation of the labour force is seen by many to be an entrenched feature of the organisation of work in North American and Western European societies.

Table 12.1 *Female share of the labour force (percentages of population aged 15–64)*

	1950	1977	1982
Canada	21.3	37.8	40.9
France	35.9	37.6	38.6
Germany	35.1	37.6	38.2
Italy	25.4	31.9	33.8
Sweden	26.3	43.7	46.2
UK	30.7	38.2	39.1
USA	28.9	40.3	42.8

Source: Organisation for Economic Co-operation and Development (1985) *The Integration of Women into the Economy*, Paris, in Jane Jenson, Elizabeth Hagen and Cealliagh Reddy, *Feminization of the Labour Force: Paradoxes and Promises* (Cambridge, Polity Press, 1988).

Although the past two decades have witnessed significant and possibly irreversible changes in women's participation in paid employment, two major changes have been occurring throughout the twentieth century in Britain, and with varying degrees of intensity in other Western European and North American countries. The first of these changes has been a gradual increase in the proportion of women working, which means that the overall *level* of women's labour force participation has been increasing steadily. In Britain it increased from 34 per cent in 1901 to 56 per cent in 1971, with most of this increase occurring after the Second World War (Hakim, 1979). In 1982, female participation rates ranged from 33 per cent in Spain to 56 per cent in Norway and the United Kingdom, and 61 per cent in the United States (OECD, 1985). In Britain, women's participation level has continued to rise steadily during the past two decades and stood at 70 per cent in 1987. Nowadays, women in Britain are spending more and more time in paid employment during their lifetime.

In the early 1980s, a major survey of women and employment in Britain found that 63 per cent of women in their sample were working (Martin and Roberts, 1984). The bulk of this increase has been accounted for by the steadily increasing participation of married women in employment. Between 1901 and 1971 there was a proportional increase in the labour-force participation of wives by almost 400 per cent; in 1901 only one married woman in ten was working, whereas by 1971 one in two was active in the labour force (Hakim, 1979). More recently, in Britain the activity rate of married women stood at 55.6 per cent. In Denmark it is higher at 66.7 per cent, but in Spain, Ireland and Luxembourg it is substantially lower, with less than a third of married women in paid employment (CEC, 1990).

The second major change has been in the typical *pattern* of women's labour-force participation during their lifetime, particularly in the reasons for, and duration of, periods out of paid employment. As already mentioned, the typical work profile of women at the beginning of the twentieth century was a period of employment when they were young and single, followed by permanent withdrawal from the labour force on marriage; a practice maintained by the ideology of domesticity, which encouraged women to regard their primary role as that of wives and mothers, as well as by discriminatory practices by employers, many of whom operated bars against married women. Some, most notably the Civil Service, discouraged women from long service by paying 'dowries' in lieu of pension rights to women leaving employment to marry, but only for up to twelve years' service (Sanderson, 1990). From the 1960s the 'two-phase' work profile began to emerge, replacing the 'marriage career'. Increasingly, women who had left employment on marriage began to return in later life, usually when their children had reached school age. In a climate of post-war labour shortages, married women were tempted back into employment by employers who introduced part-time jobs and 'twilight shifts'. Over the past thirty years the pace of change has been rapid: as women no longer typically leave employment on marriage, but usually at the birth of the first child, their periods out of employment are becoming shorter. They are increasingly returning to work in between births; and a growing minority of younger women do not plan to leave employment at all, except to take maternity leave (Martin and Roberts, 1984). Indeed, the evidence suggests that the two-phase work profile is rapidly becoming a less-than-accurate description of how a large number of women experience the labour market.

A crucial question for feminists is whether the sexual division of labour in the home has been renegotiated in the light of women's increasing involvement in paid work outside the home. The answer gleaned from research studies is a gloomy one. Despite optimistic claims by some sociologists about the emergence of 'symmetrical' families (Young and Willmott, 1975) – families where women and men allegedly engage more equally in housework, child-care and decision-making – it appears that little, in fact, has changed (Oakley, 1976a; and Morris, 1990). Women still perform the bulk of household chores, particularly child-care tasks, and assume the main burden of responsibility for the care of elderly, disabled and dependent relatives. In addition, it is women who 'mediate' between the private and public spheres of service provision by, for example, liaising with health-care workers when children are ill, taking children to the dentist and so on (Graham, 1984). If anything, the demands on women's time and energy as unpaid carers is increasing, as a result of current community care policies in health care in Britain, for example (Finch and Groves, 1983; and Ungerson, 1987). This is because care by the community in practice translates into care by the family, and this inevitably means care by women in the family. For feminists, this lack of any fundamental reorganisation in the household division of labour means that, within marriage, men still effectively enjoy the 'right' to expect a range of services from their wives or partners, whilst women are duty-bound to provide these, whether or not they also find themselves engaged in paid employment outside the home.

Gender segregation at work

I have discussed how more and more women are participating in paid employment for longer, less intermittent periods of time during their working lives. But what about the terms on which they participate in paid employment, such as the hours they work, the pay they receive and the kinds of jobs in which they find themselves, compared to men? There are two key issues here. The first is part-time and other typically feminised forms of employment; the second is gender segregation at work.

Many women work part-time. It has been the expansion of low-level, low-paying, part-time working which has facilitated the increase in the amount, as well as changes in the pattern, of female labour force participation in Britain, as it has in other European countries. In the European Community as a whole around 28 per cent of all women in employment in 1989 worked part-time, with Britain being one of the member countries with the highest proportion of part-time women workers (CEC, 1990; Dale, 1991). The creation of part-time employment in the immediate post-war years and since has been a deliberate strategy on the part of employers to tempt married women back into the labour market. In Britain, 42 per cent of women employees work part-time rather than full-time, whilst four-fifths of Britain's 5 million-strong part-time workforce are women (Equal Opportunities Commission, 1990).

A crucial question for feminists is: who benefits from part-time employment? In one sense, the increasing availability of part-time work-

ing has been an important factor in facilitating women's greater participation in paid work, by enabling them to combine paid work with the
demands of domesticity and child-care (Martin and Roberts, 1984). In
other words, part-time employment enables women to engage in paid
work and achieve a modicum of economic independence, but within the
constraints placed on their time and energy by the gendered division of
labour within the household. Whether this means that women benefit
from part-time work is debatable, as part-time workers are often seen as
marginal members of the workforce, enjoy little employment protection,
and perform work which is frequently of low status and poorly-paid.
Part-time workers are less likely to enjoy good conditions of employment such as paid holidays, sick pay or occupational pension schemes,
to have promotion and training opportunities, or to work in unionised
jobs (Martin and Roberts, 1984). In addition, women are much more
likely to experience downward occupational mobility if they return to
work on a part-time basis after child-bearing. In the Women and Employment survey (Martin and Roberts, 1984), 45 per cent of women
going back to a part-time job experienced downward occupational
mobility, returning to a lower-level job. Furthermore, it may be argued
that the feminisation of part-time work puts a brake on any real reorganisation of gender roles within the household, for as long as male partners
in households more typically have full-time employment, then the ideological underpinnings of the household division of labour remain un-
challenged, as men continue to be seen as 'main breadwinners' and
women's earnings as supplementary.

The creation of part-time work has been a gender-specific strategy
on the part of employers in order to tap pools of female labour, both
during post-war labour shortages and in the recession of the early 1990s
and period of economic restructuring. Labour flexibility and cheapness
have now become crucial employer strategies in the restructuring of the
workforce, and these are being achieved in gender-specific ways. When
women are employed, part-time jobs are created; when men are employed, short-time working, temporary contracts and overtime are used
to achieve flexibility and cheapness (Beechey and Perkins, 1987). But
men too benefit from women's part-time employment, both as husbands
or partners of women and as workers. Part-time work for married or
cohabiting women may be seen as a compromise between the conflicting
interests of men and capital (Walby, 1986); between the interests men
have in retaining women's unpaid domestic services in the household

and the interests of employers in tapping women's labour. But the creation of part-time work to tap pools of female labour is not a universal strategy. In some Nordic countries, better state provision of child-care and welfare facilities lessens the constraints on women, particularly those with children, to take part-time rather than full-time employment.

Before moving on to look at gender segregation and the kinds of jobs in which women typically find themselves, it is important to recognise that homeworking represents another highly feminised form of paid work. Homeworkers are one of the most vulnerable and low-paid groups in the workforce and are often found doing manufacturing, needlework, office and clerical work, childminding and semi-professional work. The Trades Union Congress estimated that there were 390 000 homeworkers in 1981, although it is extremely difficult to gauge the precise number of homeworkers in Britain. The debate about whether or not Black women are disproportionately represented amongst their ranks (Phizaklea, 1988; and Wolverhamption Homeworkers Project, 1984) or slightly under-represented (Hakim, 1979) should alert us to the differences between white women, Asian women and Afro-Caribbean women in Britain, not only in relation to homeworking but also in relation to part-time and full-time employment, and the kinds of jobs done. As regards part-time employment, there are important ethnic differences between women. One study showed that whilst 44 per cent of white women worked part-time, only 29 per cent of Afro-Caribbean women and 16 per cent of Asian women did (Brown, 1984). And whilst full-time work is associated with better pay and conditions for white women, the same is not true for Black women (Greater London Council, 1986). Indeed, it has been argued that the emphasis white feminists have placed on part-time work as a determinant of gender inequalities between women's and men's paid work can be seen as ethnocentric (Amos and Parmar, 1984; Barrett and McIntosh, 1985; and Bruegel, 1989). Table 12.2 shows how, in Britain, Black women are much less likely to be working part-time and appear to be constrained to work full-time; especially West Indian women, who are more likely to be the main or sole breadwinners in a family and to find themselves in poverty. Whereas for white women, rewards, prospects and the quality of work vary greatly between those who work full-time and those who work part-time, the same is not true for Black women. As Irene Bruegel (1989) suggests, white feminists need to seriously rethink their 'domestic responsibilities' model of women's disadvantaged position in the labour market, as the standard

Table 12.2   *Proportion of economically active women working full or part time*

Ethnic group	% Full time employees	% Part time	% Self employed
White	52	40	6
West Indian	71	24	2
Indian	66	21	8
Pakistani/Bangladeshi	[55]	[27]	[18]
All Black	65	25	7

Source: Labour Force Survey 1984/5/6 in Irene Bruegel (1989) 'Sex and race in the labour market', *Feminist Review*, 32, p. 56.

picture they present of the way women have negotiated their 'double burden' by taking part-time work does not necessarily apply to Black women.

If we turn to look at the kinds of industries and jobs in which women are employed, then studies reveal that women and men tend to be employed in different occupations and industries, and that women are concentrated in a much smaller number of jobs and industries than are men. This is referred to as *gender segregation*, which is now believed by feminists and policy-makers alike to be the single most important reason for the persistence of gender inequalities, particularly wage differentials, in the labour market. The existence of gender segregation explains women's lower wages compared to men's. The Equal Pay Act 1975 in Britain had the immediate effect of reducing some of the differences between women's and men's earnings, but it remains the case that women's average gross hourly earnings are less than three-quarters of those of men. In 1988, in Britain, female manual workers earned on average 70.8 per cent of the hourly earnings of male manual workers; female non-manual workers earned an average of 62.2 per cent of the hourly wage of their male equivalents (Equal Opportunities Commission, 1990). The limited impact of the Equal Pay Act has been largely due to gender segregation in the workplace, as this has meant that women and men, for the most part, are not actually engaged in the same types of work.

Gender segregation within industry takes the form of women's underrepresentation in the primary sector (agriculture, forestry and fishing, energy and water); in most manufacturing industries; in transport and communications; and, in particular, in the construction industry. But, as

Figure 12.1 shows, whilst women are under-represented in 7 out of 9 industrial divisions, they are over-represented in just 3: distribution, hotels, catering and repairs; banking, finance and insurance; and in a catch-all category, other services, which includes medical and other services. In fact, two of these industrial divisions (distribution, hotels, catering and repairs; and other services) account for around two-thirds of all female employment in Britain (Equal Opportunities Commission, 1991).

Gender segregation occurs not only within industries but also within occupations. So in what kinds of jobs are women typically found? Studies of women's and men's jobs in Britain, and more generally in

Figure 12.1   *Representation of women by industry*

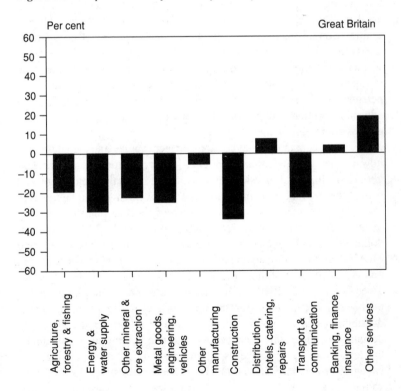

Source: Census of Employment in Equal Opportunities Commission, *Women and Men in Britain 1991* (London, HMSO, 1991).

industrial societies, show that women and men do different kinds of jobs in the labour market (Hakim, 1979; Martin and Roberts, 1984; and Walby, 1989). Occupational segregation by sex is the term used to describe the extent to which women and men work in different kinds of jobs. There are two dimensions of occupational segregation: *horizontal*, which simply describes the fact that women and men are most commonly working in different types of jobs; and *vertical*, which describes how men are most commonly found in higher-grade occupations, and women in lower-grade occupations (Hakim, 1979). Figure 12.2 shows the pattern of horizontal vertical segregation across sixteen occupational groups, showing how women are under- or over-represented in each of these. In Britain, about a quarter of of all occupations have a higher proportion of female workers than in the labour force as a whole, whilst three-quarters of all occupations have a higher proportion of male workers than in the labour force as a whole (Hakim, 1979; and Equal Opportunities Commission, 1991). This means that a quarter of occupations are 'typically female', whilst three-quarters are 'typically male'. In 1987, women accounted for around three-quarters of employees in the three occupational groupings of catering, cleaning, hairdressing and other personal services; clerical and related; and professional and related in education, welfare and health, whereas women made up 43 per cent of employees in employment.

Vertical occupational segregation between women and men describes how men tend to predominate in higher-level occupations, such as managerial and higher professional types of non-manual employment and skilled forms of manual employment, whilst women tend to be found in lower-level occupations, such as lower professional and clerical non-manual jobs, and semi-skilled or unskilled manual jobs. Men continue to dominate the ranks of management, particularly senior management, and even in 1989, women remain under-represented in management, making up only 27 per cent of those in managerial occupations (Equal Opportunities Commission, 1990). However, the number of women employed in managerial occupations (for example, office managers; managers in distribution and of hotels and clubs) and in professional and related occupations supporting management and administration (for example, the law, accountancy, advertising and marketing) nearly doubled between 1979 and 1989 (Equal Opportunities Commission, 1990). When women gain entry to or increase their presence in a particular occupation, gender segregation may still occur *within* it, however. For example, in pharmacy, although formal qualification levels of women and men

Figure 12.2 *Representation of women by occupational group in England, 1988*

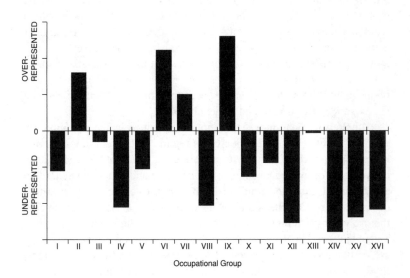

Source: Labour Force Survey in Equal Opportunities Commission, *Women and Men in Great Britain 1990* (London, HMSO, 1990).

Key: Occupational groups

I	Professional and related supporting management
II	Professional and related in education, welfare and health
III	Literary, artistic, sports
IV	Professional and related in science, engineering, technology
V	Managerial
VI	Clerical and related
VII	Selling
VIII	Security and protective services
IX	Catering, cleaning, hairdressing and other personal service
X	Farming, fishing and related
XI	Processing, making, repairing and related (excl metal and electrical)
XII	Processing, making, repairing and related (metal and electrical)
XIII	Painting, repetitive assembling, product inspecting, packaging and related
XIV	Construction and mining
XV	Transport operating, materials moving and storing and related
XVI	Miscellaneous

entering the profession are equal, women become segregated into 'prac-titioner' niches, whilst men move into 'managerial practitioner' roles (Crompton and Sanderson, 1989). Male careers in non-manual hier-archies may therefore be seen as constructed at the expense of female careers. Indeed, there are also a number of important ways in which women's activities sustain men's careers in their roles as wives, as their activities are often 'incorporated' into their husbands' careers – enter-taining clients and colleagues in the interests of their husband's business contacts and promotion, typing research papers and books, taking tele-phone calls at home or keeping the accounts for the self-employed man (Finch, 1983; and Callan and Ardener, 1984).

Although occupational segregation in Britain is influenced more by gender than by 'race' and ethnicity, as Figure 12.3 shows, it is none the less crucial to recognise that within the overall pattern of broad similarity between the occupational segregation of white and Black women, there are important 'race' and ethnic differences as the degree of concentration of Asian, Afro-Caribbean and white women varies. Asian women find themselves over-represented in lower-paid unskilled and semi-skilled manual jobs and in certain sectors of industry; whilst West Indian women are particularly under-represented in professional and managerial jobs, in which only 2 per cent of West Indian women are employed as compared to 17 per cent of white women and 20 per cent of Asian women (Brown, 1984). Over the last twenty years, 'race' and ethnic patterns have developed within the overall pattern of women's employ-ment as, for example, Asian women are highly concentrated in manu-facturing, particularly textiles and clothing, whilst Afro-Caribbean and white women are divided between the manufacturing and service sectors in a similar way (Phizacklea, 1988). In addition, within any particular sector, there are important 'race' and ethnic differences in occupational distribution. For example, within the category 'professional and scien-tific' services, whereas a high proportion of white women are adminis-trative workers, the majority of Afro-Caribbean women are found in nursing jobs and the remainder in manual work, particularly cleaning and catering (Brown, 1984; and Greater London Council, 1986).

It is therefore vital to deconstruct the category 'women', in order to pull out the differences *between* women. This applies to lesbians and women with disabilities (see Chapter 11), as well as to Black women. Women with disabilities are much more likely to be in unskilled work than either men with disabilities or women without disabilities, and they also have a greater propensity for unemployment (Lonsdale, 1990). In

Figure 12.3 *Distribution of workers by occupational grouping: by sex and ethnic origin, Great Britain, 1984–86 average*

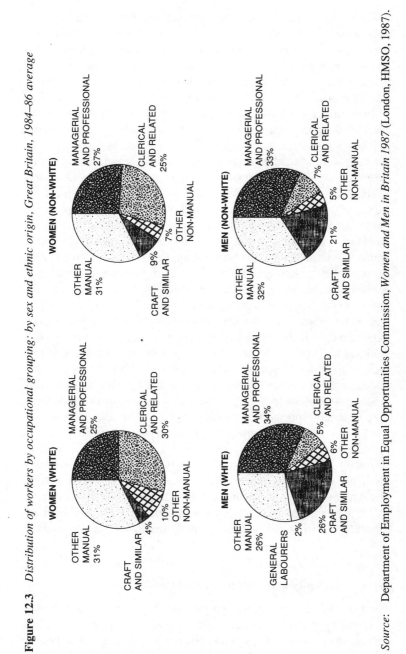

Source: Department of Employment in Equal Opportunities Commission, *Women and Men in Britain 1987* (London, HMSO, 1987).

advanced industrial countries, the feminisation of the labour force has been a steady and continuous feature in the context of changing economic conditions. From 1945 to the 1960s, economic growth and stability meant that it was the shortage of workers which drew women into the labour force in increasing numbers. However, the period of economic recession in the 1970s followed by a period of fundamental economic restructuring in the 1980s, involving the search for flexibility, has not reversed this process, but rather reinforced it. In Britain, labour market deregulation has led to the widespread expansion and promotion of forms of work which are characteristic of women's employment – part-time work, as well as temporary and casual employment (Atkinson, 1986; Pollert, 1981; and Dale, 1991). So women's employment has expanded during the current period of crisis and restructuring, as women continue to provide the flexible labour force sought by cost-cutting employers. The irony is that the 'model worker', once male with a continuous attachment to the labour market, might now become female, as employers capitalise on the weaker and more marginal position of women in the labour market (Hagen and Jenson, 1988). However, these trends might suggest a fundamental continuity in the terms on which women are employed, rather than any significant break with past practices, as more and more employment opportunities are part-time, poorly-paid and less skilled, and done largely by women workers, whilst only women in full-time employment will enjoy similar benefits to men, thus widening the wage gap between part-time and full-time women themselves (Humphries and Rubery, 1988). Surveying women's employment in comparative perspective, some general conclusions emerge (see Tables 12.3 and 12.4). Participation rates for women are continuing to increase or remain stable, whereas those for men have slowly declined over the past few decades. Women overwhelmingly work in the service sector and make up the bulk of the part-time workforce; they are concentrated in low-wage occupations; and, although there has been a narrowing of the unemployment rate differential between women and men, the unemployment rate for women is still higher in some cases (Bakkar, 1988).

Gender, sexuality and workplace relations

Feminist interest in occupational segregation by sex has not been limited to surveying the broad sweep of gender divisions in employment, although this is clearly of central importance in explaining the wages gap between women and men in Western economies (Walby, 1988). Femin-

Table 12.3 *Concentration of women workers by occupation (percentage of female labour force)*

	Clerical	Sales	Professional and technical	Administrative and managerial	Service workers
Canada	34.0	10.5	19.3	4.8	18.0
France	26.9	10.4	19.7	1.5	15.3
Germany	31.0	13.2	13.8	1.5	16.9
Italy	14.4	12.4	13.1	0.2	13.5
UK	30.8	12.2	12.2	0.9	23.3
USA	34.3	6.8	15.2	5.9	21.0

Source: Organisation for Economic Co-operation and Development (1985) *The Integration of Women into the Economy*, Paris, in Jane Jenson, Elizabeth Hagen and Cealliagh Reddy, *Feminization of the Labour Force: Paradoxes and Promises* (Cambridge, Polity Press, 1988).

Table 12.4 *Part-time employment*

	Women's share of part-time employment	
	1973	1981
Canada[a]	69.5	72.0
France	82.1	84.6
Germany	92.4	93.8
Italy	55.4	64.1
Sweden	88.0	84.5
UK	92.1	94.3
USA	68.4	70.3

[a] 1975 and 1981.

Source: Organisation for Economic Co-operation and Development (1983) *Employment Outlook*, Paris, in Jane Jenson, Elizabeth Hagen and Cealliagh Reddy, *Feminization of the Labour Force: Paradoxes and Promises* (Cambridge, Polity Press, 1988).

ists have also conducted a number of small-scale workplace studies, which explore the everyday realities of women's and men's experiences of work. The reality of occupational segregation by sex is that women and men rarely work side by side in their workplaces, and that women are rarely found supervising and managing the work of men (Martin and Roberts, 1984). Feminists have also explored the deeply-entrenched cultural and ideological constructions of women's worth as being less than men's. It is vital to appreciate that the very designation of the skill level of a job is saturated with gender bias and that the grading of jobs often depends as much, if not more, upon the gender of the person performing it than it does on the content of the job itself (Phillips and Taylor, 1980; Cockburn, 1983; and Crompton and Jones, 1984). 'Far from being an objective economic fact, skill is often an ideological category imposed on certain types of work by virtue of the sex and the power of the workers who perform it . . . It is the sex of those who do the work, rather than its content, which leads to its identification as skilled or unskilled' (Phillips and Taylor, 1980, pp. 79 and 82).

A brief consideration of gender divisions in clerical work illustrates this link between sex and skill. A study by Rosemary Crompton and Gareth Jones (1984) of clerical workers in insurance, banking and local authority employment provides grist to the mill for the argument that it is not so much the content of the job as the sex of the workers which determines its grading and classification. This study found that women are more likely than men to be in relatively demanding jobs, requiring a range of technical and social skills, but that these jobs are nevertheless placed in low clerical grades.

Workplace studies show the everyday reality of horizontal occupation segregation, and tell us more about the kinds of tasks and jobs women and men typically find themselves doing. They also reveal not only how women's work is defined as less-skilled, whatever the level of skill involved, but also that working-class women are more likely to be segregated into labour-intensive work, whilst men predominate in capitalintensive, that is, more mechanised, forms of work. Anna Pollert's (1981) study of a tobacco factory in Bristol showed women doing labour-intensive work such as weighing, packing, stripping and spinning; and men doing more mechanised jobs such as moisturising, blending and cutting in the early stage of tobacco preparation. Peter Armstrong's (1982) study of two factories, one producing footwear, the other electrical goods, similarly found that men tended to monopolise craft work (whatever the level of skill involved in the latter), whilst women's work tended to be unrecognised as skilled (whatever the actual levels of skill involved). Similarly, in her study of a car components factory, Ruth Cavendish (1982) argues that the prominent division on the shop-floor is that between women and men workers, in terms of the jobs they do (with women concentrated in semi-skilled assembly work), their opportunities for advancement and their workplace cultures. Finally, Sallie Westwood's

(1984) study of women's work in a knitting factory also showed how women were relegated to tasks such as machining and pressing which were not socially constructed as skilled, unlike the men's jobs as knitters, mechanics, dyers and managers.

Feminist workplace studies also reveal the ways in which shop floor hierarchies are gendered, not only in terms of skill classification, but also in terms of the supervision and management of work. In Ruth Cavendish's study, men on the shop floor occupied positions of varying authority: as chargehands, supervisors, quality controllers and progress chasers. Anna Pollert discusses how work discipline was mediated through men's control and how women were continually exposed to sexual harassment from male chargehands and foremen, as well as from male operatives. There are also important ways in which women are controlled and restricted in physical ways in the workplace; in sedentary jobs they are tied to machines, whereas men are permitted more physical mobility and are more able to rove freely around the shop floor.

The proliferation of workplace studies in the 1970s reflected the interest of socialist-feminists in particular, in understanding the ways in which gender divisions persist within the capitalist workplace and the class relations of capitalism. In the 1980s, broader questions concerning the interrelationship between class, gender and 'race' as different yet cross-cutting forms of oppression in the workplace began to be addressed for, as Black feminists have indicated, 'race' was often ignored in these earlier studies. More recently, there has been another challenging shift of emphasis in feminist workplace studies, which are beginning to explore sexuality and male power in the workplace. Feminist writers have begun to turn their attention to the workplace, this time as a site of sexualised power relations between women and men.

Feminist workplace studies, mainly from radical feminist perspectives, have focused on the ways in which the deployment of sexuality becomes a means whereby men control women in the office or the boardroom, as well as in the bedroom. The significance of sexuality in the workplace has been examined through discussions of sexual harassment, which is defined broadly as unwanted and intrusive sexual attention, which can be verbal, visual or physical (Stanko, 1985, 1988). Sexual harassment is seen as one of the means whereby the sexualisation of women reinforces the gendering of workplace relations and hierarchies, particularly as a means of driving women out of previously all-male spheres of employment (MacKinnon, 1978; and Stanko, 1988). Other recent work focuses more broadly on sexuality and reveals how it is a public issue, as well as an issue of power, and that it is embedded within workplace organisations, particularly managerial hierarchies (Hearn and Parkin, 1986). Another approach to the study of sexuality, power and workplace relations is represented by Rosemary Pringle's (1989) study of secretaries and bosses. Pringle argues that the sexualisation of jobs and hierarchies is a vital, yet neglected, underpinning of gender segregation at work. So, for example, she argues that it is easier to define what a secretary *is* than to specify what a secretary *does*. Secretaries are represented in gendered, sexualised and familial terms and Pringle identifies three constructions of what a secretary is: the 'office wife', the 'sexy secretary' or the 'career woman'. So Pringle is urging us not to see jobs as purely functional roles, which initially consist of gender neutral tasks, into which women are recruited and which then become sexualised. Instead, she urges us to see the three processes of job definition, gendering and sexualisation as concurrent and inseparable processes.

Pringle's work and the work of radical feminists suggests that, in a patriarchal society where male sexuality and power are so intimately bound up together, the sexualisation of workplace relations is not easily undone. This does not mean to say that women cannot resist forms of male control, such as sexual harassment. Indeed, codes of practice advising women on what constitutes sexual harassment, and how they can initiate grievance procedures, are being drawn up in many workplaces. However, other feminist analyses of women in organisations, particularly Rosabeth Kanter's (1977) study of gender and managerial hierarchies, are more optimistic, as they see the sexualisation of women as just one of the resources which men use in order to defend already gendered workplace territories. So the sexualisation of, for example, the attributes of a 'good manager' functions as an exclusionary device that rationalises women's exclusion from managerial positions rather than creates it.

This broadening focus of feminist workplace studies from 'gender' to 'sexuality' has also rendered heterosexist forms of oppression and discrimination more visible (London Strategic Policy Unit, 1987). Lesbians in organisations are liable to experience 'double jeopardy' in terms of their gender as women and in terms of their sexuality, especially as the background buzz of heterosexist assumptions continually presents issues of whether or not to disclose their lesbianism (Hall, 1989). Lesbians and gay men in Britain experience discrimination at work, in the form of employers' attitudes to recruiting and promoting lesbian and gay staff, and also from other workers. Lesbians working with heterosexual women, and gay men working with heterosexual men, may also experience profound alienation from sexualised workplace cultures. Heterosexist discrimination at work is less visible and, indeed, is not illegal in Britain.

Explaining gender divisions in employment

Feminists have engaged in lively debate about the mechanisms generating and sustaining the disadvantaged and gender-specific nature of women's participation in paid work. There are two main sources of tension within feminist accounts. The first concerns the relationship between women's oppression in the family and in the labour market. Is it women's oppression in the family that largely dictates the terms and conditions under which they engage in paid work? This approach is referred to by Irene Bruegel (1989) as the 'domestic responsibilities model'. Or is it the case that the segregation of women into low-paid and low-status jobs in paid employment is now the crucial factor sustaining patterns of male privilege in advanced industrial societies, including male dominance in the family, as women's exclusion from better-paid jobs in turn forces them into marriage and dependency on a male wage? Or is it both of these? This tension in feminist theory turns upon the relative importance of the private or the public sphere in sustaining patterns of male dominance and female subordination.

The second tension in feminist theory has emerged in the form of a debate about the structural determinants of women's oppression. Is it the dynamics of capitalism which have generated women's lower wages and gender segregation at work? Or is this too narrow an explanation? Does this ignore the actions of men, who have secured and tried to hang on to male privileges in the labour market, but at the expense of women, and who have thereby ensured that women continue to provide them with unpaid domestic and caring services in the home? This debate turns upon the question of whether or not we need a concept of patriarchy in order to understand the interrelationship between class and gender divisions in shaping women's oppression at work. The debate has more recently been recast in broader terms, as white feminists have been forced to confront the ethnocentrism of some of their accounts of the dynamics of women's oppression, which Black feminists in particular have highlighted, recognising the specific nature of Black women's oppression, and confronting the question of the complex interrelationship between class, gender and 'race'.

In seeking to explain gender segregation and inequalities in paid employment, feminist have simultaneously drawn upon and moved beyond existing concepts used within economics and sociology to explain the operation of labour markets and understand the world of work. Furthermore, feminist work has been extremely important in challenging received wisdoms and broadening frames of reference within academic disciplines. The sociology of work had traditionally tended to concentrate on white males, but on those rare occasions when women were taken into account in workplace studies, their experiences and attitudes to work were often simply assumed to derive from their family roles and activities (Brown, 1976; Feldberg and Glen, 1979; Yeandle, 1984; and Beechey, 1987). Studies of employment in the 1950s and 1960s operated with a 'masculinist' conception of work (Beechey, 1987) using a 'job-model' to analyse men's experiences and attitudes to work in terms of the conditions of work itself, but adopting a 'gender-model' to explain women's attitudes to work solely in terms of the family and their activities within it (Feldberg and Glen, 1979). Much of the research during this period focused on the problem-creating nature for the family of married women's employment, but without really questioning existing gender roles and power relations within the family. Explanations of female employment were 'theoretically subordinated to the claims of domesticity', as Jackie West (1978) neatly expressed it. Much of this research operated within a 'voluntaristic' framework, focusing on women's motives and attitudes to work and assuming that women's position in the workforce could be 'read off' or deduced from their different orientations to work and their family responsibilities.

Feminist research in the 1970s began to subject the gendered division of labour in both the household and the labour market to far more critical scrutiny. Economists had largely been content to explain gender segregation in employment and women's lower wages in terms of women typically possessing less 'human capital' – or marketable skills and expertise – because they interrupt their work careers to bear and rear children. Feminists began to point out that even if women did work continuously without breaks, they were still found in low-paid jobs. Indeed, there is now a substantial body of feminist research which also shows that when women leave paid work to rear children, they typically experience downwards occupational mobility, moving back into lower-level jobs when they return to work, so their 'human capital' is being disregarded or under-rewarded (Dex, 1987). Increasingly, then, feminists have argued that it is necessary to look at the structure and operation of the labour market in order to explain gender segregation at work, rather than relying solely on a 'domestic responsibilities model'.

One way of doing this has been offered by *dual labour market theory*,[2] which examines the ways in which labour markets are structured into two distinct sectors: a primary and a secondary sector. Primary sectors are characterised by forms of employment associated with high wages, fringe benefits, skills, opportunities for education and training, employment stability and high levels of unionisation. Secondary sectors are composed of jobs characterised more by low wages, few fringe benefits, lack of skill, few training opportunities and low levels of unionisation. The confinement of women to secondary labour markets, according to this model, provides the main reason for gender-related job segregation and the generally disadvantaged position of women in the labour market. There are five attributes which make a social group a preferred source of secondary labour from an employer's point of view: dispensability; clearly visible social differences; low interest in economic rewards; little interest in acquiring training; and lack of solidarity (Barron and Norris, 1976). Women as a social group possess these attributes, or at least employers believe they do – in fact, it is never entirely clear which of these is supposed to be the case.

There is no doubt that dual labour market theory offers some insights in the structuring of labour markets, although it by no means provides an exhaustive explanation of either the operation of labour markets or gender segregation at work. It relies wholly upon an explanation in terms of the discriminatory practices of employers and neglects the role of organised male workers, who have traditionally sought to exclude women from skilled jobs and secure privileges for male workers at the expense of women workers. Neither does it locate labour markets within wider economic, social and political processes, such as the dynamics of capitalist production, or the state's role in regulating the terms and conditions of work through employment and insurance policies.

Feminists concerned with explaining gender segregation at work have been interested in uncovering its broader structural causes, and an alternative focus on the ways in which labour markets are structured or segmented was offered from within Marxist accounts. These *theories of segmented labour markets* (Reich, Gordon and Edwards, 1980) locate analyses within the broader structural and historical context of the development of capitalism and focus particularly on how the workforce has been subjected to different forms of capitalist control. In truth, these analyses are more concerned to explore the transformation of the working class under capitalism than to explore gender divisions. Although it is argued that the segmentation of the workforce by sex has formed an integral part of the overall process of fragmentation and control of the working class, little indication is given of how precisely 'segmentation by sex' has also been linked to changing forms of capitalist control in the workplace. Indeed, it is argued that sex segmentation cannot simply be explained in terms of the workings of capitalism, but that this has a separate dynamic, although this is never specified. It fell to feminists to think this one through, and Heidi Hartmann (1979, 1981) has argued that this separate dynamic shaping gender segregation at work is one of patriarchy. But before looking at how feminists have introduced the concept of patriarchy into analyses of gender segregation, it is necessary to examine another way in which feminists have drawn upon Marxist theory in exploring gender divisions at work.

Some feminists turned to the Marxist concept of a reserve army of labour, or surplus population not yet drawn into waged labour, in order to explain the specificity of women's employment in capitalist societies. They were influenced by the work of Harry Braverman (1974) who argued that the transformation of the working class in the twentieth century, through deskilling, could not be fully understood without taking into account the fact that new forms of female employment made up the bulk of new working-class occupations. He argued that women have made up a vital part of the industrial reserve army of labour and have been drawn into employment, largely as jobs have been deskilled. Some feminists writers, notably Veronica Beechey (1977, 1987), Irene Bruegel (1979) and Jane Humphries (1983) have explored the explanatory potential of the industrial reserve-army model, which states that women are pulled into employment during periods of labour shortage and economic boom, but are the first to lose their jobs in a recession. Is this the case and, if so, why?

Veronica Beechey suggested that married women have been a preferred source of the industrial reserve army largely because of their position within the family, which makes them flexible and disposable members of the labour force. This is because they 'have a world of their very own, the family, into which they can disappear when discarded from production' (Beechey, 1977, p. 57). They are cheap too, because it is assumed that wives, unlike husbands, do not have to earn enough to support others in the family.

However, other feminists have been critical of the reserve-army hypothesis because it does not explain why women have been excluded from the labour market in the first place (Walby, 1986). Also, the existence of gender segregation may actually mitigate against women's unemployment in periods of recession, when industries and jobs in which men predominate may be the hardest hit, such as in the United States during the 1930s depression (Milkman, 1976), and indeed in Britain in the 1990s. Another criticism is that the reserve-army thesis may partly account for married women's lower pay, but it does not explain why gender segregation exists (Barrett, 1980). Irene Bruegel (1979) and Jane Humphries (1983) have both attempted to modify the reserve-army hypothesis in the light of the buoyant level of female employment in the 1970s. Irene Bruegel noted how women were more vulnerable than men to job-loss in manufacturing industries, but that the continued expansion of service-sector employment throughout the 1970s meant that, on the whole, women's employment opportunities did not deteriorate relative to men's. Jane Humphries also used data on female unemployment to suggest that women have indeed been used as an industrial reserve, but also that their cheaper labour has led to a substitution of female for male labour, which she sees as undermining gender segregation at work. As yet, however, there is no evidence to support the proposition that occupational gender segregation is declining.

Another way in which some feminists have forged connections between Marxist theory and feminism has been through *dual-systems theory*. Advocates of dual-systems theory introduce the concept of patriarchy in order to explain gender segregation at work. Dual-systems theory owes much to the pioneering analysis of 'patriarchal capitalism' by Heidi Hartmann (1979, 1981), who argues that patriarchal relations of male dominance and female subordination, far from being destroyed, have been sustained within capitalism. The basis of male power in patriarchal capitalism is men's control over women's labour within both the family and the labour market. Heidi Hartmann argues that job segregation by sex has provided the major means through which male dominance in the labour market has been secured, and that the 'family wage' (a male wage high enough to support a wife and children) has provided the pivotal means enabling men not only to ensure that working men receive higher wages than working women, but also to secure women's unpaid domestic services within the family, for women's low wages force them into marriage. Hartmann emphasises the role of trade union organisation amongst working men, which was a means not only of class struggle but also of gender struggle, as men secured gains for themselves often at the expense of working women.

So dual and segmented labour market theorists, together with feminists using the notion of a reserve army of labour, tend to focus on the actions of employers in their explanations of gender divisions in employment. Dual-systems theorists, however, insist that we also need to look at the actions of organised working men, who have excluded women from skilled and more lucrative forms of employment, particularly during the formative period of patriarchal capitalism in the nineteenth century. In other words, dual-systems theorists insist that patriarchy, as well as capitalism, structures gender divisions at work in modern Western societies.

Sylvia Walby (1986), another dual-systems theorist, argues that patriarchal relations are present in the workplace and that these exist alongside, yet in tension and conflict with, capitalist relations. At each phase of capitalist development new patriarchal strategies are pursued and new struggles between men and capitalists have produced distinct sets of gender relations in the workplace. Two main patriarchal strategies are identified by Walby. One is an exclusionary strategy, such as that used by engineering unions in the nineteenth century, based on excluding women from certain jobs. The other is a segregationary strategy based on confining women to jobs graded lower than those of men, such as those used by male clerical workers and an increasing proportion of trade unions from the last quarter of the nineteenth century.

What is particularly important about both Heidi Hartmann's and Sylvia Walby's work is their challenge to the conventional view, that the position of women in the labour market is determined by their position in the family. Both adopt a contrary position, arguing that gender segregation and patriarchal practices in the labour market are important in confining women to a subordinate position within the household (Walby, 1986, 1990). A number of other feminist writers have pioneered dual-systems analysis by engaging in detailed historical analyses of gender segregation and patriarchal practices in the printing trades (Cockburn, 1983); in silk production (Lown, 1990); in coal-mining (John, 1986; and Mark-Lawson and Witz, 1988); and in both the world wars (Braybon and Summerfield, 1987). Sallie Westwood's (1984) study of Black and white women workers in the hosiery industry not only vividly documents the role of family and factory in the creation of gender identities, but also successfully explores how Black and white women workers share in the experience of exploitation under patriarchal capitalism. She shows how racism intersects with patriarchal capitalism, subjecting Black women to a 'triple oppression' of class, gender and 'race'.

Dual-systems theorists have also explored the relation between technological change and gender segregation at work, demonstrating how the takeover of technological competence by men is an important factor generating gendered job hierarchies in, for example, medical X-ray work (Cockburn, 1985; and Witz, 1992); the printing industry; clothing manufacture; and mail-order warehouses (Cockburn, 1985). In addition, dual-systems theory has been used to examine patriarchal exclusionary strategies in professional employment, demonstrating how middle-class men have utilised professional organisations to exclude and segregate women within professional hierarchies (Witz, 1992).

The concept of patriarchy has proved vital in furthering feminist analyses of women's employment. In particular, dual-systems analyses have radically overturned the conventional view that gender divisions in employment can simply be read off from those in the family and so present a strong challenge to the 'domestic responsibilities model' of women's employment. Dual-systems theory has also provided a framework for arguments that the feminisation of the labour force in Western European societies is responsible for changing the form of patriarchy, as we are shifting from a 'private' form, which pivoted around male control over women in the family, to a 'public' form, sustained through male control over women's activities in the public sphere, particularly waged work, where gender segregation persists (Hernes, 1987; and Walby, 1990). Feminists analysing the advanced welfare states of Sweden and Denmark argue that the breakdown of the breadwinner–homemaker family has increased women's independence from their husbands but has also increased their dependence on the state as employees, clients and consumers of public services (Borchorst and Siim, 1987; and Hernes, 1987). Many of the jobs women do have been created due to the expansion of the welfare state and its administrative apparatus in Western economies: jobs such as teachers, health workers, social workers, and clerical and administrative jobs in local and central government. However, despite broadly similar trajectories from 'private' to 'public' patriarchy, there are differences in the degree of public patriarchy between different societies. In the advanced welfare states of Denmark and Sweden, women have become primarily dependent on the state as employees and as consumers of social services, whereas in Britain and the United States women are to a larger extent, still dependent either on their husbands or on the state as clients (Borchorst and Siim, 1987).

Conclusion: current issues and future prospects

Women engage in a complex web of work activities which span both public and private spheres (Balbo, 1987; and Smith, 1988). The tasks which women perform in each of these spheres are often similar and may be defined as 'servicing tasks'. These are tasks which ensure that the material conditions of life are sustained in an orderly way: tasks such as cleaning (the housewife, the chambermaid, the office cleaner, the hospital domestic, the home help); feeding (the cook, the waitress, the housekeeper, the home help, the nursery nurse); and tidying or organising (the housewife, the secretary, the filing clerk, the shop assistant). Women relieve men of many of the tasks necessary to sustain social life and the social world on a daily basis, and do so in both the private and the public spheres.

This complex interweaving of women's work activities in the household and the workplace, in formal and informal economies, is a universal feature of women's lives. Indeed, the existence of an international division of labour means that women all over the world are being pulled into the sphere of capitalist production. Feminists argue that women's oppression and patriarchy are universal phenomena, but at the same time recognise that patriarchy assumes different forms in different societies, just as existing patriarchal relations intersect with capitalist relations in different ways in different places (Mies, 1986). None the less, certain universal patterns in women's work are in evidence. Worldwide, one in three paid jobs go to women, but women make up only a quarter of employees in industry, although the rapid expansion of industrial employment in parts of Asia over the past thirty years has meant that their share of industrial jobs has been growing (Brekke *et al.*, 1985). It is in the service sector that women take the largest share of jobs worldwide, although in the developing world a quarter and in the rich world a half of service jobs are done by women. In developing countries in free-trade zones – where multinational corporations are encouraged to move in – there has been an overwhelming preference for young women workers (*World Survey: Women in Industrial Development*, 1985). Multinational capitalist employers draw upon and reproduce existing sets of patriarchal authority relations, perceiving young women as a 'docile' labour force (Elson and Pearson, 1989). Diane Elson and Ruth Pearson's work on women's employment in multinationals, in Europe and globally, demonstrates how they perpetuate an unequal gender division of labour, in which women production workers are merely 'nimble fingers', and how women are concentrated in a limited range of occupations and in positions in the bottom half of the jobs hierarchy. In white-collar jobs, women are concentrated in secretarial and clerical work (see Table 12.5), whilst in blue-collar jobs they are concentrated in work that requires 'nimble fingers' – sewing, food preparation and assembly work – classified as unskilled or semi-skilled. Just as feminists have argued for a redefinition of what counts as 'work' in industrial societies, so too have they drawn attention to the invisibility of women's work in developing countries, particularly their unacknowledged role in agriculture (which has generally been overlooked in aid programmes that benefit men at the expense of women) and in the informal economy (Joekes, 1987).

At the same time as developing analyses of the similarity between women's position in paid work worldwide, feminists emphasise the necessity of recognising the heterogeneity of women's experiences, which arise out of the complex interrelationship between different structures of oppression in any one society, where their experiences of paid work and position in the labour market will vary depending on how class, gender and 'race' intersect. For discussions of the intersection of gender with 'race' and class in Britain, see Phillips (1987), Phizacklea (1988), and Bhachu and Westwood (1988).

Table 12.5 *Percentage of female and male workforce in administrative and managerial ('bosses') and clerical ('secretaries') jobs*

	Bosses		*Secretaries*	
	Women	*Men*	*Women*	*Men*
Germany (Fed. Rep.)	1.3	4.2	34.0	9.6
Hungary	0.1	0.2	16.4	3.5
Norway	2.0	6.6	26.0	2.5
USA	3.8	10.4	27.9	5.5
Japan	0.4	6.4	18.2	9.4
Egypt	0.8	0.9	25.0	6.5
Bahrain	0.4	1.1	46.0	5.8
Singapore	1.2	8.2	14.9	5.7
Venezuela	1.6	9.2	16.7	7.6

Source: International Labour Office, *Yearbook of Labour Statistics, 1984,* copyright 1984 International Labour Organisation, Geneva; in Toril Brekke *et al.*, *Women: A World Report* (London, Methuen, 1985). It should be noted that the terms 'bosses' and 'secretaries' are *not* used by the International Labour Office, which uses the International Standard Classification of Occupations 'administration and managerial workers' and 'clerical and related workers'.

Finally, what is the future for women's employment? Demographic shifts in Western European societies mean that smaller numbers of young people are entering employment. Policy-makers, politicians and employers are, once again, looking to women to make up the predicted shortfall in the civilian labour force and seeking to devise incentives to ensure not only that women return to work in greater numbers after 'career breaks', but also that women remain in employment whilst bringing up children. The institutionalisation of women's dual role as key workers in both the private and the public spheres looks to be firmly on the agenda. Whereas some countries such as Denmark and Sweden have facilitated this dual role by socialising substantial portions of work performed within the private sphere, such as child-care, housework, and care for the elderly and infirm, other countries such as Britain have been cutting back on state welfare provision, redistributing caring activities back into the private realm and on to the shoulders of women.

Although patterns of gender segregation have mitigated against women suffering as much unemployment as men, none the less, as the current recession bites, women's jobs like men's jobs, are at risk. In the recession of the 1980s women's jobs have been insulated from its harshest effects because of their concentration in the service sector, which has not been as badly hit as the industrial sector. However, it is still true that women in the industrial sector have experienced greater job losses than men. It is difficult to assess the true rate of women's unemployment, because it has been estimated that over 40 per cent of women do not register as unemployed and so are missing from the unemployment statistics. Women's jobs tend to be more threatened than men's jobs because many are part-time or low-skilled, and more susceptible to job loss through the introduction of new technology that has been occurring in offices, manufacturing industries and the distributive trades (Dale, 1991).

To ensure that women are not the 'losers' it will be necessary for women and men to substantially renegotiate the gendered division of labour in both private and public spheres, as well as to reassess the relative worth of women's and men's work in these spheres. In the area of employment, women are still struggling to secure employment rights and benefits on a par with those of men, but are increasingly charting new demands. The persistence of job segregation by sex in the labour market and of a gendered division of labour within the household means that women participate in the public sphere on different terms than do men. Demands for equality of treatment – for equal pay and equal opportunities for the sexes – which characterised feminist workplace politics in the 1960s and 1970s are now being reformulated by some feminists to take on issues of sexual difference, opening up discussions about whether women want to be treated the same or differently (Meehan and Sevenhuijsen, 1991). The issue for feminists committed to a thorough re-evaluation of women's worth in waged work must be to confront the matter of whether women are empowered through demands for 'equal' treatment or for 'special' treatment if they are to participate in paid employment on their own terms, rather than on terms set by men.

Notes

1.   However, it has been argued that the family system of labour where the family worked under the direction and control of the male head of household survived in pockets of nineteenth-century industrial capitalism, such as coal mining, textiles, and boot and shoe manufacture, as a form of subcontracting (Mark-Lawson and Witz, 1988). It also exists today on family farms (Delphy, 1984b) and in small businesses (Phizacklea, 1988).
2.   For summaries of dual labour market theory and its application to gender divisions in employment, as well as of the other explanations of gender divisions in employment discussed in this chapter, see Dex (1985) and Beechey (1987).

Further reading

Veronica Beechey, *Unequal Work* (London, Verso, 1987). This is a collection of essays written over the past ten years exploring a number of topics such as explanations of women's work, part-time work, unemployment and the future of work. Veronica Beechey combines analysis of recent trends in women's employment with a critical analysis of sociological and economic theories, and links feminist theories with feminist workplace politics.

Sylvia Walby, *Patriarchy at Work* (Cambridge, Polity Press, 1986). Sylvia Walby develops and applies the concept of patriarchy in an analysis of women's work from 1800 to the present day. The interrelationship between capitalism and patriarchy is explored in historical case studies of women's employment in engineering, clerical work and textiles.

Cynthia Cockburn, *In the Way of Women: men's resistance to sex equality in organizations* (London, Macmillan, 1991). This study of men's reactions to equal opportunities strategies in four large organisations shows how women as a sex, Black people, lesbians and gay men, and people with disabilities are compelled to hide their 'difference' if they wish to claim a right to 'equality'.

Jane Jenson, Elizabeth Hagen and Ceallaigh Reddy (eds), *Feminization of the Labour Force: Paradoxes and Promises* (Oxford, Polity Press, 1988). This collection of papers examines trends in women's employment in a comparative perspective, looking at the terms on which women are increasing their participation in paid work in Britain, France, the Federal Republic of Germany, Sweden, Italy, Canada and the United States.

13

Women, History
and Protest
June Hannam

Writing in 1972, when the women's liberation movement was gaining momentum, Anna Davin urged women to study their own history, 'for by showing that the role and nature of women changes with each society we are helping to defeat the argument "that's how it's always been"'. As Davin suggests, the writing of women's history cannot be separated from contemporary feminist politics. Women concerned to understand their specific inequalities and to challenge institutions which perpetuate their oppression have looked to understand the roots of that oppression in the past; to discover whether such challenges had been made before and what they could learn from them (Davin, 1972, p. 224). If women saw themselves as marginal in the past it would reinforce their view of themselves as subordinate and powerless in the present. Only if a woman's role could be shown to be socially constructed and rooted in a specific historical context, rather than natural and universal, could feminists hope to argue that it was open to change.

The first organised women's movement of the late nineteenth century had already inspired an earlier generation of historians to research into women's history. Finding that 'hitherto the historian has paid little attention to the circumstances of women's lives', writers such as Alice Clark, Barbara Hutchins and Barbara Drake carried out detailed studies of women's work, trade unionism and political activities (Clark, 1968; Hutchins, 1915; and Drake, 1920). In the intervening years, however, their work became lost from view. This coincided with a fragmentation of the women's movement after the First World War. Many active feminists worked from within a variety of political groups, and feminist politics were often submerged as they grappled with issues of peace, Fascism and war.

It was only with the revival of a feminist movement in the late 1960s that interest in women's history was awakened once more. This suggests that 'women's experience has to be remembered anew with each resurgence of feminist consciousness, for between times it leaves scarcely a trace' (Alexander, 1984, p. 128). When feminists searched the history books they found that women were still largely 'hidden from history'. Nothing much seemed to have changed from when Virginia Woolf complained that although woman 'pervades poetry from cover to cover; she is all but absent from history . . . Of our fathers we always know some fact or some distinction. They were soldiers or they were sailors. They filled that office or they made that law, but of our mothers, our grandmothers, our great grandmothers what remains is nothing but a tradition. One was beautiful, one was red-haired, one was kissed by a queen. We know nothing of them except their names and the dates of their marriages and the number of children they bore' (Woolf, 1929, p. 45).

As Woolf implies, women's invisibility stemmed partly from what had long been seen as historically significant – foreign policy questions, the development of formal political institutions and the growth of industry and commerce. Women did not have a high profile in any of these areas and this could be construed as an expression of the subordinate role that they played as architects of their world. It has been all too easy for historians, products themselves of a particular social context, to accept the Victorian model of women's essential passivity and domesticity and to minimise their contribution to historical developments. Consequently, women have appeared in mainstream histories either as objects of humanitarian concern or as problems affecting male workers or administrators.

Women have not been completely absent from the history books. We know about some women and some events, although this in itself can have a distorting effect. A few 'great women' have been singled out for attention, for example Florence Nightingale, Elizabeth Fry, Josephine Butler and Elizabeth Garrett Anderson, but their lives and work have been seen as exceptional and their characters idealised to emphasise 'female' qualities of caring and saintliness. Women also tend to have been noticed when engaging in activities traditionally seen as important by historians, such as munitions work during the two world wars. It is no accident that the struggle for the vote, when women sought access to the formal political arena, has received the most consistent attention from historians and is the one campaign that is instantly recognisable to a wide audience.

Despite such exceptions, women's contribution to the development of social, economic and political change has been marginalised through their absence from mainstream historical studies (Lewis, 1981). Feminist historians in the early 1970s set out to redress the balance, and over the last two decades research and writing on aspects of women's history has steadily increased. This chapter will survey the developments that have taken place in the writing of women's history over the last twenty years. It points to changes in subject matter and approach, drawing attention to the way in which our understanding of women's lives has been altered by recent scholarship. The focus will be on British women's history from the late eighteenth century. Where appropriate, reference will also be made to research undertaken into American women's history. Here the approaches and concerns have often had a different focus, leading to a fruitful exchange of ideas between researchers in the two countries (Newton *et al.*, 1983). Finally, recent trends in women's history and the most likely developments for the future will be discussed.

Given the paucity of references to women in standard texts, one of the first tasks of feminist historians was to rediscover women's active role in the process of historical change. Sheila Rowbotham's pioneering study, aptly entitled *Hidden from History* (Rowbotham, 1973), led the way and was followed by a series of monographs on aspects of women's lives, including employment, women's organisations, family life, and sexuality. With the emphasis of the women's liberation movement on consciousness-raising, feminists saw a knowledge of their past as a source of strength and therefore drew attention to women who had achieved in the public arena. If they looked hard enough, historians could find women at the workplace, in trade unions and taking part in political and social reform movements; where they canvassed for political parties, stood for election to public bodies and were militant at times of labour unrest (Lewenhak, 1977; Burman, 1979; and Hollis, 1979). The American historian and feminist theorist, Gerda Lerner, describes such an approach as contribution history; that is, one which sought to include women within an existing male-defined history, where activities in the public and political arena were seen as of greatest historical importance (Lerner, 1981).

Other feminist historians, in particular in the United States, were more interested in focusing on the development in the nineteenth century of a separate women's sphere. They explored the predominant ideals and values which underpinned women's social role and their sexuality, and produced studies of prostitution, images of women in art and literature, the double standard of morality, and contemporary debates about women's nature and femininity (Hartman and Banner, 1974; and Vicinus, 1981). The dangers in such an approach were that women could too easily be seen as victims of male oppression and that historians could end up describing 'what men in the past have told women to do and what men in the past thought women should be' (Lerner, 1981, p. 149).

Both the research into women's activities outside the home and the interest in exploring the development of a separate sphere for women went beyond simply putting women back into an existing historical framework. It also meant a challenge to definitions of what should be seen as historically significant. The growth of social history in the 1960s and 1970s provided a context for such a redefinition. The expansion of higher education, and the proliferation of social science courses, encouraged historians to recognise the significance of subjects such as family structure and relationships, sexuality, popular culture, childhood and youth for an overall understanding of social, political and economic change (Perkin, 1976; and Judt, 1979). Using insights from other disciplines, notably sociology and social anthropology, historians began to research new topics, such as the importance of etiquette and social rituals, or birth control and family size (Davidoff, 1973). They also began to examine the interrelationship between areas often seen as separate, such as work and family; or community, culture and class.

Struggles against colonialism abroad and the development of rank-and-file movements at home, coupled with changes in Marxist theory, led to a new focus on 'history from below' (Hobsbawm, 1971). Emphasis was placed on those who had previously lacked a voice, in particular unorganised rank-and-file workers and the very poor, and an attempt was made to evaluate their experiences as expressed through their work, family life, culture and class consciousness (Thompson, 1968; and Samuel, 1981). An interest in 'history from below' did not automatically mean, however, that all hitherto neglected groups were included. It was only when the women's movement of the early 1970s sought to reclaim its past that women were put at the centre, rather than left in the background, of historical enquiry. Although feminist historians made a major contribution to broadening the focus of historical enquiry, they concentrated largely on the experiences of white middle-class and working-class women. It was not until later that the need to explore the history of Black women and lesbians was more fully recognised.

To trace the history of neglected, less-powerful groups could seem to be a daunting task. Sources might at first sight appear not to exist, in particular to those historians used to relying on records of institutions, on government statistics, or on the extensive personal papers left to posterity by the wealthy and powerful. If lesbian, Black and working-class women's experience was not seen as important, either by themselves or by others, they were unlikely to have recorded it in their own right. Lesbians in particular may have destroyed written material in order to protect themselves, and others, thereby helping to compound their invisibility. Parliamentary papers, social surveys, trade union and socialist journals were usually written by men, often drawn from the middle class, and therefore reflecting their preoccupations and biases.

And yet, by asking the right questions, historians have been able to find a surprising amount of material in already familiar sources on family life, living standards and the lives of women and children. Anna Davin found that 'accumulating information and details given incidentally in other contexts' was one of the best ways for historians to find out about ordinary life (Davin, 1972, p. 218; and Beddoe, 1983). Police court cases in newspapers, the reports of charity and missionary societies, medical officers' reports, hospital records, journal articles and photographs, for example, can provide a mine of information on life histories, diet and child-care practices. Recent studies of Black women's history have shown that, far from being invisible, Black women's experiences can also be traced through a wide variety of sources, including the private papers of planters and missionaries, government enquiries, census data, newspapers and autobiographies (Higginbotham and Watts, 1988; and Alexander, 1990).

Perhaps the single most well-known source and methodology to emerge from this interest in uncovering the experiences of 'ordinary' people has been oral history. Interviewing women and men about their past lives was not a new technique for historians, but it had been largely confined to those who had played a key role in events – for example, politicians, members of the armed forces and civil servants. In the 1970s, however, researchers sought out women and men who were not well known and interviewed them in large numbers about work, family life, childhood and sexuality.

The use of oral history has been subject to considerable debate; critics have argued that samples are not representative, the accuracy of statements made cannot be tested, and that recollections of past events are not likely to be reliable. None the less, many similar issues can be raised in relation to printed material and there is no reason why oral evidence should be seen as being inherently less reliable. There may be difficulties in assessing the relationship between individual experiences and the broader social context, while the personal interaction between the inter- viewer and the subject raises problems of undue influence and the danger of asking leading questions. On the other hand, many feminists would argue that these are important aspects of feminist research methodology and should be seen as a strength rather than as a potential weakness. There has been so much discussion of the issues raised by oral history that researchers are well aware of the potential problems, and tend to provide a more detailed account of their methodology than is usual in other studies (Gittins, 1982; Lummis, 1987; and Gluck and Patai, 1991).

Oral evidence has been particularly valuable in providing an insight into the lives of those who have left few written records; in particular, lesbians, working-class, and Black women, whose experiences might otherwise have been lost from view (Roberts, 1984; and Hall Carpenter Archives/Lesbian History Group, 1989). It has enabled historians to construct life histories, to discover networking and to 'explore the world of an individual's meanings and beliefs' (Gittins, 1979, p. 12). Personal testimony can raise unexpected issues, which lead the historian to ask new questions, and can add a more three-dimensional texture to the lives of 'ordinary' people than is usually found in the studies carried out by middle-class investigators (Booth, 1902–3). Penny Summerfield and Gail Braybon's recent study of the two world wars, for example, shows how oral evidence can be used to convey a sense of women's own experiences of home and work, unmediated by official policies and propaganda (Braybon and Summerfield, 1987).

From the discussion so far it would almost appear that women's history could simply have been subsumed in social history. The study of a hitherto neglected group, denied access to formal structures of power and thereby rendered invisible, and the challenge posed to notions of what is historically significant, could be seen as entirely compatible with the broader context and concerns of social history. But social historians have often failed to draw attention to women or to recognise the import- ance of sexual divisions.

Elizabeth Higginbotham and Sarah Watts, for example, have shown how the ground-breaking scholarship of the 1970s on the history of Afro-Americans failed to explore the specific experiences of Black

women. It was only when feminist historians, building on the work of the
activist and philosopher Angela Davis (1982) put Black women at the
centre of their analysis that new insights were gained into women's
community work, family life and paid employment. They were able to
show 'the differential effects of racial oppression on men and women'
and to argue that Black women as well as Black men played a crucial
role in helping the community to 'survive and resist the dehumanising
impacts of slavery' (Higginbotham and Watts, 1988, p. 15).

As practised by feminist historians, women's history has developed a
distinctive character of its own. Far from seeking to find out about and
describe women's lives, and to incorporate their research into an existing
historical framework, feminist historians have argued that if women's
experiences, their values and the shape of their lives have often been
different from those of men, then women's history cannot be viewed as
just another version of men's history. Gerda Lerner suggests that the key
question to ask is what history would be like if it were seen through the
eyes of women and ordered by values, they define (Lerner, 1981). Such
a woman-centred approach would mean, for example, looking at the way
in which culture is transmitted to the young, at the building of social
networks and at the way in which these have provided continuity.

Women's lives were often bound up with family concerns – with
emotional support and personal relationships. Feminist historians have
argued that these personal, subjective experiences had just as much
historical significance as the world of waged work and politics. They
have questioned the distinctions usually made between public and private life and have sought instead to explore the interconnections between
them (Davidoff and Hall, 1987). In doing so they have found that
'inequalities in the domestic world structure inequalities in the public
sphere' rather than necessarily the other way round (Lewis, 1986, p. 1).
If women's experience of family and work was different from that of
men's, then the periodisation of their history would also need to be
different. It has been suggested that this difference 'may embrace not
only the contents of historical experience, but also the experience of time
itself' (Bock, 1989, p. 8). Thus the rhythm of family lives, including
events such as marriage, childbirth and death need to be recognised, and
interrelated with, the more familiar concepts of time as affected by
changes in economic and political structures (Hareven, 1982).

The distinctive approach of feminist historians has been to insist that
women as a social group have suffered a variety of controls and restrictions on their lives which need to be explored historically. Women may

be a separate group because of their sex, or biological characteristics, but what interests the historian is the 'cultural definition of behaviour defined as appropriate to the sexes in a given society at a given time' (Lerner, 1986, p. 238).

Feminist historians argue that gender divisions and the power relationships between women and men are crucial for an understanding of the historical process, and that recognition of the importance of gender divisions must then lead to a reconstruction of history in the broadest sense. As Sally Alexander notes when writing about the history of working-class women:

> Feminist history releases women from their obscurity as the wives, mothers and daughters of working men. This does not just mean that family life, housework, the reproduction of the labour force, the transmission of ideology etc. can be added to an already constituted history, but the history of production itself will be re-written. For the history of production under capitalism, from a feminist perspective, is not simply the class struggle between the producer and the owner of the means of production. It is also the development of a particular form of the sexual division of labour in relation to that struggle. (Alexander, 1977, pp. 59–60)

In seeking to rewrite history to take account of women's specific experiences, feminist historians differ in their emphases and approach. The terms 'inequality', 'subordination' and 'oppression' are used to describe women's condition, although they all have different meanings. Anne Phillips suggests that inequality implies exclusion from what is granted to men, whereas oppression goes beyond this by drawing attention to the variety of ways in which women have been 'kept in their place'. Subordination, on the other hand, identifies the agents in such a process (Phillips, 1987b, p. 1). The particular weight given to any one of these terms is then bound to influence the concerns and analysis of individual historians.

In an attempt to explain the specific features of women's social position, many feminist historians have used the concept of patriarchy. There are differences in the way patriarchy is analysed and defined (see Chapter 3), although male power and domination over women is a central issue. Gerda Lerner cautions, however, that an emphasis on male power should not imply that women are always victims, or that they have no influence, rights and resources. She urges the historian 'to trace with precision the various forms and modes in which patriarchy appears historically, the shifts and changes in its structure and function, and the adaptations it makes to female pressure and demands' (Lerner, 1986, p. 239).

As the discussion of patriarchy suggests, while almost all feminist historians share a broadly similar perspective in placing sexual divisions and women's experiences at the centre of historical enquiry, there are fundamental differences between them in terms of emphasis and approach. These relate both to the differences within contemporary feminist theory and practice, and to the strengths of particular historical traditions in different countries. In the United States, for example, feminist research has concentrated on the development of a separate women's culture, the growth of all-female institutions, and family history. In Britain, where the study of labour history has long been of central concern, feminist historians have focused on women's waged work, their trade union organisation and their role in labour politics (Newton *et al.*, 1983).

Working within a predominantly socialist tradition, many British feminist historians have taken a particular interest in how to reconcile class and gender in their historical analysis (Phillips, 1987a). This has been an uphill task; the predominance of a Marxist approach, which emphasised the key role played by the struggles of organised male workers as agents of social change, marginalised the role of women and their specific experiences (Davin, 1981; Sargent, 1981; and Segal, 1989). And yet work by feminist historians has shown how many of these working-class struggles and political movements were concerned with gender relations in both the workplace and the home.

Barbara Taylor's study of Owenism, for example, suggests that fears about the way in which the roles of family members were changing during early industrialisation, and the uncertain position of the male breadwinner, as much as alterations in work practices, lay behind disputes in the workshop trades in the period.[1] This awareness of links between changing work and family practices were then expressed politically in the Owenite movement. It was argued that a transformation in the relationship between the sexes and in the institution of marriage would go hand-in-hand with the creation of more co-operative forms of production and a socialist society (Taylor, 1983).

By focusing on the importance of the sexual division of labour at the workplace and in the home, feminist historians have made a distinctive contribution to the study of labour history. They have drawn attention to the need to explain why the sexual division of labour took the specific form that it did in different periods, rather than taking it as 'natural'. Detailed studies of women's occupations suggest that the potential advantages to employers of mechanisation, prevailing definitions of skill, the power of male trade unions, and management practices, all played a part in the definition of jobs as female or male (John, 1986).

A crucial factor in this definition was women's identification with cheap labour, which in turn was closely related to their role within the working-class family. Women's work in the nineteenth century had a lower social and economic value than men's 'due to their primary association with reproduction rather than production and their responsibility for childcare and housework (with no economic value)' (John, 1986, p. 5). The low value placed on women's work then affected all aspects of their employment, including wages, conditions of work and the type of jobs assigned to them. Angela Phillips and Barbara Taylor, for example, argue that skill definitions were closely bound up with gender, for the very fact that women performed a task devalued it and automatically led to the label 'unskilled' (Phillips and Taylor, 1980).

We now know far more about the complex relationship between women's paid work and their work within the family (Gamarnikow *et al.*, 1983). In a recent collection of articles, Pat Hudson and Robert Lee suggest the need to explore aspects of women's work which tend to be less visible, for 'we know that much of women's work . . . has been concentrated outside of this formal economy in the vast range of tasks surrounding home and hearth and in irregular low status employments which do not readily enter historical record'. They also argue that women's work should be examined in relation to broader concerns, such as the creation of political identity, the maintenance of living standards and its impact on fertility (Hudson and Lee, 1990).

The complexities of the relationship between work and family, and the dangers of assuming too readily that there has been steady progress in women's social and economic position since early industrialisation can be illustrated by Gail Braybon and Penny Summerfield's studies of women workers during the two world wars. They question the view that war had a long-lasting effect on the nature and extent of women's employment. Drawn into production because of the emergency of wartime, women's temporary status in the labour force was underlined both by government policies relating to the replacement of skilled male workers by less-skilled female workers, and by union agreements about the position of male workers once the war was over. War also led to an increased emphasis on the importance of motherhood, which served to reinforce women's marginal status in production and to promote domesticity. Although some women may have welcomed the chance to return home and give up their double burden, those who wished to remain at work found it much more difficult to retain their position in 'nontraditional' areas of female employment (Braybon, 1981; and Summerfield, 1984).

Feminist historians working within a socialist tradition have been concerned to examine the interaction between class, 'race' and gender, but their approaches have frequently differed. A recognition that 'women have not only worked for capital, they have worked for men' (Newton *et al.* (eds), 1983, p. 3) has led historians such as Barbara Taylor and Sally Alexander to use the concept of patriarchy as a way to develop a theory of sexual antagonism, since a Marxist theory of class conflict could not answer all their questions (Alexander and Taylor, 1981). Sheila Rowbotham, on the other hand, is sceptical about the use of such a concept. She argues that it cannot help to explain, and diverts attention from, those aspects of male–female relationships which are not simply oppressive, but include varying degrees of mutual aid. She points to periods in which 'class or race solidarity are much stronger than sex–gender conflict and times when relations within the family are a source of mutual resistance to class power' (Rowbotham, 1982, p. 367).

The different approaches and emphases used by feminist historians in exploring sexual conflict within the working class can be illustrated by looking at the debates about whether nineteenth-century trade unions played a key role in determining and reinforcing women's subordinate role in the workplace. Heidi Hartmann, for example, argues that women's status as secondary workers stems from the patriarchal relations between women and men which pre-dated capitalism. When capitalist labour relations threatened to destroy the family and male power over women's labour, organised male workers rejected women as co-workers in order to maintain their dominance in both the workplace and in the home (Hartmann, 1981).

Sally Alexander and Sonya Rose, however, suggest that exclusionary practices by male workers must be seen in more complex ways. Threatened with a reduction in wages and loss of control over the pace of their work, skilled men reacted by attempting to exclude less skilled men as well as women from their trades. They were reacting as workers as well as men and therefore gender was only one factor, albeit an important one, in their overall strategy of survival (Alexander, 1980; and Rose, 1988).

A more serious divide lies between socialist feminists and radical feminists. For the latter, women's experience of history has been primarily determined by their sex. The concept of patriarchy provides a conceptual tool for explaining women's oppression over time, while male power over women is seen as the key to understanding women's subordination (Rich, 1980a). As Joan Kelly notes, 'radical feminists have been more concerned with sexuality and socialisation than with labour' and have emphasised the 'psychic, sexual and ideological structures that differentiate the sexes' (Kelly, 1983, p. 260).

For some radical feminists it is men's control over women's bodies which underpins patriarchy. Lesbian historians in particular have added a new dimension to the debate by drawing attention to the way in which heterosexuality has been used to control women. Sheila Jeffreys argues, for example, that sexuality should not be seen simply as an area of personal and private concern, but as a 'political relationship'. The sexual activity which takes place between a heterosexual couple 'represents an area in which men's power and control can be reinforced, and women's subordination reproduced' (Jeffreys, 1985, p. 178). In such a context, lesbianism can be seen as a form of strong resistance and women can form a 'female world of love and ritual' in which their strongest emotional and supportive relationships are with other women (Faderman, 1981; and London Feminist History Group, 1983, p. 6).

It would be misleading, however, to suggest that there is a neat divide between those concerned with sexuality and those who concentrate on class and labour relations. In her writings on feminist biography, for example, Liz Stanley explores the way in which her subjects were created through a process which is social, class-related and sexual political (Stanley, 1987). Similarly, Sally Alexander is concerned to examine how the unconscious enters politics and the way in which our understanding of self and sexual identity changes our understanding of class (Alexander, 1984).

Feminist historians have also started to shift from an approach which emphasised women's common experiences to a recognition of the need to explore the differences between them. The nature of men's power over women and the ways in which women offer resistance to that power are bound to be different depending on whether women are white, Black, middle-class or working-class, lesbian or heterosexual, which can then determine what kind of access they have to social and economic power (London Feminist History Group, 1983; and Stanley, 1990).

The more recent interest in the history of lesbians and Black women has tended to emphasise the importance of such differences. Despite the growth of research into women's history over more than two decades, the experience of Black women in Britain has been neglected. And yet Ziggi Alexander provides evidence to suggest that 'these islands had been home to thousands of Africans and their descendants' since the time of Roman occupation (Alexander, 1990, p. 22). She argues that white feminist historians themselves have been affected by the 'political preoccupations of the dominant culture'. Their interest in recovering women from historical invisibility, therefore, did not initially rescue Black women from obscurity.

Far more studies have been undertaken into the history of Afro-American women. These have revealed the active role that Black women played in the development and maintenance of Afro-American communities in both the public and the private sphere (Higginbotham and Watts, 1988). Evelyn Higginbotham also points out, however, that these studies make clear that 'factors of class and race make any generalisation regarding womanhood's common oppression impossible' (Higginbotham, 1990, p. 63). They highlight the need to explore Black women's lives through 'race', class and gender oppression, while also insisting that Black women themselves were not a 'monolithic' group, but had a diverse range of experiences and responses to the varied aspects of their oppression.

Over the last two decades, therefore, our understanding of women's history has been enriched, both by the opening up of new areas of enquiry and also by the search for a conceptual framework to make sense of women's specific social position (Lerner, 1986; and Riley, 1988). As a result, we now have a far more complex view of the factors which shaped women's lives, of their own aspirations and the extent to which they have experienced change. Some sense of this can best be given through examples drawn from recent work on the history of middle-class women and the organised women's movement in the nineteenth and twentieth centuries. This period is of particular importance since the Victorian ideology of separate spheres (in which men were to be bread-winners and active in the public sphere, while women were to be home-makers confined to the private sphere), and notions of what constituted masculinity and femininity, have had a long-lasting influence on the lives of women up to the present day, and on the interpretations of historians.

Recent research has changed our view of the Victorian woman from that of passive victim to active agent in the process of historical change

(Lewis, 1986; and Rendall, 1987). Whilst not denying the importance of the Victorian ideology of separate spheres, historians have challenged the familiar stereotype of the middle-class leisured woman, confined to the private sphere. It has been argued that not only did a woman's role within the family contribute to broader economic and social developments, but also that women took an increasingly active part in public life and brought their own particular values to it.

Philanthropy, for example, has long been recognised as an arena which middle-class women made their own. As a voluntary activity, and one which required caring qualities, it was seen as a suitable outlet for women's desire to do something useful with their lives for the good of a wider community (Prochaska, 1980). Research by feminist historians, however, has provided new insights into the motivations of female philanthropists and has re-assessed their contribution to the development of social policy. Mary Carpenter, Octavia Hill, Louisa Twyning and others were not just do-gooders, filling in time between social engagements. They took a serious approach to philanthropy, regarded their activities as purposeful work and helped to develop a professional standing for social work.

The consequences of their activities in redefining women's social role were more contradictory. Jane Lewis suggests that Octavia Hill, Helen Bosanquet and other social activists were all convinced that it was women's duty to serve the community and that they needed education and training for voluntary work. Their views were underpinned, however, by a belief in natural sexual difference and they were 'extremely sensitive as to where the boundary should be drawn in respect of their activities' (Lewis, 1991, p. 8). Octavia Hill, for example, thought that work among the poor should be 'quiet' and 'out of sight' and should not fall outside the bounds of propriety (Lewis, 1991, p. 9). None the less, by speaking in public, directing the work of large organisations, taking part in committees and negotiating with politicians they provided a salient example for those who argued that women had a valuable contribution to make to the public sphere (Vicinus, 1985; and Parker, 1988).

In the nineteenth century, women increasingly organised together to challenge aspects of their unequal social position. The dramatic struggle for the vote has always been a well-researched area, but we now know that this was the culmination of a much broader struggle to achieve political, social and economic equality. Women fought to gain a measure of economic independence by seeking access to higher education and the professions; they dared to speak out in public about sexuality when they fought to repeal the Contagious Diseases' Acts; and they sought to influence public affairs by standing for selection to School Boards, Boards of Guardians and local councils. From the beginning they also campaigned for the Parliamentary vote, partly on the grounds of natural justice and equality with men, and also because they saw it as a way to achieve other goals (Banks, 1981; and Levine, 1987).

In the last decade attention focused on the importance of friendship ties between women involved in these campaigns and also on the framework of ideas which guided their actions (Spender, 1983a; Garner, 1984; and Levine, 1990). The result is that we now have a much clearer and more complex view of the aims and dynamics of the nineteenth-century women's movement. In the context of separate spheres, women in the nineteenth century often found the greatest emotional support from other women, whether female relatives or friends, and created networks which linked their political and social lives. These support networks, and their importance for the development of feminism, have emerged most clearly as a result of the new interest in writing feminist biography.

Feminists have been concerned to use the biographies of individuals, or groups of women, to explore wider networks of friendship, the relationship between the public and the private, and the economic and social position of women more generally. In doing so they have questioned the approach of more traditional biography writing, with its emphasis on the great woman or unique individual, the description of her life from birth to death, and the possibility of knowing the innermost thoughts and definitive personality of the subject (Morley and Stanley, 1988). Feminist biographers have, instead, been concerned to locate their subjects within the broader social, political and intellectual context in which they lived, and to adopt a more thematic approach in their writings. Carolyn Steedman, for example, uses the life of Margaret McMillan to explore childhood in the late nineteenth and early twentieth centuries and the relationship between educational theories and reform (Steedman, 1990).

Feminists, therefore, have been at the forefront in developing new approaches to biography writing and in their critical appraisal of existing methodology. They have recognised the need to examine the relationship between the historian and the subject of the biography, and to think critically about the way in which diaries, letters and journals were produced and their use as a source (Farran, Scott and Stanley, 1986; *Gender and History*, 1990). Both Liz Stanley and Kali Israel, for example, use the image of a kaleidoscope to convey some of the complexities of historical research into women's lives. Israel feels this is particularly important in the case of middle-class women, for their lives have been 're-fracted to us through the multiple mirrors of their contemporaries' texts and art-works' (Israel, 1990, p. 39; and Stanley, 1987). Feminist biographers are also more willing than in the past to confront the unpalatable aspects of some women's lives, and to learn something from them, rather than to 'gloss these over in the search for perfect heroines' (*Gender and History*, 1990).

Recent studies of leading women, including Olive Schreiner, Maude Royden, Isabella Ford and Margaret McMillan, as well as more collective biographies of less well-known feminists, have provided important insights into the social background and motivations of those who were active in the late-nineteenth-century women's movement (Stanley, 1985; Fletcher, 1989; Hannam, 1989; and Levine, 1990). Such biographies have shown the important links between the struggle for women's rights and other social and political movements, such as anti-slavery, medical reform, animal welfare, temperance and socialism. Friendship ties sustained late Victorian feminists in their campaigns and cut across class and political boundaries, although the implications for the goals and character of the women's movement were complex. Phillippa Levine argues, for example, that social networks helped to create a distinct female identity and alternative set of values, which led women to emphasise the perceived differences between the sexes as well as demanding equality (Levine, 1987).

A shift of attention away from the political manoeuverings of various campaigns to a study of the ideas which underpinned those movements has again provided new insights into the motivations and aims of Victorian feminists. Concerned to be treated equally with men, they also accepted the importance of their role within the home as wives and mothers. Increasingly, they used the notion of 'women's special qualities', of caring and purity, to justify their demand for entry to the public sphere and to reinforce their own sense of the importance of feminine values. They wanted the possibility of economic and social independence for women, in particular for single women, while at the same time demanding a recognition of the key importance of motherhood (Garner, 1984).

Suffragists in particular used a variety of arguments in support of women's right to vote and changed their emphasis over the long period in which their campaign took place. At the beginning they had to convince a sceptical opposition that women were capable of exercising political judgement and they sought to enter public life on equal terms with men. At the same time, they did not necessarily challenge the ideology of separate spheres, and agreed that women would bring different qualities to bear in public life (Lewis, 1987). In her study of women in local government in the late nineteenth century, Patricia Hollis argues that separate spheres could be used in both conservative and radical ways; it 'reinforced stereotyping of women's nature' while encouraging women to claim a role in public life and to 'expand the contours of what elected authorities were there to do' (Hollis, 1987, p. 210).

Feminists were not just interested in the public sphere. They also sought to improve conditions for women within marriage and saw the growing political interest in motherhood after 1900 as a movement which would reinforce their claims, as mothers, to play a part in the nation's affairs (Davin, 1978). They also sought to challenge the double standard of morality. Accepting the role assigned to them as moral guardians, they insisted that men should reform their own sexual practices rather than seeking a redefinition of women's own sexuality (Walkowitz, 1980). This outlook, along with a reluctance to champion birth control and easier divorce, brought some criticism from 1970s feminists, whose goal was greater sexual and reproductive freedom for women (Rowbotham, 1977). More recently, when the potential gains for women from the 'sexual revolution' have been questioned, historians have begun to write more sympathetically about the first wave of feminists.

Sheila Jeffreys, for example, argues that a reluctance to embrace birth control made sense in a period when women were socially and economically dependent, since they feared that this would give men greater control over women's bodies. Re-examining the work of leading sexologists of the period, such as Havelock Ellis, she argues that far from contributing to a climate of greater sexual freedom for women, they imposed a heterosexual norm which served to constrict their lives, especially those of spinsters and lesbians (Jeffreys, 1985).

Lucy Bland also draws attention to the need to analyse late-nineteenth-century feminist writings and campaigns around sexuality; she argues strongly that historians should recognise the differences between such women as well as their similarities, and to make sure that they are aware of the context in which such ideas were developed. Unlike Jeffreys, she believes that feminist attempts to control male sexuality were defeated not simply by the rise of anti-feminist sex reform before the First World War, but also by the rise of eugenic and imperialist concern with the falling white, middle-class birth-rate. She also argues that it is important to recognise the class nature of feminist writing, since it was often middle-class women 'writing about and attempting to regulate working-class sexuality' (Bland, 1986; and Bland, 1989).

What has become clear is that it can be very misleading to rigidly compartmentalise either individual women or the movements of which they were a part. Any attempt to divide women neatly into different categories, such as 'equal-rights feminists' or 'social maternalists', who sought to extend their domestic influence beyond the home, breaks down once their writings are examined in detail. The same woman could employ different sets of arguments according to the circumstances in which she was involved and not consider that they were contradictory. Moreover, even if they gave most of their energies to one cause rather than another, feminists tended to support a variety of women's rights campaigns and to see them as interlinked.

Similarly, the connections between the women's movement and other social and political movements have begun to be reassessed. Frequent conflicts between feminists and the labour movement over issues such as protective legislation and women's suffrage encouraged historians to see the two movements as separate. More recent studies, however, have emphasised the links between the two, both in their ideas and in practical campaigning (Rowan, 1982; Holton, 1986; Hannam, 1987; and Collette, 1989).

In their public work, middle-class women tended to focus on the problems faced by working-class women and children. Although issues of health and morality received most attention, a minority of feminists were concerned with wages and conditions of employment. They encouraged working women to take independent action to improve their economic conditions by helping to form trade unions and by giving assistance to mixed-sex organisations.

From the mid-1880s many feminists drew closer to the labour movement, joined socialist societies and campaigned for legislation to shorten women's hours of work and improve their wages. They tried to draw the attention of the labour movement to the specific needs of working-class women and worked hard to bring the women's movement and the labour movement closer together, grappling with the conflicts between gender and class which are still issues of debate today (Middleton, 1977; Mappen, 1985; and Phillips, 1987a).

Although it was more difficult for working-class women than their middle-class counterparts, to take part in militant suffrage activities, since they could not afford to be imprisoned or separated for too long from their communities, Jill Liddington and Jill Norris have shown that Lancashire working women campaigned actively for the vote after 1900 (Liddington and Norris, 1978). The revived suffrage movement led to tensions in the labour movement between the claims of women as a sex, and class politics. It was argued that the demand for votes for women on the same terms as men threatened labour unity by emphasising women's common interests and would only enfranchise middle-class women. The refusal of the Labour Party to give support to a 'limited' franchise caused a dilemma for those women who were both socialists and feminists about where their priorities should lie. When the Labour Party finally adopted women's suffrage it was on the grounds of women's essential difference from men – the importance of their taking caring qualities from the domestic sphere to the wider community – and could be used to divert attention away from tackling women's inequality at the workplace (Holton, 1986; and Hannam, 1989). By drawing attention to the rich interconnection between the women's movement and the labour movement, such studies have transformed our understanding of both movements and of the broader relationship between class, 'race' and gender.

In 1979, Gerda Lerner argued that women and their activities in the past had been ignored because historians asked questions that were inappropriate to women. She suggested that to rectify this feminist historians should focus on a 'woman centred inquiry' and consider the possibility of the existence of a female culture within the general culture shared by men and women (Lerner, 1981, pp. 178–9). This was to be the first step in the move towards 'a new universal history, a holistic history which will be a synthesis of traditional history and women's history' (Lerner, 1981, p. 180).

After over two decades of research into women's history, what has been achieved? It is far easier now for those who are interested to study women's history. The development of new journals, such as *History Workshop*, *Feminist Studies* and *Feminist Review*, and the growth of a women's press has made research more readily available to a wide audience. Women's active contribution to historical change has been recognised, our view of what is historically significant has been altered and some of the distinctions between public and private, production and reproduction have been broken down or blurred.

We are still a long way, however, from Gerda Lerner's vision of a new history which takes full account of women's experiences. Mainstream history texts and educational courses often ignore the latest research into women's history. There has been a tendency to view women's history as being separate from other developments and something which can be studied simply by enthusiasts, leaving other historians unaffected. This has led some feminist historians to suggest the need to move away from a focus on women's history, in order to construct a different type of history which encompasses women and men and takes account of the variety of experiences within both sexes.

Jane Rendall, for example, has argued that women's history 'need not be confined to separate shelves', but its themes should inform the history of men as well as women and should focus on the varied ways in which gender differences in different societies have been constructed and understood (Rendall, 1990). Leonore Davidoff and Catherine Hall's detailed study of family and work in Birmingham during early industrialisation is a good example of such a development, in which the intricate connections between family relationships, sex roles, work and the development of class identity are explored and seen to be gendered (Davidoff and Hall, 1987).

It is surely significant that the title of one of the latest journals in the field is *Gender and History*. The first editorial claimed that the journal's intentions were to study male institutions as well as those defined as female and to address men and masculinity as well as women and femininity, in order to 'illuminate the ways in which societies have been shaped by the relations of power between men and women' (*Gender and History*, 1990).

This new emphasis on a gender-centred history is not unproblematic. Feminist critics of such a development, both in history and in other academic disciplines, argue that the category of gender is a neutral term which implies that 'the interests of the sexes have now converged and that the differences in life chances . . . that exist between women and men are matters of choice' (Evans, 1991, p. 73). This undermines alliances between women and weakens their potential for challenging the dominant culture. It is suggested that a focus on women's history and women's experiences is the only way to ensure that sexual inequalities and the power relationships between women and men remain central to historical enquiry.

As these discussions suggest, in the 1990s, there continues to be a close relationship between debates within contemporary feminist theory and politics and the approaches and concerns of historians. It is this interaction between feminist politics and historical practice that has helped to ensure that the study of women's history can still excite its students, and remains open to change. An understanding of our history is of vital importance for women, enabling us to challenge existing stereo-types and social structures and to gain the confidence to seek change. As Nancy Cott suggests, it is the 'sense of discovery and self knowledge to be gained from women's history' that continues to motivate feminist historians, no less than it did over two decades ago (Cott, 1988, p. 5).

Note

1. Owenism: a socialist movement of the early nineteenth century which drew inspiration from the writings of Robert Owen, a textile mill owner. The Owenites' vision was of a new social order that would be based on co-operative, classless communities where women and men would be equal.

Further reading

Phillippa Levine, *Feminist Lives in Victorian England* (Oxford, Blackwell, 1990). This book studies the connections between women's public and private lives, and emphasises the importance of friendship for an understanding of the nine-teenth-century women's movement. Provides a new interpretation through the use of collective biography.

Jane Lewis, *Women in England, 1870–1950: Sexual Divisions and Social Change* (Brighton, Harvester, 1984). Excellent overview, which draws together recent research by feminist historians and provides an interesting interpretation of the changes which have affected women's lives at work, in the family and in politics.

Anne Phillips, *Divided Loyalties: Dilemmas of Sex and Class* (London, Virago, 1987a). Readable introduction to debates about the relationship between sex and class in feminist history and feminist theory.

Women's Studies Quarterly, XVI (1 & 2) Spring/Summer (New York, The Feminist Press, 1988). A special edition examining new developments in Black women's history which raises issues about methodology and approach.

A book which addresses lesbian history issues is Martin Baum Duberman, Martha Vicinus and George Chauncey, *Hidden From History: Reclaiming the Gay and Lesbian Past* (Harmondsworth, Penguin, 1991).

14

Women and Education
Christine Skelton

Schools for the Boys?, *Losing Out*, *Just a Bunch of Girls* and *Learning to Lose* are all titles of books on gender and education published in the last decade. Titles of books are important because they have to summarise the contents in short, eye-catching phrases and although I could add many more to the above list, they all point to the same fact; that is, female educational experiences are different, and unequal, to those of males. In many ways, present day schooling inhibits women's and girls' confidence, skills and abilities. Whether the focus of research has been on female pupils, teachers/lecturers, or students in further and higher education, the findings have all illustrated how females *receive* and *perceive* different messages about their aptitudes and abilities from those of males, which has implications for their place in the family and the labour market. The intention in this chapter is to examine women's education but, given that this involves issues of 'race', social class and feminist perspectives, a difficult decision arises as to what should be included and what should be set aside. As a feminist, it seems to me that a starting point has to be my own experiences. In addition, this book is aimed at students who are 'new' to the theoretical underpinnings of Women's Studies courses. I can recall the confusion experienced when I was a primary school teacher interested in the area of gender issues in education but having to read sociological theory divorced from my reality. What I needed was a basic introduction to ideas, with guidance as to where I could find more in-depth discussion of specific issues. The ideas to be discussed in this chapter emerge from the questions I asked as a white, female, primary teacher with an awakened interest in gender and education.

At the beginning of the 1980s I embarked upon an Open University degree in education and sociology. Also, in 1981 the LEA (local education authority) for whom I worked declared itself an Equal Opportunities employer. This combination of factors resulted in my becoming increasingly conscious of the multiplicity of ways gender inequalities exist in all aspects of schooling – gender influences teachers' attitudes and classroom practices, resources, school organisation and administration. In an attempt to come to terms with these various aspects of gender discrimination, certain questions constantly came to the fore. How has this happened? What, specifically, do we know about the schooling experiences of girls and boys? What is being done about it?

Taking each question in turn: 'How has this happened?' To answer this question we need to look at the history of women's education and recognise the different ways 'girls'' and 'boys'' schooling has been deemed appropriate. The second question, 'What, specifically, do we know about the schooling experiences of girls and boys?', will look at the research carried out in secondary and primary schooling. Finally, 'What is being done about it?' considers approaches adopted by schools and LEAs. I am aware of many areas being left out, for example students in further and higher education, trade unions, and youth training schemes. A useful bibliography to refer to is the Open University's *Gender and Education* (1988).

History of women's education 1870–1975

The first Education Act (Forster Act 1870) in Britain made education compulsory for all children aged between five and ten years of age and was a major achievement for all those who had been campaigning for 'education for all', but particularly so for feminists. Educating middle- and upper-class boys had long been an accepted (and expected) feature of boys' preparation for adulthood. However, nineteenth-century feminists had to fight to secure acceptance of women's right to work and to receive an education. The main opposition had come from the clerical, medical and scientific professions, who based their arguments predominantly on concepts of 'natural' differences between males and females. A collection of papers, written in the nineteenth and early twentieth centuries, demonstrate how the 'female physique' was used to justify why women could not, and should not, be educated (Spender, 1987):

> Not one girl in a hundred would be able to work up the subjects required for an Indian Civil Service examination in the ways which

boys do. Her health would break down under the effort . . . if she is allowed to run the risks which to the boys are a matter of indifference, she will probably develop some disease which if not fatal, will at any rate be an injury to her for life. (Elizabeth Sewell, 1865, in Spender, pp. 144–5)

One forceful argument put forward by feminist historians to explain girls' inclusion in compulsory schooling has focused on women's roles on the domestic front. A major belief underpinning mass education was that it would help to socialise the working class; through education they would develop new attitudes to work, defer to their 'betters' (the middle classes) and raise the standard of living in their homes (Sharpe, 1976; and Davin, 1979). If educated, working-class women would acquire certain skills they could employ in the home and with their families. Physically exhausting jobs in poor working conditions for low pay and returning to overcrowded houses with little heat and no sanitation was the bleak prospect for a majority of the population; educating women would enable them to accustom their families to accepting such harsh realities. Also, it would improve the infant mortality rate by educating women for motherhood. It was clear, then, from the outset that mass education for all children was never intended to provide girls and boys with the same skills and abilities. Boys had to be equipped for their future in the labour market and girls had to acquire the skills to support and make life comfortable for their menfolk, and to care adequately for their children.

This emphasis in educational decision-making on the home and family responsibilities of girls has been called the 'ideology of domesticity', and was as relevant to middle-class as to working-class girls (Purvis, 1987). There is, however, a fundamental distinction between the 'ideology of domestication' as it applied to females from the different social classes. As June Purvis has said: 'What was considered appropriate, relevant and attainable for middle-class women was inappropriate, irrelevant and unattainable for working-class women' (Purvis, 1987, p. 255). Whilst the ideal for working-class females was the 'good woman', for their sisters in the middle classes the aim was to be a 'perfect wife and mother'. The 'good woman' was one who demonstrated her *practical* abilities and skills as housewife, wife and mother. In contrast, the 'perfect wife and mother' was achieved by middle-class women using organisational skills to provide a stable, supportive domestic environment. Ironically, this conducive home setting could only be operationalised through the paid labour of working-class women.

Educating the middle classes was not a fundamental aim in the establishment of compulsory mass education as this social group could, and usually did, make alternative arrangements in the form of private education. The structure of education for girls following the 1870 Act was based upon the perceived requirements for working-class females. Hence, in the latter part of the nineteenth century girls would spend as much as a fifth of their time in school doing needlework (a compulsory subject) and, in 1882, cookery too became a curriculum requirement. The 1876 Code stipulated that every girl entered for examination in the higher standards of elementary education had to take domestic economy as one of her subjects. As most schools only entered children for *one* subject, the vast majority of girls had no choice as to what they would be examined on. Present-day interventionist strategies have been geared towards encouraging more girls to undertake science or technology subjects at examination level; a situation which can be both compared and contrasted to the prevailing attitudes of a hundred years ago. When science was first introduced as a curriculum subject, girls were not allowed to study it and when this subject was eventually taught to girls, the scientific principles were frequently applied to domestic contexts such as ventilation and evaporation for drying and airing clothes (Sharpe, 1976). In some ways the wheel has come full circle, because one of the strategies used in the Girls Into Science and Technology (GIST) project to attract more girls to this area of study was to relate their everyday experiences and knowledge in the domestic context to scientific experiments. The fact remains that in the past science was not considered an appropriate subject for girls.

Arguably, this exclusivity contributed to science being seen as a masculine area which, as the GIST study shows, still continues today. Judith Whyte (1985) suggests that boys act in a way which makes science seem more masculine, and teachers too help create the impression that science is a macho business. For example, when a teacher warned of the dangers of chemicals and laboratory equipment boys responded with bravado, by attempting to give each other electric shocks with a 6-volt battery; the girls, on the other hand, were discouraged by the element of danger. Alison Kelly has identified four ways in which science can be argued to be masculine: 'First, the pupils, teachers and practitioners of science are overwhelmingly male in terms of numbers;

second, school science is packaged and presented to appeal to boys, not girls; third, classroom behaviours and interaction operate to reconstruct science as a male activity, and finally it has been suggested that "scientific" thinking embodies an intrinsically masculine world view' (Kelly, quoted in Whyte, 1985, p. 82). Recent research by John Archer and Maureen McDonald (1991) suggests that girls' attitudes have moved away from perceiving science as a 'masculine subject'. This change in perception may be attributed to the work of feminists in the educational sector, who have sought to demystify scientific terminology and facilitated 'girl-friendly' practical science experiments.

Education in the early part of the twentieth century lacked the benefit of feminist analysis, and so continued to provide an 'appropriate curriculum' for girls. However, the outbreak of two world wars and the subsequent shortage of 'manpower' called upon women to exercise their skills, particularly in industry but also in agriculture and commerce. To facilitate the movement of women into the workplace the government vastly increased day-care provision. This, together with the move in the 1940s for the development of a welfare state, meant that by the end of the Second World War more women than ever before were combining family responsibilities with full-time employment. Many of these women were in semi-skilled and skilled jobs, although vast numbers were employed as part-time, unskilled workers. The majority of those in employment were from the working, rather than the middle, classes. In 1944 an Education Act was passed, which, for the first time, tackled the concept of equal educational opportunities. A combination of these factors – the economy needing women's skills in the labour market, adequate day-care provision and an education act which considered equality issues – set the scene for change in what *should* have been perceived as an 'appropriate' education for girls. After all, women had demonstrated that their 'natural' abilities were not confined to the domestic front, and they had many skills to offer the labour market. All that had been missing was the opportunity for females to show their abilities in the public sector or in work.

The end of the Second World War did not herald any widening of opportunities for women: instead, they were placed firmly back in the home. This echoed what happened after the First World War; as the men returned from the war they found women doing the jobs they had once done and which they then wanted back. Also, women employed in jobs created by war industries found themselves to be redundant. In this situation of high unemployment it was clear that the secondary labour force (women) had to be disbanded and returned to its 'natural' domestic habitat. The government adopted a number of strategies intended to encourage women back into the home, starting with a vast reduction in the number of day nurseries, from over 1500 in 1945 to 903 in 1949 (Open University, 1981, E200, Block 2). These cutbacks were justified by the use of another strategy; one which played upon a mother's sense of guilt at leaving her children. A Ministry of Health circular (221/45) stated that 'in the interest of the health and development of the child . . . the proper place for a child under two is at home with his [*sic*] mother'. The expert advice on child-rearing practices reinforced such views (see Chapter 9). For example, John Bowlby's theory of 'maternal deprivation' argues that if a child is separated from the exclusive and continuous care of its *mother* at an early age, then the outcome would be 'delinquent character development and persistent misbehaviour' (Bowlby in Sharpe, 1976, p. 189).

Given that the doors which had begun to open to women at the start of the Second World War were rapidly being slammed shut, it is hardly surprising to find that the intentions laid down in the 1944 Education Act to address equal opportunities actually did nothing to further girls' educational chances. The aims of this section of the Act were twofold; firstly, to encourage social class mobility all children were provided with the right to free secondary education. Secondly, 'the meritocratic structure of the education system would guarantee that personal achievement and talent would be rewarded within a competitive setting, irrespective of the age, sex, and ethnic or class origin of individual students' (Troyna, 1987, p. 1). The way these principles were construed militated against equal educational opportunities for all being put into practice. The decision as to the type of secondary school children went to rested upon their performance in the 11-plus examination. It was found that girls achieved higher scores than boys in this examination, a fact which could have resulted in more girls than boys obtaining the prestigious grammar school placements. To rectify this 'problem', girls' performances were weighted differently from those of boys, so that girls achieved fewer places than their results demanded, and boys were awarded more places than their results merited (Deem, 1981). A further consideration is the interpretation of the phrase in the Act which called for schools to 'afford for all pupils opportunities for education offering such variety of instruction and training as may be desirable in view of their *different* ages, *abilities* and *aptitudes*' (para. 8(b)) (my emphasis). As we have seen, girls' 'natural' future, irrespective of class or 'race', was seen to be in domesticity. Therefore, an interpretation of children's 'abilities and aptitudes' could (and did) point to a different curriculum for girls and boys, with the former undertaking subjects suitable for homemaking and the latter receiving instruction in those subjects relevant to obtaining a 'good job'.

A series of educational reports, Norwood (1943), Crowther (1959) and Newsom (1963) continued to underline a girl's place as being in the home and a boy's in the workplace. There were some slight changes in views; for instance, the Crowther Report showed awareness that some women may occupy dual roles (in the home and the workforce) but this was a possibility seen as only being available to middle-class women. (For an informative and detailed examination of these reports see Rosemary Deem (1981).) The 1960s and 1970s witnessed the emergence of many groups concerned with civil liberties, not least the development of a new feminist movement in Britain. Through a series of campaigns, various acts were passed dealing with inequality, that is, the Equal Pay Act 1970, the Sex Discrimination Act 1975, and the Race Relations Act 1976. As women's education is the focal issue in this chapter the Sex Discrimination Act will be discussed in the next section, but it should be noted that the other two acts had significant implications for other aspects of inequality.

Sex Discrimination Act and government policy

A detailed account of the politics surrounding the passage of the Sex Discrimination Act 1975 can be found in Margherita Rendel (1985). Education came close to being excluded from the Act, mainly because of the opposition of the Department of Education and Science (DES) (Byrne, 1978; Rendel, 1985; and Arnot, 1987). The DES (as well as the Department of Health and Social Security, Home Office and Civil Service) argued that legislation on the grounds of sex discrimination was unnecessary and inappropriate, as this did not exist in the education service. Despite such resistance, education was included in the Act but, as Madeleine Arnot (1987) has said, a price had to be paid. First, single-sex schools and sport were exempted from the Act. Second, positive action (positive discrimination) could take the form of special access routes or courses only in the tertiary sector and not in general education. Third, the powers of the Equal Opportunities Commission (EOC), the quango set up under the auspices of the Sex Discrimination Act, were curtailed as far as education is concerned. The EOC cannot issue non-discrimination notices in relation to investigations in education. If there is a complaint about sex discrimination in a school or LEA then the EOC can investigate it, after referring it in the first instance to the Secretary of State for Education. The subsequent recommendations of the EOC to the school or LEA have to be presented to the Secretary of State, who has the power to enforce these. This is unlike the situation in other sectors whereby the recommendations of the EOC, following an investigation, form the basis of non-discrimination notices, so should these not be acted upon by the company or institution they would be breaking the law and liable to prosecution. Finally, contract-compliance (for example, providing money to build extra laboratory facilities or for science materials) was omitted from the Sex Discrimination Act; this factor was reinforced by the DES in the guidance it sent to LEAs (circular 2/76). Schools were told they should ensure that girls and boys had *access* to the same curriculum subjects. This was nothing more than a time-tabling exercise for most schools and would not tackle the discrimination taking place in the *content* of the curriculum.

The stance adopted by the DES in passing responsibility for implementing the Sex Discrimination Act on to LEAs explains the variety of approaches to equal opportunities issues. Today, many LEAs have Equal Opportunities policies which have been implemented and monitored, others have policy statements which remain at the back of the filing cabinet and others have yet to address gender inequalities (Skelton, 1989). It is also worth mentioning here that the majority of policies are 'equal opportunities' rather than anti-sexist policies. The distinction between these approaches will be discussed later, but parallels can be drawn with this and LEAs' preferred perspective when it comes to developing policies on issues of 'race' and gender. In both cases there has been a tendency to favour multi-cultural and 'equal opportunities' approaches rather than the more radical anti-racist and anti-sexist approaches, dealing as they do with issues of power (see Arnot, 1985; Weiner, 1985; Troyna, 1987). It has to be said that the DES has consistently refused to countenance the term 'anti-racist', choosing instead to define 'educational problems posed by the nonwhite presence in nonracial terms' (Kirp, 1985, p. 33). Yet it does not appear to have such a strong resistance to the term 'anti-sexist'. One reason for this has been suggested by John Boyd:

Inequality issues concerning gender are simply less threatening, more easily dismissed and more susceptible to token responses from official bodies than ones concerning race. Since 1981 especially, race has generated foreboding because of its volatility, and the threats that race issues offer to white society's sense of well-being ensures that there will continue to be government responses in the form of commissions and policies. So far, there have been no sex riots. (Boyd, 1989, p. 70)

This is a highly contentious viewpoint and Boyd falls into the trap of seeing one form of oppression as being of more significance than another. Nor does he appear to see how racism and sexism interact. The fact that there has been more official government response to 'race' issues in education than to gender does not mean that 'race' has been any less subject to token responses. It may be that Black groups have been more successful than feminists in collective and widespread action in putting 'race' on the agenda and/or 'race' has generated foreboding because of its *perceived* volatility.

The Sex Discrimination Act is a milestone in the history of women's education. The 1944 Education Act may have put 'equal opportunities' on the agenda, but the Sex Discrimination Act took the *theory* and transformed it into a *mode of practice*. Putting to one side for a moment the opposition of the DES to a whole-hearted commitment towards removing gender inequalities from schooling, the endeavours of researchers, LEAs and individual schools and teachers have illustrated where and how gender issues arise in the education system and have developed strategies to reduce the restrictive effects. The next section will identify *what* is meant by gender inequalities in schooling and *how*, amongst other things, feminist theory has influenced the various approaches adopted by LEAs.

Gender discrimination and schools

The primary and secondary sectors of education have different histories and have, in the past, been characterised by many different features. The main impetus in secondary schooling has been the development of a curriculum that encompasses both vocational training and 'subject knowledge'; the aim being to equip all secondary students with relevant skills for their future in the labour market (for some, via further and higher education). The ethos of primary schooling (particularly since the Plowden Report, 1967) has been child-centred, whereby children experience an education appropriate to their individual needs, taken at their own pace and where 'discovery learning' is a key feature. These differences in approaches to education suggest that it might be more valuable to discuss studies on gender issues in two sections. However, there are overlaps in some of the research findings of the primary and secondary phases, so the intention here is to discuss areas common to both.

In the previous section it was noted that in circular 2/76 the DES urged LEAs to ensure that schools' concern lay with according children *access* to the same curriculum subjects. The thinking of the DES is clear – if the same numbers of girls and boys undertake maths, science and modern languages, then any 'problems' regarding gender inequalities would be removed. This stance resulted in research studies and interventionist strategies which concentrated upon secondary students' option choices.

Gender inequalities in the primary school was something of a later runner as far as research studies are concerned. The DES document, *Curricular Differences for Boys and Girls* (Department of Education and Science, 1975), records how girls were inclined towards humanities subjects and boys towards science subjects at option choice time. Prior to the Sex Discrimination Act, and indeed after the passing of this Act, some schools encouraged this channelling of children into gender-stereotyped areas by timetabling a science subject against an arts subject. In the process of identifying factors mitigating against girls opting for 'male'-type subjects, evidence was found to demonstrate the impact that the 'hidden' curriculum had on these apparent choices.

There are differences between the official curriculum and the 'hidden' curriculum, although there are ambiguities in these terms (see Meighan, 1981, pp. 54–5). Broadly speaking, the official curriculum refers to the timetable and/or everything organised by teachers (including clubs and out-of-school activities). The 'hidden' curriculum has been defined as 'those aspects of learning in schools that are unofficial, or unintentional, or undeclared consequences of the way teaching and learning are organized and performed' (Davies and Meighan, 1975, p. 171). Amongst those aspects of the 'hidden' curriculum found to be discriminatory were teaching resources; organisation and administration; and teacher attitudes.

Teaching resources

There is now a wealth of evidence to support the view that the vast majority of school materials have been gender-biased. Analysis of textbooks in particular have attracted considerable attention. Women have been rendered insignificant or invisible in secondary-school English, social studies, history, geography, maths and science textbooks (Scott, 1980). At the same time, history, geography and science books abound with references to male pioneers and scientists (Turnbull *et al.*, 1983; and Kelly, 1987), and mathematics and French textbooks perpetuate male bias (Abraham, 1989). The collection edited by Janie Whyld (1983) points to the fact that the lack of females in school books is not specific to 'male subjects', as the same situation exists in areas of the curriculum with a feminine image. Not only have women been notable by their absence, but when they *are* depicted they are frequently given a submissive persona. For example, physics books have represented females as 'women pushing prams, a woman floating on the Dead Sea, girls blowing bubbles, women cooking, women as radiographers, nurses or patients, women used as sex symbols in the same way they are used to sell cars, women looking amazed or frightened or simply women doing "silly" things' (Walford, 1980, pp. 224–5).

Research into primary schooling did not initially receive the same amount of attention as had secondary schooling. Once enquiries began, however, it rapidly became evident that sexism is as much a feature of the early years as the secondary years of education. Primary schooling, for all its emphasis on child-centred education, has been found to use 'boy-centred' resources, and even quite recent studies continue to note the disparity in images of females and males in maths schemes and history textbooks (Bailey, 1988; and Cairns and Inglis, 1989). Apart from teaching children to read, reading schemes have become famous for their tendency to demarcate certain jobs, activities and temperamental dispositions as feminine or masculine. In a study of nine reading schemes, many of which are still used in schools today, Glenys Lobban (1975) discovered thirty-three different occupations were given for adult males. Only eight were shown for adult women and these were mum, granny, princess, queen, witch, handywoman about the house, teacher and shop assistant! This, of course, means that girls are being presented with two possible future roles in the paid labour market. More recent research has shown sex-role representation in reading schemes continues to be that of traditional stereotypes (Stones, 1983). To be fair, some publishers have made attempts to address 'race' and gender bias in reading schemes brought out in the 1980s, for example, *The Oxford Reading Tree*, *Story Chest*, and *Reading World*, but there is still a long way to go.

Organisation and administration

Segregation by sex as an administrative device dates back to Victorian times when the words 'Girls' and 'Boys' were engraved on stone set above separate school entrances. My mother can recall how her own secondary school, built in 1937, maintained this tradition and when she left in 1944, rigid segregation between the sexes was still being enforced. These practices were widespread well into the first half of this century and the demise of single-sex schooling in pursuit of egalitarian co-education did not mean that gender ceased to be an organisational method. Registers, record cards and cloakrooms are frequently divided on the basis of sex; children are 'lined up' as girls and boys and given separate activities within one subject, for example, games lessons with girls playing netball or hockey whilst the boys play football (Delamont, 1980). Playgrounds too have had a role in discriminating between girls' space and boys' space.

Separating children according to their sex is considered by many teachers to be a routine and easy means of organisation. When this point arises (and it always does) on 'equal opportunities' training days in schools, it comes in the form of two questions; 'Why does it matter, as it's only a way of dividing the class up?' and, 'If I stop organising my class in this way then I'll have done equal opportunities, won't I?' These two questions are, in effect, intertwined. Organisation by gender is just one of the features of classroom life which differentiates between girls and boys and is frequently used in such a way that more fundamental aspects of 'femaleness' and 'maleness' are being enforced. So, what are children learning about their gender when schools base day-to-day organisation on pupils' sex?

Dividing children into groups of girls and boys is often used by teachers as a controlling device. This may come in the form of encouraging competition between the sexes, for example in music lessons, 'Who can sing the loudest, the boys or the girls?' It is inevitably the boys who are allowed to achieve this so they are learning to be valued for their ability to 'shout down' any competition. In contrast to this, girls are valued for their ability *not* to be vocal. I have vivid memories of a device used by one headteacher to dismiss children after school assembly when they left the hall in order of 'quietness'. The girls' lines always 'won'. Teachers may also use the opposite sex as a threat. Michael Marland (1983) gives an example of a female teacher snapping at a group of girls saying that, if they did not stop fooling around they would be made to dance with the boys. Similarly, a 'naughty boy' may be punished by being made to sit with a group of girls.

This differentiation by sex effects adults in the school as much as children. Staffing structures have (and still do) present a picture of 'male superiority', with males holding positions of authority. Headteachers, heads of department and the school caretaker are more often males, whilst women are seen in the subordinate roles of teaching auxiliaries, dinner attendants, school secretaries and main professional grade teachers (that is, teachers on basic salary). This situation is even more true of primary schools, where the majority of staff are female; as M. Strober and D. Tyack (1980) have said 'Women teach and men manage'. A report in the *Times Educational Supplement* (*TES*), (27 October 1989) entitled 'Heads, he wins and she loses' examined the most up-to-date figures available for the whole teaching force. These statistics demonstrated that the tendency for males to be over-represented in higher posts has actually increased in Britain in recent years. In primary schools, one in three males occupies a headteacher role, compared with one woman teacher in fourteen. Looking at the years 1981 and 1987, there was a 6.7 per cent increase in male primary heads, but only a 5.3 per cent increase in female primary heads. A similar situation was found in secondary schools, with nearly one male in thirty being a headteacher (an increase of 7.5 per cent from 1981 to 1987). In striking contrast, less than one in 127 female secondary staff was a head in 1987 (a 6.7 per cent increase from 1981). But it is not just a matter of considering the number of males to females in positions of authority. There is also the question of *what* areas of responsibility are held by women and men teachers. Studies in the late 1970s and early 1980s all pointed to women and men teaching (and in charge of) traditional subject areas (Byrne, 1978; Delamont, 1980; and Whyld (ed.) 1983). The *TES* article referred to these differences in relation to posts of responsibility, with women more likely to be involved in 'liaison, negotiating, training, influencing people and extra out of school activities'. They can be found as heads of year of upper and lower schools, and heads of special education. Higher status positions such as head of faculty, head of sixth form, deputy head, or head of outdoor pursuits were likely to be occupied by males.

The studies referred to in this and the previous section illustrate how gender discrimination is a 'fact of life' in schools. Children are provided with educational materials which reinforce gender stereotyping, and both witness and take part in practices that confirm differing routes for women and men. Although schools may not deliberately set out to teach children that girls and boys are 'different', as Sara Delamont has argued, schools are often 'more conservative about sex roles than either homes or wider society' (Delamont, 1983, p. 93).

This discussion has, so far, focused on the way schools reinforce notions of femininity and masculinity, but this is only part of the story. We are not passive recipients of socialisation processes, but active agents in our own learning. Therefore, the attitudes and beliefs of teachers and school students, and the interaction between and within these groups have a crucial impact. What do children learn about themselves through the attitudes of their teachers? Do teachers make judgements about children in their classrooms on the basis of their gender? It is to these and other related questions we will now turn.

Teacher–pupil interaction

To discuss the evidence of all the research findings in this area would occupy more space than is available here. A simpler exercise is to summarise the findings of teacher–*male* pupil interaction. First, boys make greater use of verbal and non-verbal language. This commands more of the teacher's time, in both attention and classroom control, resulting in boys receiving more reprimands and more praise than girls. Second, in order to establish control in the primary classroom, teachers will select topics that interest boys (Skelton, 1989). Third, as boys appear more 'evident' in the classroom, teachers perceive them as more active learners. Finally, boys' domination of teachers' time leads to their work being assessed differently from that of girls, with boys' work being graded more highly (Goddard-Spear, 1989).

These points highlight the importance of teacher attitudes. In 1978, Eileen Byrne stated that 'Teacher attitudes are almost certainly the dominant influence on how children develop in school; they may well be more accountable than they realize for the persistence of different inter-ests, activities, and levels of achievement in boys and girls' (Byrne,

1978, p. 82). It would be quite unfair to accuse most teachers of deliberately treating girls and boys differently, but it has been argued that the question of what behaviour is appropriate for girls or boys, or women and men, is one of *personal* as opposed to *professional* attitudes (Clarricoates, 1983).

Boys take up more of their teacher's time in the classroom, in the form of teacher–pupil interaction, reprimands and praise, as well as receiving a different type of instruction (Serbin, 1978). There is a notable domination by boys in any classroom discussion, although Jane French and Peter French (1984, 1986), in a conversational analysis of tapes, have discovered that it is not boys *per se* who secure the maximum amount of teacher attention, but one or two boys only. This 'skill' in attracting the teacher's time is achieved in several ways. First, boys are more mobile in the classroom, and use more and larger body movements. One teacher observing her class reported: 'Even with an equal number of boys and girls, the boys dominated the discussion – not by strength of argument, nor even by their ability to articulate . . . But the boys added power to their contributions by constant movement, jostling for attention while, for the most part, the girls sat still' (Lee, 1990, p. 28). By making greater use of non-verbal language than girls they literally gain space and attention for their arguments. A second tactic that effectively engages the teacher again relies heavily on non-verbal language: that is misbehaviour. Research has not only shown that boys require, or demand, more of their teacher's attention than do girls, but also that this leads teachers to believe that boys are academically more capable than girls, and think that boys' contributions are more impressive (Goddard-Spear, 1989). This is a view which appears to stand firm even in the face of conflicting evidence. Julia Stanley (1989) has analysed DES School Leavers Statistics (1986), where she found that in the eighteen rather arbitrary subject groupings used for GCSE results, girls are outstripping boys in twelve of them and rapidly drawing level in the others. Boys continue to be more successful at geography, economics, chemistry, physics, 'other sciences' and also in maths, but here there is only a marginal difference. In primary schools, the academic performance of girls across the board also outstrips that of boys. However, it has been shown that although teachers 'know' that girls are academically more capable, the more ebullient behaviour of boys results in an undervaluing of girls' achievements (Clarricoates, 1987; and Walkerdine, 1990).

Such attitudes are continued into the assessment of children's work. Margaret Goddard-Spear's (1989) research in this area found that the majority of teachers she interviewed claimed they could distinguish between the written work of girls and boys. She asked a group of secondary school science teachers to grade samples of children's work on a number of characteristics. These samples were taken from actual handwritten work of a scientific experiment carried out by eleven-year-old children. The sex of the pupils was altered so that each work sample was given to half of the teachers as boys' work and to the remaining teachers as girls' work. When teachers believed they were marking boys' work, higher ratings were given for scientific accuracy, richness and organisation of ideas than to identical work attributed to girls. Goddard-Spears' research also suggests that the sex of the teacher was an influential factor, as the work of 'boys' assessed by a female teacher produced a generous mark, whilst the most severe marking was of 'girls'' work by a male teacher. Teachers, then, are influenced by gender specific preconceptions in the assessment of children's abilities.

School students are not oblivious to the attitudes teachers have towards them, and these expectations strongly influence their self-perceptions:

> Teacher attitudes made a great difference. The girls said they need teachers who are patient with them, who don't 'take the mickey', who explain things to them and listen to them. They felt that teachers' expectations of them made a difference to the way they perform. It was important to like the teacher: 'If you don't like the teacher, you get to hate the subject and then you don't really try'. (Jones and Jones, 1989, p. 193)

Many studies have highlighted how teachers' attitudes act in such a way as to undermine girls' self-confidence. Michelle Stanworth (1981) coined the phrase the 'faceless bunch' to describe the inability of many teachers to see through girls' more passive approach and recognise them as individuals, rather than as a conformist 'whole' group. Ultimately, this has led to a situation whereby boys are far more confident in their abilities than are girls. Girls are far more likely to underestimate their performance in a given task than boys, and they interpret failure in different ways. Boys will accord their failings to lack of effort, whilst girls will tend to attribute failure to lack of ability (Kelly, 1988; and Jones and Jones, 1989).

These, and many other, research studies illustrate the various ways gender discrimination pervades the schooling experiences of girls, but what steps have been taken to rectify the situation? In accordance with the stance adopted by the DES, one strategy carried out in the early 1980s aimed to address the 'problem' of girls' 'underachievement' by raising teachers' awareness and making a traditional male area (science) 'girl-friendly'. The project was referred to as GIST – Girls Into Science and Technology – which spanned the years 1979–83. A team of researchers from Manchester Polytechnic and University, in England, worked with ten coeducational comprehensive schools, alongside teachers with responsibility for science and technology in the lower school. In eight schools the project team collaborated with teachers to devise and implement strategies which would improve girls' attitudes to science. The two control schools participated in attitude testing but were not involved in any interventions. The team followed a sample of pupils in the schools from the time they entered secondary school until they made their option choices at the age of thirteen. The aim of this action-research project was 'to explicate the reason for girls' underachievement in physical science and technical subjects at school, and simultaneously to explore the feasibility and effectiveness of interventions aimed at improving the situation' (GIST Final Report, 1984, p. 1). The GIST Final Report presents a range of disappointing outcomes. In the first place, the project made very little impact on pupils' subject choices. Only 4 per cent more girls chose physics in the GIST cohort than in previous years. The change in percentage of girls opting for technical craft was even smaller.

In relation to attitude change, the report notes that there was only a small trend for children in the action schools to show a 'less negative' attitude to subjects than was shown by children in the control schools. The teachers who had been responsible for devising and implementing the action strategies similarly showed that the project had made little impact on their attitudes. (These strategies had included the development of more 'girl-friendly' curriculum materials, single sex clubs and classes, and teachers were encouraged to undertake classroom observations in order to increase their awareness of gender differences in classroom interaction.) Although the teachers were generally supportive of GIST, they did not feel that their own practices had altered much as a result of it. The team themselves concluded that 'Perhaps the greatest impact of the project was a ripple effect whereby interest in GIST contributed to a changing climate of opinion in which girls' underachievement in science and technology came to be seen as a serious educational issue' (GIST, 1984, p. 39).

GIST's failure to make any great impact was not just a 'one-off' for this type of equal opportunities interventionist strategy. By the mid-1980s many LEAs and individual schools had equal opportunities policies, advisory teachers for equal opportunities (gender) were evident in some LEAs, and there was evidence of growing numbers of individual teachers committed to combating discrimination in their institutions (ILEA, 1986). Yet, as in the case of GIST, research continued to show that the experience of girls and boys in school had changed very little, with boys continuing to dominate physical space, teacher time and classroom resources (Wheldall and Merrett, 1988; and Lloyd, 1989).

Encouraging more girls to undertake subjects construed as 'male areas' such as maths, science and technology fails to provide an overall picture of the breadth of of curriculum offered within secondary schooling. The introduction of vocational training into schools in the form of the Technical and Vocational Education Initiative (TVEI, launched in 1983), underlined the fact that children's schooling experiences effect their future options in the labour market. One of TVEI's briefs was actively to promote equal opportunities. The effectiveness of TVEI and a detailed analysis of the various ways schools have attempted to address equal opportunities has been considered in an informative and lucid way by Millman (1985); Wickham (1986); and Millman and Weiner (1987). A generalised summary of their analysis suggests that the initiative has failed, and that it has failed because TVEI policy did not provide an adequate framework in which LEAs and schools could address gender inequalities. This left individual authorities having to cope with a complex issue for which they had no guidance, and resulted in a number of 'hit and miss' strategies, some more sophisticated than others. Encouraging more girls and boys to enter non-traditional areas of vocational training encounters the same problems as promoting non-stereotypical option choices. As Val Millman and Gaby Weiner have said:

> Achieving equal opportunities in education is conceptually and qualitatively different from, say, acquiring computing skills or developing pupil profiles. If equality is a serious consideration of TVEI, it needs to address the psychological, social and *political* perceptions of teachers, the MSC and employers before it can tackle the pedagogical problems of how to provide equal opportunities for pupils. (Millman and Weiner, 1987, p. 175)

The principles laid down here are applicable to *all* schooling and not just the TVEI scheme. Equal opportunities initiatives were clearly having little effect in changing girls' and boys' stereotypical choices. For some feminist researchers think the reason why gender inequalities continue to pervade schooling experiences is obvious. The concept of power dynamics and its implications for classroom interaction is not a central feature of many of the studies and interventionist strategies carried out in the 1970s and early 1980s. To understand the feminist perspectives underpinning studies of gender (and more recently, gender, 'race' and social-class inequalities) the differences and similarities of 'equal opportunities' and anti-sexist approaches need explaining.

Equal opportunities and anti-sexism

These two approaches share a common view – that education and school-ing is dominated by the ideal of the white, middle-class male – but they differ as to *how* this situation should be challenged. Within the equal opportunities perspective, girls' education is regarded as a 'problem' as they 'underachieve' in certain areas of the school system. Equal oppor-tunities (or liberal) feminists aim for a situation whereby girls and women are provided with the types of skills and educational qualifica-tions that will enable them to enter areas of employment traditionally dominated by men; put crudely, a desire for equal numbers of female and male plumbers, pilots and politicians. The GIST project is an example of this stance with its emphasis on ensuring girls are given equal *access* to science and technology subjects. The DES and local authorities have favoured this 'soft' approach as opposed to the 'strong' anti-sexist per-spective (Arnot, 1985). Those supporters of anti-sexist approaches see the question of girls' educational experiences as being more than simply ensuring *access* to school resources and educational benefits; it is about girls' *treatment in* and *outcome of* their schooling. Their intention is to place girls and women at the centre of the classroom in order to chal-lenge the dominance of male experience (Weiner, 1986).

This more radical stance is evident in the work of feminists who have researched gender power dynamics; that includes such issues as sexual harassment and girls' sexuality (Mahony, 1985; Herbert, 1989). In-equalities in power dynamics are particularly evident in Black girls' accounts of their school experiences when they are confronted by both racial and sexual harassment (Bryan, Dadzie and Scafe, 1985; and Suleiman and Suleiman, 1985). It also needs pointing out that the sexual harassment of females by males assumes, in the first instance, a heterosexist position. Lesbian (and gay) teachers and pupils are also subjected to sexual harassment, but it is of a qualitatively different nature (Lees, 1986a; and Harris, 1990). The power imbalances between men and women (in general), Black women and girls, and lesbians, is an issue which liberal feminism fails to engage with.

Whereas equal opportunities advocates see girls as the 'problem' in schooling, anti-sexist supporters regard male power and privilege as the 'problem'. These two viewpoints have been neatly identified by Lyn Yates. She says that 'Even teachers who agree there is a problem regarding what happens to girls and women in this society and who want to reform the schools, do not necessarily agree on their priority: is it to re-distribute shares of the cake or to change the cake?' (Yates, 1987, p. 6). More comprehensive accounts of these approaches and their relation to feminist theory are available elsewhere (Weiner, 1985, 1986; and Weiner and Arnot, 1987). The main distinction between these perspectives is 'Whereas [Equal Opportunities supporters] fail to address the relationship between patriarchy, power and women's subordination, the [anti-sexist supporters] place it at the centre of their thinking' (Weiner, 1985, p. 9). In their chapter in *Gender and the Politics of Schooling* (1987) Gaby Weiner and Madeleine Arnot have produced a table demonstrating the practical application of these ideas in schools. For example, an equal opportunities/'girl-friendly' strategy would be persuading girls into science and technology, whilst the corresponding anti-sexist/ 'girl-centred' approach would entail recognising the importance of girl-centred study, focusing on girl- and woman-centred science and technology. As more evidence has become available illustrating the failure of equal opportunities approaches to change attitudes, advocates of this view have notably been widening their framework of analysis. Although the concept of male power remains outside their thinking, there are signs of an increasing commitment to the *outcomes* of girls' educational experiences (that is, career choices), hence moving closer to the anti-sexist viewpoint. It also needs to be stressed here that these two perspectives are not opposing viewpoints – anti-sexist supporters have often used equal opportunities strategies as a starting point for broader concerns.

It will be quite evident to anyone reading this chapter that much of the research on women's education has concentrated on gender inequalities to the virtual exclusion of other forms of inequality prevalent within schooling. The implications of this will be examined in the next and final section, which considers the possible effects of the National Curriculum on discrimination in schooling.

Where are we now?

There has been considerable and understandable criticism in recent years from Black feminists of the fact that the majority of studies on gender and education have failed to address 'race' issues (Carby, 1982b; and Bryan, Dadzie and Scafe, 1985). More recent research and discussions have attempted to redress this imbalance (for example, Williams, 1987; Tizard *et al.*, 1988; and Wolpe, 1988). Inequality issues do not fall neatly into 'gender', 'race', or 'social class' categories and so the research which attempts to do this can only present a distorted picture of students' educational experiences. As Barbara Tizard *et al.*, have argued, what needs to be considered is the *interaction* of gender, 'race' and social class on school attainment:

> Ethnic group, social class and sex are major status groups within our society. But each individual is a member not just of one group, but of all three. A child is not just a girl, but also, say, of Afro-Caribbean origin and middle-class. Her outlook and experiences may be very different in many respects from those of a working-class boy of Afro-Caribbean origin, even though similar in other ways – notably, both are exposed to the racism in British Society. (Tizard *et al.*, 1988, p. 22)

This is a powerful and valid argument and one which should rightly influence future research into educational inequalities. But it does throw up difficult questions, not least the issue of mixed versus single-sex schools.

Debates over the benefits of single-sex versus coeducational school-ing, and vice versa, have been going on since the beginning of this century (Brehony, 1984). Arguments in favour of single-sex schooling are that girls are more likely to pursue further and higher education generally; to take advanced science subjects; to have a more positive attitude to 'male' curriculum areas; and to experience women in posi-tions of power (Ormerod, 1985). In addition, some radical feminists suggest that coeducational schools are sites upon which boys can practice and establish their domination over girls and women, making mixed schools dangerous places for females to be (Jones, 1985). This latter argument implies that the move from single-sex schooling to coeducation was based upon male power, identifying another avenue through which patriarchal relations could be reproduced. But, as Kevin

Brehony (1984) has pointed out, supporters of coeducation in the 1920s and later used the same kinds of arguments that feminists in favour of single-sex schools used in the 1970s and 1980s: that these establishments provide a solution to sex differences in education. It can be seen that both forms of schooling have, at different times, been developed in order to support patriarchal demands: 'single-sex schooling was historically, the major form of the reproduction of gender relations and coeducation has emerged as a variant, not an alternative, to that form' (Buswell, 1989, p. 54).

One of the reasons why the debate continues today is because there is no real evidence to justify a widespread return to single-sex schooling. Investigations by ILEA (1982) and the National Children's Bureau (Steedman, 1983) into examination results show that, as far as *achievement* is concerned, girls and boys in single-sex schools perform little differently to children in coeducation schools.

The studies referred to earlier have identified the value of single-sex schooling for girls, but failed to include social class as an instrumental factor. In recent times the *choice* of single-sex or mixed schooling has been an option largely confined to those sections of society that can afford it (Shaw, 1984). The question now is really one of whether mixed comprehensive schooling has done equal justice to girls and boys in both a social and an academic sense (Deem, 1984)?

This is not to suggest that the implications of social class have been ignored by feminists who have a specific focus on issues concerning women and education. As Madeleine Arnot and Gaby Weiner (1987) have said, there has been considerable research in this country into social class, gender and 'race' but few attempts to bring these three bodies of research together. A substantial body of work exists which considers social class and gender; specifically that of Marxist–socialist feminists who have attempted to define the relationship between education and the sexual division of labour (that is, the different forms of labour undertaken by women and men in the home and in the labour market). Theoretical arguments presented by Marxist–socialist feminists provide a radical critique of schooling, confront the political neutrality of education and perceive its ideologies and structures as being closely linked to the needs of capital and of dominant class interests (particularly middle-class culture). This perspective can be found in the work of Claire Wallace (1987) in her work on female school leavers, and Ann-Marie Wolpe (1988) on the secondary school experience of girls in the London area.

Jenny Williams (1987) has argued that whatever stance is taken, single-sex schooling for girls is considered a legitimate demand by governments. This does not hold true when it comes to separate schools for the Black population. She goes on to suggest that whilst girls' schools have received some governmental support as a desirable alternative to coeducation, the question of 'Black schools' is perceived as a threat to harmony and integration. The tensions which exist for feminists who are also committed to anti-racist education programmes can be evidenced in the call for separate provision within comprehensive schooling. It was discussed earlier how anti-sexist approaches place girls and women at the centre of the classroom, and this may necessitate girls-only classes. Yet such a concept applied to 'race' issues does not necessarily fit comfortably into an anti-racist perspective: 'It is not a usual part of anti-racist strategies to create black-only classes within ordinary schools to prevent unfair competition with white pupils who get more than their share of teacher attention' (Williams, 1987, p. 343). One of the major concerns for feminists adopting anti-racist principles is in learning how to deal with different family values and customs. An article by Avtar Brah and Rosemary Deem (1986) considers the question of what is an anti-sexist and anti-racist schooling. They point out that although there are similarities in sexism and racism, these social divisions have their own histories and forms of development and, as such, are experienced differently in schools. Any attempt to reconcile these differences demands a variety of strategies which,

> take account of both the relative autonomy of one from the other and the close link between them. For instance, a re-examination of the debate about co-educational secondary school, in our view, must take account of the particular issues raised as a result of the demands for single-sex schools by some sections of the black communities, but this must be done in a non-racist way. Similarly, on the curriculum front, there must be an attempt at developing non-sexist curriculum practices which are also anti-racist as well as developing non-racist curriculum practices which are also anti-sexist . . . These various parallel but specific oppressions (racism and sexism) call for *different* but *linked* strategies of action if they are to be combatted. (Brah and Deem, 1986, p. 77)

The tensions that exist between anti-sexism and anti-racism have been the focus of discussion in other interesting articles (Walkling and Brannigan, 1986; and Williams, 1987).

How will equal opportunities or anti-sexist/anti-racist concerns fare under the National Curriculum? What we do know is that equal opportunities and preparation for life in a multicultural society (National Curriculum Council, 1990) are to form cross-curricular dimensions. That is, these concepts should permeate the whole of the curriculum rather than being taught as a specific subject or as part of another subject. References to equal opportunities and multicultural education in *The Whole Curriculum* (National Curriculum Council, 1990) continue to place emphasis on the 'soft' approaches to these issues: 'This means, firstly, ensuring that all pupils have access to the curriculum'. But the document does go on to say, 'This alone, however, will not remove some of the more subtle barriers which stand in the way of access to the curriculum'.

The Education Reform Act 1988 (which brought in the National Curriculum) introduced substantial changes in the way the education system is managed. Control has been taken away from LEAs and handed over to the governing bodies of schools, and this has implications for equal opportunities. Those LEAs that have implemented and are monitoring gender and 'race' inequality policies no longer have the power to ensure that schools meet the necessary requirements. The importance accorded to equal opportunities and multicultural education, and how these issues are to be tackled, will rest upon the commitment of the governing body of each school. A likely scenario for the future is for the *ad hoc* approach to equal opportunities, already identified to be taking place in LEAs (Gibbs, 1989; and Trickett, 1989), to become even more diffuse when left to individual schools.

What is the future for women's education? The work of researchers in the 1990s demonstrates the positive impact feminist ideas have had on girls' perceptions of 'masculine' curriculum subjects (such as maths, physics and technology) and their future careers (Archer and McDonald, 1991; and Connolly, 1991). The commitment of feminist teachers and teacher educators ensures that sexism in education will continue to be challenged. At the same time, the apparent recognition given to gender concerns, as evidenced in *The Whole Curriculum* (National Curriculum Council, 1990), requires a constant vigilance in order to prevent a potential subversion of female inequality issues. An illustration of this potential can be found in school staffing policies.

One of the aims of Equal Opportunities is to achieve greater numbers of female teachers of science subjects and also to ensure that women occupy more positions of responsibility in the educational hierarchy. An extension of this stance is that more male teachers should opt for the early years of education (from nursery age to seven-year-olds). A report by the NASUWT and the Engineering Council (1991) make ten recommendations, including 'That more men, if possible, be attracted into teaching in infant schools' (p. 2). However, the implications of this situation have not been thought through. An investigation into the career perceptions of male teachers of young children has shown that individual and institutional patterns of femininity and masculinity are so deeply embedded, that superficial structural changes do little to challenge gender–power inequalities (Skelton, 1991). If the policy of an LEA or school is to 'put a man in the reception class' then the question that needs to be asked is 'How will this contribute towards a reduction in female inequalities in schooling?' It is of major concern, then, for feminists in education to endorse the need for key female schooling experiences to be continually addressed and inequalities redressed. They also need to ensure that, at policy level, supposed 'equal opportunities' strategies do not undermine the achievements that have already been made by feminism.

Further reading

Madeleine Arnot and Gaby Weiner, *Gender and the Politics of Schooling* (London, Hutchinson, 1987). An overview of the perspectives, research methods and strategies adopted by researchers and teachers to investigate gender and education. The book covers the range of feminist theories conceptualising gender in relation to equality of opportunity; gender, power and schools; and studies on class, 'race' and gender. It also considers the policy responses of central and local government to issues of sex inequality.

Pat Mahony, *Schools for the Boys?* (London, Hutchinson, 1985). This book, by a radical feminist, explores the question of whether girls do better in single-sex or co-educational schools. Pat Mahony moves the focus away from girls' academic achievements on to sexual harassment. Practical suggestions are given for bringing about change in schools.

Julia Stanley, *Marks on the Memory* (Milton Keynes, Open University Press, 1989). An original account of six teenagers coming to the end of their compulsory schooling. The teenagers and their families contribute to discussions throughout the book, which considers how teenagers adapt to the social and educational demands of life in an 'average' state school.

Gaby Weiner and Madeleine Arnot, *Gender Under Scrutiny: New Inquiries in Education* (London, Hutchinson, 1987). This book provides examples of current research topics and methods used for the exploration of gender and education. There are five sections to the book – a critical analysis of theories of gender difference; exploring the past through autobiography and life history; implicit messages in school texts; gender dynamics within schools; and teachers' expectations and attempts to change practice.

Bibliography

Aaron, Jane and Sylvia Walby (eds) (1991) *Out of the Margins: Women's Studies in the Nineties* (London, Falmer Press).

Abbot, Pamela and Claire Wallace (1989) 'The Family', in P. Brown and R. Sparks (eds), *After Thatcher: Social Policy, Politics and Society* (Milton Keynes, Open University Press).

_____ (1990) *An Introduction to Sociology: Feminist Perspectives* (London, Routledge).

Abbot, Sidney and Barbara Love (1973) *Sappho Was a Right–On Woman: A Liberated View of Lesbianism* (New York, Stein and Day).

Abraham, John (1989) 'Teacher Ideology and Sex Roles', *British Journal of Sociology of Education*, 10(1) 33–51.

Adams, Maurianne (1977) 'Jane Eyre: Woman's Estate' in Arlyn Diamond and Lee R. Edwards (eds), *The Authority of Experience: Essays in Feminist Criticism* (Amherst, Mass., University of Massachusetts Press).

Afshar, Haleh (1989) 'Gender roles and the "moral economy of kin" among Pakistani women in West Yorkshire', *New Community*, 15(5).

Ainsworth, Mary D. (1992) 'Attachments and other afffectional bonds across the life cycle', in J. Stevenson-Hinde and T. Marris (eds), *Attachment Across the Life Cycle* (New York, Routledge).

Akhter, Farida (1988) 'The State of Contraceptive Technology in Bangladesh', *Reproductive and Genetic Engineering: Journal of International Feminist Analysis*, 1(2) 153–8.

Alexander, Jacqueline (1991) 'Redrafting Morality: The Post-Colonial State and the Sexual Offences Bill of Trinidad and Tobago' in C. Mohanty, A. Russo and L. Torres (eds), *Third World Women and the Politics of Feminism* (Bloomington, Ind., Indiana University Press).

Alexander, Sally (1977) 'Women's Work in Nineteenth-Century London: A Study of the Years 1820–1850' in Juliet Mitchell and Ann Oakley (eds), *The Rights and Wrongs of Women* (Harmondsworth, Penguin).

_____ (1980) 'Review Essay', *Capital and Class*, 11, Summer, 138–43.

_____ (1984) 'Women, Class and Sexual Differences in the 1830s and 1840s: Some Reflections on the Writing of a Feminist History', *History Workshop Journal*, 17, Spring, 125–49.

_____ and Barbara Taylor (1981) 'In Defense of Patriarchy' in Raphael Samuel (ed.), *People's History and Socialist Theory* (London, Routledge & Kegan Paul).

Alexander, Ziggi (1990) 'Let it Lie Upon the Table: The Status of Black Women's Biography in the U.K.', *Gender and History*, 2(1), Spring, 22–33.

Allen, Hilary (1986) 'Psychiatry and the feminine' in P. Miller and N. Rose (eds), *The Power of Psychiatry* (Cambridge, Polity Press).

Allen, Isobel (1988) *Any Room at the Top* (London, Policy Studies Institute).

Alonso, Ana Maria (1988) 'The effects of truth: re-presentations of the past and the imagining of community', *Journal of Historical Sociology*, 1(1) 33–57.

Amir, Menachem (1971) *Patterns in Forcible Rape* (Chicago University Press).

Amos, Valerie and Pratibha Parmar (1984) 'Challenging imperial feminism', *Feminist Review*, 17, 3–20.

Anderson, Michael (1980) *Approaches to the History of the Western Family* (London, Macmillan).

Ang, Ien (1985) *Watching Dallas* (London, Methuen).

Antaki, C. (1988) *Analysing Everyday Explanation* (London, Sage).

Antonis, Barbie (1981) 'Motherhood and Mothering' in Cambridge Women's Studies Group (eds), *Women in Society: Interdisciplinary Essays* (London, Virago).

Anwell, Maggie (1988) 'Lolita Meets the Werewolf: *The Company of Wolves*' in Lorraine Gamman and Margaret Marshment (eds), *The Female Gaze* (London, The Women's Press).

Archer, John (1989) 'Childhood gender roles: structure and development', *The Psychologist, Bulletin of the British Psychological Society*, 9, 367–70.

____ and Maureen McDonald (1991) 'Gender roles and school subjects in adolescent girls', *Educational Research*, 33(1) 55–64.

Arditti, Rita (1990) 'Surrogacy in Argentina', *Issues in Reproductive and Genetic Engineering: Journal of International Feminist Analysis*, 3(1) 35–43.

____ , Renate Duelli Klein and Shelley Minden (eds) (1984) *Test Tube Women: What Future for Motherhood?* (London, Pandora).

Armitt, Lucie (ed.) (1991) *Where No Man Has Gone Before: Women and Science Fiction* (London and New York, Routledge).

Armstrong, Nancy (1987) *Desire and Domestic Fiction: A Political History of the Novel* (New York and Oxford, Oxford University Press).

Armstrong, Peter (1982) 'If it's only women it doesn't matter so much' in Jackie West (ed.), *Women, Work and the Labour Market* (London, Routledge & Kegan Paul).

Arnot, Madeleine (ed.) (1985) *Race and Gender* (Oxford, Pergamon).

____ (1987) 'Political lip-service or radical reform? Central government responses to sex equality as a policy issue' in Madeleine Arnot and Gaby Weiner (eds), *Gender and the Politics of Schooling*, (London, Hutchinson).

Atkinson, James (1986) *Changing Working Patterns: How Companies Achieve Flexibility to Meet New Needs* (London Institute of Manpower Studies, National Economic Development Office).

Atkinson, Ti-Grace (1974) *Amazon Odyssey* (New York, Links Books).

Atwood, Margaret (1985) *The Handmaid's Tale* (reprinted 1987) (London, Virago).

____ (1989) *Cat's Eye* (London, Bloomsbury).

Auchmuty, Rosemary, Frances Borzello and Cheri Davis Langdell (1983) 'The Image of Women's Studies', *Women's Studies International Forum*, 6(3) 291–8.

Badinter, Elisabeth (1981) *The Myth of Motherhood* (London, Souvenir Press).

Baehr, Helen and Gillian Dyer (eds) (1987) *Boxed In: Women and Television* (London, Pandora).

Bailey, Angela (1988) 'Sex-stereotyping in primary school mathematics schemes', *Research in Education*, 39, 39–46.

Bakker, Isabella (1988) 'Women's Employment in Comparative Perspective' in Jane Jenson, Elisabeth Hagen and Ceallaigh Reddy (eds), *Feminization of the Labour Force: Paradoxes and Promises* (London, Polity Press).

Balbo, Laura (1987) 'Crazy guilts: rethinking the welfare state debate from a women's point of view' in Anne Showstack Sassoon (ed.), *Women and the State* (London, Hutchinson).

Banks, Olive (1981) *Faces of Feminism* (Oxford, Martin Robertson).

Bannerji, Himani (1987) *doing time: poems* (Toronto, Sister Vision).

Barrett, Michèle (1980) *Women's Oppression Today: Problems in Marxist Feminist Analysis* (2nd edn 1988) (London, Verso).

____ (1982) 'Feminism and the definition of cultural politics' in Rosalind Brunt and Caroline Rowan (eds), *Feminism, Culture and Politics* (London, Lawrence and Wishart).

____ and Mary McIntosh (1979) 'Christine Delphy: towards a materialist feminism?', *Feminist Review*, 1.

____ and Mary McIntosh (1980) 'The "family wage": some problems for socialists and feminists', *Capital and Class*, 2.

____ and Mary McIntosh (1982) *The Anti-Social Family* (London, Verso).

____ and Mary McIntosh (1985) 'Ethnocentrism and socialist feminist theory' *Feminist Review*, 20.

Barron, R. D. and G. M. Norris (1976) 'Sexual Division and the Dual Labour Market' in D. Leonard Barker and S. Allen (eds), *Dependence and Exploitation in Work and Marriage* (London, Longman).

Barry, Kathleen (1979) *Female Sexual Slavery* (Englewood Cliffs, NJ, Prentice-Hall).

Bartels, M. Dianne, Reinhard Priester, Dorothy E. Vawter and Arthur L. Caplan (eds) (1990) *Beyond Baby M: Ethical Issues in New Reproductive Techniques* (New Jersey, Humana Press).

Bartels, Ditta (1988) 'Built-In Obsolescence: Women, Embryo Production and Genetic Engineering', *Reproductive and Genetic Engineering: Journal of International Feminist Analysis*, 1(2) 141–52.

Barthes, Roland (1977) 'The Death of the Author' (first published 1968) in Roland Barthes *Image–Music–Text*, trans. and ed. Stephen Heath (London, Fontana).

____ (1975) *The Pleasure of The Text* (New York, Hill and Wang).

Baruch, Elaine Hoffman, Armadeo F. D'Adamo and Joni Seager (eds) (1988) *Embryos, Ethics and Women's Rights: Exploring the New Reproductive Technologies* (New York, The Haworth Press).

Batman, Gail (1988) *Commonwealth Perspectives on IVF Funding* (Canberra Commonwealth Department of Community Services and Health, Australia).

Baum Duberman, Martin, Martha Vicinus and George Chauncey (1991) *Hidden From History: Reclaiming the Gay and Lesbian Past* (London, Penguin).

Baxter, Sue and Geoff Raw (1988) 'Fast food, fettered work: Chinese women in the ethnic catering industry' in Sallie Westwood and Parminder Bhachu (eds), *Enterprising Women: Ethnicity, Economy and Gender Relations* (London, Routledge).

Beckett, H. (1986) 'Adolescent identity development' in Sue Wilkinson (ed.), *Feminist Social Psychology: Developing Theory and Practice* (Milton Keynes, Open University Press).

Beddoe, Deirdre (1983) *Discovering Women's History: A Practical Manual* (London, Pandora).

Beechey, Veronica (1977) 'Some notes on female wage labour in capitalist production', *Capital and Class*, 3, Autumn, 45–66.

_____ (1986) 'Introduction' in Veronica Beechey and Elizabeth Whitelegg (eds), *Women In Britain Today* (Milton Keynes, Open University Press).

_____ (1987) 'Recent approaches to women's employment in Great Britain' in Veronica Beechey (ed.), *Unequal Work* (London, Verso).

_____ and Tessa Perkins (1987) *A Matter of Hours: Women, Part-Time Work and the Labour Market* (Cambridge, Polity Press).

Bell, Lee (1987) 'Hearing All Our Voices: Applications of Feminist Pedagogy to Conference Speeches and Panel Presentations', *Women's Studies Quarterly*, XV(3 and 4), Fall/Winter, 74–80.

Belotti, Elena Gianni (1975) *Little Girls* (London, Writers and Readers Publishing Cooperative).

Belsey, Catherine and Jane Moore (eds) (1989) *The Feminist Reader: Essays in Gender and the Politics of Literary Criticism* (London, Macmillan).

Bennett, Paula (1990) 'The Pea That Duty Locks: Lesbian and Feminist–Heterosexual Readings of Emily Dickinson's Poetry' in Karla Jay and Joanne Glasgow (eds), *Lesbian Texts and Contexts: Radical Revisions* (New York, New York University Press).

Berer, Marge (1986) 'Breeding Conspiracies: Feminism and the New Reproductive Technologies', *Trouble and Strife*, 9, Summer, 29–35. See also letters in *Trouble and Strife* (1987) 10, Spring, 2–10.

Berger, Bridget and Peter Berger (1983) *The War Over the Family: Capturing the Middle Ground* (London, Hutchinson).

Berger, John (1972) *Ways of Seeing* (Harmondsworth, Penguin).

Bernard, Jessie (1982) *The Future of Marriage*, 2nd edn (New Haven, Conn., Yale University Press).

Betterton, Rosemary (ed.) (1987) *Looking On: Images of Femininity in the Visual Arts and Media* (London, Pandora).

Beuret, Kristine and Lynne Makings (1987) '"I've got used to being independent now": women and courtship in a recession' in P. Allah, T. Keil, A. Bryman and B. Bytheway (eds), *Women and the Life Cycle: Transitions and Turning Points* (London, Macmillan).

Bezucha, Robert J. (1985) 'Feminist pedagogy as a subversive activity' in Margo Culley and Catherine Portuges (eds), *Gendered Subjects, The Dynamics of Feminist Teaching* (London, Routledge & Kegan Paul).

Bhachu, Parminder (1988) '*Apri Marzi Kardhi*, Home and Work: Sikh Women in Britain' in Sallie Westwood and Parminder Bhachu (eds), *Enterprising Women* (London, Routledge).

Bhavnani, Kum-Kum (1990) 'What's power got to do with it? Empowerment and social research' in I. Parker and J. Shotter (eds), *Deconstructing Social Psychology* (London, Routledge).

____ (1991) *Talking Politics: A psychological framing for views from youth in Britain* (Cambridge University Press).

____ and Reena Bhavnani (1985) *A Socialist Anatomy of Britain* (Cambridge, Polity Press).

____ and Margaret Coulson (1986) 'Transforming Socialist Feminism: The Challenge of Racism', *Feminist Review*, 23, Summer, 81–92.

Birke, Lynda, Susan Himmelweit and Gail Vinces (1990) *Tomorrow's Child, Reproductive Technologies in the 90s* (London, Virago).

Birth Statistics (1989) Series FMI, No. 16, (London, HMSO).

Bland, Lucy (1986) 'Marriage Laid Bare: Middle-Class Women and Marital Sex c1880–1914', in Jane Lewis (ed.), *Labour and Love: Women's Experience of Home and Family* (Brighton, Wheatsheaf).

____ (1989) 'Review of Sheila Jeffreys (ed.) *The Sexuality Debates*', *Women's Studies International Forum*, 12.

____ (1990) '"Purifying" the Public World: Feminists and Sexual Morality in Late Victorian England' (paper given at 'New Directions for Women's Studies in the 1990's?', Annual Women's Studies Network Conference, London).

Blaxter, Mildred and Elizabeth Paterson (1982) *Mothers and Daughters: A Three Generational Study of Health Attitudes and Behaviour* (London, Heinemann).

Bleier, R. (1984) *Science and Gender* (Oxford, Pergamon).

Bobo, Jacqueline (1988) '*The Color Purple:* Black Women as Cultural Readers' in Deirdre E. Pribram (ed.), *Female Spectators* (London, Verso).

Bock, Gisela (1989) 'Women's History and Gender History: Aspects of an International Debate', *Gender and History*, 1(1) 7–30.

Bogus, SDiane A. (1990) 'The "Queen B" Figure in Black Literature' in Karla Jay and Joanne Glasgow (eds), *Lesbian Texts and Contexts: Radical Revisions* (New York, New York University Press).

Bonder, Gloria (1985) 'The educational process of Women's Studies in Argentina: reflections on theory and technique' in Margo Culley and Catherine Portuges (eds), *Gendered Subjects: The Dynamics of Feminist Teaching* (London, Routledge & Kegan Paul).

Booth, Charles (1902–3) *Life and Labour of the People in London* (3rd edn) (London, Macmillan).

Borchorst, Anette and Birte Siim (1987) 'Women and the advanced welfare state – a new kind of patriarchal power?' in Anne Showstack Sassoon (ed.), *Women and the State* (London, Hutchinson).

Boston Women's Health Book Collective (1973) *Our Bodies, Ourselves* (revised edn. 1984) (New York, Simon and Schuster).

____ (1989) *Our Bodies, Ourselves* (Harmondsworth, Penguin).

Bott, Elizabeth (1957) *Family and Social Network* (London, Tavistock).

Boulton, Mary G. (1983) *On Being a Mother* (London, Tavistock).

Boumelha, Penny (1990) *Charlotte Brontë* (Hemel Hempstead, Harvester Wheatsheaf).

Bourne, Jenny (1987) 'Homelands of the Mind: Jewish Feminism and Identity Politics', *Race and Class*, XXIX(1), Summer, 1–24.

Boutilier, Mary and Lucinda San Giovanni (1985) 'Women and Sports: reflections on health and policy' in E. Lewin and V. Olesen (eds), *Women, Health and Healing* (London, Tavistock).

Bowlby, John (1951) *Maternal Care and Mental Health* (Geneva, World Health Organisation Monograph).

Bowles, Gloria (1983) 'Is Women's Studies an academic discipline?' in Gloria Bowles and Renate Duelli Klein (eds), *Theories of Women's Studies* (London, Routledge & Kegan Paul).

____ and Renate Duelli Klein (eds) (1983) *Theories of Women's Studies* (London, Routledge & Kegan Paul).

Boxer, Marilyn J. (1982) 'For and About Women: The Theory and Practice of Women's Studies in the United States' in Nannerl O. Keohane, Michelle Z. Rosaldo and Barbara C. Gelpi (eds), *Feminist Theory: A Critique of Ideology* (Sussex, Harvester).

Boyd, John (1989) *Equality Issues in Primary Schools* (London, Paul Chapman).

Boyle, M. (1992) 'The Abortion Debate' in P. Nicholson and J. M. Ussher (eds), *The Psychology of Women's Health and Health Care* (London, Macmillan).

Brah, Avtar (1988) 'Journey to Nairobi', in Shabnum Grewal *et al.* (eds), *Charting the Journey* (London, Sheba Feminist Publishers).

____ (1991) 'Questions of Difference and International Feminism', in Jane Aaron and Sylvia Walby (eds), *Out of the Margins: Women's Studies in the Nineties* (London, Falmer Press).

____ and Rosemary Deem (1986) 'Towards anti-sexist and anti-racist schooling', *Critical Social Policy*, 16, 66–79.

Branca, Patricia (1981) *Silent Sisterhood: Middle-class Women in the Victorian Home* (London, Croom Helm).

Brannen, Julia and Peter Moss (1987) 'Dual earner households: women's financial contribution after the birth of the first child' in J. Brannen and G. Wilson (eds), *Give and Take In Families: Studies in Resource Distribution* (London, Allen and Unwin).

____ (1991) *Managing Mothers: Dual Earner Households After Maternity Leave* (London, Unwin Hyman).

Brannen, Julia and Gail Wilson (eds) (1987) *Give and Take in Families: Studies in Resource Distribution* (London, Allen & Unwin).

Braverman, Harry (1974) *Labour and Monopoly Capital* (New York, Monthly Review Press).

Braybon, Gail (1981) *Women Workers in the First World War: The British Experience* (London, Croom Helm).

____ and Penny Summerfield (1987) *Out of the Cage: Women's Experiences in Two World Wars* (London, Pandora).

Breen, Dana (1975) *The Birth of a First Child* (London, Tavistock).

Brehony, Kevin (1984) 'Co-education: perspectives and debates in the early twentieth century' in Rosemary Deem (ed.), *Co-education Reconsidered* (Milton Keynes, Open University Press).

Brekke, Toril *et al.* (1985) *Women: A World Report, A New Internationalist Book* (London, Methuen).

Brent Community Health Council (1981) *Black People and the National Health Service* (London, Brent Community Health Council).

Bridenthal, Renate, Atina Grossmann and Marion Kaplan (eds) (1984) *When Biology Became Destiny: Women in Weimar and Nazi Germany* (New York, Monthly Review Press).

Brimstone, Lyndie (1991) 'Out of the Margins and Into the Soup: Some Thoughts on Incorporation' in Jane Aaron and Sylvia Walby (eds), *Out of the Margins: Women's Studies in the 1990's* (London, Falmer Press).

Brittan, Arthur (1989) *Masculinity and Power* (Oxford, Blackwell).

Brod, Harry (ed.) (1987) *The Making of Masculinities* (Boston, Allen & Unwin).

Brontë, Charlotte (1847) *Jane Eyre* (reprinted 1966) Q. D. Leavis (ed.) (Harmondsworth, Penguin).

Brophy, Julia (1989) 'Custody law, child care and inequality in Britain' in C. Smart and S. Sevenhuijsen (eds) *Child Custody and the Politics of Gender* (London, Routledge).

____ and Carol Smart (1981) 'From disregard to disrepute: the position of women in family law', *Feminist Review*, 9.

____ and Carol Smart (eds) (1985) *Women in Law* (London, Routledge & Kegan Paul).

Brown, Colin (1984) *White and Black in Britain* (London, Policy Studies Institute).

Brown, Richard (1976) 'Women as employees: some comments on research in industrial sociology', in Diana Barker and Sheila Allen (eds), *Dependence and Exploitations in Work and Marriage* (London, Longman).

Brown, George and Tirril Harris (1978) *Social Origins of Depression* (London, Tavistock).

Brown, G. W., B. Andrews, T. O. Harris, Z. Adler and L. Bridge (1986) 'Social Support, Self-Esteem and Depression', *Psychological Medicine*, 16, 813–31.

Brownmiller, Susan (1976) *Against Our Will* (Harmondsworth, Penguin).

Bruegel, Irene (1979) 'Women as a reserve army of labour: a note on recent British experience', *Feminist Review*, 3, 12–23.

____ (1989) 'Sex and race in the labour market', *Feminist Review*, 32, 49–68.

Brunet, Ariane and Louise Turcotte (1988) 'Separatism and Radicalism' in Sarah Lucia Hoagland and Julia Penelope (eds), *For Lesbians Only: A Separatist Anthology* (London, Onlywomen Press).

Brunsdon, Charlotte (ed.) (1986) *Films for Women* (London, BFI).

Brunt, Rosalind (1988) 'Caught Looking – Feminism, Pornography and Censorship', *'Ten.8'*, 31, 56–9.

____ and Caroline Rowan (eds) (1982) *Feminism, Culture and Politics* (London, Lawrence and Wishart).

____ , Eileen Green, Karen Jones and Diana Woodward (1983) 'Sell out or challenge? The contradiction of a Masters in Women's Studies', *Women's Studies International Forum*, 6(3) 283–90.

Bryan, Beverley, Stella Dadzie and Suzanne Scafe (1985) *The Heart of the Race: Black Women's Writing in Britain* (London, Virago).

Bulkin, Elly (1980) 'Racism and Writing: Some Implications for White Lesbian Critics', *Sinister Wisdom*.

____ , Minnie Bruce Pratt and Barbara Smith (1984) *Yours in Struggle, Three feminist perspectives on anti-semitism and racism* (New York, Long Haul Press).

Bullard, D. and S. Knight (1981) *Sexuality and Physical Disability: Personal Perspectives* (St Louis, Mosby Publishers).

Burgoyne, Jacqueline, Roger Ormrod and Martin Richards (1987) *Divorce Matters* (Harmondsworth, Pelican).

Burman, Erica (ed.) (1990) *Feminists and Psychological Practice* (London, Sage).

Burman, Sandra (ed.) (1979) *Fit Work for Women* (London, Croom Helm).

Burns, J. (1992) 'The psychology of lesbian health care', in P. Nicolson and J. M. Ussher (eds), *The Psychology of Women's Health and Health Care* (London, Macmillan).

Busfield, Joan (1989) 'Sexism and Psychiatry', *Sociology* 23(3) 343–64.

Buswell, Carol (1989) *Women in Contemporary Society* (London, Macmillan).

Butler, Johnnella E. (1985) 'Toward a pedagogy of Everywoman's Studies', in Margo Culley and Catherine Portuges (eds), *Gendered Subjects: The Dynamics of Feminist Teaching* (London, Routledge & Kegan Paul).

Byrne, Eileen (1978) *Women and Education* (London, Tavistock).

Cairns, Joyce and Bill Inglis (1989) 'A Content Analysis of Ten Popular History Textbooks for Primary Schools with Particular Emphasis on the Role of Women', *Educational Review*, 41(3) 221–6.

Califia, Pat (1988) *Macho Sluts* (Boston, Alyson).

Callan, Hilary and Shirley Ardener (eds) (1984) *The Incorporated Wife* (London, Croom Helm).

Cameron, Deborah (1985) *Feminism and Linguistic Theory* (London, Macmillan).
_____ (1989) '"Released into language": the study of language outside and inside academic institutions' in Ann Thompson and Helen Wilcox, *Teaching Women: Feminism and English Studies* (Manchester, Manchester University Press).

Campbell, Beatrix (1980) 'A Feminist Sexual Politics: Now You See It, Now You Don't, *Feminist Review*, 5, 1–18.
_____ (1988) *Unofficial Secrets* (London, Virago).

Campbell, Carole A. (1990) 'Women and Aids', *Social Science and Medicine*, 30(4) 407–515.

Campbell, E. (1985) *The Childless Marriage* (London, Tavistock).

Canaan, Joyce E. and Christine Griffin (1990) 'The new men's studies: part of the problem or part of the solution?' in Jeff Hearn and David Morgan, *Men, Masculinities and Social Theory* (London, Unwin Hyman).

Capra, Fritjof (1982) *The Turning Point* (London, Wildwood House).

Carabine, Jean (1992) 'Constructing Women, Women Sexuality and Social Policy', *Critical Social Policy*, 34, 23–37.

Carby, Hazel V. (1982a) 'White woman listen! Black Feminism and the boundaries of sisterhood' in Centre for Contemporary Cultural Studies (eds), *The Empire Strikes Back: Race and Racism in 70s Britain* (London, Hutchinson).
_____ (1982b) 'Schooling in Babylon' in Centre for Contemporary Cultural Studies (eds), *The Empire Strikes Back* (London, Hutchinson).
_____ (1987) *Reconstructing Womanhood: The Emergence of the Afro-American Woman Novelist* (New York and Oxford, Oxford University Press).

Carmen, Gail, Shail and Pratibha (1984) 'Becoming Visible: Black lesbian discussions', *Feminist Review*, 17, Autumn, 53–74.

Carpenter, Michael (1977) 'The new managerialism and professionalism in nursing' in M. Stacey, M. Reid, C. Heath and R. Dingwall (eds), *Health and the Division of Labour* (London, Croom Helm).

Carr, Helen (ed.) (1989) *From My Guy to Sci-Fi: Genre and Women's Writing in the Postmodern World* (London, Pandora).

Carter, Angela (1979) *The Bloody Chamber and Other Stories* (reprinted 1981) (Harmondsworth, Penguin).

Cartwright, Ann and Robert Anderson (1981) *General Practice Revisited* (London, Tavistock).

Cavendish, Ruth (1982) *Women on the Line* (London, Routledge & Kegan Paul).

Cavin, Susan (1985) *Lesbian Origins* (San Francisco, ism Press).

Cayleff, Susan E. (1988) 'Teaching Women's History in a Medical School: Challenges and Possibilities', *Women's Studies Quarterly*, XVI(1 and 2), Spring/Summer, 97–109.

CEC (Commission of the European Communities) (1990) 'Statistical Supplement', *System Bulletin*, 3.

Central Statistical Office (1989) *Social Trends* (London, HMSO).

____ (1990) *Social Trends* (London, HMSO).

Centre for Contemporary Cultural Studies (eds) (1982) *The Empire Strikes Back: Race and Racism in 70s Britain* (London, Hutchinson).

Chambers, Deborah (1986) 'The constraints of work and domestic schedules on women's leisure', *Leisure Studies*, 5.

(charles) Helen (1992) 'Whiteness – The Importance of Politically Colouring the "non"' in Hilary Hinds, Ann Phoenix and Jackie Stacey (eds), *Working Out: New Directions for Women's Studies* (London, Falmer Press).

Charles, Nickie and Marion Kerr (1988) *Women, Food and Families* (Manchester, Manchester University Press).

Chesler, Phyllis (1972) *Women and Madness* (London, Allen Lane).

____ (1988) *Sacred Bond: Motherhood Under Siege* (New York, Times Books 1988; and London, Virago Press, 1990).

Chester, Gail and Julienne Dickey (eds) (1988) *Feminism and Censorship* (London, Prism Press).

Chodorow, Nancy (1978) *The Reproduction of Mothering* (Berkeley, Calif., University of California Press).

____ and Susan Contratto (1982) 'The fantasy of the perfect mother', in B. Thorne with M. Yalom (eds), *Rethinking the Family: Some Feminist Questions* (London, Longman).

Christian, Barbara (1987) 'The Race for Theory', *Cultural Critique*, Spring, 51–63.

____ (1990) 'The Race for Theory', in Karen V. Hansen and Ilene J. Philipson (eds), *Women, Class and the Feminist Imagination: A Socialist–Feminist Reader* (Philadelphia, Pa., Temple University Press).

Cixous, Hélène (1981) 'The Laugh of the Medusa' in Elaine Marks and Isabelle de Courtivron, *New French Feminisms* (Brighton, Harvester).

____ (1989) 'Sorties: Out and Out: Attacks/Way Out/Forays' in Catherine Belsey and Jane Moore (eds), *The Feminist Reader: Essays in Gender and the Politics of Literary Criticism* (London, Macmillan).

Clark, Alice (1968) *Working Life of Women in the Seventeenth Century* (1st edn 1919) (London, Frank Cass).

Clark, Anna (1988) *Women's Silence, Men's Violence, Sexual Assault in England 1770–1845* (London, Pandora).

Clarke, June, Mandy Merck and Diana Simmonds (1982) 'Doris Day Case Study: Stars and Exhibition' in *Star Signs: Papers From a Weekend Workshop* (London, BFI).

Clarke-Stewart, Alison (1982) *Day Care* (Glasgow, Fontana).

Clarricoates, Katherine (1983) 'Classroom Interaction' in J. Whyld (ed.), *Sexism in the Secondary Curriculum* (London, Harper and Row).

_____ (1987) 'Child Culture at School: A Clash Between Gendered Worlds?' in A. Pollard (ed.), *Children and their Primary Schools* (Lewes, Falmer).

Cockburn, Cynthia (1983) *Brothers: Male dominance and Technological Change* (London, Pluto Press).

_____ (1985) *Machinery of Male Dominance: Men, Women and Technological Change* (London, Pluto Press).

Cocks, Joan (1985) 'Suspicious pleasures: on teaching feminist theory' in Margo Culley and Catherine Portuges (eds), *Gendered Subjects: The Dynamics of Feminist Teaching* (London, Routledge & Kegan Paul).

Cohen, Bronwen (1988) *Caring for Children: Services and Policies For Childcare and Equal Opportunities In the United Kingdom* (London, Family Policy Studies Centre).

Cohen, Sherrill and Nadine Taub (eds) (1989) *Reproductive Laws For The 1990s* (New Jersey, Humana Press).

Coleman, David (1988) 'Population' in A. H. Halsey (ed.), *British Social Trends Since 1900* (London, Macmillan).

Collette, Christine (1989) *For Labour and For Women: The Women's Labour League, 1906–18* (Manchester, Manchester University Press).

Collins, Patricia Hill (1990) *Black Feminist Thought, Knowledge, Consciousness and the Politics of Empowerment* (London, Harper Collins).

Combahee River Collective (1981) 'A Black Feminist Statement' in Cherrie Moraga and Gloria Anzaldua (eds), *This Bridge Called My Back* (Watertown, Mass., Persephone Press).

Comer, Lee (1974) *Wedlocked Women* (Leeds, Feminist Books).

Connolly, Lesley (1991) *School, Science and Careers* (unpublished MA Study, E813, Milton Keynes, Open University).

Conseil Du Statut De La Femme (1988) *Sortir La Maternite Du Laboratoire* (Québec, Gouvernement du Québec).

Coonz, Stephanie (1988) *The Social Origins of Private Life: A History of American Families 1600–1900* (London, Verso).

Cooper, Fiona (1988) *Rotary Spokes* (London, Brilliance Books).

Cooperstock, Ruth and Henry L. Leonard (1979) 'Some social meanings of tranquilliser use', *Sociology of Health and Illness*, 1(3) 331–47.

Coote, Anna and Beatrix Campbell (1982) *Sweet Freedom* (London, Pan). (2nd edn published 1987, London, Basil Blackwell).

Corea, Gena (1985) *The Mother Machine: Reproductive Technologies from Artificial Insemination to Artificial Wombs* (New York, Harper and Row; and London, The Women's Press, 1988).

_____ et al. (1985) *Man-Made Woman: How New Reproductive Technologies Affect Women* (London, Hutchinson; and Indiana University Press, 1987).

____ and Susan Ince (1987) 'Report of a Survey of IVF Clinics in the US' in Pat Spallone and Deborah Lynn Steinberg (eds), *Made to Order* (Oxford, Pergamon).

Cornillon, Susan Koppelman (ed.) (1972) *Images of Women in Fiction: Feminist Perspectives* (Bowling Green, Ohio, Bowling Green University Popular Press).

Cornwell, Jocelyn (1984) *Hard Earned Lives: Accounts of Health and Illness from East London* (London, Tavistock).

Cott, Nancy F. (1988) 'Editorial', *Women's Studies Quarterly*, XVI (1 and 2), Spring and Summer, 3–5.

Coulson, Meg, Branca Magas and Hilary Wainwright (1975) 'The housewife and her labour under capitalism – A critique', *New Left Review*, 89, 59–71.

Coulson, Margaret and Kum-Kum Bhavnani (1990) 'Making a difference – questioning women's studies' in Erica Burman (ed.), *Feminists and Psychological Practice* (London, Sage).

Coveney, Lal, Margaret Jackson, Sheila Jeffreys, Leslie Kaye and Pat Mahony (1984) *The Sexuality Papers: Male Sexuality and the Social Control of Women* (London, Hutchinson).

Coward, Rosalind (1980) 'Are women's novels feminist novels?', *Feminist Review*, 5.

____ (1982) 'Sexual Violence and Sexuality', *Feminist Review*, 11.

____ (1983) *Patriarchal Precedents: Sexuality and Social Relations* (London, Routledge & Kegan Paul).

____ (1984) *Female Desire. Women's Sexuality Today* (London, Paladin).

____ (1989) 'The True Story of How I Became My Own Person' (first published 1984) in Catherine Belsey and Jane Moore (eds), *The Feminist Reader: Essays in Gender and the Politics of Literary Criticism* (London, Macmillan).

____ and Linda Semple (1989) 'Tracking Down the Past: Women and Detective Fiction' in Helen Carr (ed.), *From My Guy to Sci-Fi* (London, Pandora).

Coyner, Sandra (1983) 'Women's Studies as an academic discipline: why and how to do it' in Gloria Bowles and Renate Duelli Klein (eds), *Theories of Women's Studies* (London, Routledge & Kegan Paul).

Cranny-Francis, Anne (1990) *Feminist Fiction: Feminist Uses of Generic Fiction* (Cambridge, Polity Press).

Crompton, Rosemary and Gareth Jones (1984) *White-collar proletariat. Deskilling and gender in clerical work* (London, Macmillan).

Crompton, Rosemary and Kay Sanderson (1989) *Gendered Jobs and Social Change* (London, Unwin Hyman).

Crowe, Christine (1985) 'Women Want It: In Vitro Fertilization and Women's Motivations for Participation', *Women's Studies International Forum*, 8(6).

Crowther Report (1959) *15 to 18, A Report of the Central Advisory Council for Education* (London, HMSO).

Cruikshank, Margaret (ed.) (1982) *Lesbian Studies, Present and Future* (New York, The Feminist Press).

Crumpacker, Laurie and Eleanor Vander Haegen (1987) 'Pedagogy and Prejudice: Strategies for Confronting Homphobia in the Classroom', *Women's Studies Quarterly*, XV(3 and 4), Fall/Winter, 65–73.

Culley, Margo (1985) 'Anger and authority in the introductory Women's Studies classroom' in Margo Culley and Catherine Portuges (eds), *Gendered Subjects: The Dynamics of Feminist Teaching* (London, Routledge & Kegan Paul).

_____ and Catherine Portuges (eds) (1985) *Gendered Subjects: The Dynamics of Feminist Teaching* (London, Routledge & Kegan Paul).

_____ , Arlyn Diamond, Lee Edwards, Sara Lennox and Catherine Portuges (1985) 'The politics of nurturance' in Margo Culley and Catherine Portuges (eds), *Gendered Subjects: The Dynamics of Feminist Teaching* (London, Routledge & Kegan Paul).

Dale, Angela (1991) 'Women in the labour market: policy in perspective' in Nick Manning *et al.*, *Social Policy Review 1990–1991* (London, Longmans).

Dalla Costa, Maria Rosa and Selma James (1972) *The Power of Women and the Subversion of the Community* (Bristol, Falling Wall Press).

Dalley, Gillian (1988) *Ideologies of Caring: Rethinking Community and Collectivism* (London, Macmillan).

Dally, Ann (1982) *Inventing Motherhood: The consequences of an ideal* (London, Burnett Books).

Daly, Mary (1978) *Gyn/Ecology: The Metaethics of Radical Feminism* (Boston, Mass., Beacon Press; and London, The Women's Press, 1979).

_____ (1984) *Pure Lust: Elementary Feminist Philosophy* (London, The Women's Press).

David, Miriam (1986) 'Moral and maternal: the family and the new right' in Ruth Levitas (ed.), *The Ideology of the New Right* (Cambridge, Polity Press).

Davidoff, Leonore (1973) *The Best Circles: Society, Etiquette and the Season* (London, Croom Helm).

_____ and Catherine Hall (1987) *Family Fortunes: Men and Women of the English Middle Class 1780–1850* (London, Hutchinson).

Davies, L. and R. Meighan (1975) 'A Review of Schooling and Sex Roles', *Educational Review*, 27(3).

Davin, Anna (1972) 'Women and History' in Michelene Wandor (comp.) *The Body Politic. Women's Liberation in Britain 1969–1972* (London, Stage I).

_____ (1978) 'Imperialism and Motherhood', *History Workshop Journal*, 5, Spring, 9–65.

_____ (1979) 'Mind that you do as you are told', *Feminist Review*, 3, 89–98.

_____ (1981) 'Feminism and Labour History' in Raphael Samuel (ed.), *People's History and Socialist Theory* (London, Routledge & Kegan Paul).

Davis, Angela (1971) 'Reflections on the role of the black woman in the community of slaves', *Black Scholar*, December, 3–15.

_____ (1982) *Women, Race and Class* (London, The Women's Press).

Davis, Barbara Hillyer (1985) 'Teaching the feminist minority' in Margo Culley and Catherine Portgues (eds), *Gendered Subjects: The Dynamics of Feminist Teaching* (London, Routledge & Kegan Paul).

Deakin, Nicholas and Malcolm Wicks (1988) *Families and the State* (London, Family Policy Studies Centre).

de Beauvoir, Simone (1949) *The Second Sex* (reprinted 1972) (Harmondsworth, Penguin).

Deem, Rosemary (1981) 'State Policy and Ideology in the Education of Women, 1944–1980', *British Journal of Sociology of Education*, 2(2) 131–43.

_____ (ed.) (1984) *Co-education Reconsidered* (Milton Keynes, Open University Press).

Degener, Theresia (1990) 'Female Self-Determination Between Feminist Claims and "Voluntary" Eugenics, Between "Rights" and Ethnics', *Issues in Repro-*

ductive and Genetic Engineering: Journal of International Feminist Analysis, 3(2) 87–99.

de Lyon, Hilary (1989) 'Sexual Harassment' in Hilary de Lyon and Frances Migniuolo (eds), *Women Teachers* (Milton Keynes, Open University Press).

Delamont, Sara (1980) *Sex Roles and the School* (London, Methuen).

_____ (1983) 'The conservative school? Sex roles at home, at work and at school' in S. Walker and L. Barton (eds), *Gender, Class, Education* (Lewes, Falmer).

Delphy, Christine (1970) 'Libération des femmes année zero', *Partisans*, 50/51, Maspero. Translated in mimeo form, Edinburgh Women's Liberation Conference 1974.

_____ (1979) 'Sharing the same table: consumption and the family' in C. C. Harris (ed.), *The Sociology of the Family: New Directions for Britain*, Sociology Review Monograph 28 (Keele, University of Keele Press).

_____ (1980) 'A materialist feminism is possible', *Feminist Review*, 4.

_____ (1984a) *Close to Home: A Materialist Analysis of Women's Oppression* (London, Hutchinson).

_____ (1984b) 'The Main Enemy' in Christine Delphy, *Close to Home: A Materialist Analysis of Women's Oppression* (first published in 1977 by Women's Research and Resources Centre, London) (London, Hutchinson).

Department of Education and Science (1975) *Curricular Differences for Boys and Girls* (London, HMSO).

_____ (1976) *Sex Discrimination Act 1975*, Circular 2/76 (London, HMSO).

DE (Department of Employment) (1989) 'Labour force outlook to 2000', *Employment Gazette*, April, 159–72.

Department of Health (1990) *Health and Personal Social Services Statistics for England* (London, HMSO).

_____ (1991) *NHS Workforce in England* (London, Crown Copyright).

_____ and Social Security (1981) *Growing Older* (London, HMSO).

de Wolfe, Patricia (1980) 'Women's Studies: The Contradictions for Students' in Dale Spender and Elizabeth Sarah (eds), *Learning to Lose: Sexism and Education*, 2nd edn, 1988 (London, The Women's Press).

Dex, Shirley (1985) *The Sexual Division of Work* (Brighton, Wheatsheaf).

_____ (1987) *Women's Occupational Mobility: a lifetime perspective* (London, Macmillan).

Dick, Leslie (1989) 'Feminism, Writing, Postmodernism' in Helen Carr (ed.), *From My Guy to Sci-Fi: Genre and Women's Writing in the Postmodern World* (London, Pandora).

_____ (1987) *Without Falling* (London, Serpent's Tail).

Dinnerstein, Dorothy (1977) *The Mermaid and the Minotaur: Sexual Arrangements and the Human Malaise* (New York, Harper and Row).

Dobash, Rebecca and Russell Dobash (1980) *Violence Against Wives* (Shepton Mallet, Open Books).

_____ (1987) 'The Response of the British and American Women's Movements to Violence Against Women' in Jalna Hanmer and Mary Maynard (eds), *Women, Violence and Social Control* (London, Macmillan).

Dosanj-Matwala, N. and A. Woollett (1990) 'Asian women's ideas about contraception, family size and composition', *Journal of Reproductive and Infant Psychology*, 8, 231–2.

Douglas, Carol Anne (1990) *Love and Politics: Radical Feminist and Lesbian Theories* (San Francisco, ism Press).

Dowling, Colette (1981) *The Cinderella Complex* (Glasgow, Fontana).

Downing, Hazel (1983) 'On being automated', *Aslib Proceedings*, 35(1) 38–51.

Doyal, Lesley (1985) 'Women and the National Health Service: the carers and the careless' in E. Lewin and V. Olesen (eds), *Women, Health and Healing* (London, Tavistock).

⎯⎯ with Imogen Pennell (1979) *The Political Economy of Health* (London, Pluto Press).

⎯⎯ and Mary Ann Elston (1986) 'Women, health and medicine' in Veronica Beechey and Elizabeth Whitelegg (eds), *Women in Britain Today* (Milton Keynes, Open University Press).

Drake, Barbara (1920) *Women and Trade Unions* (London, Labour Research Department).

Driver, Emily (1989) 'Introduction' in Emily Driver and Audrey Droisen (eds), *Child Sexual Abuse* (London, Macmillan).

Dunn, Sara (1990) 'Voyages of the Valkyries: Recent Lesbian Pornographic Writing', *Feminist Review*, 34, 161–70.

Dworkin, Andrea (1981) *Pornography: Men Possessing Women* (London, The Women's Press).

⎯⎯ (1987) *Right-wing Women: The Politics of Domesticated Females* (first published 1983, New York, Perigree Books). (London, The Women's Press).

⎯⎯ (1991) Interview, *Guardian*, 5 December, p. 21.

Dyer, Richard *et al.* (1981) *Coronation Street* (London, BFI Monograph).

Edholm, Felicity (1982) 'The unnatural family' in E. Whitelegg, M. Arnot, E. Bartels, V. Beechey and L. Birke, *The Changing Experience of Women* (Oxford, Martin Robertson).

Edwards, Anne (1987) 'Male Violence in Feminist Theory' in Jalna Hanmer and Mary Maynard (eds), *Women, Violence and Social Control* (London, Macmillan).

Edwards, Robert (1989) *Life Before Birth: Reflections on the Embryo Debate* (London, Hutchinson).

⎯⎯ and Patrick Steptoe (1980) *A Matter of Life: The Story of a Medical Breakthrough* (London, Hutchinson).

Edwards, Susan (1981) *Female Sexuality and the Law* (Oxford, Martin Robertson).

Ehrenreich, Barbara and Deidre English (1979) *For Her Own Good: 150 years of the experts' advice to women* (London, Pluto Press).

Ehrenreich, Barbara, Elizabeth Hess and Gloria Jacobs (1987) *Re-making Love: The Feminization of Sex* (London, Fontana).

Eisenstein, Hester (1984) *Contemporary Feminist Thought* (London, Unwin).

Eisenstein, Zillah R. (1979) *Capitalist Patriarchy and the Case for Socialist Feminism* (New York, Monthly Review Press).

Ellman, Mary (1968) *Thinking About Women* (New York, Harcourt Brace Jovanovich).

Elson, Diane and Ruth Pearson (1989) *Women's Employment and Multinationals in Europe* (London, Macmillan).

Engels, Friedrich (1940) *The Origins of the Family, Private Property and the State* (London, Lawrence and Wishart).

Enloe, Cynthia (1989/1990) *Bananas, Beaches and Bases. Making feminist sense of international politics* (London, Pandora, 1989; Berkeley, Calif., University of California Press, 1990).

Equal Opportunities Commission (1987) *Women and Men in Great Britain 1987* (London, HMSO).

_____ (1990) *Women and Men in Great Britain 1990* (London, HMSO).

_____ (1991) *Women and Men in Great Britain 1991* (London, HMSO).

Escoffier, Jeffrey (1990) 'Inside the Ivory Closet: The Challenges Facing Lesbian and Gay Studies', *Out/Look*, Fall, 40–8.

Evans, Mary (1982) 'In Praise of Theory: The Case for Women's Studies', *Feminist Review*, 10, 61–71.

_____ (1983a) 'The teacher's tale: on teaching Women's Studies' in *Women's Studies International Forum*, 6(3) 325–30.

_____ (1983b) 'In Praise of Theory: The Case for Women's Studies' in Gloria Bowles and Renate Duelli Klein (eds), *Theories of Women's Studies* (London, Routledge & Kegan Paul).

_____ (1991) 'The Problem of Gender for Women's Studies' in Jane Aaron and Sylvia Walby (eds), *Out of the Margins: Women's Studies in the Nineties* (London, Falmer Press).

Evanson, E. (1980) *Just Me and the Kids: A Study of Single Parent Families in Northern Ireland* (Belfast, Equal Opportunities Commission of Northern Ireland).

Everywoman (1988) *Pornography and Sexual Violence: Evidence of Links* (London, Everywoman).

Ewing, Christine M. (1988) 'Tailored Genes: IVF, Genetic Engineering and Eugenics', *Reproductive and Genetic Engineering: Journal of International Feminist Analysis*, 1(1) 31–40.

_____ (1990) 'Australian Perspectives on Embryo Experimentation: An Update', *Issues in Reproductive and Genetic Engineering: Journal of International Feminist Analysis*, 3(2) 119–23.

_____ (1990) 'Draft Report on Surrogacy issued by the Australian National Bioethics Consultative Committee', *Issues in Reproductive and Genetic Engineering: Journal of International Feminist Analysis*, 3(2) 143–6.

Faderman, Lillian (1981) *Surpassing the Love of Men: Romantic Friendship and Love Between Women from the Renaissance to the Present* (London, Junction Books).

Family Policy Studies Centre (1990) *Family Policy Bulletin* No. 8.

Faraday, Annabel (1981) 'Liberating Lesbian Research' in Kenneth Plummer (ed.), *The Making of the Modern Homosexual* (London, Hutchinson).

Farran, Denise, Sue Scott and Liz Stanley (eds) (1986) *Writing Feminist Biography*, Studies in Sexual Politics (Manchester, Manchester University).

Farwell, Marilyn R. (1990) 'Heterosexual Plots and Lesbian Subtexts: Toward a Theory of Lesbian Narrative Space' in Karla Jay and Joanne Glasgow (eds), *Lesbian Texts and Contexts: Radical Revisions* (New York, New York University Press).

Feldberg, Roslyn and Evelyn Nakano Glenn (1979) 'Male and female: job versus gender models in the sociology of work', *Social Problems*, 26(5) 524–38.

Felski, Rita (1989) *Beyond Feminist Aesthetics: Feminist Literature and Social Change* (London, Hutchinson Radius).

Feminism and Psychology (1992) Special Issue on 'Heterosexuality', 2(3).

Ferguson, Ann (1989) *Blood at the Root: Motherhood, Sexuality and Male Dominance* (London, Pandora Press).

Ferguson, Marjorie (1983) *Forever Feminine: Women's Magazines and the Cult of Femininity* (London, Heinemann).

Fildes, Sarah (1983) 'The Inevitability of Theory', *Feminist Review*, 14, Summer, 62–70.

Finch, Janet (1983) *Married to the Job: wives' incorporation into men's work* (London, Allen and Unwin).

____ and Dulcie Groves (1983) *A Labour of Love: Women, Work and Caring* (London, Routledge & Kegan Paul).

Firestone, Shulamith (1971) *The Dialetic of Sex: The Case for Feminist Revolution* (London, Jonathan Cape).

Fisher, Berenice (1987) 'The Heart Has Its Reasons: Feelings, Thinking, and Community Building in Feminist Education', *Women's Studies Quarterly*, XV(3 and 4) 47–58.

Fleischer, Eva (1990) 'Ready For Any Sacrifice? Women in IVF Programmes', *Issues in Reproductive and Genetic Engineering: Journal of International Feminist Analysis*, 3(1) 1–11.

Fletcher, Sheila (1989) *Maude Royden: A Life* (Oxford, Blackwell).

Foucault, Michel (1973) *The Archaeology of Knowledge* (London, Tavistock).

____ (1979) *The History of Sexuality* (Vol. 1) (London, Allen Lane).

Frankenberg, Ruth (1988) *White Women Race Matters* (doctorate dissertation, Santa Cruz, Calif., University of California).

Franklin, Sarah and Jackie Stacey (1986) Lesbian Perspectives on Women's Studies, Women's Studies Occasional Papers (University of Kent at Canterbury).

____ (1988) 'Dyketactics for Difficult Times: a review of the "Homosexuality Which Homosexuality?" Conference', *Feminist Review*, 29, 136–51.

Franklin, Sarah, Celia Lury and Jackie Stacey (eds) (1991) *Off Centre: Feminism and Cultural Studies* (London, Harper Collins).

Fraser, Nancy (1989) *Unruly Practices: Power, discourse and gender in contemporary social theory* (Minneapolis, University of Minnesota Press).

Freeman, Jo (1979) 'The Feminist Scholar', *Quest*, 5(1) 26–36.

Freire, Paulo (1970) *Pedagogy of the Oppressed* (New York, Seabury Press).

French, Jane and Peter French (1984) 'Gender imbalances in the primary classroom', *Educational Research*, 26(2) 127–36.

____ (1986) *Gender imbalances in infant school classroom interaction* (Manchester, EOC).

French, Marilyn (1977) *The Women's Room* (reprinted 1978) (London, Sphere).

Friedan, Betty (1963) *The Feminine Mystique* (London, Gollancz); (Also Harmondsworth, Penguin, 1965).

Friedman, Susan Stanford (1985) 'Authority in the feminist classroom: a contradiction in terms?' in Margo Culley and Catherine Portuges (eds), *Gendered Subjects: The Dynamics of Feminist Teaching* (London, Routledge & Kegan Paul).

Fuss, Diane (1990) *Essentially Speaking: Feminism, Nature and Difference* (first published New York, Routledge, 1989) (London, Routledge).

Gagnon, John H. and William Simon (1973) *Sexual Conduct* (London, Hutchinson).

Gallup, Jane (1982) *Feminism and Psychoanalysis: The Daughter's Seduction* (London, Macmillan).

Gamarnikow, Eva *et al.* (eds) (1983) *Gender, Class and Work* (London, Heinemann).

Gamman, Lorraine (1988) 'Watching the Detectives: The Enigma of the Female Gaze' in Lorraine Gamman and Margaret Marshment (eds), *The Female Gaze* (London, The Women's Press).

____ and Margaret Marshment (eds) (1988) *The Female Gaze: Women as Viewers of Popular Culture* (London, The Women's Press).

Gardiner, Jean, Susan Himmelweit and Maureen Macintosh (1976) 'Women's domestic labour', *Conference of Socialist Economists*, reprinted in Ellen Malos (ed.) *The Politics of Housework* (London, Allinson and Busby).

Gardner, Katy (1981) 'Well woman clinics' in H. Roberts (ed.), *Women, Health and Reproduction* (London, Routledge & Kegan Paul).

Garner, Lesley (1984) *Stepping Stones to Women's Liberty: Feminist Ideas in the Women's Suffrage Movement, 1900–1918* (London, Heinemann).

Garnsey, Elizabeth (1978) 'Women's work and theories of class and stratification', *Sociology,* 17, 223–43.

Gavron, Hannah (1966) *The Captive Wife: Conflicts of Housebound Mothers* (reprinted 1977) (Harmondsworth, Pelican).

Gelles, Richard J. (1983) 'An Exchange/Social Control Theory of Family Violence' in David Finkelhor *et al.* (eds), *The Dark Side of Families* (California, Sage).

____ and Clark Cornell (1985) *Intimate Violence in Families* (California, Sage).

Gender and History (1990) Special Issue on Autobiography and Biography, 2(1) Spring.

Gerrard, Nicci (1989) *Into the Mainstream: How Feminism Has Changed Women's Writing* (London, Pandora).

Gibbs, John (1989) 'Equal Opportunities in Leicestershire' in Christine Skelton (ed.), *Whatever Happens to Little Women?* (Milton Keynes, Open University Press).

Giddings, Paula (1984) *When and Where I Enter, The impact of black women on race and sex in America* (New York, Bantam Books).

Gilbert, Sandra M. and Susan Gubar (1979) *The Madwoman in the Attic: The Woman Writer and the Nineteenth-Century Literary Imagination* (New Haven, Conn. and London, Yale University Press).

____ (1988/89) *No Man's Land: The Place of the Woman Writer in the Twentieth Century: Vol. 1, The War of the Words* (1988) (New Haven, Conn. and London, Yale University Press); *Vol. 2, Sexchanges* (1989) (New Haven, Conn. and London, Yale University Press).

Gilman, Charlotte Perkins (1981) *The Yellow Wallpaper* (first published 1892) (London, Virago).

GIST (1984) *Girls into Science and Technology: Final Report* (Manchester, EOC).

Gittins, Diana (1979) 'Oral History, Reliability and Recollection' (unpublished paper given to Annual British Sociological Association Conference).

____ (1982) *Fair Sex: Family Size and Structure 1900–39* (London, Hutchinson).

____ (1985) *The Family in Question* (London, Macmillan).

Gluck, Sherna B. and Daphne Patai (1991) *Women's Words: The Feminist Practice of Oral History* (London, Routledge).

Goddard-Spear, Margaret (1989) 'Differences between the Written Work of Boys and Girls', *British Educational Research Journal*, 15(3) 271–7.

Goerlich, Annette and Margaret Krannich (1989) 'The Gene Politics of the European Community', *Reproductive and Genetic Engineering: Journal of International Feminist Analysis*, 2(3) 201–18.

Goldberg, P. (1976) 'Are women prejudiced against men?' in J. Stacey *et al.* (eds), *And Jill Came Tumbling After* (New York, Dell).

Goldman-Amirav, Anna (1988) 'Behold, the Lord Hath Restrained Me from Bearing', *Reproductive and Genetic Engineering: Journal of International Feminist Analysis*, 1(3) 275–9.

Gordon, Linda (1977) *Birth Control in America: Woman's Body, Woman's Right* (Harmondsworth, Penguin).

____ (1989) *Heroes of Their Own Lives* (London, Virago).

____ and Ellen DuBois (1984) 'Seeking Ecstasy on the Battlefield: Danger and Pleasure in the Nineteenth-Century Feminist Sexual Thought' in Carole S. Vance (ed.), *Pleasure and Danger: Exploring Female Sexuality* (London, Routledge & Kegan Paul).

Gove, Walter and Jeannette Tudor (1973) 'Adult sex roles and mental illness', *American Journal of Sociology*, 78, 812.

Graham, Elspeth *et al.* (eds) (1989) *Her Own Life: Autobiographical writing by seventeenth-century Englishwomen* (London, Routledge).

Graham, Hilary (1984) *Women, Health and the Family* (Brighton, Wheatsheaf).

____ (1985) *Women, Health and Healing* (London, Tavistock).

____ (1987a) 'Women's poverty and caring' in C. Glendenning and J. Millar (eds), *Women and Poverty in Britain* (Brighton, Wheatsheaf).

____ (1987b) 'Being poor: perceptions and coping strategies of lone mothers' in J. Brannen and G. Wilson (eds), *Give and Take in Families* (London, Allen & Unwin).

____ (1987c) 'Women, health and illness', *Social Studies Review*, 3(1) 15–20.

Gray, Ann (1987) 'Behind closed doors: video recorders in the home' in Helen Baehr and Gillian Dyer (eds), *Boxed In* (London, Pandora).

Greater London Council (1986) *London Labour Plan* (London, GLC).

Green, Eileen, Sandra Hebron and Diana Woodward (1990) *Women's Leisure, What Leisure?* (London, Macmillan).

Greer, Germaine (1970) *The Female Eunuch* (London, McGibbon and Kee).

____ (1971) *The Female Eunuch* (London, Paladin Press).

____ (1988) 'The proper study of womankind', *The Times Literary Supplement*, 3–9 June, 616 and 629.

Grewal, Shabnum, Jackie Kay, Liliane Landor, Gail Lewis and Pratibha Parmar (eds) (1988) *Charting the Journey. Writings by black and third world women* (London, Sheba Feminist Publishers).

Griffiths, Vivienne (1987) 'Adolescent girls: transition from girlfriends to boyfriends?' in P. Allatt *et al.* (eds), *Women and the Life Cycle* (London, Macmillan).

Griffin, C. (1986) 'Qualitative Methods and Female Experience: Young Women from School to the Job Market' in S. Wilkinson (ed.), *Feminist Social Psy-*

chology: Developing Theory and Practice (Milton Keynes, Open University Press).

_____ (1989) 'I'm Not a Women's Libber But . . . Feminism Consciousness and Identity' in S. Skevington and D. Baker, *The Social Identity of Women* (London, Sage).

Grimstad, K. and S. Rennie (1973) *The New Woman's Survival Catalog* (New York, Coward, McCann and Geoghegan).

Gunew, Sneja (ed.) (1990) *Feminist Knowledge: Critique and Construct* (Routledge, London).

_____ (ed.) (1991) *A Reader in Feminist Knowledge* (Routledge, London).

Gupta, Jyotsna Agnihotri (1991) 'Women's Bodies: The Site for the Ongoing Conquest by Reproductive Technologies', *Issues in Reproductive and Genetic Engineering: Journal of International Feminist Analysis*, 4(2) 93–107.

Gurko, Jane (1982) 'Sexual Energy in the Classroom' in Margaret Cruikshank (ed.) *Lesbian Studies, Present and Future* (New York, The Feminist Press).

Hagen, Elizabeth and Jane Jenson (1988) 'Paradoxes and Promises: work and politics in the postwar years' in Jane Jenson, Elizabeth Hagen and Cealliagh Reddy (eds), *Feminization of the Labour Force: Paradoxes and Promises* (Cambridge, Polity Press).

Hakim, Catherine (1979) *Occupational Segregation: a comparative study of the degree and patterns of the differentiation between men's and women's work in Britain, the United States and other countries*, Department of Employment Research Paper (London, Department of Employment).

Hall Carpenter Archives/Lesbian Oral History Group (eds) (1989) *Inventing Ourselves: Lesbian Life Stories* (London, Routledge).

Hall, Catherine (1982) 'The butcher, the baker, the candlestickmaker: the shop and the family in the industrial revolution', in Elizabeth Whitelegg *et al.*, *The Changing Experience of Women* (Oxford, Martin Robertson).

_____ (1983) *The Changing Experience of Women*, Open University, U221 Course, Unit 8 (Milton Keynes, Open University Press).

_____ (1989) 'The early formation of Victorian domestic ideology', in S. Burman (ed.), *Fit Work for Women* (London, Croom Helm).

_____ and Rosemary O'Day (1983) Units 7 and 8 *The Changing Experience of Women* (Milton Keynes, Open University Press).

Hall, Marny (1989) 'Private experiences in the public domain: lesbians in organizations' in Jeff Hearn, Deborah L. Sheppard, Rita Tancred-Sheriff and Gibson Burrell (eds), *The Sexuality of Organization* (London, Sage).

Hall, Radclyffe (1928) *The Well of Loneliness* (reprinted 1982) (London, Virago).

Hall, Ruth (1985) *Ask Any Woman* (Bristol, Falling Wall Press).

Hall, Stuart (1990) 'Cultural Identity and Diaspora' in J. Rutherfold (ed.), *Identity, Community, Culture, Difference* (London, Lawrence and Wishart).

Halson, Jacquie (1989) 'The Sexual Harassment of Young Women' in Lesley Holly (ed.), *Girls and Sexuality* (Milton Keynes, Open University Press).

Hamer, Diane (1990) 'Significant Others: Lesbians and Psychoanalytic Theory', *Feminist Review*, 34, 134–51.

Hanmer, Jalna (1978) 'Violence and the Social Control of Women' in Gary Littlejohn *et al.* (eds), *Power and the State* (London, Croom Helm).

_____ (1981) 'Sex Predetermination, Artificial Insemination and the Maintenance of Male Dominated Culture' in Helen Roberts (ed.), *Women, Health and Reproduction* (London, Routledge & Kegan Paul).

_____ (1983) 'Reproductive Technology: The Future for Women' in Joan Rothchild (ed.), *Machina Ex Dea: Feminist Perspectives on Technology* (New York, Pergamon).

_____ (1985) 'Transforming Consciousness: Women and the New Reproductive Technologies' in Gena Corea *et al.*, *Man-Made Women: How the New Reproductive Technologies Affect Women* (London, Hutchinson).

_____ (1991) 'Women's Studies – A Transitional Programme', in Jane Aaron and Sylvia Walby (eds), *Out of the Margins: Women's Studies in the Nineties* (London, Falmer Press).

_____ and Pat Allen (1980) 'Reproductive Engineering: The Final Solution?' in Sandra Best and Linda Birke (eds), *Alice through the Microscope: The Power of Science Over Women's Lives* (London, Virago).

_____ and Mary Maynard (eds) (1987) *Women, Violence and Social Control* (London, Macmillan).

_____ and Elizabeth Powell-Jones (1984) 'Who's Holding the Test Tube?', *Trouble and Strife*, 3, Summer, 44–9.

_____ , Jill Radford and Elizabeth Stanko (eds) (1989) *Women, Policing and Male Violence* (London, Routledge).

_____ and Sheila Saunders (1984) *Well-Founded Fear* (London, Hutchinson).

Hannam, June (1987) '"In the Comradeship of the Sexes Lies the Hope of Progress and Social Regeneration": Women in the West Riding ILP, c1890–1914' in Jane Rendall (ed.), *Equal or Different? Women's Politics, 1800–1914* (Oxford, Blackwell).

_____ (1989) *Isabella Ford* (Oxford, Blackwell).

Haraway, Donna (1988) 'Situated knowledges: the science question in feminism and the privilege of partial perspective', *Feminist Studies*, 14(3) 575–600.

Harding, Sandra (ed.) (1987) *Feminism and Methodology* (Milton Keynes, Open University Press).

Hareven, Tamara (1982) *Family Time and Industrial Time: The Relationship Between Family and Work in a New England Industrial Community* (Cambridge University Press).

Hargreaves, Jennifer A. (1985) 'Where's the Virtue? Where's the Grace? A discussion of the social production of gender relations in and through sport', *Thesis Eleven*, 12, 109–21.

Harris, Chris (1990) *Kinship* (London, Routledge).

Harris, Olivia (1981) 'Households as natural units' in K. Young, C. Walkowitz and R. McCullagh (eds), *Of Marriage and the Market: Women's Subordination in International Perspective* (London, CSE Books).

Harris, Simon (1990) *Lesbian and Gay Issues in the English Classroom* (Milton Keynes, Open University Press).

Hartman, Mary and Lois Banner (eds) (1974) *Clio's Consciousness Raised* (London, Harper).

Hartmann, Betsy (1987) *Reproductive Rights and Wrongs: The Global Politics of Population Control and Contraceptive Choice* (New York, Harper & Row).

Hartmann, Heidi (1979) 'Capitalism, patriarchy and job segregation by sex' in

Zillah R. Eisenstein (ed.), *Capitalist Patriarchy and the Case for Socialist Feminism* (New York, Monthly Review Press).

―― (1981) 'The unhappy marriage of Marxism and Feminism: towards a more progressive union' in L. Sargent (ed.) *Women and Revolution* (New York, Monthly Review Press).

Haskell, Molly (1973) *From Reverence to Rape: The Treatment of Women in the Movies* (Harmondsworth, Penguin).

Hatty, Suzanne (1989) 'Policing and Male Violence in Australia' in J. Hanmer *et al.* (eds), *Women, Policing and Male Violence* (London, Routledge).

Haywoode, Terry L. and Laura Polla Scanlon (1987) 'World of Our Mothers: College for Neighborhood Women', *Woman's Studies Quarterly*, XV(3 and 4), Fall/Winter, 101–9.

Hearn, Jeff and Wendy Parkin (1986) *'Sex' at 'Work': The Power and Paradox of Organisation Sexuality* (Brighton, Wheatsheaf).

Hearn, Jeff and David Morgan (eds) (1990) *Men, Masculinities and Social Theories* (London, Unwin Hyman).

Henderson, Mae Gwendolyn (1990) 'Speaking in Tongues: Dialogues, Dialectics and the Black Woman Writer's Literary Tradition' in Cheryl A. Wall (ed.), *Changing Our Own Words* (London, Routledge).

Hennegan, Alison (1988) 'On Becoming a Lesbian Reader' in S. Radstone (ed.), *Sweet Dreams: Sexuality, Gender and Popular Fiction* (London, Lawrence and Wishart).

Henriques, Julian, Wendy Hollway, Cathy Urwin, Couze Venn and Valerie Walkerdine (1984) *Changing the Subject* (London, Methuen).

Hepburn, Cuca with Bonnie Gutierrez (1988) *Alive and Well. A Lesbian Health Guide* (New York, The Crossing Press).

Herbert, Carrie (1989) *Talking of Silence: The Sexual Harassment of Girls* (Lewes, Falmer Press).

Hernes, Helga Marie (1987) 'Women and the welfare state: the transition from private to public dependence' in Anne Showstack Sassoon (ed.), *Women and the State* (London, Hutchinson).

Hickman, Mary J. (1990) 'A Study of the Incorporation of the Irish in Britain with special reference to Catholic State Education' (PhD thesis, Institute of Education, University of London).

Higginbotham, Evelyn (1989) 'Beyond the Sound of Silence: Afro-American Women's History', *Gender and History*, 1(1) 50–67.

Higginbotham, Elizabeth and Sarah Watts (1988) 'The New Scholarship on Afro-American Women', *Women's Studies Quarterly*, XVI(1 & 2) Spring/Summer, 12–21.

Hinds, Hilary, Ann Phoenix and Jackie Stacey (eds) (1992) *Working Out: New Directions for Women's Studies* (London, Falmer Press).

Hite, Shere (1976) *The Hite Report* (New York, Macmillan).

―― (1988) *Women and Love: A Cultural Revolution in Progress* (London, Viking).

Hoagland, Sarah (1978) 'On The Reeducation Of Sophie' in Kathleen O'Connor Blumhagen and Walter D. Johnson (eds), *Women's Studies: An Interdisciplinary Collection* (Connecticut, Greenwood Press).

Hobby, Elaine (1989) 'Women returning to study' in Ann Thompson and Helen

Wilcox (eds), *Teaching Women: Feminism and English Studies* (Manchester, Manchester University Press).

Hobsbawm, Eric (1971) 'From Social History to a History of Society', *Daedalus*, 100, i.

Hobson, Dorothy (1978) 'Housewives: isolation as oppression' in Centre for Contemporary Cultural Studies, *Women Take Issue: Aspects of Women's Subordination* (London, Hutchinson).

Hoffman, Nancy Jo (1985) 'Breaking silences: life in the feminist classroom' in Margo Culley and Catherine Portuges (eds), *Gendered Subjects: The Dynamics of Feminist Teaching* (London, Routledge & Kegan Paul).

Holcombe, Lee (1973) *Victorian Ladies at Work: Middle-Class Working Women in England and Wales, 1850–1914* (Newton Abbot, David and Charles).

Holland, Janet, Caroline Ramazanoglu, Sue Scott, Sue Sharpe and Rachel Thomson (1991) 'Between Embarrassment and Trust: Young Women and the Diversity of Condom Use' in Peter Aggleton, Graham Hart and Peter Davies (eds), *AIDS: Responses, Interventions and Care* (London, Falmer).

Hollis, Patricia (1979) *Women in Public: The Women's Movement 1850–1900* (London, Allen & Unwin).

_____ (1987) 'Women in Council: Separate Spheres, Public Space' in Jane Rendall (ed.), *Equal or Different? Women's Politics, 1800–1914* (Oxford, Blackwell).

Holmes, Helen Bequaert (1989) 'Hepatitis – Yet Another Risk of In Vitro Fertilization?', *Reproductive and Genetic Engineering: Journal of International Feminist Analysis*, 2(1) 29–37.

_____ , Betty Hoskins and Michael Gross (eds) (1981) *The Custom-Made Child? Women-Centred Perspectives* (New Jersey, Humana Press).

Holton, Sandra (1986) *Feminism and Democracy* (Cambridge University Press).

Homans, Hilary (ed.) (1985) *The Sexual Politics of Reproduction* (Aldershot, Gower).

Home Office (1990) *Criminal Statistics. England and Wales 1989*, Cm 1322 (London, HMSO).

hooks, bell (1982) *Ain't I a Woman: Black Women and Feminism* (London, Pluto Press).

_____ (1984) *Feminist Theory: From Margin to Center* (Boston, Mass., South End Books).

_____ (1989) *Talking Back: Thinking Feminist – Thinking Black* (London, Sheba).

_____ (Gloria Watkins) (1991) 'Sisterhood: Political Solidarity Between Women' in Sneja Gunew (ed.), *A Reader in Feminist Knowledge* (London, Routledge).

Hooper, Carol-Ann (1987) 'Getting Him Off The Hook – The Theory and Practice of Mother-Blaming in Child Sexual Abuse', *Trouble and Strife*, 12.

Hubbard, Ruth (1990) *The Politics of Women's Biology* (New Brunswick, NJ, Rutgers University Press).

Hudson, Diane (1987) 'You Can't Commit Violence Against an Object: Women, Psychiatry and Psychosurgery' in Jalna Hanmer and Mary Maynard (eds), *Women, Violence and Social Control* (London, Macmillan).

Hudson, Pat and Robert Lee (eds) (1990) *Women's Work and the Family Economy in Historical Perspective* (Manchester, Manchester University Press).

Hughes, M., B. Mayall, P. Moss, J. Perry, P. Petri and G. Pinkerton (1980) *Nurseries Now* (Harmondsworth, Penguin).

Hughes, Mary and Mary Kennedy (1983) 'Breaking Out – Women in Adult Education', *Women's Studies International Forum*, 6(3) 261–9.

Hull, Gloria T., Patricia Bell Scott and Barbara Smith (eds) (1982) *All the Women Are White, All the Blacks Are Men, But Some of Us Are Brave: Black Women's Studies* (New York, The Feminist Press).

Humm, Maggie (1986) *Feminist Criticism: Women as Contemporary Critics* (Brighton, Harvester).

____ (1988) 'Amenorrhea and Autobiography' *Reproductive and Genetic Engineering: Journal of International Feminist Analysis*, 1(2) 159–65.

____ (1989a) *The Dictionary of Feminist Theory* (Brighton, Harvester Wheatsheaf).

____ (1989b) 'Subjects in English: autobiography, women and education' in Ann Thompson and Helen Wilcox (eds), *Teaching Women: Feminism and English Studies* (Manchester, Manchester University Press).

____ (1991) '"Thinking of things in themselves": Theory, Experience, Women's Studies' in Jane Aaron and Sylvia Walby (eds) (1991) *Out Of The Margins: Women's Studies in the Nineties* (London, Falmer).

____ (1992) *Feminism: A Reader* (Brighton, Harvester Wheatsheaf).

Humphries, Jane (1983) 'The emancipation of women in the 1970s and 1980s: from latent to the floating', *Capital and Class*, 20, 6–28.

____ and Jill Rubery (1988) 'Recession and Exploitation: British women in a changing workplace, 1979–1985' in Jane Jenson, Elisabeth Hagen and Ceallaigh Reddy (eds), *Feminisation of the Labour Force: Paradoxes and Promises* (Cambridge, Polity Press).

Hunt, M. (1975) *Sexual Behaviour in the 1970s* (New York, Dell).

Hunt, Margaret (1990) 'The De-Eroticization of Women's Liberation: Social Purity Movements and the Revolutionary Feminism of Sheila Jeffreys', *Feminist Review*, 34, Spring, 23–46.

Hunt, Pauline (1980) *Gender and Class Consciousness* (London, Macmillan).

Hutcheon, Linda (1989) *The Politics of Postmodernism* (London, Routledge).

Hutchins, Barbara (1915) *Women in Modern Industry* (London, G. Bell).

Hutson, Susan and Richard Jenkins (1989) *Taking the Strain: Families, Unemployment and the Transition to Adulthood* (Milton Keynes, Open University Press).

Hynes, H. Patricia (ed.) (1989a) *Reconstructing Babylon: Essays on Women and Technology* (London, Earthscan).

____ (1989b) *The Recurring Silent Spring* (New York, Pergamon Press).

____ (1989c) 'Biotechnology in Agriculture: An Analysis of Selected Technologies and Policy in the United States', *Reproductive and Genetic Engineering: Journal of International Feminist Analysis*, 2(1) 39–49.

ILEA (Inner London Education Authority) (1982) *Sex Differences in Educational Achievement: ILEA Research and Statistics Reports 823/82* (London, ILEA).

____ (1986) *Primary Matters* and *Secondary Issues* (London, ILEA).

Illich, Ivan (1975) *Medical Nemesis: The Expropriation of Health* (London, Caldar and Boyars).

International Solidarity for Safe Contraception, Amsterdam and X–Y Movement, Amsterdam (1990) *Report of a Working Day on Changing Trends in Population Control, Impact on Third World Women and the Role of the World*

Health Organisation (Amsterdam, International Solidarity for Safe Contraception and X–Y Movement).

Irigaray, Luce (1985a) *This Sex Which Is Not One*, trans. Catherine Porter with Carolyn Burke (first published 1977) (Ithaca, NY, Cornell University Press).

_____ (1985b) *Speculum of the Other Woman* (Ithaca, NY, Cornell University Press).

Israel, Kali (1990) 'Writing Inside the Kaleidoscope: Re-Representing Victorian, Women Public Figures', *Gender and History*, 2(1) 40–8.

Jackson, Margaret (1984) 'Sexology and the Universalization of Male Sexuality' in Lal Coveney *et al.*, *The Sexuality Papers* (London, Hutchinson).

Jackson, Stevi (1982) *Childhood and Sexuality* (Oxford, Blackwell).

_____ (1991) 'Towards A Historical Sociology of Housework: A Materialist Feminist Analysis', *Women's Studies International Forum*, 14(6).

Jacobs, Brian (1988) *Racism in Britain* (London, Croom Helm).

Jacobs, Harriet (1861) *Incidents in the Life of a Slave Girl* (reprinted 1988) (New York and Oxford, Oxford University Press).

Jacobus, Mary (1981) 'Review of *The Madwoman in the Attic*', *Signs*, 6(3) 517–23.

Jaggar, Alison (1983) *Feminist Politics and Human Nature* (Brighton, Harvester).

Jay, Karla and Joanne Glasgow (eds) (1990) *Lesbian Texts and Contexts: Radical Revisions* (New York, New York University Press).

Jayaratne, Toby Epstein (1983) 'The value of quantitative methodology for feminist research' in Gloria Bowles and Renate Duelli Klein (eds), *Theories of Women's Studies* (London, Routledge & Kegan Paul).

Jeffreys, Sheila (1985) *The Spinster and Her Enemies: Feminism and Sexuality 1880–1930* (London, Pandora).

_____ (1990) *Anticlimax: A Feminist Perspective On The Sexual Revolution* (London, The Women's Press).

Joekes, Susan P. (1987) *Women in the World Economy*, United Nations International Research and Training Institute for the Advancement of Women (Oxford University Press).

John, Angela (ed.) (1986) *Unequal Opportunities: Women's Employment in England 1800–1918* (Oxford, Blackwell).

Johnson, Jill (1973) *Lesbian Nation: A Feminist Solution* (New York, Simon and Schuster).

Jones, Ann Rosalind (1986) 'Writing the Body: Toward an Understanding of *l'Écriture féminine*', in Elaine Showalter (ed.), *The New Feminist Criticism: Essays on Women, Literature and Theory* (London, Virago).

Jones, Carol (1985) Sexual Tyranny: Male violence in a mixed secondary school in Gaby Weiner (ed.), *Just a Bunch of Girls* (Milton Keynes, Open University Press).

Jones, L. G. and L. P. Jones (1989) Context, confidence and the able girl, *Educational Research*, 31(3) 189–94.

Judt, Tony (1979) 'A Crown in Regal Purple: Social History and the Historians', *History Workshop Journal*, 7, Spring, 66–94.

Kaluzynska, Eva (1980) 'Wiping the floor with theory – a survey of writings on housework', *Feminist Review*, 6.

Kane, Elizabeth (1988) *Birth Mother: The Story of America's First Legal Surrogate Mother* (San Diego, Calif., Harcourt Brace Jovanovich).

____ (1989) 'Surrogate Parenting: A Division of Families, not a Creation', *Reproductive and Genetic Engineering: Journal of International Feminist Analysis*, 2(2) 105–9.

Kane, Penny (1991) *Women's Health: From Womb to Tomb* (London, Macmillan).

Kanter, Rosabeth Moss (1977) *Men and Women of the Corporation* (New York, Basic Books).

Kaplan, Cora (1986a) 'Language and Gender' (first published 1976) in Cora Kaplan, *Sea Changes: Essays on Culture and Feminism* (London, Verso).

____ (1986b) 'Pandora's Box: Subjectivity, Class and Sexuality in Socialist Feminist Criticism' in Cora Kaplan, *Sea Changes: Essays on Culture and Feminism* (first published 1985) (London, Verso).

____ (1986c) *Sea Changes: Essays on Culture and Feminism* (London, Verso).

Kaplan, E. Ann (ed.) (1980) *Women in Film Noir* (London, BFI).

Katz, Jonathan (1976) *Gay American History: Lesbians and Gay Men in the USA* (New York, Thomas and Cromwell).

Kaufmann, Caroline L. (1988) 'Perfect Mothers, Perfect Babies: An Examination of the Ethics of Fetal Treatment', *Reproductive and Genetic Engineering: Journal of International Feminist Analysis*, 1(2) 133–9.

Kaupen-Haas, Heidrun (1988) 'Experimental Obstetrics and National Socialism: The Conceptual Basis of Reproductive Technology Today', *Reproductive and Genetic Engineering: Journal of International Feminist Analysis*, 1(2) 127–32.

Keesing, Roger M. (1975) *Kin Groups and Social Structure* (New York, Holt, Rinehart and Winston).

Kelly, Alison (ed.) (1987) *Science for Girls* (Milton Keynes, Open University Press).

____ (June 1988) 'The customer is always right . . . girls' and boys' reactions to science lessons', *School Science Review*, 69(249) 662–75.

Kelly, Joan (1983) 'The Doubled Vision of Feminist Theory' in Judith Newton *et al.* (eds), *Sex and Class in Women's History* (London, Routledge & Kegan Paul).

Kelly, Liz (1985) 'Feminists v Feminists – Legislating Against Porn in the USA', *Trouble and Strife*, 7, Winter, 4–10.

____ (1988a) *Surviving Sexual Violence* (Oxford, Polity Press).

____ (1988b) 'What's in a Name?: Defining Child Sexual Abuse', *Feminist Review*, 28, Spring.

Kennedy, Mary and Brec'hed Piette (1991) 'Issues around Women's Studies on Adult Education and Access Courses' in Jane Aaron and Sylvia Walby (eds), *Out of The Margins: Women's Studies in the Nineties* (London, Falmer).

Keyssar, Hélène (1984) *Feminist Theatre: An Introduction to Plays of Contemporary British and American Women* (London, Macmillan).

Kiernan, Kathleen and Malcolm Wicks (1990) *Family Change and Future Policy* (London, Family Policy Studies Centre).

Kimmel, Michael (1988) 'The gender blender', *Guardian*, 29 September, 20.

Kingston, Maxine Hong (1977) *The Woman Warrior: Memoirs of a Girlhood Among Ghosts* (first published 1976) (Harmondsworth, Penguin).

Kinsey, C. Alfred, Wardell B. Pomeroy, Clyde E. Martin, and Paul H. Gebhard (1953) *Sexual Behavior in the Human Female* (Philadelphia, Pa., Saunders).

Kirejczyk, Marta (1990) 'A Question of Meaning? Controversies about the New Reproductive Technologies in the Netherlands', *Issues in Reproductive and Genetic Engineering: Journal of International Feminist Analysis*, 3(1) 23–33.

Kirp, David (1985) 'Racial Inexplicitness and Education Policy' in Madeleine Arnot (ed.), *Race and Gender* (Oxford, Pergamon).

Kishwar, Madhu (1985/87) 'The Continuing Deficit of Women in India and the Impact of Amniocentesis' in Gena Corea *et al. Man-Made Women: How the New Reproductive Technologies Affect Women* (London, Hutchinson, 1985; Bloomington, Ind., Indiana University Press, 1987).

_____ and Ruth Vanita (eds) (1984) *In Search of Answers* (London, Zed).

Kitzinger, Sheila (1978) *Women as Mothers* (Glasgow, Fontana).

Klein, Renate Duelli (1983) 'A brief overview of the development of Women's Studies in the UK', *Women's Studies International Forum*, 6(3) 255–60.

_____ (ed.) (1989) *Infertility: Women Speak Out About Their Experiences of Reproductive Medicine* (London, Pandora).

_____ (1990) 'IVF Research: A question of feminist ethics', *Issues in Reproductive and Genetic Engineering: Journal of International Feminist Analysis*, 3(3) 234–51.

_____ (1991) 'Passion and Politics in Women's Studies in the 1990's' in Jane Aaron and Sylvia Walby (eds), *Out of the Margins: Women's Studies in the Nineties* (London, Falmer).

_____ and Robyn Rowland (1988) 'Women as Test-Sites for Fertility Drugs: Clomiphene Citrate and Hormonal Cocktails', *Reproductive and Genetic Engineering: Journal of International Feminist Analysis*, 1(3) 251–73.

Koch, Lene (1990) 'IVF: An irrational choice?', *Issues in Reproductive and Genetic Engineering: Journal of International Feminist Analysis*, 3(3) 235–42.

Koedt, Anne (1974) 'The Myth of the Vaginal Orgasm' in The Radical Therapist Collective (eds), *The Radical Therapist* (Harmondsworth, Penguin).

Kollek, Regine (1990) 'The Limits of Experimental Knowledge: A Feminist Perspective on the Ecological Risks of Genetic Engineering', *Issues in Reproductive and Genetic Engineering: Journal of International Feminist Analysis*, 3(2) 125–35.

Kramarae, Cheris and Paula A. Treichler (1985) *A Feminist Dictionary* (London, Pandora).

Kristeva, Julia (1986) *The Kristeva Reader* (Toril Moi (ed.)) (Oxford, Blackwell).

Land, Hilary (1979) 'The boundaries between the State and the family' in C. C. Harris (ed.), *The Sociology of the Family: New Directions for Britain*, Sociological Review Monograph 28.

_____ (1983) 'Who still cares for the family? Recent developments in income maintenance, taxation and family law' in Jane Lewis (ed.), *Women's Welfare, Women's Rights* (London, Croom Helm).

Lasker, Judith and Susan Borg (1987) *In Search of Parenthood: Coping with Infertility and High-Tech Conception* (Boston, Beacon Press).

Lawrence, Errol (1984) 'Just plain common sense: the "roots" of racism' in Centre for Contemporary Cultural Studies (ed.), *The Empire Strikes Back: Race and Racism in 70s Britain* (London, Hutchinson).

Lee, Dorothy (1990) 'Chatterboxes', *Child Education*, 67(7) 26–7.

Leeds Revolutionary Feminist Group (1981) 'Political Lesbianism: the case against Heterosexuality' in Onlywomen Press (eds), *Love Your Enemy? The Debate between Heterosexual Feminism and Political Lesbianism* (London, Onlywomen Press).

Lees, Sue (1986a) *Losing Out: Sexuality and Adolescent Girls* (London, Hutchinson).

____ (1986b) 'Sex, race and culture: feminism and the limits of cultural pluralism', *Feminist Review*, 22.

____ (1991) 'Feminist Politics and Women's Studies: Struggle, Not Incorporation', in Jane Aaron and Sylvia Walby (eds), *Out of the Margins: Women's Studies in the Nineties* (London, Falmer).

Lefanu, Sarah (1988) *In the Chinks of the World Machine: Feminism and Science Fiction* (London, The Women's Press).

Leonard, Diana (1978) 'The regulation of marriage: repressive benevolence' in G. Littlejohn, B. Smart, J. Wakefield and N. Yuval-Davis (eds), *Power and the State* (London, Croom Helm).

____ (1980) *Sex and Generation: A Study of Courtship and Weddings* (London, Tavistock).

Leonard, P. (1984) *Personality and Ideology* (London, Macmillan).

Lerner, Gerda (1981) *The Majority Finds Its Past* (Oxford University Press).

____ (1986) *The Creation of Patriarchy* (Oxford University Press).

Leuzinger, Monika and Bigna Rambert (1988) '"I Can Feel It – My Baby is Healthy": Women's experiences with Prenatal Diagnosis in Switzerland', *Reproductive and Genetic Engineering: Journal of International Feminist Analysis*, 1(3) 239–49.

Levine, Phillippa (1987) *Victorian Feminism, 1850–1900* (London, Hutchinson).

____ (1990) *Feminist Lives in Victorian England* (Oxford, Blackwell).

Lewallen, Avis (1988) '*Lace*: Pornography for Women?' in Lorraine Gamman and Margaret Marshment (eds), *The Female Gaze* (London, The Women's Press).

Lewenhak, Sheila (1977) *Women and Trade Unions* (London, Benn).

Lewin, Ellen and Virginia Olesen (1985) 'Occupational health and women: the case of clerical work' in Ellen Lewin and Virginia Olesen (eds), *Women, Health and Healing* (London, Tavistock).

Lewis, Charlie (1986) *Becoming a Father* (Milton Keynes, Open University Press).

____ and Margaret O'Brien (eds) (1987) *Reassessing fatherhood* (London, Sage).

Lewis, Gail (1990) 'Audre Lorde: Vignettes and Mental Conversations', *Feminist Review*, 34, Spring, 100–14.

Lewis, Jane (1981) 'Women Lost and Found: The Impact of Feminism on History' in Dale Spender (ed.), *Men's Studies Modified: The Impact of Feminism on the Academic Disciplines* (London, Pergamon).

____ (1984) *Women in England 1870–1950: Sexual divisions and social change* (Brighton, Wheatsheaf).

____ (1991) *Women and Social Action in Victorian and Edwardian England* (London, Edward Elgar).

____ (ed.) (1986) *Labour and Love: Women's Experience of Home and Family* (Oxford, Blackwell).

____ (ed.) (1987) *Before the Vote Was Won: Arguments For and Against Women's Suffrage* (London, Routledge & Kegan Paul).

Liddington, Jill and Jill Norris (1978) *One Hand Tied Behind Us: The Rise of the Women's Suffrage Movement* (London, Virago).

Light, Alison (1984) '"Returning to Manderley" – Romance Fiction, Female Sexuality and Class', *Feminist Review*, 16, Summer, 7–25.

Lilly, Mark (ed.) (1990) *Lesbian and Gay Writing* (London, Macmillan).

Lingam, Lakshmi (1990) 'New Reproductive Technologies in India: A Print Media Analysis', *Issues in Reproductive and Genetic Engineering: Journal of International Feminist Analysis*, 3(1) 13–21.

Littlewood, Roland and Maurice Lipsedge (1988) 'Psychiatric illness among British Afro-Caribbeans', *British Medical Journal*, 296, 950–1.

Lloyd, Barbara (1989) 'Rules of the gender game', *New Scientist*, December, 60–4.

Lobban, Glenys (1975) 'Sex Roles in Reading Schemes', *Educational Review*, 27(3) 202–10.

London Feminist History Group (1983) *The Sexual Dynamics of History: Men's Power, Women's Resistance* (London, Pluto).

London Strategic Policy Unit (1987) *Danger! Heterosexism At Work* (London, Industry and Employment Branch of the Greater London Council).

Lonsdale, Susan (1990) *Women and Disability: The Experience of Physical Disability Among Women* (London, Macmillan).

Lonzi, Carla (1972) *Sputiamo su Hegel* (Milan, Scritti di Rivolta Feminile Available in English (mimeo) London) Reprinted as 'Let's Spit on Hegel' in Paola Bono and Sandra Kemp (eds) *Italian Feminist Thought: A Reader* (London, Blackwell, 1991).

Lorde, Audre (1983) 'My Words Will Be There' in Mari Evans (ed.), *Black Women Writers* (London, Pluto).

____ (1984a) *Sister Outsider: Essays and Speeches* (New York, The Crossing Press).

____ (1984b) 'The Master's Tools Will Never Dismantle the Master's House', in Audre Lorde, *Sister Outsider: Essays and Speeches* (New York, The Crossing Press).

____ (1984c) 'An Open Letter to Mary Daly' in *Sister Outsider: Essays and Speeches* (New York, The Crossing Press).

Lovell, Terry (1987) *Consuming Fiction* (London, Verso).

____ (ed.) (1990) *British Feminist Thought* (Oxford, Blackwell).

Lowe, Marian and Margaret Lowe Benston (1991) 'The Uneasy Alliance Of Feminism And Academia' in Sneja Gunew (ed.), *A Reader in Feminist Knowledge* (London, Routledge).

Lowe, Nigel V. (1982) 'The legal status of fathers: past and present' in L. McKee and M. O'Brien (eds), *The Father Figure* (London, Tavistock).

Lown, Judy (1990) *Women and Industrialisation: gender and work in nineteenth-century England* (Cambridge, Polity Press).

Lubelska, Cathy (1991) 'Teaching Methods in Women's Studies: Challenging the Mainstream' in Jane Aaron and Sylvia Walby (eds), *Out of the Margins: Women's Studies in the Nineties* (London, Falmer Press).

Lummis, T. (1982) 'The Historical Dimension of Fatherhood' in L. McKee and M. O'Brien (eds), *The Father Figure* (London, Tavistock).

MacCabe, Colin (1976) 'Realism and Cinema: notes on some Brechtian theses', *Screen*, 17, Autumn (3).

MacCormack, Carol P. (1989) 'Technology and Women's Health in Developing Countries', *International Journal of Health Services*, 19(4) 681–92.

____ and Marilyn Strathern (eds) (1980) *Nature, Culture and Gender* (Cambridge University Press).

Macintyre, S. (1976) 'Who Wants Babies? The Social Construction of Instincts' in D. Barker and S. Allen (eds), *Sexual Divisions in Society* (London, Tavistock).

MacKeith, Nancy (1978) *The New Women's Health Handbook* (London, Virago).

MacKinnon, Catherine (1978) *Sexual Harassment of Working Women* (New Haven, Conn., Yale University Press).

____ (1982) 'Feminism, Marxism, Method and the State: An Agenda for Theory', *Signs*, 7(3) 515–44.

Maclean, Mavis (1987) 'Households after divorce: the availability of resources and their impact on children' in J. Brannen and G. Wilson, *Give and Take in Families* (London, Allen and Unwin).

____ and John Eekelaar (1984) 'Financial provision on divorce: a reappraisal' in Michael Freeman (ed.), *State, Law and the Family: Critical Perspectives* (London, Tavistock).

MacLeod, Mary and Esther Saraga (1988) 'Challenging the Orthodoxy: Towards a Feminist Theory and Practice', *Feminist Review*, 28, Spring.

Maconachie, Moira (1987) in Janet Sayers, Mary Evans and Nanneke Redclift (eds), *Engels Revisited: New Feminist Essays* (London, Tavistock).

Maher, Frances (1985) 'Classroom pedagogy and the new scholarship on women', in Margo Culley and Catherine Portuges (eds), *Gendered Subjects: The Dynamics of Feminist Teaching* (London, Routledge & Kegan Paul).

Mahony, Pat (1983) 'Boys will be Boys: Teaching Women's Studies In Mixed-Sex Groups', *Women's Studies International Forum* 6(3) 331–4.

____ (1985) *Schools for the Boys? Co-education Reassessed* (London, Hutchinson).

Mair, Lucy (1972) *Marriage* (New York, Pica Press).

Malos, Ellen (ed.) (1980) *The Politics of Housework* (London, Allinson and Busby).

Mama, Amina (1989) *The Hidden Struggle. Statutory and voluntary sector responses to violence against black women in the home* (London, London Race and Housing Research Unit).

Mani, Lata (1990) 'Multiple Mediations: Feminist Scholarship in the Age of Multi-National Reception', *Feminist Review*, 35, Summer, 24–41.

Mansfield, Penny and Jean Collard (1988) *The Beginning Of The Rest Of Your Life: A Portrait Of Newly-Wed Marriage* (London, Macmillan).

Mappen, Ellen (1985) *Helping Women at Work: The Women's Industrial Council, 1889–1914* (London, Hutchinson).

Margolies, David (1982) 'Mills and Boon – guilt without sex', *Red Letters*, 14.

Mark-Lawson, Jane and Anne Witz (1988) 'From family labour to family wage?: the case of women's labour in 19th century coalmining', *Social History*, 13(2).

Marks, Elaine and Isabelle de Courtivron (eds) (1981) *New French Feminisms: An Anthology* (Brighton, Harvester).

Marland, Michael (ed.) (1983) *Sex Differentiation and Schooling* (London, Heinemann).

Marsden, Dennis (1973) *Mothers Alone: Poverty and the Fatherless Family* (Harmondsworth, Pelican).

Martin, Emily (1987) *The Woman in the Body. A Cultural Analysis of Reproduction* (Milton Keynes, Open University Press).

Martin, Jean and Ceridwin Roberts (1984) *Women and Employment: A Lifetime Perspective* (London, HMSO).

Marxist Feminist Literature Collective (1978) 'Women's Writing: *Jane Eyre, Shirley, Villette, Aurora Leigh*' in Francis Barker *et al.* (eds), *1848: The Sociology of Literature* (University of Essex).

Maynard, Mary (1989) 'Privilege and Patriarchy: Feminist Thought in the Nineteenth Century' in Susan Mendus and Jane Rendall (eds), *Sexuality and Subordination* (London, Routledge & Kegan Paul).

_____ (1990) 'The Re-shaping of Sociology?: Trends in the Study of Gender', *Sociology*, 24(2) 269–90.

McCann, Kathy (1985) 'Battered Women and the Law' in Julia Brophy and Carol Smart (eds), *Women-in-Law* (London, Routledge & Kegan Paul).

McDaniel, Judith (1985) 'Is there room for me in the closet? Or, my life as the only lesbian professor' in Margo Culley and Catherine Portuges (eds), *Gendered Subjects: The Dynamics of Feminist Teaching* (London, Routledge & Kegan Paul).

McDonnell, Kathleen (1986) *Adverse Effects: Women and the Pharmaceutical Industry* (Penang, Malaysia, International Organization of Consumers Unions Regional for Asia and the Pacific).

McDowell, Linda (1989) 'Gender Divisions' in Chris Hamnett, Linda McDowell and Philip Sarre (eds), *Restructuring Britain: The Changing Social Structure* (London, Sage/Open University Publications).

McIntosh, Mary (1981) 'The homosexual role' in Kenneth Plummer (ed.), *The Making of the Modern Homosexual* (London, Hutchinson).

McNeil, Maureen (1992) 'Pedagogical Praxis and Problems: Reflections on Teaching About Gender Relations' in Hilary Hinds, Ann Phoenix and Jackie Stacey (eds), *Working Out: New Directions For Women's Studies* (London, Falmer).

_____ , Ian Varcoe and Steven Yearley (eds) (1990) *The New Reproductive Technologies* (New York, St Martin's Press).

McNeill, Sandra (1987) 'Flashing: Its effect on Women' in Jalna Hanmer and Mary Maynard (eds), *Women, Violence and Social Control* (London, Macmillan).

McRobbie, Angela (ed.) (1989) 'Second-Hand Dresses and the Role of the Ragmarket' in Angela McRobbie (ed.), *Zoot Suits and Second-Hand Dresses: An Anthology of Fashion and Music* (London, Unwin Hyman).

Meehan, Elizabeth and Selma Sevenhuijsen (eds) (1991) *Equality Politics – Gender* (London, Sage).

Meighan, Roland (1981) *A Sociology of Educating* (Eastbarne, Holt, Rinehart and Winstin).

Mernissi, Fatima (1988) (trans. Mary Jo Lakeland), *Doing Daily Battle. Interviews with Moroccan women* (London, The Women's Press).

Middleton, Chris (1983) 'Patriarchal exploitation and the rise of English capital-ism' in Eva Gamarnikow, Daniel Morgan, June Purvis and Daphne Taylorson (eds), *Gender, Class and Work* (London, Heinemann).

_____ (1988) 'The familiar fate of the famulae: gender division in the history of wage labour' in Ray Pahl (ed.), *On Work: Historical, Comparative and Theoretical Approaches* (Oxford, Blackwell).

Middleton, Lucy (ed.) (1977) *Women in the Labour Movement: The British Experience* (London, Croom Helm).

Mies, Maria (1983) 'Towards a methodology for feminist research', in Gloria Bowles and Renate Duelli Klein (eds), *Theories of Women's Studies* (London, Routledge & Kegan Paul).

_____ (1986) *Patriarchy and Accumulation on a World Scale: Women in the International Division of Labour* (London, Zed Books).

_____ (1988) 'From the Individual to the Dividual: In the Supermarket of "Repro-ductive Alternatives"', *Reproductive and Genetic Engineering: Journal of International Feminist Analysis*, 1(3) 225–37.

Milkman, Ruth (1976) 'Women's work and the economic crisis: some lessons of the Great Depression', *Review of Radical Political Economy*, 8 (1) Spring.

Millar, Jane and Caroline Glendenning (1987) 'Invisible women, invisible pov-erty' in Jane Millar and Caroline Glendenning (eds), *Women and Poverty in Britain* (Brighton, Wheatsheaf).

Millett, Kate (1970) *Sexual Politics* (London, Abacus) reprinted in 1977 (Lon-don, Virago).

Millman, Val (1985) 'The new vocationalism in secondary schools: its influence on girls' in J. Whyte *et al.* (eds), *Girl-friendly Schooling* (London, Methuen).

_____ and Gaby Weiner (1987) 'Engendering Equal Opportunities: The Case of TVEI' in D. Gleeson (ed.), *TVEI and Secondary Education* (Milton Keynes, Open University Press).

Mills, Sara, Lynne Pearce, Sue Spaull and Elaine Millard (1989) *Feminist Readings/Feminists Reading* (Hemel Hempstead, Harvester Wheatsheaf).

Ministry of Health Circular 221/45 in J. Tizard, P. Moss and J. Perry (1976) *All Our Children* (London, Temple-Smith).

Mitchell, Juliet (1966) 'Women: The Longest Revolution', *New Left Review*, 40, 11–37.

_____ (1971) *Woman's Estate* (Harmondsworth, Penguin).

_____ (1974) *Psychoanalysis and Feminism* (Harmondsworth, Penguin).

_____ and Jacqueline Rose (1982) *Feminine Sexuality: Jacques Lacan and the Ecole Freudienne* (London, Macmillan).

Mitter, Swasti (1986) *Common Fate, Common Bond: Women in the Global Economy* (London, Pluto Press).

Modleski, Tania (1982) *Loving With a Vengeance: Mass-produced Fantasies for Women* (reprinted 1988) (London, Routledge).

Moers, Ellen (1978) *Literary Women* (first published 1976) (London, The Wo-men's Press).

Mohanty, Chandra Talpade (1988) 'Under Western Eyes: Feminist Scholarship and Colonial Discourses', *Feminist Review*, 30, Autumn, 61–89.

Moi, Toril (1985) *Sexual/Textual Politics: Feminist Literary Theory* (London, Methuen).

_____ (ed.) (1987) *French Feminist Thought: A Reader* (Oxford, Blackwell).

Montague, Ann (1991) 'Doctors who are in double pain', *Guardian*, 18 September, 36.

Montefiore, Jan (1987) *Feminism and Poetry: Language, Experience, Identity in Women's Writing* (London, Pandora).

Moore, Henrietta L. (1988) *Feminism and Anthropology* (Cambridge, Polity).

Moraga, Cherrie and Gloria Anzaluda (eds) (1981) *This Bridge Called My Back: Writings by Radical Women of Color* (Watertown, Mass., Persephone Press).

Morgan, David (1985) *The Family, Politics and Social Theory* (London, Routledge & Kegan Paul).

Morley, Ann with Liz Stanley (1988) *The Life and Death of Emily Wilding Davison* (London, The Women's Press).

Morris, Lydia (1984) 'Redundancy and patterns of household finance', *Sociological Review*, 32(3).

____ (1990) *The Workings of the Household* (first published 1984) (Cambridge, Polity Press).

Morrison, Toni (1973) *Sula* (reprinted 1982) (London, Triad Granada).

____ (1987) *Beloved* (reprinted 1988) (London, Picador).

Moss, P., G. Bolland, R. Foxman and C. Owen (1983) *Marital Relationships During the Transition to Parenthood* (unpublished paper, Thomas Coram Research Unit).

Mulvey, Laura (1975) 'Visual Pleasure and Narrative Cinema', *Screen*, 16(3), reprinted in Laura Mulvey (1989) *Visual and Other Pleasures* (London, Macmillan).

____ (1989) *Visual and Other Pleasures* (London, Macmillan).

Murcott, Anne (1983) '"It's a pleasure to cook for him": food, mealtimes and gender in some South Wales households' in E. Gamarnikow, D. Morgan, J. Purvis and D. Taylorson, *The Public And The Private* (London, Heinemann).

Myers, Kathy (1989) 'Towards a Feminist Erotica', *Camerawork*, 24, 14–16 and 19.

Myrdal, Alva and Viola Klein (1970) *Women's Two Roles* (London, Routledge & Kegan Paul).

Nain, Gemma Tang (1991) 'Black women, sexism and racism: Black or anti-racist feminism?', *Feminist Review*, 37, 1–22.

Nair, Sumati (1989) *Imperialism and the Control of Women's Fertility: New hormonal contraceptives population control and the WHO* (Amsterdam, Campaign Against Long Acting Hormonal Contraceptives).

Namjoshi, Suniti (1985) *The Conversations of Cow* (London, The Women's Press).

NASUWT/The Engineering Council (1991) *Gender, Primary Schools and the National Curriculum* (Birmingham, NASUWT).

Nathanson, Constance A. (1975) 'Illness and the Feminine Role: A Theoretical Review', *Social Science and Medicine*, 9, 57–62.

National Curriculum Council (1990) *The Whole Curriculum* (York, NCC).

National Perinatal Statistics Unit/Fertility Society of Australia (1988) *IVF and GIFT Pregnancies, Australia and New Zealand, 1987* (Sydney, National Perinatal Statistics Unit).

Nelson, Sarah (1987) *Incest: Fact and Myth* (Edinburgh, Stramullion).

Nestle, Joan (1988) *A Restricted Country: Essays and Short Stories* (London, Sheba).

Newsom Report (1963) *Half Our Future; A Report of the Central Advisory Council for Education* (London, HMSO).

Newton, Judith, Mary Ryan and Judith Walkowitz (eds) (1983) *Sex and Class in Women's History* (London, Routledge & Kegan Paul).

Nichols, Grace (1984) *The Fat Black Woman's Poems* (London, Virago).

Nichols, Margaret (1987) 'Lesbian Sexuality: Issues and Developing Theory' in Boston Lesbian Psychologies Collective (eds), *Lesbian Psychologies* (Chicago, University of Illinois Press).

Nicolson, Paula (1988) 'The Social Psychology of Postnatal Depression' (unpublished PhD thesis, University of London).

_____ (1990) 'Brief Report of Women's Expectations of Men's Behaviour in the Transition to Motherhood', *Counselling Psychology Quarterly*, 3(4) 353–61.

_____ (1991) 'Virgins and Wise Women', *The Psychology of Women Section Newsletter*, 7, 5–8.

_____ (1992) 'Towards a Psychology of Women's Health and Health Care' in P. Nicolson and J. M. Ussher (eds), *The Psychology of Women's Health and Health Care* (London, Macmillan).

Norwood Report (1943) *Curriculum and Examination in Secondary Schools, A Report of the Secondary Schools Examination Council* (London, HMSO).

Oakley, Ann (1976a) *Housewife* (Harmondsworth, Penguin).

_____ (1976b) 'Wisewoman and Medicine Man; Change in the Management of Childbirth' in Juliet Mitchell and Anne Oakley (eds), *The Rights and Wrongs of Women* (Harmondsworth, Penguin).

_____ (1980) *Women Confined. Towards a Sociology of Childbirth* (Oxford, Martin Robertson).

_____ (1984) *The Sociology of Housework*, 2nd edn (Oxford, Blackwell).

_____ (1989) 'Smoking in pregnancy: smokescreen or risk factor? Towards a materialist analysis', *Sociology of Health and Illness*, 11(4).

_____ and Juliet Mitchell (eds) (1976) *The Rights and Wrongs of Women* (Harmondsworth, Penguin).

O'Brien, Mary (1981) *The Politics of Reproduction* (London, Routledge & Kegan Paul).

_____ (1989) *Reproducing The World: Essays in Feminist Theory* (Boulder, Col.,Westview Press).

O'Brien, N. (1984) 'Fathers Without Wives' (unpublished PhD thesis, University of London).

O'Connor, Margaret Ann (1987) 'Health/Illness in Healing/Caring – a feminist perspective' in J. Orr (ed.), *Women's Health in the Community* (Chichester, John Wiley).

O'Day, Rosemary (1983) *The Changing Experience of Women*, Open University U221 Course, Unit 7 (Milton Keynes, Open University Press).

OECD (Organisation for Economic Co-operation and Development) (1985) *The Integration of Women into the Economy*.

Office of Population, Censuses and Surveys (1988) *The Prevalence of Disability Among Adults* (London, HMSO).

Office of Population Censuses and Surveys (1988) *General Household Survey*, No. 19 (London, HMSO).

Omolade, Barbara (1984) 'Hearts of Darkness' in Ann Snitow, Christine Stansell and Sharon Thompson (eds), *Desire: The Politics of Sexuality* (London, Virago).

_____ (1987) 'A Black Feminist Pedagogy', *Women's Studies Quarterly*, XV(3 and 4) Fall/Winter, 32–9.

Onlywomen Press (eds) (1981) *Love Your Enemy? The Debate between Heterosexual Feminism and Political Lesbianism* (London, Onlywomen Press).

Open University (1981) 'Day care outside the family', *E200 Contemporary Issues in Education* (Milton Keynes, Open University Press).

_____ (1988) Gender and Education Bibliography (Milton Keynes, Open University Press).

Ormerod, M. (1985) 'Subject preference and choice in co-educational and single-sex secondary schools', *British Journal of Psychology*, 45, 257–67.

O'Rourke, Rebecca (1979) 'Summer Reading', *Feminist Review*, 2.

_____ (1989) *Reflecting on 'The Well of Loneliness'* (London, Routledge).

Overall, Christine (1987) *Ethics and Human Reproduction: A Feminist Analysis* (London, Allen & Unwin).

Pahl, Jan (1983) 'The Allocation of Money and the Restructuring of Inequality Within Marriage', *Sociological Review*, 31(2) 237–62.

_____ (1984) 'The allocation of money within the household' in M. Freeman, *State, Law and the Family* (London, Tavistock).

_____ (1985) (ed.) *Private Violence and Public Policy* (London, Routledge & Kegan Paul).

_____ (1989) *Money and Marriage* (London, Macmillan).

Palmer, Paulina (1989) *Contemporary Women's Fiction: Narrative Practice and Feminist Theory* (Hemel Hempstead, Harvester Wheatsheaf).

_____ (1990) 'Contemporary Lesbian Feminist Fiction: Texts for Everywoman' in Linda Anderson (ed.), *Plotting Change: Contemporary Women's Fiction* (London, Edward Arnold).

Parke, R. D. (1981) *Fathering* (Glasgow, Fontana).

Parker, Julia (1988) *Women and Welfare: Ten Women in Public Social Service* (London, Macmillan).

Parker, Rozsika and Griselda Pollock (1981) *Old Mistresses: Women, Art and Ideology* (London, Pandora).

Parmar, Prathibha (1982) 'Gender, race and class: Asian women in resistance' in Centre for Contemporary Cultural Studies, *The Empire Strikes Back* (London, Hutchinson).

_____ (1988) 'Gender, race and power: the challenge to youth work practice' in P. Cohen and H. S. Baines (eds), *Multi-Racist Britain* (London, Macmillan).

Parsons, Claire D. F. (1990) 'Drugs, Science and Ethics: Lessons from the Depo-Provera Story', *Issues in Reproductive and Genetic Engineering: Journal of Feminist Analysis*, 3(2) 101–10.

Parsons, T. and R. F. Bales (1953) *Family Socialisation and Interaction Process* (New York, Free Press).

Patel, Vibhuti (1989) 'Sex-Determination and Sex Pre-Selection Tests in India: Recent Techniques in Femicide', *Reproductive and Genetic Engineering: Journal of International Feminist Analysis*, 2(2) 111–19.

Payne, Irene and Dale Spender (1980) 'Feminist Practices in the Classroom' in Dale Spender and Elizabeth Sarah (eds), *Learning to Lose: Sexism and Education*, 2nd edn, 1988 (London, The Women's Press).

Perkin, Harold (1976) 'Social History in Britain' *Journal of Social History*, 10(2) Winter, 129–43.

Pfeffer, Naomi and Allison Quick (1988) *Infertility Services: A Desperate Case* (London, Greater London Association of Community Health Councils).

Phillips, Angela and Jill Rakusen (1978) (eds) *Our Bodies, Ourselves* (2nd edn 1989) (Harmondsworth, Penguin).

Phillips, Angela and Barbara Taylor (1980) 'Sex and Skill: Notes Towards a Feminist Economics', *Feminist Review*, 6, 79–88.

Phillips, Anne (1987a) *Divided Loyalties: Dilemmas of Sex and Class* (London, Virago).

____ (ed.) (1987b) *Feminism and Equality* (Oxford, Blackwell).

Philp, M. (1985) 'Madness, Truth and Critique. Foucault and Anti-Psychiatry', *Psych Critique*, 1(2) 155–70.

Phizacklea, Annie (1983) (ed.) *One Way Ticket. Migration and Female Labour* (London, Routledge & Kegan Paul).

____ (1988) 'Gender, racism and occupational segregation', in Sylvia Walby (ed.), *Gender Segregation at Work* (Milton Keynes, Open University Press).

Phoenix, Ann (1988) 'Narrow definitions of culture: the case of early motherhood' in S. Westwood and P. Bhachu (eds), *Enterprising Women: Home, Work and Culture Among Minorities in Britain* (London, Routledge).

____ (1991) 'Mothers Under Twenty: Outsider and Insider Views' in A. Phoenix, A. Woollett and E. Lloyd (eds), *Motherhood, Meanings, Practices and Ideologies* (London, Sage).

Pierce-Baker, Charlotte (1990) 'A Quilting of Voices: Diversifying the Curriculum/Canon in the Traditional Humanities, *College Literature*, 17(2–3) 152–61.

Pill, Roisin and Nigel C. H. Stott (1982) 'Concepts of illness causation and responsibility: some preliminary data from a sample of working class mothers', *Social Science and Medicine*, 60, 43–52.

Place, Janey (1980) 'Women in Film Noir' in E. Ann Kaplan (ed.), *Women in Film Noir* (first published 1978) (London, BFI).

Pleck, Elizabeth (1987) *Domestic Tyranny* (Oxford, Oxford University Press).

Plowden Report (1967) *Children and their Primary Schools. A Report of the Central Advisory Council for Education* (London, HMSO).

Plummer, Kenneth (1975) *Sexual Stigma: An Interactionist Account* (London, Routledge & Kegan Paul).

Politi, Jina (1982) '*Jane Eyre* Class-ified', *Literature and History*, 8(1) Spring, 56–66.

Pollert, Anna (1981) *Girls, Wives, Factory Lives* (London, Macmillan).

Pollock, Griselda (1977) 'What's wrong with images of women?', *Screen Education*, 24, Autumn, reprinted in Rosemary Betterton (ed.) 1987, *Looking On: Images of Femininity in the Visual Arts and Media* (London, Pandora).

Pribram, Deirdre E. (ed.) (1988) *Female Spectator: Looking At Film and Television* (London, Verso).

Pringle, Rosemary (1989) *Secretaries Talk: Sexuality, Power and Work* (London, Verso).

Prochaska, Frank (1980) *Women and Philanthropy in Nineteenth-Century England* (Oxford, Clarendon Press).

Puckering, C. (1989) 'Maternal Depression', *Journal of Child Psychology and Psychiatry*, 30(6) 807–18.

Purvis, June (1987) 'Social class, education and ideals of femininity in the nineteenth century', in Madeleine Arnot and Gaby Weiner (eds), *Gender and the Politics of Schooling* (London, Macmillan).

Rack, Philip (1982) *Race, Culture and Mental Disorder* (London, Tavistock).

Radicalesbians (1973) 'The Woman-Identified Woman', in Anne Koedt, Ellen Levine and Anita Rapone (eds), *Radical Feminism* (New York, Quadrangle Books).

Radstone, Susannah (1988) (ed.) *Sweet Dreams: Sexuality, Gender and Popular Fiction* (London, Lawrence & Wishart).

Radway, Janice (1987) *Reading the Romance: Women, Patriarchy and Popular Literature* (first published 1984) (London, Verso).

Rakusen, Jill and Nick Davidson (1982) *Out of Our Hands: What Technology Does To Pregnancy* (London, Pan).

Ramazanoglu, Caroline (1986) 'Ethnocentrism and socialist feminist theory: a response to Barrett and McIntosh', *Feminist Review*, 22.

_____ (1989) *Feminism and the Contradictions of Oppression* (London, Routledge).

Rapoport, R. and R. Rapoport (1976) *Dual Career Families Revisited* (Oxford, Martin Robertson).

Raymond, Janice G. (1985) 'Women's Studies: a knowledge of one's own' in Margo Culley and Catherine Portuges (eds), *Gendered Subjects: The Dynamics of Feminist Teaching* (London, Routledge & Kegan Paul).

Raymond, Janice (1986) *A Passion For Friends: Towards a Philosophy of Female Affection* (London, The Women's Press).

_____ (1988a) 'The Spermatic Market: Surrogate Stock and Liquid Assets', *Reproductive and Genetic Engineering: Journal of International Feminist Analysis*, 1(1) 65–75.

_____ (1988b) 'At Issue: In the Matter of Baby M; Rejudged', *Reproductive and Genetic Engineering: Journal of International Feminist Analysis*, 1(2) 175–81.

_____ (1989) 'The International Traffic in Women: Women Used in Systems of Surrogacy and Reproduction', *Reproductive and Genetic Engineering: Journal of International Feminist Analysis*, 2(1) 51–7.

Reamy, K. J. and S. E. White (1987) 'Sexuality in the puerperium: A Review', *Archives of Sexual Behaviour*, 16(2) 165–87.

Reich, Michael, David M. Gordon and Richard C. Edwards (1980) 'A theory of labour market segmentation' in Anne Amsden (ed.), *The Economics of Women and Work* (Harmondsworth, Penguin).

Reis, Regina Gomes dos (1990) 'Norplant in Brazil: Implantation Strategy in Guise of "Scientific Research"', *Issues in Reproductive and Genetic Engineering: Journal of International Feminist Analysis*, 3(2) 111–18.

Rendall, Jane (1985) *The Origins of Modern Feminism* (London, Macmillan).

_____ (1987) (ed.) *Equal or Different? Women's Politics, 1800–1914* (Oxford, Blackwell).

_____ (1990) 'Review Article: Women's History: Beyond the Cage?', *History*, 75, February 63–72.

Rendal, Margherita (1985) 'The Winning of the Sex Discrimination Act' in M. Arnot (ed.), *Race and Gender* (Oxford, Pergamon).

Re W (1991) (Minors) (Surrogacy) Family Division, *Family Law*, 180, 1 FLR, 385.

Reynolds, Margaret (ed.) (1991) *Erotica: An Anthology of Women's Writing* (London, Pandora).

Rhys, Jean (1968) *Wide Sargasso Sea* (first published 1966) (Harmondsworth, Penguin).

Rich, Adrienne (1977) *Of Woman Born: Motherhood as Experience and Institution* (first published 1976) (London, Virago).

____ (1980a) *On Lies, Secrets and Silence: Selected Prose 1966–1978* (London, Virago).

____ (1980b) 'Compulsory Heterosexuality and Lesbian Existence', *Signs*, 5(4) 631–60. Also published 1981, London, Onlywomen Press.

____ (1980c) 'Jane Eyre: The Temptations of a Motherless Woman', in Adrienne Rich *On Lies, Secrets and Silence* (London, Virago).

____ (1980d) 'When We Dead Awaken: Writing as Re-vision', in Adrienne Rich *On Lies, Secrets and Silence*, (London, Virago).

____ (1981) 'Disobedience is what NWSA is Potentially About', *Women's Studies Quarterly*, 9(3) Fall, 4–5.

____ (1984) 'Compulsory Heterosexuality and Lesbian Existence', in Ann Snitow, Christine Stansell and Sharon Thompson (eds), *Desire: The Politics of Sexuality* (London, Virago).

Richards, Janet Radcliffe (1982) *The Sceptical Feminist* (Harmondsworth, Penguin).

Richardson, Diane (1989) *Women and the AIDS Crisis* (2nd edn) (London, Pandora).

____ (1990) 'AIDS Education and Women: Sexual and Reproductive Issues' in Peter Aggleton, Peter Davies and Graham Hart (eds), *AIDS: Individual, Cultural and Policy Dimensions* (London, Falmer).

____ (1992a) *Women, Motherhood and Child Rearing* (London, Macmillan).

____ (1992b) 'Constructing Lesbian Sexualities' in Kenneth Plummer (ed.), *Modern Homosexualities* (London, Routledge).

Riegler, Johanna (1989) 'IVF Doctor Sues: Update from Austria', *Reproductive and Genetic Engineering: Journal of International Feminist Analysis*, 2(3) 251.

Riegler, Johanna and Aurelia Weikert (1988) 'Product Egg: Egg Selling in an Austrian IVF Clinic', *Reproductive and Genetic Engineering: Journal of International Feminist Analysis*, 1(3) 221–3.

Rights of Women (1984) *Lesbian Mothers On Trial* (London, Community Press).

Riley, Denise (1983) *War in the Nursery: Theories of the Child and Mother* (London, Virago).

____ (1984) *Am I That Name? Feminism and the Category of 'Women' in History* (London, Macmillan).

Roach, Sharyn L. (1989) 'New Reproductive Technologies and Legal Reform', *Reproductive and Genetic Engineering: Journal of International Feminist Analysis*, 2(1) 11–27.

Roberts, Elizabeth (1984) *A Woman's Place: An Oral History of Working-Class Women* (Oxford, Blackwell).

Roberts, Helen (ed.) (1981a) *Doing Feminist Research* (London, Routledge & Kegan Paul).

_____ (1981b) 'Male hegemony in family planning' in Helen Roberts (ed.), *Women, Health and Reproduction* (London, Routledge & Kegan Paul).

_____ (ed.) (1992) *Women's Health Matters* (London, Routledge).

Roberts, Michèle (1978) *A Piece of the Night* (London, The Women's Press).

Robinson, Victoria (1993) 'Heterosexuality: Beginnings and Connections' in Sue Wilkinson and Celia Kitzinger (eds), *Heterosexuality: A Feminism and Psychology Reader* (London, Sage).

Rodgerson, Gillian and Elizabeth Wilson (eds) (1991) *Pornography and Feminism by Feminists Against Censorship* (London, Lawrence and Wishart).

Rogers, Barbara (1980) *The Domestication of Women* (London, Tavistock).

Rosaldo, Michelle Zimbalist and Louise Lamphere (eds) (1974) *Women, Culture and Society* (Stanford, Cal., University of California Press).

Rose, Hilary and Jalna Hanmer (1976) 'Women's Liberation, Reproduction and the Technological Fix' in Diana Leonard Barker and Sheila Allen (eds), *Sexual Divisions and Society: Process and Change* (London, Tavistock).

Rose, Jacqueline (1986) *Sexuality in the Field of Vision* (London, Verso).

Rose, Sonya (1988) 'Gender Antagonism and Class Conflict: Exclusionary Strategies of Male Trade Unionists in Nineteenth Century Britain', *Social History*, 13, May, 191–208.

Rosenfelt, D. (1984) 'What women's studies programs do that mainstreaming can't', *Women's Studies International Forum*, 7(3) 167–76.

Rosier, Pat (1989) 'The Speculum Bites Back: Feminists Spark an Inquiry Into the Treatment of Carcinoma in Situ at Auckland's National Women's Hospital', *Reproductive and Genetic Engineering: Journal of International Feminist Analysis*, 2(2) 121–32.

Ross, Ellen (1983) 'Survival Networks: Women's Neighbourhood Sharing in London Before World War One', *History Workshop Journal*, 15, Spring, 4–27.

Ross Muir, Anne (1988) 'The Status of Women Working in Film and Television' in Lorraine Gammon and Margaret Marshment (eds), *The Female Gaze* (London, The Women's Press).

Rothman, Barbara Katz (1989) *Recreating Motherhood: Ideology and Technology in a Patriarchal Society* (New York, W. W. Norton).

Rowan, Caroline (1982) 'Women and the Labour Party', *Feminist Review*, 12, 74–91.

Rowbotham, Sheila (1973) *Women's Consciousness, Man's World* (Harmondsworth, Penguin).

_____ (1977) *A New World for Women* (London, Pluto).

_____ (1982) 'The Trouble with Patriarchy' in Mary Evans (ed.), *The Women Question* (Oxford, Fontana).

_____ (1990a) *The Past Is Before Us: Feminism in Action Since the 1960s* (London, Penguin).

_____ (1990b) *Hidden from History* (1st edn 1973) (London, Pluto).

_____ , Lynne Segal and Hilary Wainwright (1979) *Beyond the Fragments: Feminism and the Making of Socialism* (London, Merlin Press).

Rowland, Robyn (1990) 'Response to the Draft report of the National Bioethics Consultative Committee, Surrogacy', *Issues in Reproductive and Genetic Engineering: Journal of International Feminist Analysis*, 3(2) 147–57.

Ruddick, S. (1982) 'Maternal Thinking' in Barry Thorne with Marilyn Yalom (eds), *Rethinking the Family: Some Feminist Questions* (London, Longman).

Rubin, Gayle (1975) 'The Traffic in Women: Notes on the "political economy" of sex' in R. R. Reiter (ed.), *Toward an Anthropology of Women* (New York, Monthly Review Press).

Rule, Jane (1975) *Lesbian Images* (also published 1982) (Trumansburg, New York, The Crossing Press).

Rumbold, Judy (1991) 'My vile bodies', *Guardian*, 10 January.

Russ, Joanna (1975) *The Female Man* (reprinted 1985) (London, The Women's Press).

Russell, Diana (1982) *Rape in Marriage* (New York, Macmillan).

_____ (1984) *Sexual Exploitation* (California, Sage).

_____ (1986) *The Secret Trauma* (New York, Basic Books).

Russell, Michele (1985) 'Black-eyed blues connections: teaching black women' in Margo Culley and Catherine Portuges (eds), *Gendered Subjects: The Dynamics of Feminist Teaching* (London, Routledge & Kegan Paul).

Saadawi, Nawal el (1980) *The Hidden Face of Eve* (London, Zed).

Sachs, Albie and Joan Hoff Wilson (1978) *Sexism and the Law* (Oxford, Martin Robertson).

Sadrozinski, Renate (1989) '"Kinder oder keine-entscheiden wir alleine" On the Abolition of the Law Against Abortion and the Patriarchal Needs to Protect Embryos', *Reproductive and Genetic Engineering: Journal of International Feminist Analysis*, 2(1) 1–9.

Said, Edward (1978) *Orientalism* (London, Routledge & Kegan Paul).

Salomone, Jo (1991) 'Report on the 6th International Women and Health Meeting, November 3–9, 1990, Manila, Philippines', *Issues in Reproductive and Genetic Engineering: Journal of International Feminist Analysis*, 4(1) 77–85.

Samuel, Raphael (1981) (ed.) *People's History and Socialist Theory* (London, Routledge & Kegan Paul).

Sanderson, Kay (1990) 'Meanings of class and social mobility: the public and private lives of women civil servants' in Helen Corr and Lynne Jamieson (eds), *Politics of Everyday Life* (London, Macmillan).

Sargent, Lydia (1981) (ed.) *The Unhappy Marriage of Marxism and Feminism: A Debate on Class and Patriarchy* (London, Pluto).

Sashidharan, S. P. (1989) 'Schizophrenic – or just black?', *Community Care*, 5 October, 14–15.

Sayers, Janet (1982) *Biological Politics* (London, Tavistock).

_____ (1986) *Sexual Contradictions* (London, Methuen).

_____ (1988) 'Feminist Therapy: Forgetting the Father?', *Psychology of Women Section Newsletter*, 2, Autumn, 18–22.

Schilb, John (1985) 'Pedagogy of the oppressors?' in Margo Culley and Catherine Portuges (eds), *Gendered Subjects: The Dynamics of Feminist Teaching* (London, Routledge & Kegan Paul).

Schleiermacher, Sabine (1990) 'Racial Hygiene and "Deliberate Parenthood": Two Sides of Demographer Hans Harmsen's Population Policy', *Issues in Reproductive and Genetic Engineering: Journal of International Feminist Analysis*, 3(3) 201–10.

Schniedewind, Nancy and Frinde Maher (1987) 'Editorial', *Women's Studies Quarterly: Feminist Pedagogy*, XV(3 and 4) Fall/Winter, 4.

Schulman, Sarah (1990) *After Delores* (first published 1988) (London, Sheba).

Schur, Edwin M. (1984) *Labelling Women Deviant* (New York, Random House).

Scott, Marion (1980) 'Teach her a Lesson: Sexist Curriculum in Patriarchal Education' in Dale Spender and Elizabeth Sarah (eds), *Learning to Lose* (London, The Women's Press).

Scott, Sara (1987) 'Sex and Danger: Feminism and AIDS', *Trouble and Strife*, 11, 13–18.

Scutt, Jocelynne A. (1988) (ed.) *The Baby Machine: Commercialisation of Motherhood* (Carlton, Australia, McCulloch).

Segal, Lynne (1987) *Is the Future Female? Troubled Thoughts on Contemporary Feminism* (London, Virago).

_____ (1989) 'Slow Change or No Change?: Feminism, Socialism and the Problem of Men', *Feminist Review*, 31, Spring, 5–21.

_____ (1990a) *Slow Motion: Changing Masculinities, Changing Men* (London, Virago).

_____ (1990b) 'Pornography and Violence: What the "Experts" Really Say', *Feminist Review*, 36.

Sellers, Susan (1989) 'Biting the teacher's apple: opening doors for women in higher education' in Ann Thompson and Helen Wilcox (eds), *Teaching Women, Feminism and English Studies* (Manchester, Manchester University Press).

Serbin, Lisa (1978) 'Teachers, peers and play preference' in B. Sprung (ed.), *Perspectives on Non-Sexist Early Childhood Education* (New York, Teachers College Press).

Seymour, Julie (1990) 'Women's time – a household resource?' (paper presented to the British Sociological Association Annual Conference, University of Surrey).

Shalev, Carmel (1989) *Birth Power: The Case for Surrogacy* (New Haven, Conn., and London, Yale University Press).

Shapiro, Jean (1987) *Ourselves, Growing Older* (London, Fontana).

Sharan-Shan, Ject (1985) *In My Own Name: An Autobiography* (London, The Women's Press).

Sharpe, Sue (1976) *Just Like a Girl: How Girls Learn to be Women* (Harmondsworth, Penguin).

_____ (1984) *Double Identity* (Harmondsworth, Pelican).

Shaw, Jenny (1984) 'The politics of single-sex schools' in Rosemary Deem (ed.), *Co-education Reconsidered* (Milton Keynes, Open University Press).

Sheba (eds) (1989) *Serious Pleasure: Lesbian Erotic Stories and Poetry* (London, Sheba).

_____ (eds) (1990) *More Serious Pleasure* (London, Sheba).

Sheridan, Susan (1990) 'Feminist Knowledge, Women's Liberation and Women's Studies' in Sneja Gunew (ed.), *Feminist Knowledge: Critique and Construct* (London, Routledge).

_____ (1991) 'From Margin to Mainstream, Situating Women's Studies' in Sneja Gunew (ed.), *A Reader in Feminist Knowledge* (London, Routledge).

Shiva, Vandana (1988) *Staying Alive: Women, Ecology and Development* (London, Zed).

Showalter, Elaine (1978) *A Literature of Their Own: British Women Novelists from Brontë to Lessing* (first published 1977) (London, Virago).

_____ (1979) 'Towards a Feminist Poetics' in Mary Jacobus (ed.), *Women Writing and Writing about Women* (London, Croom Helm).

_____ (ed.) (1986) *The New Feminist Criticism: Essays on Women, Literature and Theory* (London, Virago).

_____ (1987) 'Critical Cross-Dressing: Male Feminists and the Woman of the Year' in Alice Jardine and Paul Smith (eds), *Men In Feminism* (London, Methuen).

Shrewsbury, Carolyn M. (1987) 'What is Feminist Pedagogy?', *Women's Studies Quarterly: Feminist Pedagogy*, XV(3 and 4) Fall/Winter, 6–14.

Simson, Rennie (1984) 'The Afro-American Female: The Historical Context of the Construction of Sexual Identity', in Ann Snitow, Christine Stansell and Sharon Thompson (eds), *Desire: The Politics of Sexuality* (London, Virago).

Singer, Peter and Deane Wells (1984) *The Reproduction Revolution: New Ways of Making Babies* (Oxford, University Press).

Skelton, Christine (ed.) (1989) *Whatever Happens to Little Women?* (Milton Keynes, Open University Press).

_____ (1991) 'A Study of the Career Perspectives of Male teachers of Young Children', *Gender and Education*, 3(3) 279–89.

Sluckin, W., M. Herbert and A. Sluckin (1983) *Maternal Bonding* (Oxford, Blackwell).

Smart, Carol (1984) *The Ties That Bind: Law, Marriage and The Reproduction Of Patriarchal Relations* (London, Routledge & Kegan Paul).

_____ (1989a) 'Power and the politics of child custody' in C. Smart and S. Sevenhuijsen, *Child Custody And The Politics Of Gender* (London, Routledge).

_____ (1989b) *Feminism and the Power of the Law* (London, Routledge).

Smith, Barbara (1986) 'Toward a Black Feminist Criticism' (first published 1977) in Elaine Showalter (ed.), *The New Feminist Criticism* (London, Virago).

_____ (1982) 'Racism and Women's Studies' in G. Hull *et al.*, *But Some of Us Are Brave* (New York, The Feminist Press).

_____ (ed.) (1983) *Home Girls: A Black Feminist Anthology* (New York, Kitchen Table, Women of Color Press).

Smith, Dorothy (1988) *The Everyday World as Problematic: A Feminist Sociology* (Milton Keynes, Open University Press).

Smith, Lorna (1989) *Domestic Violence: An Overview of the Literature* (London, HMSO).

Smith, Paul (1978) 'Domestic Labour and Marx's theory of value' in Annette Kuhn and Ann Marie Wolpe, *Feminism and Materialism* (London, Routledge & Kegan Paul).

Smith, Valerie (1990) 'Black Feminist Theory and the Representation of the "Other"' in Cheryl A. Wall (ed.), *Changing Our Own Words* (London, Routledge).

Smyth, Cherry (1990) 'The Pleasure Threshold: Looking at Lesbian Pornography on Film', *Feminist Review*, 34, 152–9.

Snitow, Ann Barr (1983) 'Mass Market Romance: Pornography for Women is Different', in Ann Snitow, Christine Stansell and Sharon Thompson (eds) *Powers of Desire: The Politics of Sexuality* (New York, Monthly Review Press).

_____ , Christine Stansell and Sharon Thompson (eds) (1983/4) *Desire: The Politics of Sexuality* (London, Virago, 1984; New York, Monthly Review Press, 1983).

Snoek, Diedrick (1985) 'A male feminist in a women's college classroom' in Margo Culley and Catherine Portuges (eds), *Gendered Subjects: The Dynamics of Feminist Teaching* (London, Routledge & Kegan Paul).

Solomon, Alison (1988) 'Integrating Infertility Crisis Counselling Into Feminist Practice', *Reproductive and Genetic Engineering: Journal of International Feminist Analysis*, 1(1) 41–9.

Sontag, Susan (1983) *Illness as Metaphor* (Harmondsworth, Penguin).

Spallone, Patricia (1988) *Beyond Conception: The New Politics of Reproduction* (London, Macmillan).

_____ and Deborah Lynne Steinberg (eds) (1987) *Made to Order: The Myth of Reproductive and Genetic Progress* (Oxford, Pergamon).

Spelman, Elizabeth V. (1985) 'Combating the marginalization of black women in the classroom' in Margo Culley and Catherine Portuges (eds), *Gendered Subjects: The Dynamics of Feminist Teaching* (London, Routledge & Kegan Paul).

_____ (1988) *Inessential Woman: Problems of Exclusion in Feminist Thought* (Boston, Mass., Beacon Press).

Spencer, Jane (1986) *The Rise of the Woman Novelist: From Aphra Behn to Jane Austen* (Oxford, Blackwell).

Spender, Dale (1980) *Man Made Language* (London, Routledge & Kegan Paul).

_____ (ed.) (1981) *Men's Studies Modified: The Impact of Feminism on the Academic Disciplines* (Oxford, Pergamon).

_____ (ed.) (1983a) *Feminist Theorists: Three Centuries of Women's Intellectual Traditions* (London, The Women's Press).

_____ (1983b) *Women of Ideas (And What Men Have Done To Them)* (London, Ark).

_____ (1986a) *Mothers of the Novel: 100 Good Women Novelists Before Jane Austen* (London, Pandora).

_____ (1986b) 'Still crazy after all these years', *Trouble and Strife*, 9, 40–5.

_____ (ed.) (1987) *The Education Papers: Women's Quest for Equality in Britain 1850–1912* (London, Routledge & Kegan Paul).

_____ and Elizabeth Sarah (eds) (1988) *Learning to Lose: Sexism and Education*, 2nd edn (London, The Women's Press).

Spivak, Gayatri Chakravorty (1985) 'Strategies of vigilance' in *Block*, 5, 5–9.

_____ (1987) *In Other Worlds: Essays in Cultural Politics* (London, Methuen).

_____ (1989) 'Three Women's Texts and a Critique of Imperialism' in Catherine Belsey and Jane Moore (eds), *The Feminist Reader: Essays in Gender and the Politics of Literary Criticism* (London, Macmillan).

Squirrell, Gillian (1989) 'Teachers and Issues of Sexual Orientation', *Gender and Education*, 1(1) 17–34.

Stacey, Jackie (1991) 'Promoting Normality: Section 28 and the Regulation of Sexuality' in Sarah Franklin, Celia Lury and Jackie Stacey (eds), *Off Centre: Feminism and Cultural Studies* (London, Unwin Hyman).

Stanko, Betsy (1991) 'Angst and Academia', *Trouble and Strife*, 22, 19–21.

Stanko, Elizabeth A. (1985) *Intimate Intrusions* (London, Routledge & Kegan Paul).

_____ (1988) 'Keeping women in and out of line: sexual harassment and occupational segregation', in Sylvia Walby (ed.), *Gender Segregation at Work* (Milton Keynes, Open University Press).

Stanley, Julia (1989) *Marks on the Memory* (Milton Keynes, Open University Press).

Stanley, Liz (1985) 'Feminism and Friendship: Two Essays on Olive Schreiner', *Studies in Sexual Politics*, 8 (Manchester University).

_____ (1987) 'Biography as Microscope or Kaleidoscope? The Case of "Power" in Hannah Cullwick's Relationship with Arthur Munby', *Women's Studies International Forum*, 10(1) 19–31.

_____ (ed.) (1990a) *Feminist Praxis: Research, Theory and Epistemology in Feminist Sociology* (London, Routledge).

_____ (1990b) 'Recovering Women in History from Feminist Deconstructionism', *Women's Studies International Forum*, 13(1/2) 151–8.

_____ and Sue Wise (1983) *Breaking Out: Feminist Consciousness and Feminist Research* (London, Routledge & Kegan Paul).

Stanworth, Michelle (1981) *Gender and Schooling* (London, Hutchinson).

_____ (ed.) (1987) *Reproductive Technologies, Gender, Motherhood and Medicine* (Cambridge, Polity Press).

Steedman, Carolyn (1986) *Landscape for a Good Woman: A Story of Two Lives* (London, Virago).

_____ (1990) *Childhood, Culture and Class in Britain: Margaret McMillan, 1860–1939* (London, Virago).

Steedman, J. (1983) *Examination Results in Mixed and Single-Sex Schools: Findings from the National Child Development Study* (Manchester, EOC).

Stetson, Erlene (1985) 'Pink elephants: confessions of a black feminist in an all-white, mostly male English department of a white university somewhere in God's country', in Margo Culley and Catherine Portuges (eds), *Gendered Subjects: The Dynamics of Feminist Teaching* (London, Routledge & Kegan Paul).

Stimpson, Catherine (1988) *Where the Meanings Are, Feminism and Cultural Spaces* (New York, Routledge).

Stolcke, Verena (1988) 'New Reproductive Technologies: The Old Quest for Fatherhood', *Reproductive and Genetic Engineering: Journal of International Feminist Analysis*, 1(1) 5–19.

Stones, Rosemary (1983) *Pour Out the Cocoa Janet* (York, Longman).

Straus, Murray (1980) 'A Sociological Perspective on the Causes of Family Violence' in Michael Green (ed.), *Violence and the Family* (Boulder, Col., West View Press).

Strober, M. and D. Tyack (1980) 'Why do women teach and men manage? A report on research on schools', *Signs*, 5(3) 494–504.

Stuart, Andrea (1988) '*The Color Purple*: In Defence of Happy Endings' in Lorraine Gamman and Margaret Marshment (eds), *The Female Gaze* (London, The Women's Press).

Suleiman, Leila and Susan Suleiman (1985) 'Mixed Blood – That Explains a Lot of Things' in Gaby Weiner (ed.), *Just a Bunch of Girls* (Milton Keynes, Open University Press).

Summerfield, Penny (1984) *Women Workers in the Second World War* (London, Croom Helm).

Sydie, Rosalind A. (1987) *Natural Women Cultured Men: A Feminist Perspective on Sociological Theory* (Milton Keynes, Open University Press).

Sykes, Roberta (1989) *Black Majority: An Analysis of 21 years of Black Australian experience as emancipated Australian citizens* (Hawthorn, Australia, Hudson).

Taking Liberties Collective (1989) *Learning The Hard Way: Women's Oppression in Men's Education* (London, Macmillan).

Tan, Amy (1989) *The Joy Luck Club* (reprinted 1990) (London, Minerva).

Tandon, K. (1987) 'Lumps and Bumps in Racism and Sexism' in Sue O'Sullivan (ed.) *Women's Health: a Spare Rib Reader* (London, Pandora).

Taylor, Barbara (1983) *Eve and the New Jerusalem* (London, Virago).

Taylor, Helen (1989) *Scarlett's Women: Gone with the Wind and its Female Fans* (London, Virago).

Thompson, Edward (1968) *The Making of the English Working Class* (Harmondsworth, Penguin).

Thompson, Martha E. (1987) 'Diversity in the Classroom: Creating Opportunities for Learning Feminist Theory', *Women's Studies Quarterly*, XV(3 and 4) Fall/Winter, 81–9.

Thompson, Thea (1981) *Edwardian Childhoods* (London, Routledge & Kegan Paul).

Thorogood, Nicki (1987) 'Race, class and gender: the politics of housework' in J. Brannen and G. Wilson (eds), *Give and Take In Families* (London, Allen & Unwin).

Tizard, Barbara, Peter Moss and Jane Perry (1976) *All Our Children: Pre-School Services in a Changing Society* (London, Temple Smith/New Society).

Tizard, Barbara, P. Blatchford, J. Burke, C. Farquhar and P. Lewis (1988) *Young Children at School in the Inner City* (Hove, Lawrence/Erlbaum).

Tong, Rosemary (1989) *Feminist Thought: A Comprehensive Introduction* (London, Unwin Hyman).

Townsend, Peter and Nick Davidson (1982) *Inequalities in Health: The Black Report* (Harmondsworth, Penguin Books).

Trickett, Denise (1989) 'Leeds Primary Needs Programme and Gender', in Christine Skelton (ed.), *Whatever Happens to Little Women?* (Milton Keynes, Open University Press).

Trivedy, Parita (1984) 'To Deny Our Fullness: Asian Women in the Making of History', *Feminist Review*, 17, 37–52.

Troyna, Barry (1987) (ed.) *Racial Inequality in Education* (London, Tavistock).

Turnbull, A., J. Pollock and S. Bruley (1983) 'History' in J. Whyld (ed.), *Sexism in the Secondary Curriculum* (London, Harper & Row).

Tuttle, Lisa (1987) *Encyclopedia of Feminism* (London, Arrow Books).

UBINIG (1990) 'Research Report: Norplant: The Five Year Needle: An Investigation of the Norplant Trial in Bangladesh from the User's Perspective', *Issues in Reproductive and Genetic Engineering: Journal of International Feminist Analysis*, 3(3) 211–28.

——— (1991a) '"The Price of Norplant is TK.2000! You Cannot Remove It." Clients are Refused Removal of Norplant Trial in Bangladesh', *Issues in Reproductive and Genetic Engineering: Journal of International Feminist Analysis*, 4(1) 45–6.

____ (1991b) *Declaration of Comilla: Proceeding of FINRRAGE–UBINIG International Conference, 1989* (Bangladesh, UBINIG).

Ungerson, Clare (ed.) (1985) *Women and Social Policy: a Reader* (London, Macmillan).

____ (1987) *Policy is Personal: sex, gender and informal care* (London, Tavistock).

____ (1988) *The Times Higher Education Supplement*, 3 June, 22 and 24.

____ (ed.) (1990) *Gender and Caring* (Hemel Hempsted, Harvester Wheatsheaf).

Urry, John (1981) *The Anatomy of Capitalist Societies* (London, Macmillan).

Ussher, Jane Maria (1990) 'Negative Images of Female Sexuality and Reproduction: Reflecting Misogyny or Misinformation?', *Psychology of Women Section Newsletter*, 5, Spring, 17–29.

Vance, Carole S. (ed.) (1984) *Pleasure and Danger: Exploring Female Sexuality* (London, Routledge & Kegan Paul).

____ (1989) 'Social Construction Theory: Problems in the History of Sexuality' in Dennis Altman *et al.*, *Which Homosexuality?*, (London, Gay Men's Press).

Varela, Maria Jose and Verena Stolcke (1989) 'The New Spanish Law: A Model for Europe?', *Reproductive and Genetic Engineering: Journal of International Feminist Analysis*, 2(3) 231–5.

Versluysen, Margaret Connor (1981) 'Midwives, medical men and poor women labouring of child: lying-in hospitals in eighteenth-century London' in H. Roberts (ed.), *Women, Health and Reproduction* (London, Routledge & Kegan Paul).

Vicinus, Martha (ed.) (1981) *Suffer and Be Still: Women in the Victorian Age* (London, Methuen).

____ (1985) *Independent Women: Work and Community for Single Women, 1850–1920* (London, Virago).

Viinikka, Simmy (1989) 'Child Sexual Abuse and the Law' in Emily Driver and Audrey Droisen (eds), *Child Sexual Abuse* (London, Macmillan).

Visram, Rosina (1986) *Ayahs, Lascars and Princes* (London, Pluto Press).

Voluntary Licensing Authority (VLA) (1989) *IVF Research in the UK: A Report on Research Licensed by the Interim Licensing Authority (ILA) for Human In Vitro Fertilisation and Embryology 1985–1989* (London, ILA). See Annual Reports from 1986.

Walby, Sylvia (1986) *Patriarchy at Work: patriarchal and capitalist relations in employment* (Cambridge, Polity Press).

____ (1988) 'Introduction' in Sylvia Walby (ed.), *Gender Segregation at Work* (Milton Keynes, Open University Press).

____ (1989) 'Theorising patriarchy', *Sociology*, 23(2).

____ (1990) *Theorising Patriarchy* (Oxford, Blackwell).

Waldby, Cathy, Atosha Clancy, Jan Emetchi, Caroline Summerfield for Dympna House (1989) 'Theoretical Perspectives on Father–Daughter Incest' in Emily Driver and Audrey Droisen (eds) *Child Sexual Abuse* (London, Macmillan).

Waldschmidt, Anne (1991) 'The Embryo as a Legal Entity – Woman as a Fetal Environment. The New German Laws on Reproductive Engineering and Embryo Research', *Issues in Reproductive and Genetic Engineering: Journal of International Feminist Analysis*, 4(3) 209–22.

Walford, Geoffrey (1980) 'Sex bias in physics textbooks', *School Science Review*, 1(62) 224–5.

Walker, Alice (1982) *The Color Purple* (reprinted 1983) (London, The Women's Press).

___ (1984) *In Search of Our Mothers' Gardens: Womanist Prose* (London, The Women's Press).

Walkerdine, Valerie (1984) 'Developmental Psychology and the Child Centred Pedagogy' in J. Henriques, W. Holloway, C. Urwin, C. Venn and V. Walkerdine, *Changing the Subject* (London, Methuen).

___ (1990) *Schoolgirl Fictions* (London, Verso).

Walkling, Philip and Chris Brannigan (1986) Anti-sexist/Anti-racist Education: A Possible Dilemma, *Journal of Moral Education*, 15(1) 16–25.

Walkowitz, Judith (1980) *Prostitution and Victorian Society: Women, Class and the State* (Cambridge University Press).

Wall, Cheryl A. (ed.) (1990) *Changing Our Own Words: Essays on Criticism, Theory and Writing by Black Women* (London, Routledge).

Wallace, Claire (1987) 'From girls and boys to women and men: the social reproduction of gender' in M. Arnot and G. Weiner (eds), *Gender and the Politics of School* (London, Hutchinson).

Wallace, Michele (1979) *Black Macho and the Myth of the Superwoman* (London, John Calder).

Ward, Elizabeth (1984) *Father–Daughter Rape* (London, The Women's Press).

(Warnock Report) Department of Health and Social Security (1984) *Report of the Committee of Inquiry Into Human Fertilisation and Embryology*, Cmnd 9314 (London, HMSO).

Warren, Mary Anne (1986) 'The Social Construction of Sexuality' in N. Grieve and A. Burns (eds), *Australian Women: New Feminist Perspectives* (Melbourne, Oxford University Press).

Washington, Mary Helen (1985) 'How racial differences helped us discover our common ground' in Margo Culley and Catherine Portuges (eds), *Gendered Subjects: The Dynamics of Feminist Teaching* (London, Routledge & Kegan Paul).

Watt, Shantu and Juliet Cook (1991) 'Racism: Whose Liberation? Implications for Women's Studies' in Jane Aaron and Sylvia Walby (eds), *Out of the Margins: Women's Studies in the Nineties* (London, Falmer).

Wearing, B. (1984) *The Ideology of Motherhood* (London, Allen & Unwin).

Webb, Christine (1987) 'Defining women and their health: the case of hysterectomy' in J. Orr (ed.), *Women's Health in the Community* (Chichester, John Wiley and Sons).

Weedon, Chris (1987) *Feminist Practice and Post-Structuralist Theory* (Oxford, Blackwell).

Weeks, Jeffrey (1990) *Sex, Politics and Society*, 2nd edn (London, Longman).

Weiner, Gaby (ed.) (1985) *Just a Bunch of Girls* (Milton Keynes, Open University Press).

___ (1986) 'Feminist education and equal opportunities: unity or discord?', *British Journal of Sociology of Education*, 7(3) 265–74.

___ and Madeleine Arnot (1987) 'Teachers and gender politics' in M. Arnot and G. Weiner (eds), *Gender and the Politics of Schooling* (London, Hutchinson).

Weldon, Fay (1975) *Female Friends* (reprinted 1977) (London, Picador).

West, D. J., C. Roy and L. F. Nichols (1978) *Understanding Sexual Attacks* (London, Heinemann).

West, Jackie (1978) 'Women, sex and class' in A. Kuhn and A. M. Wolpe (eds), *Feminism and Materialism* (London, Routledge & Kegan Paul).

Westwood, Sallie (1984) *All Day, Every Day: Factory and Family in the Making of Women's Lives* (London, Pluto Press).

____ and Parminder Bhachu (eds) (1988) *Enterprising Women: Ethnicity, Economy and Gender Relations* (London, Routledge).

Wheldall, Kevin and Frank Merrett (1988) 'Which classroom behaviours do primary school teachers say they find most troublesome?', *Educational Review*, 40(1) 13–27.

Whitbeck, C. (1984) 'The Maternal Instinct' in J. Treblicott, *Mothering: Essays in Feminist Theory* (New Jersey, Rowan and Allanheld).

White, Evelyn C. (ed.) (1990) *The Black Women's Health Book. Speaking for Ourselves* (Seattle, The Seal Press).

Whyld, Janie (ed.) (1983) *Sexism in the Secondary Curriculum* (London, Harper and Row).

Whyte, Judith (1985) 'Girl friendly science and the girl friendly school' in J. Whyte *et al.* (eds), *Girl-friendly Schooling* (London, Methuen).

Wichterich, Christa (1988) 'From the Struggle Against "Overpopulation" to the Industrialization of Human Production', *Reproductive and Genetic Engineering: Journal of International Feminist Analysis*, 1(1) 21–30.

Wickham, Ann (1986) *Women and Training* (Milton Keynes, Open University Press).

Wilkinson, Sue (1991) 'Why Psychology (Badly) Needs Feminism' in Jane Aaron and Sylvia Walby (eds), *Out of the Margins: Women's Studies in the Nineties* (London, Falmer).

Williams, Anne (1987) 'Making sense of feminist contributions to women's health' in J. Orr (ed.), *Women's Health in the Community* (Chichester, John Wiley).

Williams, Fiona (1989) *Social Policy: A Critical Introduction* (Cambridge, Polity Press).

Williams, Jenny (1987) 'The construction of women and black students as educational problems: re-evaluating policy on gender and "race" ' in M. Arnot and G. Weiner (eds), *Gender and the Politics of Schooling* (London, Hutchinson).

Williams, Linda (1988) 'It's Gonna Work For Me', *Birth* 15 March, 153–6.

____ (1990) 'Wanting Children Badly: A study of Canadian women seeking in vitro fertilisation and their husbands', *Issues in Reproductive and Genetic Engineering: Journal of International Feminist Analysis*, 3(3) 229–34.

____ (1991) 'Motherhood, Ideology, and the Power of Technology: In Vitro Fertilization Use by Adoptive Mothers', *Women's Studies International Forum*, 13(6) 543–52.

Williamson, Judith (1978) *Decoding Advertisements: Ideology and Meaning in Advertising* (London, Marion Boyars).

____ (1986a) 'Woman is an island' in Tania Modleski (ed.), *Studies in Entertainment* (Bloomington, Ind. and Indianapolis, Indiana University Press).

____ (1986b) *Consuming Passions: The Dynamics of Popular Culture* (London, Marion Boyars).

Willis, Susan (1987) *Specifying: Black Women Writing the American Experience* (reprinted 1990) (London, Routledge).

Wilson, Amrit (1978) *Finding a Voice: Asian Women in Britain* (London, Virago).

Wilson, Barbara (1986) *Sisters of the Road* (reprinted 1987) (London, The Women's Press).

Wilson, E. A. (1978) *On Human Nature* (Cambridge, Mass., Harvard University Press).

Wilson, Elizabeth (1977) *Women and the Welfare State* (London, Tavistock).

_____ (1981) 'Psychoanalysis: Psychic Law and Order', *Feminist Review*, 8, 63–78.

_____ (1983) *What is to be Done about Violence Against Women?* (Harmondsworth, Penguin).

_____ (1985) *Adorned in Dreams: Fashion and Modernity* (London, Virago).

_____ (1988) 'Tell It Like It Is: Women and Confessional Writing' in S. Radstone (ed.) *Sweet Dreams: Sexuality, Gender and Popular Fiction* (London, Lawrence & Wishart).

Wilson, Gail (1987) 'Money: patterns of responsibility and irresponsibility in marriage' in J. Brannen and G. Wilson, *Give and Take in Families* (London, Allen & Unwin).

Wings, Mary (1986) *She Came Too Late* (London, The Women's Press).

Winkler, Ute (1988) 'New U.S. Know-How in Frankfurt – A "Surrogate Mother" Agency', *Reproductive and Genetic Engineering: Journal of International Feminist Analysis*, 1(2) 205–7.

Winship, Janice (1987) *Inside Women's Magazines* (London, Pandora).

Winterson, Jeanette (1985) *Oranges Are Not the Only Fruit* (London, Pandora).

Wise, Sue and Liz Stanley (1987) *Georgie Porgie: Sexual Harassment in Everyday Life* (London, Pandora).

Witherspoon, Sharon (1988) 'A Woman's Work' in R. Jowell, S. Witherspoon and L. Brook (eds), *Black Social Attitudes: The 5th Report* (Aldershot, Gower).

Wittig, Monique (1975) *The Lesbian Body* (New York, Morrow).

_____ (1981) 'One is Not Born a Woman', *Feminist Issues*, 1(2) 47–54.

Witz, Anne (1992) *Professions and Patriarchy* (London, Routledge).

Wollstonecraft, Mary (1792) *Vindication of the Rights of Woman* (Harmondsworth, Penguin, 1982).

Wolpe, Ann-Marie (1988) *Within School Walls* (London, Routledge & Kegan Paul).

Wolverhampton Homeworkers Project (1984) *Report* (Wolverhampton Trades Council).

Women and AIDS Project Report (1991) (New York, New York State Division for Women).

Women and Work Hazards Group (1987) 'Danger – women's work' in S. O'Sullivan (ed.), *Women's Health: a spare rib reader* (London, Pandora Press).

Women in Mind (1986) *Finding Our Own Solutions* (London, Mind).

Women's Studies International Forum (1983) 6(3) (Oxford, Pergamon).

Women's Studies Quarterly (1987) 'Special Feature: Feminist Pedagogy', XV(3 and 4) Fall/Winter.

_____ (1988) 'Special Feature: Teaching the New Women's History', XVI(1 and 2) Spring/Summer.

Woolf, Virginia (1929) *A Room of One's Own* (reprinted 1977) (London, Grafton).

_____ (1938) *Three Guineas* (reprinted 1986) (London, Hogarth Press).

Woollett, A. (1987) 'Why Motherhood is Popular: An Analysis of Accounts of Mothers and Childless Women' (paper presented at the second 'Women in Psychology' Conference at Brunel University, Uxbridge).

_____ (1991) 'Having Children: Accounts of Childless Women and Women with Reproductive Problems' in A. Phoenix, A. Woollett and E. Lloyd (eds), *Motherhood, Meanings, Practices and Ideologies* (London, Sage).

_____ (1992) 'The Psychology of Infertility and Infertility Investigations' in P. Nicolson and J. M. Ussher (eds), *The Psychology of Women's Health and Health Care* (London, Macmillan).

Yates, Lyn (1987) *Girls and Democratic Schooling* (Sydney, New South Wales Education Department and Curriculum Development Centre).

Yeandle, Susan (1984) *Women's Working Lives: Patterns and Strategies* (London, Tavistock).

Yllo, Kersti and Michele Bograd (eds) (1988) *Feminist Perspectives on Wife Abuse* (California, Sage).

Young, Kate and Olivia Harris (1982) 'The Subordination of Women in Cross-cultural Perspective' in Mary Evans (ed.), *The Woman Question* (Oxford, Fontana).

Young, Lola (1990) 'A Nasty Piece of Work: A Psychoanalytic Study of Sexual and Racial Difference in "Mona Lisa"' in J. Rutherford (ed.), *Identity, Community, Culture, Difference* (London, Lawrence and Wishart).

Young, Michael and Peter Wilmott (1966) *Family and Kinship in East London* (Harmondsworth, Penguin).

_____ (1975) *The Symmetrical Family* (Harmondsworth, Penguin).

Young, Shelagh (1988) 'Feminism and the Politics of Power: Whose Gaze is it Anyway?' in Lorraine Gamman and Margaret Marshment (eds), *The Female Gaze* (London, The Women's Press).

Zimmerman, Susan (1990) 'Industrial Capitalism's "Hostility to Childbirth" "Responsible Childbearing" and Eugenic Reproductive Politics in the First Third of the 20th Century', *Issues in Reproductive and Genetic Engineering: Journal of International Feminist Analysis*, 3(3) 191–200.

Zimmermann, Bonnie (1986) 'What Has Never Been: An Overview of Lesbian Feminist Literary Criticism' (first published 1981) in E. Showalter, *The New Feminist Criticism: Essays on Women, Literature and Theory* (London, Virago).

Zmroczek, Christine and Claire Duchen (1989) 'Gender Specifics', *The Times Higher Education Supplement*, 2 June, 24 and 30.

_____ (1991) 'What *are* those Women up to? Women's Studies and Feminist Research in the European Community' in Jane Aaron and Sylvia Walby (eds), *Out of the Margins: Women's Studies in the Nineties* (London, Falmer).

Author Index

Subject Index

411